REVITALIZING WORDS FOR HUNGRY HEARTS

AND THIRSTY SOULS: "As the deer pants for the water brooks, so pants my soul for You, O God. My soul thirsts for God, for the Living God."

Psalm 42:1-2a

Gerry Alderink

Gerry Alderink

xulon PRESS

Copyright © 2005 by Gerry Alderink

Revitalizing Words For Hungry Hearts
by Gerry Alderink

Printed in the United States of America

ISBN 1-59781-565-9

All rights reserved solely by the author. The author guarantees all contents are original and do not infringe upon the legal rights of any other person or work. No part of this book may be reproduced in any form without the permission of the author. The views expressed in this book are not necessarily those of the publisher.

Unless otherwise indicated, Scriptures are from the New King James Version. Copyright © 1982 by Thomas Nelson. Used by permission.

Verses marked KJV are taken from the King James Version of the Bible. Authorized King James Version.

Verses marked NIV are taken from the New International Version® of the Bible. Copyright © 1973, 1978, 1984 by the International Bible Society, published by the Zondervan Corporation, Grand Rapids, MI.

Verses marked NLT are taken from the New Living Translation of the Bible. Copyright © 1996 by the Tyndale House Publishers, Inc., Wheaton, IL.

www.xulonpress.com

COME ON IN — MEET THE AUTHOR

My life long friend, Gerry Alderink, has been the greatest God fearing witness in my life. She never tires of praising God and is always searching His Word to find what God will have her do. She so wants everyone to know of God's love and forgiveness. I hope this book will show others the way to God's plan for their lives.

Emily DeWitt, Grand Rapids, MI

Christians believe that God's Word is the one Perfect Book written by the Perfect One. Many commentaries have sprung forth to help people apply those truths to life. Gerry Alderink has created a treatise that is most helpful, covering many aspects of our interest. Devoted to Jesus Christ from her youth, she continues to serve in various capacities. I've known her for 35 years, witnessing her in action, especially while we taught, worked with and prayed for clients who called for counseling on the Christian Lifelines, Inc. which she founded and directed in Central Indiana for several years. She speaks from extensive research and personal experiences in a way that is heartfelt, practical, easy to read and understand.

Joan Salz, Carmel, IN

Gerry has been such a joy in my life. When I was in a very desperate situation in my life, she took me in for several days. I felt so safe. She was the first one to tell me about the ministry of the Holy Spirit, which made a lot of difference for me. Jesus became more real than I thought possible. People enjoy her writing about the Bible because they can understand what she is saying. I've shared her articles with many people, even by mail to another state. They continue asking for more. Her letters have also given me encouragement and helped me face several hardships. I am so happy to share a few words to honor my friend. You will want this book.

Doyce Chase Indianapolis, IN

Gerry Alderink was my first Bible study teacher and has become my spiritual mother and dear friend over the last twelve years. I had the privilege of working along side her as she led Compassion Helplines, Inc. as Executive Director from Jan. 1996 to Nov. 1997. This Christian telephone ministry reached out to lost and broken people. I can testify that Gerry is a woman after God's own heart! She is a true servant of our Lord Jesus Christ by ministering God's grace to the poor and needy. God has granted Gerry great wisdom and truth because of her unquenchable hunger and thirst for His Word. You will find refreshment for your soul as you journey through these pages. They contain life and truth that our Heavenly Father longs to give you. Enjoy!

Cherri Gaza, Indianapolis, IN

To Gerry Alderink— My love and heartfelt gratitude. A vibrant example of Christ, whose zealousness for the Lord breathes into my soul Words of Life.

June Cretors, Greenwood, IN

The words in this book were inspired by the Holy Spirit. Gerry has searched God's Word thousands of times to know His ways and His desire for us to live each and every day. Many times she would call me early in the morning after she had been searching and writing during the night. As she read those messages I experienced the power of the Holy Spirit minister to my heart.

She trusts the Lord with all of her heart, mind, and being, and has been the best teacher of all as she helped me to understand what God is saying in His Word. She has helped me to identify problems and the consequences of our actions when not following God's ways to overcome in the midst of struggles and hurts. She would bring me right to the exact Scripture for each situation.

I had breast cancer in 1991, and she prayed multiple times for me and trusted God by faith for my healing. She walked with me through that difficult time, helping me to overcome and trust God's Word. I give God all the glory because He completely healed me. Through her prayers, leadership, counseling and loving kindness, Gerry has helped me to become a better servant for our Lord Jesus Christ.

There are a couple special things she taught me. She took me on 'faith trips' for many years. My first reaction was, "What's that?" As we took van loads of clothing and so forth, through prayer God led us to needy places where we were to bring them. Each time our joy was overflowing! Another one is 'seeing God's love for us' when we found pennies. God has likened sparrows to pennies in connection with what God has said in the Word. The song says, "His eye is on the sparrow and I know He cares for me."

God has given her many amazing gifts, and I'm thankful to the Lord that she is my very wonderful and special friend.

Edith Sergent, Indianapolis, IN

My dear, most precious friend Gerry Alderink and I met on a mission cruise in Russia in 1993. She immediately became my prayer partner and encourager. As she shared her dreams of helping people around the world to know God's perfect love, she told me of her involvement in ministering to hurting people for several years in Indianapolis, IN as Founder and Director of a crisis line—Christian Lifelines, which later became Compassion Helplines.

She also shared another dream of writing a book on her love and admiration of the Word of God in a simplistic form, so anyone could read and understand the Gospel of Jesus Christ. It is with great joy and delight that I honor her dedication and devotion to the Lord with the release of REVITALIZING WORDS FOR HUNGRY HEARTS for such a time as this. Lovingly,

Marilyn James, Lakewood CA

This book is very special to me. It reveals a person with a great desire to be closer to God, to respond to almost any adversity we can meet in life and do it according to His Word. It is actually a guide for a happy and successful life for everyone who seeks true meaning to our existence.

Elena V. Batrakova, Ph.D, Asst. Prof. of Pharm. Sc.
Univ. of Nebraska Medical Center in Omaha

Gerry has been a spiritual mom to me. She loves the Word of God and has encouraged and prayed it with me and for me. It is because of this, our hearts have been joined with the Holy Spirit in our prayer times, and when the Lord put each of us on the other one's heart. The Lord has used these devotions for me in going through trials and tribulations, plus daily life for growth and understanding. I've been very blessed and grateful to know her.

Sharon Tanner, Omaha, NE

Gerry has been an inspiration to me since the day I met her. I knew instantly she is a person full of the Holy Spirit. I lost my mother at an early age and am honored to call her my "spiritual mom." I have learned so much from her about God. We laugh together, cry together, but most of all, we pray together.

Lee Acklie, Omaha, NE

My precious and vivacious friend, Gerry, loves the Word of God. Her personal relationship with Jesus Christ spills out into every inch of her life. Picture yourself sitting in the most comfortable chair in the front room of Gerry's home. Read this book as if she is conversing directly with you. Allow the truths of "God's Living Word" to sink into your whole being. Be transformed!

Carol Landrey, Elkhorn-Omaha, NE
Wife of the President of T.O.P.I.C. Ministry

Here is a book worth grabbing hold of. Gerry Alderink is a trusted author, and a woman worth following. In her book Revitalizing Words for Hungry Hearts, she uses Scriptures, parables and personal experiences to give you a deeper understanding of who God is, and brings life to the texts for application to the readers. If you are hungry and thirsty of heart, Gerry's grace saturated words with stylistic originality and power, not only reveals an artist at work, but will draw you into the presence of God to know Him more perfectly.

Mary Caltenco, Freelance Writer,
Bradenton, FL

The Preface of Gerry's book, and the chapter about forgiveness, especially touched me with the tender but direct explanation of God's truth. It explains the calling to forgive and the benefits of a heart filled with forgiveness. Gerry covers all angles of the necessary freedom of forgiveness to free the soul from the bondage of bitterness and grief—an important reminder to all Christians.

Jan Eckles, Orlando, FL
Author of- Trials of Today, Treasures for Tomorrow

DEDICATION

First of all I want to dedicate this book to my husband, R. Wayne Alderink, who went to be with Jesus Dec. 27, 2003. We enjoyed serving the Lord together in various forms of ministry, especially in Nursing Home ministry in segments of time across most of our 53 years of marriage. Today he is most probably singing in Heaven's Hallelujah Chorus and at other times trying out all the instruments of God's Glorious Orchestra. His sweet smile, as I proofread my messages to him, is still vivid in my mind. How great is our God!

I also dedicate this book to my four children and to their spouses who are precious gems in my heart and life; each one with their special God given qualities: Rod and Cheryl Brunsting, Tom and Marlene Lathers, Michael and Doris Alderink, and Stephen Alderink. They have added 14 most precious grandchildren, 2 granddaughters-in-law, and last year, 2 great-grandsons to enrich our family. God's grace has abundantly blessed all of us! To God be the glory, great things He has done!!!

ACKNOWLEDGMENTS

My heart overflows with gratitude to my Pastor David Haynes for what he has poured into my life through his preaching the Word of God and his compassion as he ministers to people. Wayne and I were recipients of this during Wayne's most desperate time of suffering. Pastor David has also encouraged me in exceptional ways to pursue the work of this book, my teaching on the subject of prayer and ministering to prisoners. A tremendous blessing!

This book has drawn in the help of many people who were diligent in editing for a more desirable presentation. The Lord provided the dearest busy bees to assist in the preparation. Realizing how important each one is, it is hard to properly thank them and give adequate acknowledgment. Toward the beginning Phyllis Beatty was there with her expertise. Later Joyce Brock became involved and Karen Kumpf as they provided excellent recommendations. Then my daughter Cheryl offered to help, and Carol Landrey, Bernie Bruning and James Jackson; each one offering very valuable insights along with cheering me on to the goal line. Special thanks also to Rob Pugh and James Jackson who are helping me send all the materials to the publisher. I have felt encouragement from all of these caring hearts and strength from their fervent prayers.

I need to add to the above precious people, another group of loving prayer warriors and encouragers. There's one huge concern in my heart; that somehow I could overlook anyone at this moment. If I do, please forgive! These come to mind in a special way, because their uplifting prayers are constantly my blessing: Edith Sergent, her daughters Sherry and Jami, Emily DeWitt, Jewell

Withers, Marilyn James, Joan Salz, June Cretors, Sandy Ploughe, Doyce Chase, Julia Davis, Todd Brown, Cherri Gaza, Cindy Evans, Beulah Lucas, Elizabeth Rogers, Evelyn Earl, Sharon Tanner, Sandy Heide, Ed & Margaret Karas, Elena Batrakova, Jeanne Effrein, Julie Osborn, Lee Acklie, Linda Cole, Jo Cecil, Bob & Alice Garvey, Don & Marcy Rowe, Larry & Sue Brazau, Steve & Ami Mortensen, Joel & Sherry Brandt, Mary Caltenco, Lydia Chorpening, Jan Eckles.

As I acknowledge you for the many ways that you have blessed me, it is my prayer that each of you will be richly supplied with God's provisions for every possible area of your lives, so that you may become productive and fruitful in an overflowing measure to the praise of His glory!

FOREWORD

Ever since Gerry asked me to write the forward to her book and sent me several chapters, I have had all sorts of things going through my mind about 'Words." I love words! Listening to them and proclaiming them make up a major part of my life as Pastor and Teacher of the Word of God. At a conference recently I heard a speaker say that he was addicted to words. "No, more than that," he said, "I am a dealer!" Our very ability to use words, (hear, read, recognize, and understand) is God given, and His first purpose in this is that we might know Him through His written Word. And then He has given us the capacity to write and speak and teach and preach that we might pass along His words to others!

Proverbs 25:11 says, "A word aptly spoken is like apples of gold in settings of silver." It was words well chosen, properly sequenced, defined, applied and aptly spoken that made the gospel irresistible to me the night I accepted Christ. Of the smitten Job it was said by Eliphaz, "Your words have supported those who stumbled; you have strengthened (by words) faltering knees." Jesus said that words come from the overflow of the heart that indeed when the tongue speaks or the pen writes it is our heart that is on parade. To Jesus words were very important! He urged us to be careful of every word because there would be an accounting.

I am amazed at what I hear these days concerning words. Words and the meaning of words and the usage of words is not important at all to growing numbers of people. How do we know a word means a certain thing? Who has the authority to stand behind all words and say in truth, "this is what this word means?" Remember this one? "How I answer your question depends on the meaning of the words "is!" Words, according to some can mean whatever the hearer wants them to mean. Isn't it interesting that the first words of temptation in the Garden begin, "Did God really say...?

I find it interesting that Fredrick Nietzche said, "We cannot get rid of God until we get rid of grammar." Was he saying that as long as we used words, the right words, using them correctly according to their meaning, that people would have no choice, at least intellectually, than to believe in God? In order to rid the world of God he attacked words and the meaning and use of words! Wonder how he would have gotten along with his agenda had he not used words which he carefully defined?

I'm very glad that this dear Christian woman who loves words has written this important, practical, well researched and well written book. But before I speak further concerning the book I would like to speak of the author. For the past several years it has been my very great privilege to be Gerry Alderink's Pastor. When I think about her and the way she conducts her life in Christ I remember that Augustine said that "A Christian should be a hallelujah from head to toe!" That fits Gerry so well! And her life now is even more remarkable to me because of the major hurdles she has had to overcome. When she was 2 and one half years old she was stricken with Group "A" Strep. It is an infection that eats the flesh. As a little girl a significant portion of one side of her face was eaten away and for 4 weeks the doctors fought to keep her alive and this was in the days before antibiotics. Her Christian parents prayed fervently, as did many other people, that her life would be spared. God answered their prayers and the flesh eating infection was stopped. It was as if God said, "This far and no further!" But the infection had done its work and beginning when Gerry was six she had nine reconstructive surgeries and according to her own testimony she had to deal with rejection in one form or another for what she describes as a few decades.

But Gerry would come to have power in her inner being through God's Spirit. She also would possess a beautiful soul. She lives according to the deep desire of earlier Christians who had this slogan, "to live all their life in the presence of God, under the authority of God, to the Glory of God."

This book is a direct result of that desire. She believes it is in response to a mandate from God. Out of her passion for God and her passion for words well understood and used correctly for the blessing they can be to us and others, she has written us a book! Keep it handy and close when you study and read God's Word. Refer to it when it is your task to preach or teach or lead a small group. As you cruise along with Gerry you will find so many aptly spoken words and when you do they will be "like apples of gold in settings of silver!" Take much joy in your journey!

Aristophanes, a Greek philosopher said, "by words the mind is winged." Thank you Gerry for using your life to praise, honor and give glory to the WORD. And thank you for helping us have words concerning His Word, that would enable our minds to soar!

David A. Haynes,
Assistant Professor of Pastoral Ministry
Nebraska Christian College
Norfolk, Nebraska

PREFACE

My personal invitation to you,

COME, COME, COME! Come with me on a cruise. This book is my ship. I've been preparing for years to have the greatest ship, with every cupboard, closet, nook and cranny loaded with the finest promises and blessings, with instructions how to use them from the Word of God. I've been fishing for glorious treasures too, and I pray that your heart will be stirred to go fishing while on this cruise. Maybe it will even give you a break-through in discovering how to find greater treasures than you ever thought were possible. There are so many more treasures for you to discover.

This ship has an 'all you can eat' buffet. Wow! Think about that! Remember, like I said, it's loaded. You'll find the finest delicacies and full-course meals in each concordance attached to the entrees. "Seek first the kingdom of God and His righteousness, and all these things (listed in previous verses) shall be added to you," is the major instruction our Captain has given for this voyage. Let me slip this in here, there are more cruises in the making. Oh yes, completely new menus.

Many years ago, it's seems like ages, my heart was yearning to understand God's Word. At first it seemed too hard. I didn't understand very much. But as I continued to yield to the Holy Spirit's urgings it became easier, and then I would spend hours just gulping as I became so hungry and thirsty for truth.

After writing and re-writing across the years, and yes, re-writing again, it's time to share some of these treasures with you, who are also searching for truth. I want to tell the whole world that God truly is Almighty God, and there's only One. I also feel an urgency to let people know that "God so loved the world that He gave His only begotten Son, that whoever believes in Him, should not perish, but have eternal life." Many of you already know the verse so well, but we can easily forget the depth of its meaning. It tells me that He is not just sitting in heaven waiting for opportunities to klonk us every time He sees us doing something that doesn't please Him. Not at all. His arms are wide open as He calls us to a love relationship!

That doesn't mean that He ignores sin in our lives, but His love is full of mercy, and He is so gracious that He will go great lengths to draw us from sin unto Himself, and to desire His ways; to depart from sin and avoid sin like a plague. He wants us to be free from the bondages that our life's choices, habits, cravings, false teachings and stuff like that have gotten us into. In John 8:31-32 and 36 we find that truth—"Then Jesus said to those Jews who believed Him, 'If you abide in My word, you are My disciples indeed. And you shall know the truth, and the truth shall make you free. ...Therefore if the Son makes you free, you shall be free indeed." Only Jesus can set you free; it's not head knowledge, not works, not pleasing people, not becoming religious, not working 60 hours a week, nor by earning points for reading through the Bible yearly—only in Jesus can we become free! With just that good news we can move toward freedom in the Spirit.

You may question why you should go on such a cruise as this, to read a book I've written. I questioned it too, until I recognized God's voice and the leading of the Holy Spirit. Back in 1984 He asked me to begin a Christian Crisis Line in Indianapolis, Indiana. I couldn't imagine that He was asking me to do that. We had many discussions—not arguments; I just had to ask many questions, over a period of weeks, to make sure I was hearing a request from Him, not just my imagination without validity. In the midst of a discussion, I became sure that I was too old already to spend 40 years on the back side of the desert, as Moses did. That would put me in my 90s—too late to produce fruit for God's glory!

I became aware that when we ignore the Lord's urgings, nudging, calling, or whatever else He uses, He may never call on us again. That gripped my heart, so I said, "Yes, Sir, I'll do whatever you wish, but You have to lead me." His answer came quickly, "I'm glad you recognize that, for I'm the boss, you're my secretary." So that's how I've responded to the urgency of preparing this ship of God's grace; absolutely all glory belongs to HIM!

My heart rejoices to think that you've decided to come with me,
Gerry Alderink

INTRODUCTION TO REVITALIZING WORDS FOR HUNGRY HEARTS

AND THIRSTY SOULS: "*As the deer pants for the water brooks, so pants my soul for You, O God. My soul thirsts for God, for the Living God.*" *Psalm 42:1-2a*

God has given us a book of history, promises, direction, instructions, warnings, and much more. **Words** are powerful; however, God's Word is the absolute **truth**, and is the final word relating to any subject, whether it involves creation, which is God's masterpiece, the history and development of nations, philosophy, psychology, science, health, and all other subject matters.

God's **grace** has provided **redemption** and **forgiveness** through the shed blood of Jesus Christ. He wants us to experientially enjoy His **reconciliation** and **restoration** through the work of the Holy Spirit in our hearts. All of this is possible as we surrender self in exchange for Christ's **righteousness** and **partake** of His Divine nature.

He desires to **reveal** Himself and His **glory** to each one of us, for He is Almighty God, the only True God. He is the King of kings and Lord of lords; His **kingdom** is an eternal kingdom that cannot be shaken or destroyed, therefore His **judgment** stands over all the nations of the earth as their Creator and Judge.

God is persistently calling people from all nations, encouraging them to **come,** because He is not willing that any should perish. So **listen** carefully and **seek the Lord**, for this wonderful **new** vibrant way of living is for all who **believe** on the Lord Jesus Christ and **follow** Him. When we **acknowledge** God as the Supreme Being, we are enabled to gain **understanding** and we're able to **trust** Him through all kinds of circumstances. He urges us to **abide** in Him, and **walk** with **steadfastness** in the security of His love. He becomes our **refuge** and **deliverer** in time of trouble, and He offers **strength** for all our daily experiences.

Come, let us **rejoice** in the Lord together, and **WORSHIP** Him wholeheartedly with gratitude and praise!

WORDS

WORDS ARE POWERFUL

WORDS are powerful. They are used in court; they make up important documents, including the Constitution of the United States. Words are crafted to draw people to buy certain products. Words are used in playing games, but also used for instruction in class rooms all through our school years and then we are instructed at our place of business. Even the President of the United States receives instructions for his various daily tasks.

Words are an extremely important means of communication through many avenues. They can either make your day, or break it. They bring comfort and encouragement, or fear and discouragement. Words can give clear direction or total confusion. They bond a relationship, or destroy it. Words may be expressed gently, or unreasonably harsh.

Have you noticed how words can come flowing into your mind like a gentle stream, and another time negative thoughts come like hurricane winds threatening to flatten you out? You may begin your day with hope and anticipation, but as you're working, other thoughts come forcefully ushering in despair. We often do not consider that we can control our thoughts. It appears as though we have to take them as they come, and try to work with them the best we can. Words seem to take over, like it or not, but God's Word reveals that we make choices. We are so blessed to have His Word to give us direction and understanding.

GOD'S WORD REVEALS HIS CHARACTER

Throughout the Bible we find many words and phrases referring to the integrity and the strength of the words God spoke to the people, carrying their power throughout all generations. In Genesis 26:1-5, we find an excellent example. There was a famine in the land, which had also happened during Abraham's time, and Isaac went to king Abimelech. Then the Lord appeared to him and told him not to go down to Egypt, but to stay there in Gerar. He promised to bless him and his descendants by giving him all those lands, just as He had sworn to Abraham, his father. God had promised that his seed would be multiplied as the stars of heaven, and that all the nations of the earth would be blessed on this basis: "...because Abraham obeyed My voice and kept My charge, My commandments, My statutes, and My laws." All of these refer to the words God spoke. They are full of hope and promises that God fulfilled. He never fails!

We find other words expressed, particularly in Psalm 119, which give great importance to whatever God says to His people, such as: His precepts, testimonies, and righteous judgments. The important observation is—whatever God says, His words are profound and weighty. They are never 'just words, take them or leave them.' When God spoke, His words were unchangeable, Isaiah 40:8. His Words are forever established in heaven, Psalm 119:89.

In Isaiah 14 there are two other outstanding verses which verify these truths. Verse 24 says: "The Lord of hosts has sworn, saying, 'Surely, as I have thought, so it shall come to pass, and as I have purposed, so it shall stand.'" And verse 27 says: "For the Lord of hosts has purposed, and who will annul it? His hand is stretched out, and who will turn it back?" In these verses we see that even what God thought, would come to pass, and whatever He purposed would stand, absolutely immovable. Remember, God spoke, and His creation came into being from nothing, and during the first five days there was not a man or animal to hear Him. And no one could ever alter His choices. Can man choose to remove any river, or another body of water to transplant it in another location? Can man choose to move a mountain from one country to another, or change the position of a planet in the heavens? Can man choose to rearrange the seasons within the year?

God's Word tells us in Psalm 33:11, "The counsel of the Lord stands forever, the plans of His heart to all generations." In Proverbs 21:30 we read, "There is no wisdom or understanding or counsel against the Lord." Also Isaiah 55:11 says, "So shall My word be that goes forth from My mouth; it shall not return to Me void, but it shall accomplish what I please, and it shall prosper in the thing for which I sent it." How clearly these verses show us the determination and power of God's words.

The written Word has come to us through the Holy Spirit, as He breathed the words upon the writers. In 2 Peter 1:19-21, Peter tells us: "And so we have the prophetic word confirmed, which you do well to heed as a light that shines in a dark place, until the day dawns and the morning star rises in your hearts; knowing this first, that no prophecy of Scripture is of any private interpretation, for prophecy never came by the will of man, but holy men of God spoke as they were moved by the Holy Spirit." Another writer, Timothy, says it in these words, "All Scripture is given by inspiration of God, and is profitable for doctrine, for reproof, for correction, for instruction in righteousness" *2 Timothy 3:16*.

These truths are so very important to grasp in your heart and mind, for then the WORD becomes alive for you. His Word is 'spirit and life' according to John 6:63. Psalm 119:105 refers to the Word as "a lamp to my feet and a light to my path." Possibly you have thought that God's Word seems 'old fashioned and needs to be more up-to-date'; or that the words are too demanding, and impossible to obey. However, the Word of God is as important, as anointed, and as precious for our everyday living now, as it was in Bible times. As you study the Word, and believe the truths that are set forth, you can be set free from any bondage, as is promised in John 8:31, 32 and 36. Read the whole chapter for greater understanding.

It may seem like God is asleep, and doesn't really know what's going on in the world today, and even more particularly in your life. Do not be deceived. God is a NOW GOD, all eternity past, throughout all eternity future. God sees and knows everything, all the time. He doesn't choose to handle things our way, for His wisdom and knowledge far surpass ours. Isaiah 55:8 and 9 says, "For My thoughts are not your thoughts, nor are your ways My ways," says the Lord. "For as the heavens are higher than the earth, so are My ways higher than your ways, and My thoughts than your thoughts."

CAUTION FOR HOW WE USE WORDS

Thoughts are words. They become more powerful when they are expressed, so we need to pay very close attention to what we even think, for these words have a way of spilling out, sometimes in words, sometimes in our body language, and sometimes in our deeds. They can be a blessing, or be destructive. Possibly you haven't considered how powerful your words can be.

We are especially instructed about the words of our mouth, or lips, in the Psalms, Proverbs and Ecclesiastes. Many are listed in our Scriptures for this word. The Gospels also give us some very strong guidance. You see, we have a choice about the kind of words that will come forth from our mouths today. Will you bless or curse? Will you express God's love and grace from a heart that abides with Jesus day by day, or respond abruptly to circumstances and how others have spoken to you? Sometimes we are very critical of others, or speak harshly because of disturbed emotions. But we can choose a mind-set that we will bless everyone that we communicate with in some way today. We can choose to give spiritual gems that will give encouragement, hope, and purpose in their lives. We can provide a reason to smile and to be glad in their hearts.

The words we speak will judge us, according to what Jesus was teaching the multitudes in Matthew 12:35-37, where it says, "A good man out of the good treasure of his heart brings forth good things, and an evil man out of the evil treasure brings forth evil things. But I say to you that for every idle word men may speak, they will give account of it in the Day of Judgment. For by your words you will be justified, and by your words you will be condemned."

PAUL IS CAUTIOUS IN PRESENTING THE GOSPEL

Paul gives interesting insights about his preaching, as he wrote to the Corinthian Christians. In 1 Corinthians 1:17, he says, "For Christ did not send me to baptize, but to preach the gospel, not with wisdom of words, lest the cross of Christ should be made of no effect." And in 1 Corinthians 2:4, 5 and 13: "And my speech and my preaching were not with persuasive words of human wisdom, but in demonstration of the Spirit and of power, that your faith should not be in the wisdom of men but in the power of God. These things we also speak, not in words which man's wisdom teaches but which the Holy Spirit teaches, comparing spiritual things with spiritual."

Paul was very cautious about how he presented the gospel message; not wanting to sound persuasive, or coercive. He found it vitally important to yield to the Holy Spirit so He could demonstrate His power, and the people would know that it's not man's wisdom, but God's power that changes lives. In no way did he want to present his personal opinions. He taught what he had learned from the Scriptures and the Apostles' teachings with an anointing of the Holy Spirit. He recognized that only the Holy Spirit could impact people's hearts with the gospel in a way that would change lives for the glory of God. If you teach the Word to anyone, it is well to consider Paul's personal concern.

We can never realize the full impact that our words may have on someone who is listening casually, and possibly it is someone we didn't even know was listening. Then at other times we may be trying hard to impress our children with a powerful word from the Lord, and wonder if it will have much effect on their lives.

Just before Christmas 2004, I received a marvelous book The God Who Hung On the Cross, from the International Cooperating Ministries.[1] It is marvelously written by its Founder Dois Rosser, and Helen Vaughn. They each share their part in how this ministry was formed and about several of their mission stories, which reveal how dependent they were and are for God's power to work out the impossible situations. I am including this especially for a powerful incident that is shared in the book and has influenced the book title.

There were many villagers ordered out of their huts and the village to an area where they were forced to dig a trench, which they expected would be their grave. They expected they would be "bludgeoned to death" as many others had gone down before. After laying down their tools for digging, some screamed to Buddha and other sources for their intervention. "Then one woman began to cry, intuitively, to one of her earliest memories—the faint echo of a story told her by her mother about the God who hung on the cross. She called out to that God. Surely the One who had suffered Himself might have compassion on those about to die. Time stopped. The humid jungle air lay still.

"Suddenly the screams around her became one great wail, as the entire village called out as one, crying for their lives to the God who hung on the cross. There was only silence. They sobbed into the darkness of the pit before them. Silence. A flicker of hope. And then the people turned, one by one by one. The jungle was empty. The soldiers were gone. And ever since that astounding day in 1979, the people of that village had been waiting . . . waiting for someone to come and tell them more . . .more about the God who hung on the cross."

They waited for 20 years. That woman's mother, in the midst of Buddhism, spiritism and many other religions, except Christianity, somehow had heard of the God who hung on a cross, and must have expressed it often enough to her children that this daughter was enabled by the Holy Spirit to recall this truth at such a time as this. God answered her heart-cry!

Words are powerful! When we fill ourselves with the Word of God, which is a great cleanser of the heart and mind, we are not so apt to express words that would dishonor Him. Yet, may this also help us to recognize the mandate that God has given us to spread the gospel. It may be that your children's friends are the ones to begin with. Then think about the other children in your neighborhood; what can the Lord accomplish through you? Can you imagine your gathering becoming a 'Sunday School' class in your home? Besides teaching the Word of God, missionary stories from the YWAM books [2] would make a great addition. It's not only what we can do, but through our commitment and believing prayers, 'what God can do' with the words we speak!

I give you these words from Colossians 3:16 and 17 as a closing: "Let the word of Christ dwell in you richly in all wisdom, teaching and admonishing one another in psalms and hymns and spiritual songs, singing with grace in your hearts to the Lord. And whatever you do in word or deed, do all in the name of the Lord Jesus, giving thanks to God the Father through Him." May the grace of the Lord Jesus Christ be with you!

SCRIPTURES FOR WORDS

Importance of God's words – His instructions and commands—-

Ex. 19:3-9 And Moses went up to God, and the Lord called to him from the mountain, saying, "Thus you shall say to the house of Jacob, and tell the children of Israel: 'You have seen what I did to the Egyptians, and how I bore you on eagles' wings and brought you to Myself. Now therefore, if you will indeed obey My voice and keep My covenant, then you shall be a special treasure to Me above all people; for all the earth is Mine. And you shall be to Me a kingdom of priests and a holy nation.' These are the **words** which you shall speak to the children of Israel." So Moses came and called for the elders of the people, and laid before them all these **words** which the Lord commanded him. Then all the people answered together and said, "All that the Lord has spoken we will do." So Moses brought back the **words** of the people to the Lord. And the Lord said to Moses, "Behold, I come to you in the thick cloud that the people may hear when I speak with you, and believe you for ever." So Moses told the **words** of the people to the Lord.

Deut. 5:22 These **words** *(the Ten commandments)* the Lord spoke to all your assembly, in the mountain from the midst of the fire, the cloud, and the thick darkness, with a loud voice; and He added no more. And He wrote them on two tablets of stone and gave them to me *(Moses)*.

Deut. 8:13 So He humbled you, allowed you to hunger, and fed you with manna which you did not know nor did your fathers know, that He might make you know that man shall not live by bread alone; but man lives by every **word** that proceeds from the mouth of the Lord. *Quoted in Matt. 4:4 and Luke 4:4.*

Deut. 11:18 Therefore you shall lay up these **words** of Mine in your heart and in your soul, and bind them as a sign on your hand, and they shall be as frontlets between your eyes. *Also see verses 19-25 and 6:5-25.*

Deut. 17:19 And it shall be with him, and he *(the king)* shall read it all the days of his life, that he may learn to fear the Lord His God and be careful to observe all the **words** of this law and these statutes.

Ps. 119:160-162 The entirety of Your **word** is truth, and every one of Your righteous judgments endure forever. Princes persecute me without a cause, but my heart stands in awe of Your **word**. I rejoice at Your **word** as one who finds great treasure.

Prov. 22:20-21 Have I not written to you excellent things of counsels and knowledge, that I may make you know the certainty of the **words** of truth, that you may answer **words** of truth to those who send to you?

Jer. 26:2 "Thus says the Lord: 'Stand in the court of the Lord's house, and speak to all the cities of Judah, which come to worship in the Lord's house, all the **words** that I command you to speak to them. Do not diminish a **word**.'"

Rev. 22:19 "….and if anyone takes away from the **words** of this prophecy, God will take away his part from the Book of Life, from the holy city, and from the things which are written in this book."

The word of the Lord is—-

2 Sam. 22:31 As for God, His way is perfect, the **word** of the Lord is proven; He is a shield to all who trust in Him.

Ps. 12:6 The **words** of the Lord are pure words like silver tried in a furnace of earth, purified seven times.

Ps. 33:4 For the **word** of the Lord is right, and all His work is done in truth.

Ps. 119:103-105 How sweet are Your **words** to my taste, sweeter than honey to my mouth! Through Your precepts I get understanding; therefore I hate every false way. Your **word** is a lamp to my feet and a light to my path.

Prov. 30:5 Every **word** of God is pure; He is a shield to those who put their trust in Him.

Jer. 15:16 Your **words** were found, and I ate them, and Your **word** was to me the joy and rejoicing of my heart; for I am called by Your name, O Lord God of hosts.

Jer. 20:8-9 For when I spoke I cried out; I shouted, "Violence and plunder!" Because the **word** of the Lord was made to me a reproach and a derision daily. Then I said, "I will not make mention of Him, nor speak anymore in His name." But His **word** was in my heart like a burning fire shut up in my bones; I was weary of holding it back, and I could not.

John 1:1, 14 In the beginning was the **Word**, and the **Word** was with God, and the **Word** was God *(Jesus)*. ....And the **Word** became flesh and dwelt among us, and we beheld His glory as of the only begotten of the Father, full of grace and truth.

John 6:63, 68 "It is the Spirit who gives life; the flesh profits nothing. The **words** that I *(Jesus)* speak to you are spirit and they are life." ....But Simon Peter answered Him, "Lord to whom shall we go? You have the **words** of eternal life."

John 17:14, 17 "I have given them *(Jesus' disciples)* Your **word**; and the world has hated them because they are not of the world, just as I am not of the world. ....Sanctify them by Your truth. Your **word** is truth."

The faithfulness and power of God's eternal Word —-

1 Kings 8:56 "Blessed be the Lord, who has given rest to His people Israel, according to all that He promised. There has not failed one **word** of all His good promise, which He promised through His servant Moses.

Ps. 33:6 By the **word** of the Lord the heavens were made, and all the host of them by the breath of His mouth.

Ps. 119:89 Forever, O Lord, Your **word** is settled in heaven. *See Isa. 40:8, Matt. 24:35*

Ps. 119:130 The entrance of Your **word** gives light; it gives understanding to the simple.

Isa. 45:22-23 "Look to Me, and be saved, all you ends of the earth! For I am God, and there is no other. I have sworn by Myself; the **word** has gone out of My mouth in righteousness, and shall not return, that to Me every knee shall bow, every tongue shall take an oath."

Isa. 55:11 So shall My **word** be that goes forth from My mouth; it shall not return to Me void, but it shall accomplish what I please, and it shall prosper in the thing for which I sent it.

Jer. 23:28-30 "The prophet who has a dream, let him tell a dream; and he who has My **word**, let him speak My **word** faithfully. What is the chaff to the wheat?" says the Lord. "Is not My **word** like a fire?" says the Lord, "and like a hammer that breaks the rock in pieces? Therefore behold, I am against the prophets," says the Lord, "who steal My **words** every one from his neighbor."

Luke 14:44 *Jesus was with His disciples—* Then He said to them, "These are the **words** which I spoke to you while I was still with you, that all things must be fulfilled which were written in the Law of Moses and the Prophets and the Psalms concerning Me."

Eph. 6:17 And take the helmet of salvation; and the sword of the Spirit, which is the **word** of God.

2 Tim. 2:8-9 Remember that Jesus Christ, of the seed of David, was raised from the dead according to my gospel, for which I suffer trouble as an evildoer, even to the point of chains; but the **word** of God is not chained.

Heb. 1:1-3 God, who at various times and in various ways spoke in time past to the fathers by the prophets, has in these last days spoken to us by His son, whom He has appointed heir of all things, through whom also He made the worlds; who being the brightness of His glory and the express image of His person, and upholding all things by the **word** of His power, when He had by Himself purged our sins, sat down at the right hand of the Majesty on high....

Heb. 4:12 For the **Word** of God is living and powerful, and sharper than any two-edged sword, piercing even to the division of soul and spirit and of joints and marrow, and is a discerner of the thoughts and intents of the heart.

Heb. 11:3 By faith we understand that the worlds *(universe)* were framed by the **word** of God, so that the things which are seen were not made of things which are visible.

1 Peter 1:23-25 ...having been born again, not of corruptible seed but incorruptible, through the **word** of God which lives and abides forever, because "All flesh is as grass, and all the glory of man as the flower of the grass. The grass withers, and its flower falls away, but the **word** of the Lord endures forever." Now this is the **word** which by the gospel was preached to you.

Prayers—-

Ps. 5:1 Give ear to my **words**, O Lord, consider my meditation. Give heed to the voice of my cry, my King and my God.

Ps. 19:14 Let the **words** of my mouth and the meditation of my heart be acceptable in Your sight, O Lord, my strength and my Redeemer.

Ps. 119:41-44 Let Your mercies come also to me, O Lord—Your salvation according to Your **word**. So shall I have an answer for him who reproaches me, for I trust in Your **word**. And take not the **word** of truth utterly out of my mouth, for I have hoped in Your ordinances. So shall I keep Your law continually, forever and ever.

Ps. 139:4 For there is not a **word** on my tongue, but behold, O Lord, You know it altogether.

Instructions to listen and to be cautious of the words we speak —-

Prov. 4:20-22 My son, give attention to my **words**; incline your ear to my sayings. Do not let them depart from your eyes; keep them in the midst of your heart; for they are life to those who find them, and health to all their flesh.

Prov. 15:1-2 A soft answer turns away wrath, but a harsh **word** stirs up anger. The tongue of the wise uses knowledge rightly, but the mouth of fools pours out foolishness.

Prov. 15:23 A man has joy by the answer of his mouth, and a **word** spoken in due season, how good it is!

Prov. 16:23-24 The heart of the wise teaches his mouth, and adds learning to his lips. Pleasant **words** are like a honeycomb, sweetness to the soul and health to the bones.

Prov. 18:4, 8 The **words** of a man's mouth are deep water; the wellspring of wisdom is a flowing brook. ....The **words** of a talebearer are like tasty trifles, and they go down into the inmost body. *See Prov. 20:19.*

Prov. 23:12 Apply your heart to instruction, and your ears to **words** of knowledge.

Prov. 25:11 A **word** fitly spoken is like apples of gold in settings of silver.

Isa. 30:21 Your ears shall hear a **word** behind you; saying, "This is the way, walk in it," whenever you turn to the right hand or whenever you turn to the left.

Matt. 12:35-37 "A good man out of the good treasure of his heart brings forth good things, and an evil man out of the evil treasure brings forth evil things. But I *(Jesus)* say to you that for every idle **word** men may speak, they will give account of it in the day of judgment. For by your **words** you will be justified, and by your **words** you will be condemned."

John 12:47-48 "And if anyone hears My **words** and does not believe, I do not judge him; for I did not come to judge the world but to save the world. He who rejects Me, and does not receive My **words**, has that which judges him—the **word** that I have spoken will judge him in the last day."

Rom. 10:16-18 But they have not all obeyed the gospel. For Isaiah says, "Lord, who has believed our report *(words)*?" So then faith comes by hearing, and hearing by the **word** of God. But I say, have they not heard? Yes indeed: "Their sound has gone out to all the earth, and their **words** to the ends of the world." *See Ps. 19:4.*

Col. 3:16-17 Let the **word** of Christ dwell in you richly in all wisdom, teaching and admonishing one another in psalms and hymns and spiritual songs, singing with grace in your hearts to the Lord. And whatever you do in **word** or deed, do all in the name of the Lord Jesus, giving thanks to God the Father through Him.

2 Tim. 2:14-15 Remind them of these things, charging them before the Lord not to strive about **words** to no profit, to the ruin of the

hearers. Be diligent to present yourself approved to God, a worker who does not need to be ashamed, rightly dividing the **word** of truth.

2 Tim. 4:2 Preach the **word**! Be ready in season and out of season. Convince, rebuke, exhort, with all longsuffering and teaching.

James 1:21-22 Therefore lay aside all filthiness and overflow of wickedness, and receive with meekness the implanted **word**, which is able to save your souls. But be doers of the **word**, and not hearers only, deceiving yourselves.

1 John 1:9-10 If we confess our sins, He is faithful and just to forgive us our sins and to cleanse us from all unrighteousness. If we say that we have not sinned, we make Him a liar, and His **word** is not in us.

1 John 2:5 But whoever keeps His **word**, truly the love of God is perfected in him. By this we know that we are in Him.

Warnings—-

Prov. 10:19-21 In the multitude of **words** sin is not lacking, but he who restrains his lips is wise. The tongue of the righteous is choice silver; the heart of the wicked is worth little. The lips of the righteous feed many, but fools die for lack of wisdom.

Eccl. 5:2-3 Do not be rash with your mouth, and let not your heart utter anything hastily before God. For God is in heaven, and you on earth; therefore let your **words** be few. For a dream comes through much activity, and a fool's voice is known by his many **words**.

Eccl. 9:16-17 Then I said: "Wisdom is better than strength. Nevertheless the poor man's wisdom is despised, and his **words** are not heard. **Words** of the wise, spoken quietly, should be heard rather than the shout of a ruler of fools.

Ezek. 12:25, 28 *The word of the Lord kept coming to Ezekiel also.* "For I am the Lord. I speak, and the **word** which I speak will come to pass; it will no more be postponed; for in your days, O rebellious house, I will say the **word** and perform it," says the Lord God. ...."Therefore say to them, 'Thus says the Lord God: "None of My **words** will be postponed any more, but the **word** which I speak will be done." says the Lord God.'"

Rev. 22:18-19 For I testify to everyone who hears the **words** of the prophecy of this book: If anyone adds to these things, God will add to him the plagues that are written in this book; and if anyone takes away from the **words** of the book of this prophecy, God shall take away his part from the Book of Life, from the holy city, and from the things which are written in this book.

Where His Word can be effective—-

John 15:3-4, 7 *Jesus is speaking*—-"You are already clean because of the **word** which I have spoken to you. Abide in Me, and I in you. As the branch cannot bear fruit of itself, unless it abides in the vine, neither can you, unless you abide in Me. ....If you abide in Me, and My **words** abide in you, you will ask what you desire, and it shall be done for you."

Rom. 10:8-10 But what does it say? "The **word** is near you, in your mouth and in your heart" (that is, the **word** of faith which we preach): that if you confess with your mouth the Lord Jesus and believe in your heart that God has raised Him from the dead, you will be saved. For with the heart one believes unto righteousness, and with the mouth confession is made unto salvation.

1 Thess. 2:13 For this reason we also thank God without ceasing, because when you received the **word** of God which you heard from us, you welcomed it not as the **word** of men, but as it is in truth, the **word** of God, which also effectively works in you who believe.

Heb. 4:2 For indeed the gospel was preached to us as well as to them; but the **word** which they heard did not profit them, not being mixed with faith in those who heard it.

The ministry of the word of God —-

Acts 6:2-4 Then the twelve summoned the multitude of the disciples and said, "It is not desirable that we should leave the **word** of God and serve tables. Therefore, brethren, seek out from among you seven men of good report reputation, full of the Holy Spirit and wisdom, whom we may appoint over this business; but we will give ourselves continually to prayer and to the ministry of the **word**."

Acts 13:48-49 Now when the Gentiles heard this, they were glad and glorified the **word** of the Lord, and as many as had been appointed to eternal life believed. And the **word** of the Lord was being spread throughout the region.

1 Cor. 1:17 NIV For Christ did not send me to baptize, but to preach the gospel—not with **words** of human wisdom, lest the cross of Christ be emptied of its power.

1 Cor. 2:4-5, 13 And my speech and my preaching were not with persuasive **words** of human wisdom, but in demonstration of the Spirit and of power, that your faith should not be in the wisdom of men but in the power of God. ....These things we also speak, not in **words** which man's wisdom teaches but which the Holy Spirit teaches, comparing spiritual things with spiritual.

2 Cor. 2:17 For we are not, as so many, peddling the **word** of God; but as of sincerity, but as from God, we speak in the sight of God in Christ.

2 Cor. 4:2 But we have renounced the hidden things of shame, not walking in craftiness nor handling the **word** of God deceitfully, but by manifestation of the truth commending ourselves to every man's conscience in the sight of God.

Rev. 22:7-9 "Behold, I *(Jesus)* am coming quickly! Blessed is he who keeps the **words** of the prophecy of this book." Now I, John, saw and heard these things. And when I heard and saw, I fell down to worship before the feet of the angel who showed me these things. Then he said to me, "See that you do not do that. For I am your fellow servant, and of your brethren the prophets, and of those who keep the **words** of this book. Worship God."

TRUTH

CHARACTERISTICS OF TRUTH

What is truth? Evidently many people choose for themselves what truth is. In court the witnesses are to swear that they will tell the truth, nothing but the truth, so help me God. And then they say what they want to say, oftentimes hiding the truth in a cunning way, and skirting around the truth, making a lie sound like the truth. Although there are stories in the Bible of wicked people who did not speak the truth, what is being presented in the Word of God is true, inspired by the Holy Spirit through chosen men of God, to tell the truth. Psalm 119:160 says, "The entirety of Your word is truth, and every one of Your righteous judgments endures forever."

Taking the Old Testament Scriptures, we find these words associated with truth: mercy; gracious longsuffering and abounding in goodness; love, sincerity, faithfulness, salvation, lovingkindness; compassion and merciful kindness. These great words do not associate with the expression of emotions, or the actions of the person who is lying. Usually there are several things in their speech and actions that raise red flags, betraying the one who is lying.

Of one thing you can be sure: God will never forsake His mercy and truth; He is infallible and faithful to His divine nature. He cannot lie! Every attribute of God portrays a Sovereign Being who is unquestionably, absolutely true, and all He says is completely true. Jesus, who is the way, the truth, the life, as the Son of God is the same as His heavenly Father. Our children can differ from us in their personalities, their choices in life, and many other differences, but not so with Jesus and His Father, they are one in Spirit and essence, in righteousness and holiness.

When Jesus said, "I tell you the truth," He could speak no other way. We often read in the gospels where Jesus prefaced His preaching and teachings with those very words. Therefore, whatever facts Jesus gave, were absolutely true and we can believe what He says. This makes it exceedingly important that we listen carefully to everything He says, and plant our faith in Him.

THE POWER OF TRUTH

Ephesians 6: 10-18 gives instructions about putting on the armor of God, so that we might be able to stand against the wiles of the devil. Just hearing that makes one know the Word shows urgency for studying to know what God has to say to us. Verse 14 says, "Stand therefore, having girded your waist with truth, having put on the breastplate of righteousness." What could 'girded with truth' mean? One who is girded is wearing a girdle—a belt, or a sash; something that encircles around the waist, giving support. Truth is not something that you can put on like a piece of clothing. Truth has to be learned, from reading, or from a teacher. So putting this all together—a girdle of truth must be like having the knowledge of God's Word that would give the support you need for any unusual and unexpected situation, hardship or spiritual battle.

This reminds me of Jesus, just after His baptism and the outpouring of the Holy Spirit. His Father, Almighty God, had just anointed Him for His ministry. Then He was led by the Spirit into the wilderness to be tempted by the devil. *See Matthew 4:1-11.* This was the test that proved Christ Jesus' divinity. As Jesus was being tempted by the devil, He was not struggling to figure out what to do about these three temptations. Not at all! He was definitely girded with truth, for He is truth. He was able to recite a Scripture for each one, and each Scripture broke the power of Satan in that particular temptation.

It has happened often in my life when I had no clue how to deal with certain situations, but as I prayed, and waited quietly before Him, His answer would come to me by way of a Scripture I knew, or a spiritual song. When I was in my teens, I asked the Lord to plant a hungering and thirsting in my heart for His Word. He surely did answer that prayer; it is a prayer that He always delights to answer! Many of Satan's temptations, so cunningly camouflaged, could draw us into his snares, but Jesus, the truth, is able to help us recall exactly the right Scriptures. The light of His truths that are anchored in our hearts will reveal the hidden snare awaiting us, and can keep us from falling, if we choose to listen and obey.

But there is another reason we need to know the truths of the Word. We are to spread the good news. However, we can't do that if we hardly know these truths for our own lives. We need to help others get out of their ditches, and only in the power of God's Word and the name of Jesus, can we give them something solid to hold on to in order to climb out. Truth is also the only way to become free from bondages. People are in bondages because they have believed a lie. One of the biggest lies, which is so cunningly set out there before all of us, is that we need entertainment in order to relax in our busy lives.

Even ball games, video games and card games can fill your time, so there's none left for a personal relationship with the Lord. Let me give you a secret, studying God's Word and having a sanctified prayer time is the most relaxing, blessed thing you can do for yourself. But let's not be selfish; invite a few other couples to share this wonderful time with you. This is true refreshment for your whole being! Christian bookstores have a variety of Bible study books to choose from.

THE HOLY SPIRIT – THE SPIRIT OF TRUTH

The Holy Spirit is the Spirit of truth. There is a category for these Scriptures in the attached concordance. Read the surrounding verses in your Bible too, so that you can much better understand the basic truths.

For those who haven't become Christians yet, when you invite Jesus into your heart, the Spirit of truth will come to live within you. He's totally prepared to bring to your remembrance the Word that you've read or studied, and even provides new ones. Psalm 145:18-19 are so encouraging—"The Lord is near to all who call upon Him, to all who call upon Him in truth. He will fulfill the desire of those who fear *(respect, honor and reverence)* Him; He also will hear their cry and save them."

Remember to gird yourself with truth daily, then you will have a good Scriptural foundation. If you happen to hear a false prophet, who is teaching false doctrines; truth will show you the lie. The message of John 8:31, 32 sheds light on this: "Then Jesus said to those Jews who believed Him, 'If you abide in My word, you are my disciples indeed. And you shall know the truth, and the truth shall make you free.'" Then verse 36: "Therefore if the Son makes you free, you shall be free indeed." Isn't that powerful truth!

I pray that you are challenged to search for those fabulous, freeing Scriptures that relate to every situation of your life. Keep on going beyond the basic requirements, for that's where the depth of truth will become visual and alive to you by the guidance of the Holy Spirit!

SCRIPTURES FOR
TRUTH

The Lord God is the God of Truth—

Gen 24:27 And he said, "Blessed be the Lord God of my master Abraham, who has not forsaken His mercy and **truth** toward my master. As for me, being on the way, the Lord led me to the house of my master's brethren."

Ex. 34:6 And the Lord passed before him and proclaimed, The Lord, the Lord God, merciful and gracious, longsuffering, and abounding in goodness and **truth**...."

Ps. 31:5 Into Your hand I commit my spirit; You have redeemed me, O Lord God of **truth**.

Ps. 33:4 For the word of the Lord is right, and all His work is done in **truth**.

Ps. 40:10-11 I have not hidden Your righteousness within my heart; I have declared Your faithfulness and Your salvation; I have not concealed Your lovingkindness and Your **truth** from the great assembly. Do not withhold Your tender mercies from me, O Lord; let Your lovingkindness and Your **truth** continually preserve me.

Ps. 86:15 But You, O Lord, are a God full of compassion, and gracious, longsuffering and abundant in mercy and **truth**.

Ps. 115:1 Not unto us, O Lord, not unto us, but to Your name give glory, because of Your mercy, because of Your **truth**.

Ps. 117:1-2 Praise the Lord, all you Gentiles! Laud Him, all you peoples! For His merciful kindness is great toward us, and the **truth** of the Lord endures forever. Praise the Lord!

Jesus—the way, the truth, the life—

In Matthew and John (NIV), often times Jesus said, "I tell you the **truth**...."

John 1:14, 17 And the Word became flesh and dwelt among us, and we beheld His glory, the glory as of the only begotten of the Father, full of grace and **truth**. ....For the law was given through Moses, but grace and **truth** came through Jesus Christ.

John 8:44-46 *Jesus is speaking*— "You are of your father the devil, and the desires of your father you want to do. He was a murderer from the beginning, and does not stand in the **truth**, because there is no **truth** in him. When he speaks a lie, he speaks from his own resources, for he is a liar and the father of it. But because I tell the **truth**, you do not believe Me. Which of you convicts Me of sin? And if I tell the **truth**, why do you not believe Me?"

John 14:6 Jesus said to him, "I am the way, the **truth**, and the life. No one comes to the Father except through Me."

John 18:37-38a Pilate therefore said to Him, "Are You a king then?" Jesus answered, "You say rightly that I am a king. For this cause I was born, and for this cause I have come into the world, that I should bear witness to the **truth**. Everyone who is of the **truth** hears My voice." Pilate said to Him, "What is **truth**?"

Spirit of truth—

John 14:16-18 "And I will pray the Father, and He will give you another Helper, that He may abide with you forever—the **Spirit of truth** whom the world cannot receive, because it neither sees Him nor knows Him; but you know Him, for He dwells with you and will be in you. I will not leave you orphans; I will come to you."

John 15:26 "But when the Helper comes, whom I shall send to you from the Father, the **Spirit of truth** who proceeds from the Father, He will testify of Me."

John 16:13 "However, when He, the **Spirit of truth** has come, He will guide you into all **truth**; for He will not speak on His own authority, but whatever He hears He will speak; and He will tell you things to come."

1 John 5:6 This is He who came by water and blood – Jesus Christ; not only by water, but by water and blood. And it is the Spirit who bears witness, because the **Spirit is truth.**

His Word is truth —-

Ps. 119:142 Your righteousness is an everlasting righteousness, and Your law is **truth**.

Ps. 119:160 The entirety of **Your Word is truth**, and every one of Your righteous judgments endures forever.

John 17:16-19 "They are not of this world, just as I am not of the world. Sanctify them by Your **truth**. As You sent Me into the world, I also have sent them into the world. And for their sakes I sanctify Myself, that they also may be sanctified by the **truth**."

Gal. 2:4-5 And this occurred because of false brethren secretly brought (who came in by stealth to spy out our liberty which we have in Christ Jesus, that they might bring us into bondage), to whom we did not yield submission even for an hour, that the **truth of the gospel** might continue with you.

Eph. 6:14 Stand therefore, having girded your waist with **truth**, having put on the breastplate of righteousness.

Col. 1:5, 6 ...because of the hope which is laid up for you in heaven, of which you heard before in the **word of the truth of the gospel**, which has come to you, as it has also in all the world, and is bringing forth fruit, as it is also among you since the day you heard and knew the grace of God in **truth**...

1 Thess. 2:13 For this reason we also thank God without ceasing, because when you received the **word of God** which you heard from us, you welcomed it not as the word of men, but as it is in **truth, the word of God**, which also effectively works in you who believe.

We are to live and serve in truth–

1 Sam. 12:24 "Only fear the Lord, and serve Him in **truth** with all your heart; for consider what great things He has done for you."

1 Kings 2:1-4 Now the days of David drew near that he should die, and he charged Solomon his son, saying : "I go the way of all the earth; be strong, therefore, and prove yourself a man. And keep the charge of the Lord your God: to walk in His ways, to keep His statutes, His commandments, His judgments, and His testimonies, as it is written in the Law of Moses, that you may prosper in all that you do and wherever you turn; that the Lord may fulfill His word which He spoke concerning me, saying, 'If your sons take heed to their way, to walk before me in **truth** with all their heart and with all their soul,' He said, 'you shall not lack a man on the throne of Israel.' "

Ps. 15:1-2 Lord, who may abide in Your tabernacle? Who may dwell in Your holy hill? He who walks uprightly, and works righteousness and speaks **truth** in his heart.

Ps. 51:6 Behold, You desire **truth** in the inward parts, and in the hidden part You will make me to know wisdom.

Ps. 85:10-11 Mercy and **truth** have met together; righteousness and peace have kissed. **Truth** shall spring out of the earth, and righteousness shall look down from heaven.

Ps. 119:30 I have chosen the way of **truth**; Your judgments I have laid before me.

Ps. 145:18 The Lord is near to all who call upon Him, to all who call upon Him in **truth**.

Ps. 146:5-6 Happy is he who has the God of Jacob for his help, whose hope is in the Lord his God, who made heaven and earth, the sea, and all that is in them; who keeps **truth** forever.

Prov. 3:3-4 Let not mercy and **truth** forsake you, write them on the tablet of your heart, and so find favor and high esteem in the sight of God and man.

Prov. 8:7 For my mouth will speak **truth**; wickedness is an abomination to my lips.

Prov. 14:22 Do they not go astray who devise evil? But mercy and **truth** belong to those who devise good.

Prov. 16:6 In mercy and **truth** atonement is provided for iniquity; and by the fear of the Lord one departs from evil.

Prov. 22:20-21 Have I not written to you excellent things of counsels and knowledge, that I may make you know the certainty of the words of **truth**, that you may answer words of **truth** to those who send to you?

Prov. 23:23 Buy the **truth**, and do not sell it, also wisdom and instruction and understanding.

Zech. 8:16 'These are the things you shall do: speak each man the **truth** to his neighbor; give judgment in your gates for **truth**, justice, and peace.'

John 3:21 "But he who does the **truth** comes to the light, that his deeds may be clearly seen, that they have been done in God."

John 4:23-24 "But the hour is coming, and now is, when the **true** worshipers will worship the Father in spirit and **truth**; for the Father is seeking such to worship Him. God is Spirit, and those who worship Him must worship in spirit and **truth**."

John 5:32-33 "There is another who bears witness of Me, and I know that the witness which He witnesses of Me is **true**. You have sent to John, and he has borne witness to the **truth**."

John 8:31-32 Then Jesus said to those Jews who believed Him, "If you abide in My word, you are My disciples indeed. And you shall know the **truth**, and the **truth** shall make you free."

Acts. 26:24-25 Now as he thus made his defense, Festus said with a loud voice, "Paul, you are beside yourself! Much learning is driving you mad!" But he said, "I am not mad, most noble Festus, but speak the words of **truth** and reason."

1 Cor. 5:8 Therefore let us keep the feast, not with old leaven, nor with the leaven of malice and wickedness, but with the unleavened bread of sincerity and **truth**.

2 Cor. 13:8 NIV For we cannot do anything against the **truth**, but only for the **truth**.

Gal. 5:6-7 For in Christ Jesus neither circumcision nor uncircumcision avails anything, but faith working through love. You ran well. Who hindered you from obeying the **truth**?

Eph. 4:14-15 ...that we should no longer be children, tossed to and fro and carried about with every wind of doctrine, by the trickery of men, in the cunning craftiness of deceitful plotting, but, speaking the **truth** in love, may grow up in all things into Him who is the head–Christ....

2 Tim. 2:15 Be diligent to present yourself approved of God, a worker who does not need to be ashamed, rightly diving the word

of **truth**.

Heb. 10:26 For if we sin willfully after we have received the knowledge of the **truth**, there no longer remains a sacrifice for sins....

1 Peter 1:22 Since you have purified your souls in obeying the **truth** through the Spirit in sincere love of the brethren, love one another fervently with a pure heart....

2 Peter 1:12 For this reason I will not be negligent to remind you always of these things, though you know and are established in the present **truth**.

1 John 2:21 I have not written to you because you do not know the **truth**, but because you know it, and that no lie is of the **truth**.

1 John 3:18-19 NIV Dear children, let us not love with words or tongue but with actions and in **truth**. This then is how we know that we belong to the **truth**, and how we set our hearts at rest in His presence...

1 John 4:6 NIV We are from God, and whoever knows God listens to us; but whoever is not from God does not listen to us. This is how we recognize the Spirit of **truth** and the spirit of falsehood.

Prayers—

Ps. 25:5 Lead me in Your **truth** and teach me, for You are the God of my salvation; on You I wait all the day.

Ps. 43:3 Oh, send out Your light and Your **truth**! Let them lead me; let them bring me to Your holy hill and to Your tabernacle.

Ps. 86:11 Teach me Your way, O Lord; I will walk in Your **truth**; unite my heart to fear (*reverence, honor*) Your name.

Jerusalem, the City of Truth—

Zech. 8:3 "Thus says the Lord: 'I will return to Zion, and dwell in the midst of Jerusalem. Jerusalem shall be called the **City of Truth**, the Mountain of the Lord of hosts, the Holy Mountain.'"

Those who hate truth—

Rom. 1:18-19 For the wrath of God is revealed from heaven against all ungodliness and unrighteousness of men, who suppress the **truth** in unrighteousness, because what may be known of God is manifest in them, for God has shown it to them.

Rom. 1:24-25 Therefore God also gave them up to uncleanness, in the lusts of their hearts, to dishonor their bodies among themselves, who exchange the **truth** of God for the lie, and worshiped and served the creature rather than the Creator, who is blessed forever. Amen.

1 Tim. 6:3-5 If anyone teaches otherwise and does not consent to wholesome words, even the words of our Lord Jesus Christ, and to the doctrine which accords with godliness, he is proud, knowing nothing, but is obsessed with disputes and arguments over words, from which come envy, strife, reviling, evil suspicions, useless wranglings of men of corrupt minds and **destitute of the truth**, who suppose that godliness is a means of gain. From such withdraw yourself.

2 Thess. 2:10-12 ...And with all unrighteous deception among those who perish, because they did not receive the love of the **truth**, that they might be saved. And for this reason God will send them strong delusion, that they should believe the lie, that they all may be condemned who did not believe the truth but had pleasure in unrighteousness.

How to be saved—

2 Thess. 2:13 But we are bound to give thanks to God always for you, brethren, beloved by the Lord, because God from the beginning chose you for salvation through sanctification by the Spirit and **belief in the truth.**

1 Tim. 2:3, 4, 7 For this is good and acceptable in the sight of God our Savior, who desires all men to be saved and come to the **knowledge of the truth.** ....for which I was appointed a preacher and an apostle– I am speaking the **truth** in Christ and not lying– a teacher of the Gentiles in faith and **truth**.

GRACE

GOD'S GRACE COVERS ALL

What a magnificent word this is. A word encompassing the broad spectrum of the blessings God has for His people, His family. I picture a rainbow in the sky, more broadly painted with brilliant colors than we ordinarily see, representing God's grace. And God, our Father who is in heaven, desires for His children to receive it all, for our invitation to receive comes from His compassionate and gracious heart.

Within that rainbow of grace and mercy is salvation in all its aspects, such as: redemption, healing, His righteousness and justice. Grace covers it all. You cannot speak of any gift from God such as His compassion, provisions, protection, healing, forgiveness, and all the loving desires He has for His people, without speaking about His grace. Nothing is earned. All of these treasures come from His most gracious, generous, loving heart.

"Noah found grace in the eyes of the Lord." The Lord saw Noah through eyes of grace. This grace must be like the sun's rays pouring down upon Noah and his family, preserving them from all the evil that the others had fallen into so deeply. Several Scriptures speak of God's grace being given to the humble; those who love Him and recognize Him as the Holy One, the Sovereign God, and honor Him with their whole heart.

Then in Zechariah we read that God would pour out the 'Spirit of grace' upon the house of David and the inhabitants of Jerusalem. Even though the nation of Israel had not honored Jesus as the promised Messiah, God still blessed them with His mercy and grace. His grace also has preserving power, no matter how threatening the enemies are around God's people.

GOD'S GRACE COMES THROUGH JESUS CHRIST

Today we receive grace through Jesus Christ. These wonderful words are in John 1:14, 16-17: "And the Word became flesh and dwelt among us, and we beheld His glory, the glory as of the only begotten of the Father, full of grace and truth. ...And of His fullness we have all received, and grace for grace. For the law was given through Moses, but grace and truth came through Jesus Christ." We could not exist without God's grace; every blessing we receive is part of His broad scope of grace.

This is so great a truth for us to assimilate! We need to sit quietly before the Lord meditating upon the Scriptures to drink it in. As we do, we'll receive understanding; just like sitting in the sunshine absorbing its warmth, nutrients and vitality.

In the book of Acts we find many accounts of God's grace upon the believers. His grace was drawing them to believe the truths that the Apostles were preaching and teaching, and to exercise their spiritual gifts. The grace of God was seen in the behavior of these new Christians, and was visible on the countenance of their faces. It was empowering them to be steadfast in their walk with the Lord in the midst of severe persecution as His presence sustained them.

No other god can give grace. None! They have no life, no power to be gracious, or to give any loving gift. They are empty, hollow and lifeless. And any religion without the resurrection power of the living Christ Jesus working in them is empty, hollow and lifeless. But the One true living God is a gracious God, and can give out of His fullness to all who are yearning to receive. Jesus, His Son, is very God, full of grace and truth. He is alive! Those who believe in Him are experiencing the abundant life that He offers to you. His life in them is eternal.

His grace was so evident in Stephen, that those who were evil resisted him. They could not tolerate such tremendous grace in this man of God. They responded violently as He testified about the truths of the gospel of Jesus: that He died for our sins, was resurrected by the power of God, and ascended into heaven, preparing a place for believers.

Many believers suffered persecution in that day, which caused them to spread to other regions; yet they remained faithful and steadfast in their faith. God's grace was sustaining power and is "able to build them up and give them an inheritance among all those who were sanctified," according to Acts 20:32. This is for all believers today too!

In Romans 5:1-2 we hear, "Therefore having been justified by faith, we have peace with God through our Lord Jesus Christ, through whom also we have access by faith into this grace in which we stand." Let me say that last phrase again, "into this grace in which we stand." His grace is a covering over us; it surrounds us, and shines down on us. Through faith we have access into this gift of God's grace.

In Romans we also see that God gives this grace in abundance through Jesus Christ. It has a tremendously important place as it is to "reign through righteousness to eternal life through Jesus Christ our Lord." Grace is active, not like an emblem, or certificate to prove sainthood. God's grace changed Paul, actually changed all the Apostles, and all who become born-again believers. The grace of God enabled Paul to labor diligently and selflessly, with amazing energy, in spite of all the persecutions. He risked everything, including his life.

Paul reprimanded the Christians in Galatia for "turning from Him who called them in the grace of Christ, to a different gospel." And in chapter 5:4, he calls it 'estrangement from Christ' as they attempted to be justified by law. He makes it clear that we can fall from grace by choice, but I know it is not easy to fall, for God graciously, yet with magnetic urgency, calls each one to return to Him.

WE ARE SAVED BY GRACE

In Romans 11, he shows that grace and works are opposites in regard to our being accepted by the Lord. We cannot earn our salvation or a relationship by works of the law. Ephesians 2:4-9 shows this clearly: "But God, who is rich in mercy, because of His great love with which He loved us, even when we were dead in trespasses, made us alive together with Christ (by grace you have been saved), and raised us up together, and made us sit together in heavenly places in Christ Jesus, that in the ages to come He might show the exceeding riches of His grace in His kindness toward us in Christ Jesus. For by grace you have been saved through faith, and that not of yourselves; it is a gift of God, not of works, lest anyone should boast."

This is not a negative statement. God has provided grace to cover every kind of need, including bringing us to repentance and salvation. His grace sufficiency is available to every one who believes on the Lord Jesus Christ. You see, we're not called according to our abilities or honorary degrees, but according to His purposes, linked with grace. *See 2 Tim. 1:9.* Also Titus 2:11 tells us: "The grace of God that brings salvation has appeared to all men." That shows that no one is left out.

Recently a friend of mine and I were seated near a pool, watching over my grandchildren, when a Jewish gentleman, after walking back and forth past us several times, began to talk with us. He seemed so lonely and somehow drawn to us. Then as he stopped by for about the fourth time, he asked my friend if she had gone to the Billy Graham crusade. We both thought this was an expression of his delight in Billy Graham's messages, however, in further conversation we discovered that he didn't even believe in the Old Testament truths about God. When we told him that Jesus, the Son of God, came to save us from sin, his harsh, angry response was, "Saved from what? Man takes care of everything for himself. All life came from the sea."

We talked a little longer, but then he was on his way again. We may well have been among God's line-up of witnesses of the gospel truths to this man. I believe that God is following him; revealing the truths about salvation through Jesus the Christ. We prayed for Him, and I trust it was God's purpose in this most unusual episode.

HUMBLED BY GOD'S GRACE

I have heard and read about so many testimonies of people who had resisted the calling of the Lord for years. Then one day it was as though the truths of God's grace struck them like an arrow way down deep in their hearts and they humbled themselves before Him. When Jesus took over in their lives, they lost all interest in the things of this world. Some gave away earthly goods, for it had no value to them anymore. Some were instantly delivered from drugs and/or alcohol, and other enslaving sins. Incredible miracles began to happen in their lives. Families were reunited and there were physical healings. God's grace is available for you too, if you'll just surrender all that stuff that seems so important to you at the moment. Maybe it is already losing its luster. They've supported you like crutches, but you can feel they're deteriorating, ready to crumble and take you way down to the ground. Possibly you have been sensing the working of God's grace in your heart and even your body. It's time to run to the Savior. His name is Jesus, the only one who can save you and give you a new life, in Him!

The Scriptures on grace are so rich and wonderful; read them again and again. Make lists of various categories that reveal the fullness and broadness of God's grace and how they can affect your life with enormous blessings. The name of Jesus is powerful, He is Lord! He is the only channel for receiving the riches of God's grace. Without Him there is no abiding love, peace and joy.

Come to 'His throne of grace' and draw from His fullness of truth and righteousness. This is where you can find the true riches, which last for all eternity!

SCRIPTURES FOR
G R A C E

God's grace and grace of God—

Acts 11:22-23 Then news of these things came to the ears of the Church in Jerusalem, and they sent out Barnabas to go as far as Antioch. When he came and had seen the **grace of God**, he was glad, and encouraged them all that with purpose of heart they should continue with the Lord.

Acts 13:43 Now when the congregation had broken up, many of the Jews and devout proselytes followed Paul and Barnabas, who, speaking to them, persuaded them to continue in the **grace of God**.

Acts 14:26 From there they sailed to Antioch, where they had been commended to the **grace of God** for the work which they had completed.

Acts 20:24 But none of these things move me; nor do I count my life dear to myself, so that I may finish my race with joy, and the ministry which I received from the Lord Jesus, to testify to the gospel of the **grace of God.**

Rom 5:15, 17 But the free gift is not like the offense. For if by the one man's offense many died; much more the **grace of God**, the gift by the **grace** of the one Man, Jesus Christ, abounded to many. ....For if by the one man's offense death reigned through the one, much more those who receive abundance of **grace** and of the gift of righteousness will reign in life through the One, Jesus Christ.

1 Cor. 15:9-10 For I am the least of all the apostles, who am not worthy to be called an apostle, because I persecuted the Church of God. But by the **grace of God** I am what I am, and **His grace**

toward me was not in vain; but I labored more abundantly than they all; yet not I, but the **grace of God** which was with me.

Gal. 2:21 I do not set aside the **grace of God**; for if righteousness comes through the law, then Christ died in vain.

2 Thess. 1:12 ...that the name of our Lord Jesus Christ may be glorified in you, and you in Him, according to the **grace of our God and the Lord Jesus Christ.**

Titus 2:11 For the **grace of God** that brings salvation has appeared to all men.

Heb. 2:19 But we see Jesus, who was made a little lower than the angels, for the suffering of death crowned with glory and honor, that He, by the **grace of God**, might taste death for everyone.

Heb. 12:15 NIV See to it that no one misses the **grace of God** and that no bitter root grows up to cause trouble and defile many.

1 Peter 5:10 But may the God of all **grace**, who called us to His eternal glory by Christ Jesus, after you have suffered a while, perfect, establish, strengthen, and settle you.

Grace in relationship to Jesus—

Ps. 45:2 You are fairer than the sons of men (*speaking of the Messiah, Jesus*); **grace** is poured upon Your lips; therefore God has blessed You forever.

Luke 2:40 And the Child (*Jesus*) grew and became strong in the spirit, filled with wisdom, and the **grace of God** was upon Him.

John 1:14, 16-17 And the Word became flesh and dwelt among us, and we beheld His glory, the glory as of the only begotten of the Father, full of **grace** and truth. ....And of His fullness we have all received, and **grace for grace**. For the law was given through

Moses, but **grace** and truth came **through Jesus Christ.**

Rom. 1:7a, and 16:24 *From the opening and closing of Paul's letter—* To all who are in Rome, beloved of God, called to be saints: **Grace** to you and peace **from God our Father and the Lord Jesus Christ.** ....The **grace of our Lord Jesus Christ** be with you all. Amen

Rom. 5:1-2 Therefore, having been justified by faith, we have peace with God through our Lord Jesus Christ, through whom also we have access by faith into this **grace** in which we stand, and rejoice in hope of the glory of God.

Rom. 5:20-21 NIV The law was added so that the trespass might increase. But where sin increased, **grace** increased all the more, so that, just as sin reigned in death, so also **grace** might reign through righteousness to bring eternal life through Jesus Christ our Lord.

2 Cor. 8:9 For you know the **grace of our Lord Jesus Christ**, that though He was rich, yet for your sakes He became poor, that you through His poverty might become rich.

2 Cor. 13:14 The **grace of our Lord Jesus Christ**, and the love of God, and the communion of the Holy Spirit be with you all. Amen

Gal. 1:6-7 NIV I am astonished that you are so quickly deserting the one who called you by the **grace of Christ** and are turning to a different gospel—which is really no gospel at all. Evidently some people are throwing you into confusion and trying to pervert the Gospel of Christ.

Gal. 5:4 You have become estranged from Christ, you who attempted to be justified by law; you have fallen from **grace.**

Eph. 1:7-8 NIV In Him we have redemption through His blood, the forgiveness of sins, in accordance with the riches of **God's grace** that He lavished on us with all wisdom and understanding.

Eph. 2:4-9 But God, who is rich in mercy, because of His great love with which He loved us, even when we were dead in trespasses, made us alive together with Christ (by **grace** you have been saved), and raised us up together, and made us sit together in heavenly places in Christ Jesus, that in the ages to come He might show the exceeding riches of **His grace** in His kindness toward us in Christ Jesus. For by **grace** you have been saved through faith, and that not of yourselves; it is the gift of God, not of works, lest anyone should boast.

1 Tim. 1:14 And the **grace of our Lord** was exceedingly abundant, with faith and love which are in Christ Jesus.

2 Tim. 1:9 Who has saved us and called us with a holy calling, not according to our works, but according to His own purpose and **grace** which was given to us **in Christ Jesus** before time began...

2 Tim. 2:1 You therefore, my son, be strong in the **grace that is in Christ Jesus.**

Heb. 10:2 Of how much worse punishment, do you suppose, will he be thought worthy who has trampled the Son of God underfoot, counted the blood of the covenant by which he was sanctified a common thing, and insulted the **Spirit of grace**?

God's grace toward specific people —

Gen 6:8 But Noah found **grace** in the eyes of the Lord.

Zech 12:10 And I will pour on the house of David and on the inhabitants of Jerusalem the **Spirit of grace** and supplication; then they will look on Me whom they pierced. Yes, they will mourn for Him (*the Messiah, Jesus*) as one mourns for his only son, and give for Him as one grieves for a firstborn.

Acts 4:33 And with great power the apostles gave witness to the resurrection of the Lord Jesus. And great **grace** was upon them all.

Acts 6:8 NIV Now Stephen, a man full of **God's grace** and power, did great wonders and miraculous signs among the people.

Rom 1:7 To all who are in Rome, beloved of God, called to be saints: **Grace to you** and peace from God our Father and the Lord Jesus Christ. *Note: Most of Paul's letters begin with this greeting within the first few verses.*

Rom. 4:16 Therefore it is of faith that it might be according to **grace**, so that the promise might be sure to all the seed, not only to those who are of the law, but also to those who are of the faith of Abraham, who is the father of us all *(who are believers- Romans 4:11).*

Gal. 1:15 ....it pleased God, who separated me *(Paul)* from my mother's womb and called me through **His grace**.

Eph. 3:6-8 ....that the Gentiles should be fellow heirs, of the same body, and partakers of His promise in Christ through the gospel of which I became a minister according to the gift of the **grace of God** given to me by the effective working of His power. To me, who am less than the least of all the saints, this **grace** was given, that I should preach among the Gentiles the unsearchable riches of Christ.

Eph. 4:7 But to each one of us **grace** was given according to the measure of Christ's gift.

Eph. 6:23-24 Peace to the brethren, and love with faith from God the Father and the Lord Jesus Christ. **Grace** be with all those who love our Lord Jesus Christ in sincerity. Amen

The recipients of His grace are—

Ps. 84:11 For the Lord God is a sun and shield; the Lord will give **grace** and glory; no good thing will He withhold from those who walk uprightly.

Ps. 3:33-34 The curse of the Lord is on the house of the wicked, but He blesses the home of the just. Surely He scorns the scornful, but gives **grace** to the humble.

Heb. 4:15-16 For we do not have a High Priest, who cannot sympathize with our weaknesses, but was in all points tempted as we are, yet without sin. Let us therefore come boldly to the **throne of grace**, that we may obtain mercy and find **grace** to help in time of need.

The benefits of His grace—

Acts 20:32 So now, brethren, I commend you to God and to the word of **His grace**; which is able to build you up and give you an inheritance among all those who are sanctified.

Rom. 3:23-24 For all have sinned and fall short of the glory of God, being justified freely by **His grace** through the redemption that is in Christ Jesus.

Rom 4:16 Therefore it is of faith that it might be according to **grace**, so that the promise might be sure to all the seed, not only to those who are of the law, but also to those who are of the faith of Abraham, who is the father of us all.

Rom. 5:1-2 Therefore, having been justified by faith, we have peace with God through our Lord Jesus Christ, through whom also we have access by faith into this **grace** in which we stand, and rejoice in hope of the glory of God.

Rom. 5:20-21 Moreover the law entered that the offense might abound much more, so that as sin reigned in death, even so **grace** might reign through righteousness to eternal life through Jesus Christ our Lord.

2 Cor. 4:15 For all things are for your sakes, that **grace**, having spread through many, may cause thanksgiving to abound to the glory of God.

2 Cor. 12:9 And He said to me, "**My grace** is sufficient for you, for My strength is made perfect in weakness."

2 Thess. 2:16-17 Now may our Lord Jesus Christ Himself and our God and Father, who has loved us and given us everlasting consolation and good hope by **grace**, comfort your hearts and establish you in every good word and work.

Titus 3:4-7 But when the kindness and the love of God our Savior toward man appeared, not by works of righteousness which we have done, but according to His mercy He saved us, through the washing of regeneration and renewing of the Holy Spirit, whom He poured out on us abundantly through Jesus Christ our Savior, that having been justified by **His grace** we should become heirs according to the hope of eternal life.

Instructions and warnings —

Rom. 6:1-2, 14-15 What shall we say then? Shall we continue in sin that **grace** may abound? Certainly not! How shall we who died to sin live any longer in it? ...For sin shall not have dominion over you, for you are not under law but under **grace**. What then? Shall we sin because we are not under law but under **grace**? Certainly not!

Rom. 11:5-6 Even so then, at this present time there is a remnant according to the election of **grace**, then it is no longer of works; otherwise **grace** is no longer **grace**. But if it is of works, it is no longer **grace**; otherwise work is no longer work.

Col. 4:6 Let your speech always be with **grace**, seasoned with salt, that you may know how you ought to answer each one.

2 Peter 3:17-18 NIV Therefore, dear friends, since you already know this, be on your guard so that you may not be carried away by the error of lawless men and fall from your secure position. But grow in the **grace** and knowledge of our Lord and Savior Jesus Christ.

REDEMPTION

GOD'S PLAN FOR REDEMPTION

To redeem is to buy back, or purchase, what once belonged to you. It was yours, but someone through a disguised strategy has gained possession. Now you are forced to pay a high price in order to regain possession. This could be anything, such as land, houses, people, vehicles, cattle, jewels, sports equipment, or anything that has value to you.

In the first chapter of Genesis we are given the history of God's process of creating everything the universe consists of, everything that exists on this earth, in the heavens and in the sea. All that He created belonged to Him, without dispute, and man was His highest creation.

What appears to be a very short time later, but we do not know what period of time has elapsed, there's a voice coming from a snake in the garden. He is so cunning. His deception is cloaked with some truth, but Eve didn't recognize the trick question. As she accepted fruit from the 'tree of knowledge of good and evil', she sinned, and then Adam did the same. They fell into sin, and Satan gained dominion. Sin came upon the whole human race. God's first promise of redemption is in Genesis 3:15, the promise that the Seed of the woman would bruise his head. There's a summary in Romans 5:12-21, speaking of the first Adam and contrasting Jesus Christ, our Savior, as a second Adam.

Man became so sinful that God caused a flood to cover all the earth, destroying all mankind except Noah and his family, besides selected animals and birds, giving a new start on this earth. This was another part of God's judgment on sin and fulfilling His redemption plan. This happened around 2,000 years after creation and 2,000 years before Christ.

That of course didn't destroy sin, but let's pick up with the story of redemption in the lives of the Israelites in Egypt. When Jacob's family moved to Egypt, through the leadership of his son Joseph, and by the invitation of the reigning King Pharaoh, they were given a beautiful plot of land in Goshen, with an abundance of provisions.

But some years later, as the family grew and the older members of the family were dead, another Pharaoh became King. This changed everything; now they're being treated cruelly. There was no special treatment anymore. By now they are called Israelites, named after Jacob, whose name God changed to Israel. God has called Moses to be their leader, and instructs him in Exodus 6:6, "Therefore say to the children of Israel, 'I am the Lord: I will bring you out from under the burden of the Egyptians. I will rescue you from their bondage, and I will redeem you with an outstretched arm with great judgments.'"

From chapter 6 of Exodus through chapter 14, we read about the way the Lord proceeded to deliver the Israelites from their bondage in Egypt, and chapter 15 contains the song of Moses, as He blesses the Lord for their deliverance. In verse 13 Moses says, "You in Your mercy have led forth the people whom You have redeemed; You have guided them in Your strength to Your holy habitation."

Many years later, David is expressing thanks to the Lord for what He has done for the Israelites. These words are in 2 Samuel 7:22-24: "Therefore You are great, O Lord God. For there is none like You, nor is there any God besides You, according to all that we have heard with our ears. And who is like Your people, like Israel, the one nation on the earth whom God went to redeem for Himself as a people, to make for Himself a name—and to do for Yourself great and awesome deeds for Your land—before Your people whom You redeemed for Yourself from Egypt, the nations and their gods? For You have made Your people Israel Your very own people forever; and You, Lord, have become their God."

REDEMPTION THROUGH THE BLOOD OF JESUS

There are many more references to God's redeeming His people during this time of their history in several other Old Testament books. However, it seems wise to limit them somewhat in this book, especially so that we might devote some space to our redemption through the blood of Jesus Christ. God's spectacular plan of redemption is threaded *(or woven)* all the way through the Scriptures, but Jesus was to come to the earth in accordance with God's timetable. We cannot fully understand God's wisdom in regard to His 'fullness of time' for the promised Messiah, Jesus, to be born, but the Scriptures present Him in this manner, and we must take this truth by faith. *See Gal. 4:4.*

Jesus Christ, God's Son, was preordained to provide redemption from sin, from the curse of the law and from death. Jesus Christ is God's provision for us; the promised Messiah. By His death on the cross, shedding of His blood, all who believe on Him shall be saved. *See John 3:16-18.* Although there will be some overlapping, let's take these one by one—deliverance from sin—the curse of the law—from death.

Saved from sin—- Matthew 1:21 tells us: "And she will bring forth a Son, and you shall call His name Jesus, for He will save His people from their sins." And Romans 5:8, 9 says: "But God demonstrates His own love toward us, in that while we were still sinners, Christ died for us. Much more then, having now been justified by His blood, we shall be saved from wrath through Him." All of Romans 6 deals with our subject, and needs to be read completely and slowly so you can observe all the details of God's provision for our redemption.

Colossians 1:13-14 give another view of this, "He has delivered us from the power of darkness and conveyed us into the kingdom of the Son of His love, in whom we have redemption through His blood, the forgiveness of sins." There is so much valuable information in each of these Scriptures. As we put them together, we have a clear picture of what Jesus Christ has accomplished on our behalf. He didn't owe it to us. He loved us that much!

In Hebrews, there are several verses—

9:12: "Not with the blood of goats and calves, but with His own blood He entered the Most Holy Place once for all, having obtained eternal redemption."

9:27, 28: "And as it is appointed for men to die once, but after this the judgment, so Christ was offered once to bear the sins of many. To those who eagerly wait for Him He will appear a second time, apart from sin, for salvation."

10:11, 12: "And every priest stands ministering daily and offering repeatedly the same sacrifices, which can never take away sins. But this Man, after He had offered one sacrifice for sins forever, sat down at the right hand of God."

Reading carefully and meditatively through all of Hebrews, chapters 9 and 10 will give you a more complete picture of what the above verses mean for you today.

In the Old Testament writings we see a people that God chose to be redeemed from sin; separating them for Himself. He taught them His laws through His chosen leaders, and He judged them accordingly. The whole world was filled with sin. They refused to honor God as Sovereign God, worshiping idols instead. If God had not drawn a people to Himself, and kept His eyes of love upon them, no one would ever have been saved. Man was in bondage to sin. Under the Old Testament laws, the people had to kill animals according to the instructions God had given to them. This shedding of blood was their sacrifice for sin, signifying salvation from sin for that time in history, only as a temporary measure, for this could not cleanse forever. *See Hebrews 9:12 again.*

Then, in God's timing, Jesus was born. He came for the purpose of being God's supreme sacrifice; the gift of His only begotten Son *(John 3:16-18)*. This was the final blood sacrifice. Jesus was the perfect Man, who was able to take all the sins of mankind on Himself, so we, who believe on Him, might be eternally saved by His shed blood. Jesus is the fulfillment of God's redemption plan. When Jesus said from the cross, "It is finished," redemption was completed in Christ Jesus. The debt was paid, and through faith in Him, we may be saved. It is the only way.

Saved from the curse of the law — The book of Galatians has the most information on the 'curse of the law'. Here in Galatians

3:10-13 we read: "For as many as are of the works of the law are under the curse; for it is written, 'Cursed is everyone who does not continue in all things which are written in the book of the law, to do them.' But that no one is justified by the law in the sight of God is evident, for 'the just shall live by faith.' Yet the law is not of faith, but 'the man who does them shall live by them.' Christ has redeemed us from the curse of the law, having become a curse for us..." In Romans 8:2, we find this, "For the law of the Spirit of life in Christ Jesus has made me free from the law of sin and death." There's an additional thought in Acts 13:39, "...and by Him *(Jesus)* everyone who believes is justified from all things from which you could not be justified by the law of Moses." Another text is Romans 6:14: "For sin shall not have dominion over you, for you are not under law but under grace." *More information can be found in Romans, chapters 3 and 4.*

Saved from eternal death—- Remember that John 3:16 says "whoever believes in Him should not perish, but have everlasting life," and Romans 6:23 says, "For the wages of sin is death, but the gift of God is eternal life in Christ Jesus our Lord." As sinners, we were sentenced to eternal damnation, unless we receive Christ Jesus into our hearts, for He is eternal life. *(1 John 5:11, 12, 20)* This is the only way to conquer over eternal death.

Let's look at Romans 5:12-14, "Therefore, just as through one man sin entered the world, and death through sin, and thus death spread to all men, because all sinned—(For until the law sin was in the world, but sin is not imputed when there is no law. Nevertheless death reigned from Adam to Moses, even over those who had not sinned according to the likeness of the transgression of Adam, who is a type of Him who was to come....)."

In 1 Corinthians 15 Paul is teaching about the resurrection of Jesus, which is our assurance of victory over death. Just taking a few verses, 20-22: "But now Christ is risen from the dead, and has become the firstfruits of those who have fallen asleep. For since by man came death, by Man also came the resurrection of the dead. For as in Adam all die, even so in Christ all shall be made alive." Also verses 53-57, "For this corruptible must put on incorruption, and this mortal must put on immortality. So when this corruptible has put on incorruption, and this mortal has put on immortality, then shall be brought to pass the saying that is written: 'Death is swallowed up in victory. O Death, where is your sting? O Hades, where is your victory?' The sting of death is sin, and the strength of sin is the law. But thanks be to God, who gives us the victory through our Lord Jesus Christ."

We can see by all the above Scriptures that we could never have saved ourselves. We were born under a spiritual death sentence, but God sent His only begotten Son, the Lord Jesus, to pay our sin debt; to redeem us from the bondages attached to sin. In I Corinthians 1:30, 31, we have a kind of a summary: "But of Him you are in Christ Jesus, who became for us wisdom from God—and righteousness and sanctification and redemption—that, as it is written, 'He who glories, let him glory in the Lord.'"

In closing, if you already know Him as your Redeemer, you have so much to be grateful for; reason to just praise the Lord with your whole heart; expressing this praise by the way you live and heartily shout praises to Him. It is also reason to share your testimony about how the Lord revealed Himself to you as the Savior of sinners, and then go on to share your wealth of understanding of the Word at this point in your life, giving all glory to His name!

If you don't know Him, this message is especially for you, that you might recognize the tremendous price that God has paid to redeem you in sacrificing His only begotten Son, Jesus Christ. Is He calling your heart to surrender to Him? Please don't put off this special moment! There may not be another day for you to run to Him. He wants you to receive all the blessings of Christ's abundant life, replacing the death sentence of sin for the free gift of eternal life.

There's an old hymn that says it like this: "Redeemed, how I love to proclaim it. Redeemed by the blood of the Lamb." Yes, Jesus came to this earth so that we may spend eternity with Him. What a price He paid! What a tremendous gift of life He gives!

He loves you. He really does!

SCRIPTURES FOR REDEMPTION

NOTE: There is only a slight variation between the first and second grouping. Often they may overlap, and could be in either category.

Redeemed as a people for God, Himself—-

2 Sam. 7:22-23 NIV How great You are, O Sovereign Lord! There is no one like You, and there is no God but You, as we have heard with our own ears. And who is like Your people Israel—the one nation on earth that God went out to **redeem** as a people for Himself, and to perform great and awesome wonders by driving out nations and their gods from before Your people, whom You **redeemed** from Egypt?

Job 19:25-26 For I know that my **Redeemer** lives, and He shall stand at last on the earth; and after my skin is destroyed, this I know, that in my flesh I shall see God.

Ps. 49:7-9, 15 NIV No man can **redeem** the life of another or give to God a ransom for him – the ransom for a life is costly, no payment is ever enough – that he should live on forever and not see decay. ….But God will **redeem** my soul from the grave; He will surely take me to Himself.

Ps. 103:4 Who **redeems** your life from destruction, who crowns you with lovingkindness and tender mercies.

Ps. 130:7-8 O Israel, hope in the Lord; for with the Lord there is mercy, and with Him is abundant **redemption**. And He shall **redeem** Israel from all his iniquities.

Isa. 29:22-24 "Therefore thus says the Lord, who **redeemed**

Abraham, concerning the house of Jacob: "Jacob shall not now be ashamed, nor shall his face now grow pale; but when he sees his children, the work of My hands, in his midst, they will hallow My name, and hallow the Holy One of Jacob, and fear the God of Israel. These also who erred in spirit will come to understanding, and those who complained will learn doctrine."

Isa. 43:1 But now, thus says the Lord, who created you, O Jacob, and He who formed you, O Israel: "Fear not, for I have **redeemed** you: I have called you by your name, you are Mine."

Isa. 44:6 "Thus says the Lord, the King of Israel, and His **Redeemer**, the Lord of hosts: 'I am the first and I am the Last; besides Me there is no God.'"

Jer. 15:20-21 "And I will make you to this people a fortified bronze wall; and they will fight against you, but they shall not prevail against you; for I am with you to save you and deliver you," says the Lord. "I will deliver you from the hand of the wicked, and I will **redeem** you from the grip of the terrible."

Luke 1:67-68, 74-75 Now his father Zacharias was filled with the Holy Spirit, and prophesied, saying: "Blessed is the Lord God of Israel, for He has visited and **redeemed** His people, ...To grant us that we, being delivered from the hand of our enemies, might serve Him without fear, in holiness and righteousness before Him all the days of our life."

Redeemed, rescued from an enemy—-

Ex. 6:6 "Therefore say to the children of Israel: 'I am the Lord; I will bring you out from under the burdens of the Egyptians, I will rescue you from their bondage, and I will **redeem** you with an outstretched arm and with great judgments.'"

Ps. 106:8-10 Nevertheless He saved them for His name's sake, that He might make His mighty power known. He rebuked the Red Sea also, and it dried up; so He led them through the depths, as through the wilderness. He saved them from the hand of him who hated them, and **redeemed** them from the hand of the enemy.

Ps. 107:1-2 O, give thanks to the Lord, for He is good! For His mercy endures forever. Let the **redeemed** of the Lord say so, whom He has redeemed from the hand of the enemy.

Isa. 51:10-11 Are You not the One who dried up the sea, the waters of the great deep; that made the depths of the sea a road for the **redeemed** to cross over? So the ransomed of the Lord shall return, and come to Zion with singing, with everlasting joy on their heads. They shall obtain joy and gladness; sorrow and sighing shall flee away.

Mic. 4:10 Be in pain, and labor to bring forth, O daughter of Zion, like a woman in birth pangs. For now you shall go forth from the city, you shall dwell in the field, and to Babylon you shall go. There you shall be delivered; there the Lord will **redeem** you from the hand of your enemies.

Prayers—

Ps. 25:20-22 Keep my soul, and deliver me; let me not be ashamed, for I put my trust in You. Let integrity and uprightness preserve me, for I wait for You. **Redeem** Israel, O God, out of all their troubles!

Ps. 31:1-5 In You, O Lord, I put my trust; let me never be ashamed; deliver me in Your righteousness. Bow down Your ear to me, deliver me speedily; be my rock of refuge, a fortress of defense to save me. For You are my rock and my fortress; therefore, for Your name's sake, lead me and guide me. Pull me out of the net which they have secretly laid for me, for You are my strength. Into Your hand I commit my spirit; You have **redeemed** me, O Lord God of truth.

Ps. 44:24-26 Why do You hide Your face, and forget our affliction and our oppression? For our soul is bowed down to the dust; our body clings to the ground. Arise for our help, and **redeem** us for Your mercies' sake.

Ps. 69:17-18 And do not hide Your face from Your servant, for I am in trouble; hear me speedily. Draw near to my soul, and **redeem** it; deliver me because of my enemies.

Redemption through the blood of Jesus—

Luke 2:38 And coming in that instant she *(Anna, the prophetess, daughter of Phanuel)* gave thanks to the Lord, and spoke of Him to all those who looked for **redemption** in Jerusalem.

Rom. 3:21-26 But now the righteousness of God apart from the law is revealed, being witnessed by the Law and the Prophets, even the righteousness of God, through faith in Jesus Christ, to all and on all who believe. For there is no difference, for all have sinned and fall short of the glory of God, being justified freely by His grace through the **redemption** that is in Christ Jesus, whom God set forth as a propitiation by His blood, through faith, to demonstrate His righteousness, because in His forbearance God had passed over the sins that were previously committed, to demonstrate at the present time His righteousness that He might be just and the justifier of the one who has faith in Jesus.

1 Cor. 1:30-31 But of Him you are in Christ Jesus, who became for us wisdom from God—and righteousness and sanctification and **redemption** – that, as it is written, "He who glories, let him glory in the Lord."

Gal. 3:13-14 Christ has **redeemed** us from the curse of the law, having become a curse for us (for it is written, "Cursed is everyone who hangs on a tree"), that the blessing of Abraham might come upon the Gentiles in Christ Jesus, that we might receive the promise of the Spirit through faith.

Gal. 4:4-5 But when the fullness of the time had come, God sent forth

His Son, born of a woman, born under the law, to **redeem** those who were under the law, that we might receive the adoption as sons.

Eph. 1:7-9 In Him we have **redemption** through His blood, the forgiveness of sins, according to the riches of His grace which He made to abound toward us in all wisdom and prudence, having made known to us the mystery of His will, according to His good pleasure which He purposed in Himself.

Col. 1:13-14 He has delivered us from the power of darkness and conveyed us into the kingdom of the Son of His love, in whom we have **redemption** through His blood, the forgiveness of sins.

Heb. 9:11-15 But Christ came as High Priest of the good things to come, with the greater and more perfect tabernacle not made with hands, that is, not of this creation. Not with the blood of goats and calves, but with His own blood He entered the Most Holy Place once for all, having obtained eternal **redemption**. For if the blood of bulls and goats and the ashes of a heifer, sprinkling the unclean, sanctifies for the purifying of the flesh, how much more shall the blood of Christ, who through the eternal Spirit offered Himself without spot to God, cleanse your conscience from dead works to serve the living God? And for this reason He is the Mediator of the new covenant, by means of death, for the **redemption** of the transgressions under the first covenant that those who are called may receive the promise of the eternal inheritance.

Titus 2:13-14 ...looking for the blessed hope and glorious appearing of our great God and Savior Jesus Christ, who gave Himself for us, that He might **redeem** us from every lawless deed and purify for Himself His own special people, zealous for good works.

1 Peter 1:17-19 And if you call on the Father, who without partiality judges according to each one's work, conduct yourselves throughout the time of your stay here in fear; knowing that you were not **redeemed** with corruptible things, like silver or gold, from your aimless conduct received by tradition from your fathers, but with

the precious blood of Christ, as of a lamb without blemish and without spot.

Rev. 5:9-10 And they sang a new song, saying: "You are worthy to take the scroll, and to open its seals; for You were slain, and have **redeemed** us to God by Your blood out of every tribe and tongue and people and nation, and have made us kings and priests to our God; and we shall reign on the earth."

A future redemption—

Luke 21:27-28 "Then they will see the Son of Man coming in a cloud with power and great glory. Now when these things begin to happen, look up and lift up your heads, because your **redemption** draws near."

Gal. 4:30 And do not grieve the Holy Spirit of God, by whom you were sealed for the day of **redemption**.

Eph. 1:13-14 In Him you also trusted, after you heard the word of truth, the gospel of your salvation; in whom also, having believed, you were sealed with the Holy Spirit of promise, who is the guarantee of our inheritance until the **redemption** of the purchased possession, to the praise of His glory.

FORGIVENESS

UNFORGIVENESS IS A SERIOUS MATTER

Although our Scriptures begin with our relationship to God, and our need for forgiveness from Him, let's talk about our relationship with one another first. We all have difficulties with relationships at times. We are all so different; we have different personalities, different expectations of one another, and differing ideas in regard to who should be doing, or saying something, also regarding the where, when, and how things should be done. There are so many ways in which we bump into one another, causing a bruised or fractured relationship.

Some situations cause a greater disturbance in our hearts than others, but unforgiveness may move in quickly no matter what has happened. Sometimes we don't recognize that we have high expectations of the other person, which they do not feel obligated to fill. Our expectations may become like an undercurrent of demands, and if they don't do what we want, we're miffed. Then the other person prefers to stay away from us. The enemy enjoys adding fuel to the fire, and by that time he has built a real bon-fire. We may believe that the other person has trespassed on our territory, or taken advantage of us in some way. Possibly the person spoke harshly to you, or you feel you were left out of something of importance. There are so many possibilities.

We all know the pain in our hearts from the unforgiveness we hold toward others. As long as we try to feel justified, we will go into deeper suffering, and it often causes sickness in the mind and body. It came to me just last night, that unforgiveness is like moldy food which has been left too long in the refrigerator. Like something fermenting in your emotions. It's also like some creepy-crawly bugs pestering you, demanding your attention.

It is also very hard when someone else is unforgiving in his or her heart toward us, especially when you feel that you've done nothing wrong. It is extremely hard to resolve the issue as long as each one continues to hold on to unforgiveness. This is declaring, "I'm right and you're wrong, so there, wake up and fly right!" When problems remain unresolved, our lack of forgiveness can cause a tormenting root of bitterness, and the result will be diseases and many other ways of suffering deeply. This not only grieves our hearts, but also the Holy Spirit.

JESUS FORGAVE US – SO WE MUST FORGIVE

It's no wonder that the Bible speaks about the need to forgive one another. Ephesians 4:32 says, "And be kind to one another, tenderhearted, forgiving one another, even as God in Christ forgave you." And then in Colossians 3:12-13 we find another list to help us overcome the negative emotions that can overtake us: "Therefore, as the elect of God, holy and beloved, put on tender mercies, kindness, humility, meekness, longsuffering; bearing with one another, and forgiving one another, if anyone has a complaint against another; even as Christ forgave you, so you also must do." What a huge difference can transpire when we follow these instructions. This takes an attitude change. Maybe it requires way beyond that for we can have large blind spots in regard to how righteous we believe we are. Our pride may be almost an insurmountable obstacle to humbling ourselves in obedience to God's Word.

Our heavenly Father is well aware of what is going on deep within us, even though we may hide it from the people living around us. Whenever another unpleasant experience bumps these negative emotions, they are apt to splash someone with unkind words, a sharp tongue or in some other way, which causes more hurts. Sin has a way of expressing itself, and sometimes we are caught in sin without intending to be so openly expressive.

The situation may be where you feel obliged to let the other person know how they have trampled on you. They may well have struck an area of your special qualities, or skills, or they lack respect for your position. We think we're just defending ourselves with 'righteous indignation', but pride can react in ways that will even shock ourselves. In time we can observe that we haven't gained any respect, but heaped ourselves with more problems and more pain. Consider this: Why would it be so right for you to act unkindly in any way toward the person you believe has hurt you, yet become so exasperated when this same reaction is turned around—coming back toward you?

As we look at the above Scriptures, we see that it takes effort to make wiser choices of these possible situations. We have to make a definite choice to respond God's way, according to His rulebook. His rules are always for our good—always! Any anger, bitterness, malice, gossip, or rejection can also hurt others around you, not just the person who is upsetting you, and you are getting hurt the most! It's like a flu bug, or a painful sliver under the fingernail, both of these affect the whole body. There is no way that only a tiny little area is disturbed.

FORGIVENESS REQUIRES TENDER MERCIES

God's Word tells us to put on tender mercies like a piece of clothing to wear. Tender mercies and unforgiveness can't dwell together, either the one stays, or the other, but not both. So it comes down to obedience, or disobedience. We are to put on humility and meekness. This is not a simple transaction. When we are humbled before God and our fellow man, we are also meek and gentle and we become tenderhearted and considerate in relating with other people; not ready to take offense easily at all.

In 1 John 3:10-23 we are given God's view about loving one another. Verses 16-19 NIV says, "This is how we know what love is: Jesus Christ laid down His life for us. And we ought to lay down our lives for our brothers. If anyone has material possessions and sees his brother in need, but has no pity on him, how can the love of God be in him? Dear children, let us not love with words or tongue but with actions and in truth. This then is how we know that we belong to the truth, and how we set our hearts at rest in His presence." God's love in our hearts enables us to be merciful, to drop charges and begin to reach out to that person, or persons, with compassion. When we sincerely pray for the other person, and realize that we need their prayers too, there's no place left for unforgiveness. We can then accept being moved over, even put down or ignored without exploding, because we know the power of God's love in our hearts can win over any undesirable situation. Jesus is our perfect example as he prayed on the cross, "Father, forgive them for they do not know what they do." Stephen said similar words as he was being stoned to death, and I can imagine that Paul may have prayed that prayer aloud during the times he suffered severe persecution.

POSITIVE CHANGES BRING PEACE

Assurance in God's promises in Romans 8:28 can provide calmness within our heart. With that calmness we can be more longsuffering, whereas we had the tendency to respond negatively over some small detail before. If we accept God's merciful, loving ways in our difficult situations, evil cannot displace what God has given to us.

Take another look at those positive words: humility, meekness, gentleness and kindness, merciful and longsuffering; they are the fruit of the Spirit of God. They are powerful, and enable us to walk securely in the midst of the storms of life. They are definitely not produced by our human nature, but will emerge and grow as we surrender to God's Spirit within us, thereby giving us internal strength to stand and walk with ease when the going is rough.

Besides, the last phrase in Colossians 3:12 and 13 is—"even as God in Christ forgave you, so you also must do." We have the perfect example in Jesus Christ throughout his lifetime, but more than that—we have received a forgiveness that we could never work hard enough to pay for, nor inherit enough money to negotiate for it. The only way to receive God's forgiveness is through the receiving of His marvelous gift, which was purchased by the blood of Jesus, through the horrendous abuse to His body, and ultimately His death on the cross. He paid the price for you, and for me, to experience this absolutely undeserved forgiveness.

If we allow any of these— "bitterness, wrath, anger, clamor, and evil speaking, with malice," to have a place in our hearts, they will automatically take over. We have to 'unseat' them, kick them out. Giving no place for the devil! We cannot have friendly terms with even one of them, for they are closely associated to one another and will gradually overpower you; then your peace is gone. This gives us the ability to see that we've made the wrong choice.

God's Word says in Isaiah 55: 6 and 7: "Seek the Lord while He may be found. Call upon Him while He is near. Let the wicked forsake his way, and the unrighteous man his thoughts; let him return to the Lord, and He will have mercy on him; and to our God, for He will abundantly pardon."

UNFORGIVENESS AFFECTS OUR RELATIONSHIP WITH GOD

In the New Testament 1 John 1:6-9, contains a most essential enlightening truth! This truth is: "If we say that we have fellowship with Him, and walk in darkness, we lie and do not practice the truth. But if we walk in the light as He is in the light, we have fellowship with one another, and the blood of Jesus Christ His Son cleanses us from all sin. If we say that we have no sin, we deceive ourselves, and the truth is not in us. If we confess our sins, He is faithful and just to forgive us our sins and to cleanse us from all unrighteousness." God has already shown us that unforgiveness is unrighteousness in the heart—it is sin, and must be dealt with in the way God prescribes. In fact, we need to attack it like we deal with garbage and roaches, out with it all! Refuse any more discussions with that harassing spirit.

Matthew 6:14-15 give another dimension of this truth: "For if you forgive men their trespasses, your heavenly Father will also forgive you. But if you do not forgive men their trespasses, neither will your Father forgive your trespasses." When unforgiveness holds you hostage, you are a slave to evil. It holds on to you in many ways, so it is wise to choose God's way—forgiveness. We cannot live joyfully without His forgiveness.

It's not a matter of whether or not the person deserves it, but remembering the magnitude of our sins that God has forgiven.

Forgiveness releases us from being in bondage to others. It not only brings freedom, but also washes away the debris that caused friction and division. Forgiveness often comes through a process. Reconciliation will take place if you ask the Lord to help you to genuinely forgive, as well as seek their forgiveness for whatever they believe you have done against them.

    Pray for the other person's well being, and for the Lord to bless them abundantly even as you are experiencing His tender mercies. Please don't allow another day to pass by without responding to God's instructions. You will be amazed how quickly His peace will return to your heart. Peace, peace, the wonderful peace of Jesus!

SCRIPTURES FOR
F O R G I V E N E S S

Prayers for forgiveness—

Num. 14:17-19 "And now, I *(Moses)* pray, let the power of My Lord be great just as You have spoken saying, 'The Lord is longsuffering and abundant in mercy, **forgiving** iniquity and transgression; but He by no means clears the guilty, visiting the iniquity of the fathers on the children to the third and fourth generation.' Pardon the iniquity of this people, according to the greatness of Your mercy, just as You have **forgiven** this people, from Egypt even until now."

1 Kings 8:38-40 NIV *(Solomon's prayer)* "And when prayer or plea is made by any of Your people Israel–each one aware of the afflictions of his own heart; and spreading out his hands toward this temple–then hear from heaven, Your dwelling place. **Forgive** and act; deal with each man according to all he does, since You know his heart for You alone know the hearts of all men, so they will fear You all the time they live in the land You gave our fathers." *Also 2 Chron. 6:21,22.*

Neh. 9:17 NIV *The Levite leaders were leading the Israelites in prayer—-* "They refused to listen and failed to remember the miracles you performed among them. They became stiff-necked and in their rebellion appointed a leader in order to return to their slavery. But You are a **forgiving** God, gracious and compassionate, slow to anger and abounding in love."

Dan. 9:9, 19 *Daniel's prayer for the people—-* To the Lord our God belong mercy and **forgiveness**, though we have rebelled against Him. ...."O Lord, hear! O Lord, **forgive**! O Lord, listen and act! Do not delay for Your own sake, my God, for Your city and Your people are called by Your name."

Matt. 6:12 *From Jesus' model prayer*— "And **forgive** us our debts, as we **forgive** our debtors."

God forgives—

2 Chron. 7:14-15 "....if My people who are called by My name will humble themselves, and pray and seek My face, and turn from their wicked ways, then I will hear from heaven, and will **forgive** their sin and heal their land. Now my eyes will be open and my ears attentive to prayer made in this place."

Ps. 32:1 Blessed is he whose transgression is **forgiven**, whose sin is covered. *Also Rom. 4:6-8.*

Ps. 86:5 For You, Lord are good, and ready to **forgive**, and abundant in mercy to all those who call upon You.

Ps. 103:2-3 Bless the Lord, O my soul, and forget not all His benefits: Who **forgives** all your iniquities, who heals all your diseases.

Ps. 130:3-4 If You, Lord, should mark iniquities, O Lord, who could stand? But there is **forgiveness** with You, that You may be feared.

Isa. 33:24 And the inhabitant will not say, "I am sick"; the people who dwell in it will be **forgiven** their iniquity.

Jer. 31:33-34 But this is the covenant that I will make with the house of Israel after those days, says the Lord: I will put My law in their minds, and write it on their hearts: and I will be their God, and they shall be My people. No more shall every man teach his neighbor, and every man his brother say, 'Know the Lord,' for they all shall know Me, from the least of them to the greatest of them, says the Lord. For I will **forgive** their iniquity, and their sin I will remember no more."

Col. 2:13-14 And you, being dead in your trespasses and the uncircumcision of your flesh, He has made alive together with Him, having **forgiven** you all trespasses, having wiped out the handwriting of requirements that was against us, which was contrary to us. And He has taken it out of the way, having nailed it to the cross.

Jesus has power to forgive—

Matt. 9:2-6 Then behold they brought to Him a paralytic lying on a bed. When Jesus saw their faith, He said to the paralytic, "Son, be of good cheer; your sins are forgiven you." And at once some of the scribes said within themselves, "This Man blasphemes!" But Jesus, knowing their thoughts, said, "Why do you think evil in your hearts? For which is easier, to say, 'Your sins are **forgiven** you,' or to say, 'Arise and walk'? But that you may know that the Son of Man has power on earth to **forgive** sins"–then He said to the paralytic, "Arise, take up your bed, and go to your house." *Also Mark 2:5-11 and Luke 5:20-24.*

Acts 5:30-31 "The God of our fathers raised up Jesus whom you murdered by hanging on a tree. Him God has exalted to His right hand to be Prince and Savior, to give repentance to Israel and **forgiveness** of sins."

Acts 13:38-39 "Therefore let it be known to you, brethren, that through this Man is preached to you the **forgiveness** of sins; and by Him everyone who believes is justified from all things from which you could not be justified by the law of Moses."

Acts 26:15-18 *Paul is testifying before King Agrippa in regard to his conversion experience; the first account being recorded in Acts 9:1-19—-* "So I said, 'Who are You, Lord?' And He said, 'I am Jesus, whom you are persecuting, but rise and stand on your feet; for I have appeared to you for this purpose, to make you a minister and a witness both of the things which you have seen and of the things which I will yet reveal to you. I will deliver you from the Jewish people, as well as from the Gentiles to whom I now send you, to open their eyes in order to turn them from darkness to light, and from the power of Satan to God, that they may receive **forgiveness** of sins and an inheritance among those who are sanctified by faith in Me.'"

Eph. 1:7-8 In Him we have redemption through His blood, the **forgiveness** of sins, according to the riches of His grace which He made to abound toward us in all wisdom and prudence. *Also Col. 1:14.*

Forgiven - or - Not forgiven —

Matt. 6:14-15 For if you **forgive** men their trespasses, your heavenly Father will also forgive you. But if you do not **forgive** men their trespasses, neither will your Father **forgive** your trespasses. *Also Mark 11:25, 26.*

Matt. 12:31-32 "Therefore I say to you, every sin and blasphemy will be **forgiven** men, but the blasphemy against the Spirit will not be **forgiven** men. Anyone who speaks a word against the Son of Man, it will be **forgiven** him; but whoever speaks against the Holy Spirit, it will not be **forgiven** him, either in this age or in the age to come." *Also Mark 3:28, 29.*

Those who receive God's forgiveness are commanded to forgive others —

Matt. 18:21-35
  21-23 — Then Peter came to Him and said, "Lord, how often shall my brother sin against me, and I **forgive** him? Up to seven times?" Jesus said to him, "I do not say to you, up to seven times, but up to seventy times seven. Therefore the kingdom of heaven is like a certain king who wanted to settle accounts with his servants."
  24-31 — (In these verses Jesus was teaching about **forgiveness**. He went on to tell how this king dealt with someone who had a huge debt. When this man begged for **forgiveness**, the king granted it. But the one who had been forgiven turned around and dealt

mercilessly with someone who owed him a very small amount, particularly in comparison with the debt he had been **forgiven**.)

32-35— "Then his master, after he had called him, said to him, 'You wicked servant! I **forgave** you all that debt because you begged me. Should you not also have had compassion on your fellow servant, just as I had pity on you?' And his master was angry, and delivered him to the torturers until he should pay all that was due to him. So My heavenly Father also will do to you if each of you, from his heart, does not **forgive** his brother his trespasses."

Luke 7:40-50 And Jesus answered and said to him, "Simon *(a Pharisee who had invited Jesus to his house)*, I have something to say to you." So he said, "Teacher, say it."

"There was a certain creditor who had two debtors. One owed five hundred denarii *(one denarii was considered a day's wages)*, and the other fifty. And when they had nothing with which to repay, he freely **forgave** them both. Tell me, therefore, which of them will love him more?" Simon answered and said, "I suppose the one whom he **forgave** more." And He said to him, "You have rightly judged."

Then He turned to the woman and said to Simon, "Do you see this woman? I entered your house; you gave Me no water for My feet, but she has washed My feet with her tears and wiped them with the hair of her head. You gave Me no kiss, but this woman has not ceased to kiss My feet since the time I came in. You did not anoint My head with oil, but this woman has anointed My feet with fragrant oil. Therefore I say to you, her sins, which are many, are **forgiven**, for she loved much. But to whom little is **forgiven**, the same loves little." Then he said to her, "Your sins are **forgiven**."

And those who sat at the table with Him began to say to themselves, "Who is this who even **forgives** sins?" Then He said to the woman, "Your faith has saved you. Go in peace."

Eph. 4:31-32 Let all bitterness, wrath, anger, clamor *(being vehement, making a lot of noise)*, and evil speaking be put away from you, with all malice. And be kind to one another, tenderhearted,

forgiving one another, even as God in Christ **forgave** you.

Col. 3:12-13 Therefore, as the elect of God, holy and beloved, put on tender mercies, kindness, humility, meekness, longsuffering; bearing with one another, and **forgiving** one another, if anyone has a complaint against another; even as Christ **forgave** you, so you also must do.

Repentance precedes forgiveness—

Isa. 55:6, 7 Seek the Lord while He may be found. Call upon Him while He is near. Let the wicked forsake his way, and the unrighteous man his thoughts; let him return to the Lord, and He will have mercy on him; and to our God, for He will abundantly **pardon** *(forgive)*.

Luke 17:1-4 Then He said to the disciples, "It is impossible that no offenses should come, but woe to him through whom they do come! It would be better for him if a millstone were hung around his neck, and he were thrown into the sea, than that he should offend one of these little ones. Take heed to yourselves. If your brother sins against you, rebuke him; and if he repents, **forgive** him. And if he sins against you seven times in a day, and seven times in a day returns to you saying, 'I repent,' you shall **forgive** him."

Acts 8:22-23 "Repent therefore of this your wickedness, and pray God if perhaps the thought of your heart may be **forgiven** you. For I see that you are poisoned by bitterness and bound by iniquity."

1 John 1:6-9 If we say that we have fellowship with Him, and walk in darkness, we lie and do not practice the truth. But if we walk in the light as He is in the light, we have fellowship with one another, and the blood of Jesus Christ His Son cleanses us from all sin. If we say that we have no sin, we deceive ourselves, and the truth is not in us. If we confess our sins, He is faithful and just to **forgive** us our sins and to cleanse us from all unrighteousness.

Other important Scriptures on forgiveness—

John 20:22-23 And when He (Jesus) had said this, He breathed on them, and said to them, "Receive the Holy Spirit. If you **forgive** the sins of any, they are **forgiven** them; if you retain the sins of any, they are retained."

2 Cor. 2:10-11 Now whom you **forgive** anything, I *(Paul)* also **forgive**. For if indeed I have **forgiven** anything, I have **forgiven** that one for your sakes in the presence of Christ, lest Satan should take advantage of us, for we are not ignorant of his devices.

2 Tim. 3:1-5 But know this, that in the last days perilous times will come: for men will be lovers of themselves, lovers of money, boasters, proud, blasphemers, disobedient to parents, unthankful, unholy, unloving, **unforgiving**, slanderers, without self-control, brutal, despisers of good, traitors, headstrong, haughty, lovers of pleasure rather than lovers of God, having a form of godliness but denying its power. And from such people turn away!

James 5:14-15 Is anyone among you sick? Let him call for the elders of the church, and let them pray over him, anointing him with oil in the name of the Lord. And the prayer of faith will save the sick, and the Lord will raise him up. And if he has committed sins, he will be **forgiven**.

RECONCILIATION

RECONCILED TO GOD THROUGH JESUS

The words reconciled and reconciliation are not commonly used. We seldom hear them. So let's see what the Webster's New World Dictionary says: To make friendly again, or win over to a friendly attitude; to settle a quarrel, or dispute, bring into harmony, becoming compatible.

Now as we approach our Scriptures, we can better understand what God has done for us, and what He expects of us too. In Romans 5, the whole chapter is explaining reconciliation between God and mankind. In verses 8 and 9 it says, "But God demonstrates His own love toward us, in that while we were still sinners, Christ died for us. Much more then, having now been justified by His blood, we shall be saved from wrath through Him." Also look at Hebrews 2:17 in our Scriptures. Do you see what it cost God to reconcile us to Himself? Our sin toward God is much greater than any other person's flaws, shortcomings, weaknesses, and deliberate sins toward us!

Then in Romans 5:10 and 11 we read, "For if when we were enemies we were reconciled to God through the death of His Son, much more, having been reconciled we shall be saved by His life. And not only that, we also rejoice in God through our Lord Jesus Christ, through whom we have now received reconciliation." We couldn't have contributed anything. Only because of what Jesus has done for us, are we privileged to be reconciled to God.

RECONCILIATION WITH OTHERS

He urges us to be reconciled to one another. In fact, He doesn't even want us to bring gifts to Him until we have made things right with one another. Granted, you may already have tried and it didn't work. The other person may not have accepted your offering. Take it to the Lord in prayer. Sincere, fervent prayer is our next step. Ask the Lord to prepare the hearts of all involved, so they may be released from the heavy burden of fractured relationships. Truly, we all lack wisdom, but in James 1:5, we're told to ask God for His wisdom. When we are obedient toward Him and His Word, we can count on His ready answer, and His enabling power to forgive.

We know full well that things don't just straighten out automatically. Someone has to be loving and gracious enough to lay down all the battle gear, and choose to forget the scars in order to work through the problems. Reconciliation requires forgiveness, so there is a point of making a decision about what is most important. Is it more important to hold on to thinking you are the only one who could be right, or is the relationship more valuable? Can you humble yourself, in obedience to the Lord? In Matthew 20:20-28 we find the disciples having a discussion with Jesus about importance. And Jesus finalized it this way: "And whoever desires to be first among you, let him be your slave—just as the Son of Man did not come to be served, but to serve, and to give His life a ransom for many."

Each one of us, who has experienced God's reconciliation, knows that he has forgiven us for a multitude of sins, and that we could never have paid the price for God's love and mercy. Considering God's great mercy toward us, why would we not desire to be merciful toward those who have offended us in some way?

In the Sermon on the Mount we read, "Blessed are the merciful, for they will be shown mercy" *Matthew 5:7 NIV*. Could we possibly find a better plan than God has given to us, remembering that mercy was His way of reconciling us to Himself? When Jesus came to the earth, His mercy heart compelled Him to be a servant to mankind, even unto death on the cross, rather than as a King with swift, harsh authority.

We could never pay the price that Jesus paid— "For it pleased the Father that in Him all the fullness should dwell, and by Him to reconcile all things to Himself, by Him, whether things on earth or things in heaven, having made peace through the blood of His cross. And you, who once were alienated and enemies in your mind by wicked works, yet now He has reconciled in the body of His flesh through death, to present you holy, and blameless, and above reproach in His sight—" *Colossians 1:19-22*. There is no true peace without reconciliation. In most of Paul's epistles, within his introductory paragraph he says: "Grace to you and peace from God our Father and the Lord Jesus Christ;" and he could speak these words with absolute assurance that God was sending His grace and peace to all who believed on Jesus as the Christ. He had experienced it, so it flowed through him onto the pages of his letters, and right to the hearts of the believers in each congregation.

THE MINISTRY OF RECONCILIATION

Now God gives the ministry of reconciliation to those who have experienced the new relationship with God as Father, and Lord. You may know how important it is to be released from all the bondages of sin that were holding you down in despair and hopelessness. What a privilege to be a spokesman for the Lord; God's ambassadors for peace and righteousness. Right after being told that anyone who is in Christ becomes a new creation, we read in 2 Corinthians 5:18-20, "Now all things are of God, who has reconciled us to Himself through Jesus Christ, and has given us the ministry of reconciliation, that is, that God was in Christ reconciling the world to Himself, not imputing their trespasses to them, and has committed to us the word of reconciliation. Now then, we are ambassadors for Christ as though God were pleading through us: we implore you on Christ's behalf, be reconciled to God."

It is a part of "loving one another as Jesus loved us." *See John 13:34*. Many Christians are ecstatic about the blessing of testifying what God has done for them. They have had tremendous breakthroughs because of what Jesus has done for them, and can hardly wait to tell others. Have you enjoyed that excitement in your heart? It is inspiring to listen to such testimonies on Christian television channels, or to read about them in books.

As you hear and read about what God has done in the lives of others, because the power of His compassionate and merciful heart had reached down to transfer them from the kingdom of darkness into the kingdom of light, it encourages us to tell others about Jesus. You know how dark your life had been and how needy you were to know the story of God's love. From the love of Jesus dwelling in your heart, and the knowledge you have gained, I pray that you are compelled to go tell others so they may become reconciled to God and find the true peace and joy that the Lord Jesus has for them.

Let us seek the Lord for His compassion to fill our hearts, a compassion that is beyond ourselves, that only God can give; and with a new determination to bring reconciliation where it is needed, beginning with our own relationships. See what the Lord says in 1 Corinthians 15:57-58, then call upon the Holy Spirit to lead you.

God bless you as you seek to please the Lord in all your ways.

SCRIPTURES FOR RECONCILIATION

Being reconciled to God—

Rom. 5:8-11 But God demonstrates His own love toward us, in that while we were still sinners, Christ died for us. Much more then, having now been justified by His blood, we shall be saved from wrath through Him. For if when we were enemies we were **reconciled** to God through the death of His Son, much more, having been **reconciled**, we shall be saved by His life. And not only that, we also rejoice in God through our Lord Jesus Christ, through whom we have now received **reconciliation**.

2 Cor. 5:18-21 Now all things are of God, who has **reconciled** us to Himself through Jesus Christ, and has given us the ministry of **reconciliation**, that is, that God was in Christ **reconciling** the world to Himself, not imputing their trespasses to them, and has committed to us the word of **reconciliation**. Now then, we are ambassadors for Christ as though God were pleading through us: we implore you on Christ's behalf, be **reconciled** to God. For He made Him who knew no sin to be sin for us, that we might become the righteousness of God in Him.

Col. 1:19-23 For it pleased the Father that in Him all the fullness should dwell, and by Him to **reconcile** all things to Himself, by Him, whether things on earth or things in heaven, having made peace through the blood of His cross. And you, who once were alienated and enemies in your mind by wicked works, yet now He has **reconciled** in the body of His flesh through death, to present you holy, and blameless, and above reproach in His sight—if indeed you continue in the faith, grounded and steadfast, and are not moved away from the hope of the gospel which you heard, which was preached to every creature under heaven, of which I,

Paul, became a minister.

Heb. 2:17 Therefore, in all things He had to be made like His brethren, that He might be a merciful and faithful High Priest in things pertaining to God, to make propitiation *(reconciliation KJV)* for the sins of the people.

Reconciliation for Jews and Gentiles—-

Rom. 11:15 For if their being cast away is the **reconciling** of the world, what will their acceptance be but life from the dead? For if the firstfruit is holy, the lump is also holy, and if the root is holy, so are the branches. *See Romans—chapters 9 – 11.*

Eph. 2:14-18 For He Himself is our peace, who has made both one, and has broken down the middle wall of separation, having abolished in His flesh the enmity that is, the law of commandments contained in ordinances, so as to create in Himself one new man from the two, thus making peace, and that He might **reconcile** them both to God in one body through the cross, thereby putting to death the enmity. And He came and preached peace to you who were afar off and to those who were near. For through Him we both have access by one Spirit to the Father.

Col. 1:19-23 For it pleased the Father that in Him all the fullness should dwell, and by Him to **reconcile** all things to Himself, by Him, whether things on earth or things in heaven, having made peace through the blood of His cross. And you, who once were alienated and enemies in your mind by wicked works, yet now He has **reconciled** in the body of His flesh through death, to present you holy, and blameless, and above reproach in His sight – if indeed you continue in the faith, grounded and steadfast, and are not moved away from the hope of the gospel which you heard, which was preached to every creature under heaven, of which I, Paul, became a minister.

Reconciliation between one another —-

Matt. 5:23-24 "Therefore, if you bring your gift to the altar, and there remember that your brother has something against you, leave your gift there before the altar, and go your way. First be **reconciled** to your brother, and then come and offer your gift."

1 Cor. 7:10-11 Now to the married I command, yet not I but the Lord: A wife is not to depart from her husband. But even if she does depart, let her remain unmarried or be **reconciled** to her husband, and a husband is not to divorce his wife.

RESTORATION

GOD'S RESTORATION IS DEEP

When God restores, He also deals with the cause of the break down. He brings that person, couple, group, church, nation or land to wholeness. This is most probably beyond where we might think it needs to be. Let's take restoring a marriage, for example. Restoration would bring that couple back to what point in their relationship? What do they really need? What would change their lives so they won't sink into the same ditch again and again? Whatever the need might be: physical, emotional, spiritual or in any other area, we must relinquish ourselves to the Lord so that He might work in our hearts and show us the way to complete restoration.

There are so many possibilities for the kinds of changes that need to be made; how time is spent, the choice of companions, change in thought patterns, or lifestyle. It may not be easy to understand or accept the changes you need to make. The foods we eat, the non-foods and drinks that our bodies have to deal with, and exercise are very important factors, because they affect our behavior too. Oftentimes we think such things couldn't possibly be involved with our present need.

God's restoration is deep; bringing us to perfection. He wants us to know Him more perfectly and experience His personal interaction with us on a daily basis. He really desires to broaden our understanding of truth for godly living and bring us to an understanding of His righteousness, so we might become more like Him. This will help us to avoid the unwise choices we have been making. We will most probably become better equipped to warn others of hidden pitfalls that threaten to cause harm to them and may be blocking their spiritual growth.

In Galatians 6:1 and 2, we find this exhortation to help others who need restoration: "Brethren, if a man is overtaken in any trespass, you who are spiritual restore such a one in a spirit of gentleness, considering yourself, lest you also be tempted. Bear one another's burdens and so fulfill the law of Christ." God's compassionate heart is expressed here. It is just the way that Jesus lived here in the midst of suffering humanity, in a spirit of meekness and gentleness, as a burden bearer. He was more concerned about restoring us to the level of wholeness in which God created us, than He was about protecting Himself, or deriving any personal benefits.

SURRENDER AND OBEDIENCE ARE NECESSARY

Psalm 23, the most familiar of all the psalms, says, "He restores my soul." This wonderful truth is surrounded with these major statements: "He makes me to lie down in green pastures; He leads me beside the still waters; and, He leads me in the paths of righteousness for His name's sake." This alerts me to the importance of obediently following the Lord every day as my Shepherd. Look at this again, more thoughtfully—He makes me..., He leads me..., He guides me... NIV, so I must allow Him the freedom to do whatever He desires to do. If we choose something other than the path the Lord sets before us, trouble is very likely awaiting our next step. You can easily think of some of the troubles that you have already encountered, and the discomforts you've felt, or even the excruciating pain that you had to endure before arriving at the place of being willing to surrender to the Lord's choices, and finally, after crying out in repentance before the Lord, experienced His rescue and restoration.

Depending upon the situation, our cry may not be instantly answered; at least not in the manner we wanted it, or in accordance with our time-frame. In First Peter, chapters three and four speak a great deal about suffering in a godly manner, and we find that much of this suffering is for righteousness' sake *(3:14)*. God is always in charge, for He is Sovereign God. His purposes are always for our spiritual growth. Through suffering we find the deep need to cling to

Him and search His Word for the truths and promises we desperately need. We even ask Him more often what His will is in the affairs of our lives. In 1 Peter 5:10 NIV, we read: "And the God of all grace, who called you to His eternal glory in Christ, after you have suffered a little while, will Himself restore you and make you strong, firm and steadfast." In this Scripture we are told that this suffering is necessary. The KJV says it this way: "...after that ye have suffered a while, make you perfect, stablish, strengthen, settle you."

I think this gives us keen insight about God's way of restoring His children. He is stabilizing us, so we can stand strong through all kinds of circumstances. He wants to do far more than just bring us to a place of contentment with ourselves and satisfaction with 'the way life is treating me', as the saying goes. He's not providing us with every privilege available on this earth so that we can become spoiled children. God is conforming us to the image of Jesus, which is complete restoration. We need to spend time fellowshipping in His presence and gleaning from the truths that Jesus taught while He was here on the earth.

CONTINUOUS NEED FOR RESTORATION

Psalm 80:3 is my cry to the Lord: "Restore us, O God; cause Your face to shine and we shall be saved!" Salvation is more than just a ticket to heaven so we won't go to hell. Salvation and restoration will bring us from darkness— to light; from struggle— to freedom; depression— to a new lease on life; aloneness— to fellowship; don't care—to what's new? Yes, even from the gray blaahs— to rejoicing, and more! There is a sure victory when we trust the Lord for restoration, by letting go and surrendering all; handing the reins over to Him.

There is much more about restoration in the Scriptures given with this meditation. If you get into the Word to observe what God has done, and continues to do, you may really get a jump-start, genuinely motivated to increase your understanding. He wants to restore your health, your relationships, peace of mind and bring you to financial freedom. Restoration is a continual process. It involves a life-time of moving toward God's goal.

His desire is for you to experience the fullness of Christ Jesus in you, the hope of glory. He wants you to find a deep settled peace, with joy unspeakable and full of glory! He desires to restore all that has been taken from you by the enemy of our souls, so you might enjoy life far beyond where you are today. And, if you falter along the way, know this – He is waiting to hear your plea for restoration, knowing that only He can restore you! Praise God for His boundless love! "Now to Him who is able to do exceedingly abundantly above all that we ask or think according to the power that works in us, to Him be glory in the church by Christ Jesus to all generations, forever and ever. Amen. *Ephesians 3:20-21 NIV.*

SCRIPTURES FOR
RESTORATION

God restores—-

Job 33:26 *Elihu is speaking—-* He shall pray to God, and He will delight in him, He shall see His face with joy, for He **restores** to man His righteousness.

Ps. 23:3 He **restores** my soul; He leads me in the paths of righteousness for His name's sake.

Nah. 2:2 For the Lord will **restore** the excellence of Jacob like the excellence of Israel, for the emptiers have emptied them out and ruined their vine branches.

Acts 1:6 Therefore, when they had come together, they asked Him *(Jesus)* saying, "Lord, will You at this time **restore** the kingdom of Israel?"

I Peter 5:10 NIV And the God of all grace, who called you to His eternal glory in Christ, after you have suffered a little while, will Himself **restore** you and make you strong, firm and steadfast.

Prayers for restoration—-

Ps. 51:12 **Restore** to me the joy of Your salvation, and uphold me by Your generous Spirit.

Ps. 80:3 **Restore** us, O God; cause Your face to shine, and we shall be saved!

Jer. 31:18 "I have surely heard Ephraim bemoaning himself: 'You have chastened me, and I was chastised, like an untrained bull;

restore me, and I will return, for You are the Lord my God."

Lam. 5:20-21 Why do You forget us forever, and forsake us for so long a time? Turn us back to You, O Lord, and we will be **restored**; renew our days as of old.

God promises to restore—-

Isa. 1:26 "I will **restore** your judges as at the first, and your counselors as at the beginning. Afterward you shall be called the city of righteousness, the faithful city."

Isa. 57:17-18 For the iniquity of his covetousness I was angry and struck him; I hid and was angry, and he went on backsliding in the way of his heart. I have seen his ways, and will heal him; I will also lead him, and **restore** comforts to him and to his mourners.

Isa. 58:11-12 "The Lord will guide you continually, and satisfy your soul in drought, and strengthen your bones; you shall be like a watered garden, and like a spring of water, whose waters do not fail. Those from among you shall build the old waste places; you shall raise up the foundations of many generations; and you shall be called the Repairer of the Breach, The **Restorer** of Streets to Dwell In."

Jer. 27:21-22 "...yes, thus says the Lord of hosts, the God of Israel, concerning the vessels that remain in the house of the Lord, and in the house of the king of Judah and of Jerusalem: 'They shall be carried to Babylon, and there they shall be until the day that I visit them,' says the Lord. 'Then I will bring them up and **restore** them to this place.'"

Jer. 30:17 "...'For I will **restore** health to you and heal you of your wounds,' says the Lord,
'Because they called you an outcast saying: "This is Zion; no one seeks her."'" *The description of the restoration of Israel and Judah begins in Jeremiah 30:1 and then through many chapters following.*

Dan. 9:25 "Know therefore and understand, that from the going forth of the command to **restore** and build Jerusalem until Messiah the Prince, there shall be seven weeks and sixty-two weeks; the street shall be built again and the wall, even in troublesome times."

Joel 2:25-27 "So I will **restore** to you the years that the swarming locust has eaten, the crawling locust, the consuming locust, and the chewing locust, my great army which I sent among you. You shall eat in plenty and be satisfied, and praise the name of the Lord God, who has dealt wondrously with you; and My people shall never be put to shame. Then you shall know that I am in the midst of Israel: I am the Lord your God and there is no other. My people shall never be put to shame."

Zech. 9:11-13 "As for you also, because of the blood of your covenant, I will set your prisoners free from the waterless pit. Return to the stronghold, you prisoners of hope even today I declare that I will **restore** double to you. For I have bent Judah, My bow, fitted the bow with Ephraim, and raised up your sons, O Zion, against your sons, O Greece, and made you like the sword of a mighty man."

Matt. 17:11-12 Jesus answered and said to them, "Indeed Elijah is coming first and will **restore** all things. But I say to you that Elijah has come already, and they did not know him but did to him whatever they wished. Likewise the son of Man is also about to suffer at their hands." *Also Mark 9:12*

Acts 3:19-21 "Repent therefore and be converted, that your sins may be blotted out, so that times of refreshing may come from the presence of the Lord, and that He may send Jesus Christ, who was preached to you before, whom heaven must receive unto the times of **restoration** of all things, which God has spoken by the mouth of all His holy prophets since the world began."

Restoration through healing—-

Mark 3:1, 5 And He *(Jesus)* entered the synagogue again, and a man was there who had a withered hand. And when He had looked around at them with anger, being grieved by the hardness of their hearts, He said to the man, "Stretch out your hand." And he stretched it out, and his hand was **restored** as whole as the other. *Also Matt. 12:13 and Luke 6:10*

Mark 8:24-25 And he looked up and said, "I see men like trees, walking." Then He *(Jesus)* put His hands on his eyes again and made him look up. And he was **restored** and saw everyone clearly.

Gal. 6:1-2 Brethren, if a man is overtaken in any trespass, you who are spiritual **restore** such a one in a spirit of gentleness, considering yourself lest you also be tempted. Bear one another's burdens and so fulfill the law of Christ.

Instructions regarding restoration—-

Deut. 22:1-3 "You shall not see your brother's ox or his sheep going astray, and hide yourself from them; you shall certainly bring them back to your brother. And if your brother is not near you, or if you do not know him, then you shall bring it to your own house, and it shall remain with you until your brother seeks it; then you shall **restore** it to him. You shall do the same with his donkey, and so shall you do with his garment; with any lost thing of your brother's, which he has lost and you have found, you shall do likewise; you must not hide yourself."

Neh. 5:9-12 Then I said, "What you are doing is not good. Should you not walk in the fear of our God because of the reproach of the nations, our enemies? I also, with my brethren and my servants, am lending them money and grain. Please, let us stop this usury! **Restore** now to them, even this day, their lands, their vineyards, their olive groves, and their houses, also a hundredth of the money and the grain, the new wine and the oil, that you have charged them." So they said, "We will **restore** it and will require nothing from them; we will do as you say." Then I called the priests, and required an oath from them that they would do according to this promise.

Prov. 6:30-31 People do not despise a thief if he steals to satisfy himself when he is starving. Yet when he is found, he must **restore** sevenfold; he may have to give up all the substance of his house.

Luke 19:8-10 Then Zacchaeus stood and said to the Lord, "Look, Lord, I give half of my goods to the poor; and if I have taken anything from anyone by false accusation, I **restore** fourfold." And Jesus said to him, "Today salvation has come to this house, because he also is a son of Abraham, for the Son of Man has come to seek and to save that which was lost."

RIGHTEOUSNESS

GOD IS RIGHTEOUS

We have great reason to praise the Lord for this wonderful word. As we recognize our sinful and helpless condition we become desperate for some means of changing our nature and the direction we are going. If God was not righteous, there would be no hope for us. But God is righteous and He loves righteousness. His countenance beholds the upright, according to Psalm 11:7. So let's take a look at what the word 'righteousness' expresses to us.

It means that it conforms to truth; it is correct, accurate, moral, honest, legal and appropriate. Rightness lines up with the proper measurements, size, color; it just fits the bill.

In the spiritual sense God alone is perfect, holy and righteous. He has called us to live righteously, and provided the way for us to do so through Jesus Christ. In Psalm 71:19 it says, "Also Your righteousness, O God, is very high, You who have done great things: O God, who is like You?" In Jeremiah 23:5-6 we have a prophecy of the coming of Jesus Christ, which proves His righteousness too. He was not born of man, but conceived by the Holy Spirit. As God's only begotten Son, He was already righteous at the time of His birth. "Behold, the days are coming," says the Lord, "that I will raise to David a Branch of righteousness; A King shall reign and prosper, and execute judgment and righteousness in the earth. In His days Judah will be saved, and Israel will dwell safely. Now this is His name by which He will be called: THE LORD OUR RIGHTEOUSNESS."

HOW WE BECOME RIGHTEOUS IN JESUS CHRIST

In 1 Corinthians 1:30-31 we see how the righteousness of Jesus applies to believers. "But of Him you are in Christ Jesus, who became for us wisdom from God—and righteousness and sanctification and redemption—that, as it is written, 'He who glories, let him glory in the Lord." We cannot be righteous on our own, for God's Word makes it clear that "there is none righteous, no, not one; there is none who understands; there is none who seeks after God" "...for all have sinned and fall short of the glory of God" as it says in Romans 3:10-11 and 23.

We can understand more as we read chapters 5 and 6 in Romans, where we can read a lot about righteousness. Here is Romans 5:17, "For if by the one man's offense *(Adam in the garden of Eden)* death reigned through the one, much more those who receive abundance of grace and of the gift of righteousness will reign in life through the One, Jesus Christ." Then in Romans 6:10-14 we can see more of what Jesus has done—"For the death that He *(Jesus)* died, He died to sin once for all; but the life that He lives, He lives to God. Likewise you also, reckon yourselves to be dead indeed to sin, but alive to God in Christ Jesus our Lord. Therefore do not let sin reign in your mortal body, that you should obey it in its lusts. And do not present your members as instruments of unrighteousness to sin, but present yourselves to God as being alive from the dead, and your members as instruments of righteousness to God. For sin shall not have dominion over you, for you are not under the law but under grace." This is really great news! Jesus died for our sins, so that when His Spirit takes residence in us, we do not have to obey its lusts. We can rebuke the enemy of our souls and refuse to continue living in unrighteousness. That is a big WOW!

In 1 Peter 2:24 we learn more about this: "Jesus bore our sins in His own body on the tree, that we, having died to sins, might live for righteousness—by whose stripes you were healed." Even though we seem to be going backward as we go to Hosea 10:12, it is very fitting right here for it still applies to our generations—"Sow for yourselves righteousness; reap in mercy; break up your fallow ground, for it is time to seek the Lord, till He comes and rains righteousness on you." As we draw near to the Lord to obey Him, He draws near to us so we are enabled to obey. That sounds too good to be true, but it is truly the Word of God.

The more we read the Word of God, the more we are drawn to please Him. We become conscientious in keeping ourselves on the path that God has chosen; this is the way of righteousness. Even in the Old Testament through obedience and faith as "Abraham believed God, it was accounted to him for righteousness" we are told in Romans 4:3. Abraham didn't earn that blessing and we can't either; it is God's gift. This was first said of Abraham in Genesis 15:6 and also repeated in Galatians 3:6. We can see by that how important a statement this is, for it is a powerful truth from God, and applies to all who will believe.

SEEK HIS RIGHTEOUSNESS

Psalm 37:5-6 says, "Commit your way to the Lord, trust also in Him, and He shall bring it to pass. He shall bring forth your righteousness as the light, and your justice as the noonday." This is in harmony with all the other Scriptures given above and it reminds me of Isaiah 58:6-9, where we have some pertinent information about true righteousness with reference to God's blessings. "Is this not the fast that I have chosen: to loose the bonds of wickedness, to undo the heavy burdens, to let the oppressed go free, and that you break every yoke? Is it not to share your bread with the hungry, and that you bring to your house the poor who are cast out; when you see the naked, that you cover him, and not hide yourself from your own flesh? Then your light shall break forth like the morning, your healing shall spring forth speedily, and your righteousness shall go before you; the glory of the Lord shall be your rear guard. Then you shall call, and the Lord will answer; you shall cry, and He will say, 'Here I am.'" This enlightens us to what can make the difference for experiencing good health and God's most wonderful blessings. Obedience to His Word—living righteously can bring us to Praise Mountain!

Matthew 6:33 has one of the most powerful instructions for our lives—"Seek first the kingdom of God and His righteousness, and all these other things shall be added to you." I've been reminded of this often. It's as though the Lord is insisting that I awaken early in the morning to see 6:33 on my digital clock so my heart will be set and my focus directed to the words of that verse. We can easily read through these familiar verses without hearing God's voice. But when we really desire His will and ways, we're more alert to hear His voice and ready to die to self. God is saying here, "If you focus on My kingdom and My righteousness, giving Me top priority with your attention, then I will make a way for all your other needs to be met!"

Dying to self is dying to our own righteousness. It is dying to all our ideas of how we want to live, getting the most out of life for self; buying as many recreational things as possible to make ourselves happy. Planning all the exciting things we can possibly think of so we won't miss out on the happiness that we think we deserve; fully a focus on self. This focus makes us more and more a part of the world, rather than just a temporary resident until Jesus comes to take us to our eternal home.

I was reading a booklet this week entitled, Down Mercy Road, by Vicki Penwell.[3] I am so thankful that the Lord put this in my hands before this manuscript had gone off to the printer. She tells of her special journey down the Samaritan road which began in the late seventies. She had a call to follow Jesus in the ministry of medical missions. She went to the third world countries where she found life to be "brutal and difficult." As she shares about the merciless treatments even by the medical people in the hospitals, and the selfish demands of husbands of their wives, along with all the extreme poverty with filth beyond my imagination, it especially points to the selfishness in the lives of almost all who have so much in America. My heart is torn, that anyone has to live like that; I want so much for them to have the blessings that I am so privileged to enjoy.

My main point is that Vicki was so tremendously blessed that God had called her to be His servant in such adverse conditions, giving her an opportunity to save lives, physically and spiritually. They definitely would have been lost without God's saving grace sending her there. She was awed with God's miraculous power flowing through her time after time, as human blood flowed over her. Her unselfishness brought greater joy than any million dollar plans a person could make; and God counted it for righteousness on her account.

I must quickly add that I know there are a multitude of ministries that God has called into being, much like the creation days as He called the sun, the moon, the stars and much more into being during those six days. It's hard to imagine, but it's true, He's using simple people like you and me to get His work accomplished, and He counts it for righteousness! Wonder of wonders!

There has been many a time when I have cried out to the Lord, "I need you to speak to me through a megaphone, because for some reason I can't hear You! Please, Lord, put a spotlight on my path. I can't find Your feet to follow and I don't know why, but I can't seem to find your hand either." When I have called out with that kind of earnestness, then I've heard Him whisper, "Be still, and know that I am God." This marvelously helped me to take hold of His promise in Isaiah 41:10, "Fear not, for I am with you; be not dismayed, for I am your God. I will strengthen you, yes, I will help you, I will uphold you with My righteous right hand." God is faithful! Vast numbers of believers have found Him to be faithful to all His Word. Please remember that!

Hebrews 12:1-2 says it this way, "Therefore we also, since we are surrounded by so great a cloud of witnesses, let us lay aside every weight, and the sin which so easily ensnares us, and let us run with endurance the race that is set before us, looking unto Jesus, the author and finisher of our faith, who for the joy that was set before Him endured the cross, despising the shame, and has sat down at the right hand of the throne of God." Do you see that "great cloud of witnesses?" And do you see Jesus, not only as the author and finisher of our faith, but as "THE LORD OUR RIGHTEOUSNESS?"

SCRIPTURES FOR
RIGHTEOUSNESS

God's righteousness—-

Ps. 9:8 He shall judge the world in **righteousness**, and He shall administer judgment for the peoples in **uprightness**.

Ps. 11:7 For the Lord is **righteous**, He loves **righteousness**; His countenance beholds the **upright**.

Ps. 33:4-5 For the word of the Lord is **right**, and all His work is done in truth. He loves **righteousness** and justice; the earth is full of the goodness of the Lord.

Ps. 40:10 I have not hidden Your **righteousness** within my heart; I have declared Your faithfulness and Your salvation; I have not concealed Your lovingkindness and Your truth from the great assembly.

Ps. 50:6 Let the heavens declare His **righteousness**, for God Himself is Judge.

Ps. 71:15-16 My mouth shall tell of Your **righteousness**, and Your salvation all the day, for I do not know their limits. I will go in the strength of the Lord God; I will make mention of Your **righteousness**, yours only.

Ps. 71:19 Also Your **righteousness**, O God, is very high, You who have done great things; O God, who is like You?

Ps. 89:14-16 **Righteousness** and justice are the foundation of Your throne; mercy and truth go before Your face. Blessed are the people who know the joyful sound! They walk, O Lord, in the light of Your countenance. In Your name they rejoice all day long, and in Your **righteousness** they are exalted.

Ps. 119:137-138 **Righteous** are You, O Lord, and **upright** are your judgments. Your testimonies, which You have commanded, are **righteous** and very faithful.

Ps. 119:172 My tongue shall speak of Your word, for all Your commandments are **righteousness**.

Ps. 145:6-7 Men shall speak of the might of Your awesome acts, and I will declare Your greatness. They shall utter the memory of Your great goodness, and shall sing of Your **righteousness.**

Isa. 5:16 But the Lord of hosts shall be exalted in judgment, and God who is holy shall be hallowed in **righteousness**.

Isa. 11:5 **Righteousness** shall be the belt of His loins, and faithfulness the belt of His waist.

Isa. 41:10 Fear not, for I am with you; be not dismayed, for I am your God. I will strengthen you, yes, I will help you, I will uphold you with My **righteous** right hand.

Isa. 45:8 "Rain down, you heavens, from above, and let the skies pour down **righteousness**; let the earth open, let them bring forth salvation, and let **righteousness** spring up together. I, the Lord, have created it."

Isa. 45:19 "I have not spoken in secret, in a dark place of the earth; I did not say to the seed of Jacob, 'Seek Me in vain'; I, the Lord, speak **righteousness**, I declare things that are right."

Isa. 45:23-24a "I have sworn by Myself; the word has gone out of My mouth in **righteousness**, and shall not return, that to Me every knee shall bow every tongue shall take an oath. He shall say, 'Surely in the Lord I have **righteousness** and strength.'"

Jer. 9:24 "But let him who glories glory in this, that he understands and knows Me, that I am the Lord, exercising lovingkindness, judgment, and **righteousness** in the earth. For in these I delight," says the Lord.

The righteousness of Jesus — His righteousness is a gift to believers—

Ps. 72:1-3 Give the king Your judgments, O God, and Your **righteousness** to the king's Son. He will judge Your people with **righteousness**, and Your poor with justice. The mountains will bring peace to the people, and the little hills, by **righteousness.**

Jer. 23:5-6 "Behold, the days are coming," says the Lord**,** "that I will raise to David a Branch of **righteousness**; A King shall reign and prosper, and execute judgment and **righteousness** in the earth. In His days Judah will be saved, and Israel will dwell safely. Now this is His name by which He will be called: THE LORD OUR **RIGHTEOUSNESS**." *Repeated in Jeremiah 33:15-16*

Matt. 3:14-15 And John tried to prevent Him, saying, "I need to be baptized by You, and are You coming to me?" But Jesus answered and said to him, "Permit it to be so now, for thus it is fitting for us to fulfill all **righteousness**." Then he allowed Him.

Rom. 5:17 For if by the one man's offense death reigned through the one, much more those who receive abundance of grace and of the gift of **righteousness** will reign in life through the One, Jesus Christ. *See also verses 12-21 and Ephesians 4:20-24.*

Rom. 10:3-4 For they being ignorant of God's **righteousness**, and seeking to establish their own **righteousness**, have not submitted to the **righteousness** of God. For Christ is the end of the law for **righteousness** to everyone who believes. *Also verses 5-10 and Galatians 2:21.*

2 Cor. 5:21 For He made Him who knew no sin to be sin for us, that we might become the **righteousness** of God in Him.

Gal. 5:5-6 For we through the Spirit eagerly wait for the hope of **righteousness** by faith, for in Christ Jesus neither circumcision nor uncircumcision avails anything, but faith working through love.

Phil. 1:11 ...being filled with fruits of **righteousness** which are by Jesus Christ, to the glory and praise of God.

Phil. 3:9 ...and be found in Him, not having my own **righteousness**, which is from the law, but that which is through faith in Christ, the **righteousness** which is from God by faith...

2 Tim. 4:8 Finally, there is laid up for me the crown of **righteousness**, which the Lord, the **righteous** Judge, will give to me on that Day, and not to me only but also to all who loved His appearing.

2 Peter 1:1 Simon Peter, a bondservant and apostle of Jesus Christ, to those who have obtained like precious faith with us by the **righteousness** of our God and Savior Jesus Christ.

2 Peter 3:13 Nevertheless we, according to His promise, look for new heavens and a new earth in which **righteousness** dwells.

1 John 2:29 If you know that He is **righteous**, you know that everyone who practices **righteousness** is born of Him.

1 John 3:7 Little children, let no one deceive you. He who practices **righteousness** is **righteous**, just as He is **righteous**.

Rev. 19:11 Now I saw heaven opened, and behold, a white horse. And He who sat on him was called Faithful and True, and in **righteousness** He judges and makes war.

We are to live righteously—

Lev. 19:15 "You shall do no injustice in judgment. You shall not be partial to the poor, nor honor the person of the mighty. In **righteousness** you shall judge your neighbor."

Hosea 10:12 Sow for yourselves **righteousness**; reap in mercy; break up your fallow ground, for it is time to seek the Lord, till He comes and rains **righteousness** on you.

Matt. 5:20 *Jesus is speaking—* "For I say to you, that unless your **righteousness** exceeds the **righteousness** of the scribes and Pharisees, you will by no means enter the kingdom of heaven."

Matt. 6:33 "But seek first the kingdom of God and His **righteousness** and all these things shall be added to you."

Luke 1:73-75 *Zacharias is prophesying—* "The oath which He swore to our father Abraham: to grant us that we, being delivered from the hand of our enemies, might serve Him without fear, in holiness and **righteousness** before Him all the days of our life."

Rom. 6:13 And do not present your members as instruments of **unrighteousness** to sin, but present yourselves to God as being alive from the dead, and your members as instruments of **righteousness** to God. *Also see verses 16-23 and Romans 8:3-4, 10.*

1 Tim. 6:11 But you, O man of God, flee these things and pursue **righteousness**, godliness, faith, love, patience, gentleness.

2 Tim. 2:22 Flee also youthful lusts; but pursue **righteousness**, faith, love, peace with those who call on the Lord out of a pure heart.

James 1:20 ...for the wrath of man does not produce the **righteousness** of God.

1 Peter 2:24 ...who Himself bore our sins in His own body on the tree, that we, having died to sins, might live for **righteousness**—by whose stripes you were healed.

2 Peter 2:21 For it would have been better for them not to have known the way of **righteousness**, than having known it, to turn from the holy commandment delivered to them.

Rev. 19:7-8 "Let us be glad and rejoice and give Him glory, for the marriage of the Lamb has come, and His wife has made herself ready." And to her it was granted to be arrayed in fine linen, clean and bright, for the linen is the **righteous** acts of the saints.

God's favor and blessings are on the righteous—

Deut. 33:18-19 And of Zebulun he *(Moses)* said: "Rejoice, Zebulun, in your going out, and Issachar in your tents! They shall call the peoples to the mountain; there they shall offer sacrifices of **righteousness**; for they shall partake of the abundance of the seas and of treasures hidden in the sand."

2 Sam. 22:21 "The Lord rewarded me *(David)* according to my **righteousness**; according to the cleanness of my hands He has recompensed me." *Psalm 18:24*

Ps. 23:3 He restores my soul; He leads me in the paths of **righteousness** for His name's sake.

Ps. 37:5-6 Commit your way to the Lord, trust also in Him, and He shall bring it to pass. He shall bring forth your **righteousness** as the light, and your justice as the noonday.

Ps. 37:25 I have been young, and now am old; yet I have not seen the **righteous** forsaken, nor his descendants begging bread.

Ps. 37:39-40 But the salvation of the **righteous** is from the Lord; He is their strength in the time of trouble. And the Lord shall help them and deliver them; He shall deliver them from the wicked, and save them, because they trust in Him.

Ps. 84:11 For the Lord God is a sun and shield; the Lord will give grace and glory; no good thing will He withhold from those who walk uprightly.

Ps. 106:3 Blessed are those who keep justice, and he who does **righteousness** at all times!

Ps. 112:1-4 Praise the Lord! Blessed is the man who fears the Lord, who delights greatly in His commands. His descendants will be mighty on earth; the generation of the **upright** will be blessed. Wealth and riches will be in his house, and his **righteousness** endures forever. Unto the **upright** there arises light in the darkness. *Read verses 5-10 also.*

Prov. 8:17-18 I *(wisdom)* love those who love me, and those who seek me diligently will find me. Riches and honor are with me, enduring riches and **righteousness.**

Prov. 10:25 When the whirlwind passes by, the wicked is no more, but the **righteous** has an everlasting foundation.

Prov. 15:9 The way of the wicked is an abomination to the Lord, but He loves him who follows **righteousness.**

Prov. 21:21 He who follows **righteousness** and mercy finds life, **righteousness** and honor.

Isa. 48:18 "Oh, that you had heeded My commandments! Then your peace would have been like a river, and your **righteousness** like the waves of the sea."

Isa. 54:17 "No weapon formed against you shall prosper, and every tongue which rises against you in judgment you shall condemn. This is the heritage of the servants of the Lord, and their **righteous-**

ness is from Me," says the Lord.

Matt. 5:6 "Blessed are those who hunger and thirst for **righteousness**, for they shall be filled."

Acts 10:34-35 Then Peter opened his mouth and said: "In truth I perceive that God shows no partiality. But in every nation whoever fears Him and works **righteousness** is accepted by Him."

The characteristics and fruit of the righteous—

Ps. 15:1-5 Lord, who may abide in Your tabernacle? Who may dwell in Your holy hill? He who walks **uprightly**, and works **righteousness**, and speaks the truth in his heart; he who does not backbite with his tongue; nor does evil to his neighbor, nor does he take up a reproach against a friend; in whose eyes a vile person is despised, but he honors those who fear the Lord; he who swears to his own hurt and does not change; he who does not put out his money at usury, nor does he take a bribe against the innocent. He who does all these things shall never be moved.

Ps. 24:3-5 Who may ascend into the hill of the Lord? Or who may stand in His holy place? He who has clean hands and a pure heart, who has not lifted up his soul to an idol, nor sworn deceitfully. He shall receive blessing from the Lord, and **righteousness** from the God of his salvation.

Ps. 37:21 The wicked borrows and does not repay, but the **righteous** shows mercy and gives.

The following portions from Proverbs are a partial list—
Prov. 10:11a The mouth of the **righteous** is a well of life,
Prov. 10:16a The labor of the **righteous** leads to life,
Prov. 10:28a The hope of the **righteous** will be gladness,
Prov. 10:29a The way of the Lord is strength for the **upright**,
Prov. 10:31a The mouth of the **righteous** brings forth wisdom,
Prov. 10:32a The lips of the **righteous** know what is acceptable,

Prov. 11:18b But he who sows **righteousness** will have a sure reward.
Prov. 11:30 The fruit of the **righteous** is a tree of life, and he who wins souls is wise.
Prov. 13:25a The **righteous** eats to satisfy his soul,
Prov. 14:2a He who walks in **uprightness** fears the Lord,
Prov. 20:7a The **righteous** man walks in his integrity;
Prov. 29:6b But the **righteous** sings and rejoices.
Prov. 29:7a The **righteous** considers the cause of the poor,

Isa. 26:7-9 The way of the just is **uprightness**; O Most **Upright**, You weigh the path of the just. Yes, in the way of Your judgments, O Lord, we have waited for You; the desire of our soul is for Your name and for the remembrance of You. With my soul I have desired You in the night, yes, by my spirit within me I will seek You early; for when Your judgments are in the earth, the inhabitants of the world will learn **righteousness**.

Isa. 32:17 The work of **righteousness** will be peace, and the effect of **righteousness**, quietness and assurance forever.

Isa. 54:14 "In **righteousness** you shall be established; you shall be far from oppression, for you shall not fear; and from terror, for it shall not come near you."

PARTAKE

PARTAKERS OF THE DIVINE NATURE

When I think of the tremendous Scriptures telling of partaking of God's nature, it is hard to imagine that we could be recipients of so great a blessing. It is truly important to consider what God says about being partakers of His spiritual provisions.

The Scripture that clearly introduces this is in 2 Peter 1:2-4; where it says, "Grace and peace be multiplied to you in the knowledge of God and of Jesus our Lord, as His divine power has given to us all things that pertain to life and godliness, through the knowledge of Him who called us by glory and virtue, by which have been given to us exceedingly great and precious promises, that through these you may be partakers of the divine nature, having escaped the corruption that is in the world."

What Peter has given to us in his two letters to the churches, is overflowing with great truths of God's precious promises for those who believe on the Lord Jesus Christ. As he begins the second letter, he lays out this foundational truth—"as His divine power has given to us all things that pertain to life and godliness," however everything is attached to believing what God has provided. Our part is to believe in order to be a partaker, for "through the knowledge of Him" comes by way of the 'stepping stones' of hearing and believing. When we partake of that knowledge, we are enabled to experience those wonderful spiritual things that God's Word is speaking of.

This is one of those 'precious promises' that Jesus provided for us. It takes time to grasp this tremendous blessing. Many settle for just improving their behavior without the true surrender of self to partake of the nature of Jesus Christ. One thing for sure, we can't serve the Lord Jesus and serve self at the same time without encountering huge problems. Can this be the answer to some of those undesirable difficulties that keep on badgering many Christians, in spite of their fervent prayers? Are they holding on to the things of this world to satisfy the cravings of the flesh, and trying to experience God's promised blessings at the same time? Then it can appear as though: "God doesn't care. He's not helping me find the answers." Where does the real problem lie? Kenneth and Gloria Copeland have written numerous books; among them is Understanding Who You Are in Christ.[4] I highly recommend this book for further study on this wonderful subject of being partakers of the divine nature.

WE ARE TO BE PARTAKERS OF HIS PROMISES

We are to be partakers of His promises, partakers of His grace, and partakers of the inheritance of the saints in the light. The list goes on— partakers of the heavenly calling, partakers of His holiness, and partakers of His glory, yet to be revealed. This is awesome! However, it doesn't just happen like magic. It doesn't arrive by express in the morning. God gives very clear instructions: "Set your mind on things above, not on earthly things." ..."Put to death, therefore, whatever belongs to your earthly nature: sexual immorality, impurity, lust, evil desires and greed, which is idolatry. Because of these things the wrath of God is coming." *Colossians 3:2, 5, 6.*

Even as I listed those wonderful phrases above, it becomes clear that we need to study the word "promises," and find more of those promises that are in His Word. Then study the word "grace," which is in this book. Taking each one of these, gives a great deal of home-work, but also disciplines us to understand them and learn how to apply the instructions in regard to becoming a partaker. There are many more Scriptures confirming these truths. Going through all the corresponding Scriptures will anchor these wonderful promises and provide warnings against ignoring the boundaries that God has compassionately given for our welfare, not for condemnation.

YOU PARTAKE OF WHAT YOU FEED INTO YOUR MIND

"Setting your mind on things above" requires discipline. We live in this world, but are not of the world. That's not easy, is it? Philippians 4:8 says, "...whatever things are true, whatever things are noble, whatever things are just, whatever things are pure, whatever things are lovely, whatever things are of good report, if there is any virtue and if there is anything praiseworthy—meditate on these things." In the New Living Translation, it is expressed this way: "Fix your thoughts on what is true and honorable and right. Think about things that are pure and lovely and admirable. Think about things that are excellent and worthy of praise."

Whatever you and I spend time thinking about, or meditating on, becomes a part of our mind-set, and that becomes a part of our nature. If you are taken up with unwholesome thoughts, or caught in the net of some ungodly stuff in magazines, movies, internet, television shows, or any other sources, they will seriously affect your life and can damage the lives of others around you. We naturally absorb whatever we submit our hearts and minds to think about.

Romans 6:19 says, "I speak in human terms because of the weakness of your flesh. For just as you presented your members as slaves of uncleanness, and of lawlessness leading to more lawlessness, so now present your members as slaves of righteousness for holiness." We must be conscientious about obeying what God's Word has instructed us to do, and be careful to not live in disobedience. Disobedience always hinders experiencing the spiritual blessings that God wants us to enjoy.

PARTAKERS OF GODLINESS BEAR GOOD FRUIT

God has high ideals for His children. In Romans 8:29, we learn, "For whom He foreknew, He also predestined to be conformed to the image of His Son." And Second Corinthians 3:18 says, "But we all, with unveiled face, beholding as in a mirror the glory of the Lord, are being transformed into the same image from glory to glory, just as by the Spirit of the Lord." This shows the power of God continuously working in the lives of believers. A working that is transforming us so that we become more and more like Jesus.

It says, "beholding as in a mirror the glory of the Lord." This means to be so focused on the 'glory of the Lord', as though a mirror was giving us the exact image to behold. What transforming power that is! We are to have Jesus' love for Father God, His compassion for people, His readiness to go and to do whatever is needed with His determination to fulfill all the Father has for Him to do and say. While Jesus was here on the earth He was preaching, teaching, healing and winning souls for His Father's glory. Jesus was a burden bearer, and bondage breaker. This is our calling as members of the Body of Christ.

Christians are called to bear the 'fruit of the Spirit'. This is only possible if we are partakers of His divine nature, partakers of His Spirit. Think about this— Unless His Spirit lives in us, and has full control; we cannot bear the fruit of love, joy, peace, longsuffering, gentleness, goodness, faith, meekness, and temperance." *Galatians 5:22- 23.* Every one of them is produced by the flow of the Holy Spirit and is involved in communicating with other people. We cannot allow anything to stifle that flow, for without God's Spirit, we will not be fruitbearers.

THE MATURE CHRISTIAN

It seems that the greatest expression of mature partakers is found in Galatians 2:20, where Paul says, "I have been crucified with Christ; it is no longer I who live, but Christ lives in me; and the life which I now live in the flesh I live by faith in the Son of God, who loved me and gave Himself for me." This is a picture of the mature Christian; each one who has put on more and more of Christ's nature through surrendering to the Holy Spirit. *Also see Colossians 3:8-14.*

You may be wondering how to begin to become a mature Christian. Paul speaks of plowing in hope. *1 Corinthians 9:10.* Plowing expresses effort in preparing ground for planting seed. The seeds take time to germinate, so there is nothing to observe for a period of time, just as faith stands for that which cannot yet be seen. This hope is not a 'hope so', or 'I sure hope it works'. It is a hope solidly based on the security of God's Word; what God said through His chosen servant writers. Hope is heart assurance—because God said so. The song so beautifully expresses it in these words—"My hope is built on nothing less than Jesus' blood and righteousness." He shed His own blood to cleanse us of our sins, and provided the way to become the righteousness of God in Him. It's all there in His Word for us to believe and receive.

What are you partaking of? Are you a partaker "of the inheritance of the saints in the light?" At this point, what does that mean to you? What draws you to search the Word more deeply? Are you ready to minister to others, compelled by the love of Christ?

It is my prayer that this message has given you light on this very important truth from God's precious Word. As you meditate on all the aspects of this truth, you will hunger for more and more of what God has to offer you from His Word. We live in a time of wars, much turmoil, and increasing strife even in Christian homes. Only God has the answer for us, which is through partaking of His Word and His divine nature, so we can remain strong in Him! We can then enjoy the abundant life in a greater measure!

SCRIPTURES FOR
PARTAKE

Partakers of spiritual things—

Rom. 15:27 It pleased them *(The Christians from Macedonia & Achaia)* indeed, and they are their debtors. For if the Gentiles have been **partakers** of their spiritual things, their duty is also to minister to them in material things.

1 Cor. 9:10-14 Or does He say it altogether for our sakes? For our sakes, no doubt, this is written, that he who plows should plow in hope, and he who threshes in hope should be **partaker** of his hope. If we have sown spiritual things for you, is it a great thing if we reap your material things? If others are **partakers** of this right over you, are we not even more? Nevertheless we have not used this right, but endure all things lest we hinder the gospel of Christ. Do you not know that those who minister the holy things eat of the things of the temple, and those who serve at the altar **partake** of the offerings of the altar? Even so the Lord has commanded that those who preach the gospel should live from the gospel.

1 Cor. 9:19, 22-23 For though I am free from all men, I have made myself *(Paul)* a servant to all, that I might win the more; ....to the weak I became as weak, that I might win the weak. I have become all things to all men; that I might by all means save some. Now this I do for the gospel's sake, that I may be **partaker** of it with you.

Eph. 3:1-6 For this reason I, Paul, the prisoner of Christ Jesus for you Gentiles—if indeed you have heard of the dispensation of the grace of God which was given to me for you, how that by revelation He made known to me the mystery (as I have briefly written already, by which, when you read, you may understand my knowledge in the mystery of Christ), which in other ages was not made known to the sons of men, as it has now been revealed by the Spirit to His holy apostles and prophets: that the Gentiles should be fellow heirs, of the same body, and **partakers** of His promise in Christ through the gospel.

Phil. 1:3-7 I thank my God upon every remembrance of you, always in every prayer of mine making request for you all with joy, for your fellowship in the gospel from the first day until now, being confident of this very thing, that He who has begun a good work in you will complete it until the day of Jesus Christ; just as it is right for me to think this of you all, because I have you in my heart, inasmuch as both in my chains and in the defense and confirmation of the gospel, you all are **partakers** with me of grace.

Col. 1:9-12 For this reason we also, since the day we heard it, do not cease to pray for you, and to ask that you may be filled with the knowledge of His will in all wisdom and spiritual understanding; that you may walk worthy of the Lord, fully pleasing Him, being fruitful in every good work and increasing in the knowledge of God; strengthened with all might, according to His glorious power, for all patience and longsuffering with joy; giving thanks to the Father who has qualified us to be **partakers** of the inheritance of the saints in the light.

Heb. 3:1 Therefore, holy brethren, **partakers** of the heavenly calling, consider the Apostle and High Priest of our confession, Christ Jesus, who was faithful to Him who appointed Him, as Moses also was faithful in all His house.

2 Peter 1:2-4 Grace and peace be multiplied to you in the knowledge of God and of Jesus our Lord, as His divine power has given to us all things that pertain to life and godliness, through the knowledge of Him who called us by glory and virtue, by which have been given to us exceedingly great and precious promises, that through these you may be **partakers** of the divine nature, having escaped the corruption that is in the world.

Partakers of suffering—

2 Cor. 1:7 And our hope for you is steadfast because we know that as you are **partakers** of the sufferings, so also you will **partake** of the consolation.

2 Tim. 1:8-9 KJV Be not thou therefore ashamed of the testimony of our Lord, nor of me his prisoner; but be thou **partaker** of the afflictions of the gospel according to the power of God: Who hath saved us, and called us with an holy calling, not according to our works, but according to His own purpose and grace, which was given us in Christ Jesus before the world began.

1 Peter 4:12-14 Beloved, do not think it strange concerning the fiery trial which is to try you, as though some strange thing happened to you; but rejoice to the extent that you **partake** of Christ's sufferings, that when His glory is revealed, you may also be glad with exceeding joy. If you are reproached for the name of Christ, blessed are you, for the Spirit of glory and of God rests upon you. On their part He is blasphemed, but on your part He is glorified.

Teachings on a variety of subjects—

1 Cor. 10:17-18 For we, though many, are one bread and one body; for we all **partake** of that one bread. Observe Israel after the flesh: are not those who eat of the sacrifices **partakers** of the altar?

1 Cor. 10:27-28, 30-31 If any of those who do not believe invites you to dinner, and you desire to go, eat whatever is set before you, asking no question for conscience' sake. But if anyone says to you, "This was offered to idols," do not eat it for the sake of the one who told you, and for conscience' sake; for "the earth is the Lord's, and all its fullness." ....But if I **partake** with thanks, why am I evil spoken of for the food over which I give thanks? Therefore, whether you eat or drink, or whatever you do, do all to the glory of God.

1 Tim. 6:2 KJV And they that have believing masters *(bosses, supervisors, trainers)*, let them not despise them, because they are brethren; but rather do them service, because they are faithful and beloved, **partakers** of the benefit. These things teach and exhort.

2 Tim. 2:6-7 The hardworking farmer must be first to **partake** of the crops. Consider what I say, and may the Lord give you understanding in all things.

Heb. 2:14-15 Inasmuch as the children have **partaken** of flesh and blood, He Himself (Jesus) likewise shared in the same, that through death He might destroy him who had the power of death, that is, the devil, and release those who through fear of death were all their lifetime subject to bondage.

Heb. 3:1-2 Therefore, holy brethren, **partakers** of the heavenly calling, consider the Apostle and High Priest of our confession, Christ Jesus, who was faithful to Him who appointed Him, as Moses also was faithful in all His house.

Heb. 12:7-10 If you endure chastening, God deals with you as with sons; for what son is there whom a father does not chasten? But if you are without chastening, of which all have become **partakers**, then you are illegitimate and not sons. Furthermore, we have had human fathers who corrected us, and we paid them respect. Shall we not much more readily be in subjection to the Father of spirits and live? For they indeed for a few days chastened us as seemed best to them, but He for our profit, that we may be **partakers** of His holiness.

1 Peter 5:1-4 The elders who are among you I exhort, I who am a fellow elder and a witness of the sufferings of Christ, and also a **partaker** of the glory that will be revealed: Shepherd the flock of God which is among you, serving as overseers, not by compulsion but willingly, not for dishonest gain but eagerly; nor as being lords over those entrusted to you, but being examples to the flock; and

when the Chief Shepherd appears, you will receive the crown of glory that does not fade away.

Warnings—

Ps. 50:16-19 But to the wicked God says: "What right have you to declare My statutes, or take My covenant in your mouth, seeing you hate instruction and cast My words behind you? When you saw a thief, you consented with him, and have been a **partaker** with adulterers. You give your mouth to evil, and your tongue frames deceit.

Matt. 23:29-31 *Jesus is speaking*—- "Woe to you, Scribes and Pharisees, hypocrites! Because you build the tombs of the prophets and adorn the monuments of the righteous, and say, 'If we had lived in the days of our fathers, we would not have been **partakers** with them in the blood of the prophets.' Therefore you are witnesses against yourselves that you are sons of those who murdered the prophets."

Rom. 11:16-18 For if the firstfruit is holy, the lump is also holy; and if the root is holy, so are the branches. And if some of the branches *(Jews)* were broken off, and you, being a wild olive tree *(Gentile)* were grafted in among them, and with them became a **partaker** of the root and fatness of the olive tree, do not boast against the branches. But if you do boast, remember that you do not support the root, but the root supports you. *Remember from John 15, that Jesus is the vine and believers are the branches.*

1 Cor. 10:19-22 What am I saying then? That an idol is anything, or what is offered to idols is anything? Rather, that the things which the Gentiles sacrifice they sacrifice to demons and not to God, and I do not want you to have fellowship with demons. You cannot drink the cup of the Lord and the cup of demons; you cannot **partake** of the Lord's table and of the table of demons. Or do we provoke the Lord to jealousy? Are we stronger than He?

Eph. 5:6, 7 Let no one deceive you with empty words, for because of these things the wrath of God comes upon the sons of disobedience. Therefore do not be **partakers** with them.

1 Tim. 5:22 KJV Lay hands suddenly on no man, neither be **partaker** of other men's sins: keep thyself pure.

Heb. 3:12-14 Beware, brethren, lest there be in any of you an evil heart of unbelief in departing from the living God; but exhort one another daily, while it is called "Today," lest any of you be hardened through the deceitfulness of sin. For we are **partakers** of Christ if we hold the beginning of our confidence steadfast to the end.

Heb. 6:4-6 For it is impossible for those who were once enlightened, and have tasted the heavenly gift, and have become **partakers** of the Holy Spirit, and have tasted the good word of God and the powers of the age to come, if they fall away, to renew them again to repentance, since they crucify again for themselves the Son of God, and put Him to an open shame.

2 John vss.9-11 KJV Whosoever transgresseth, and abideth not in the doctrine of Christ, hath not God. He that abideth in the doctrine of Christ, he hath both the Father and the Son. If there come any unto you, and bring not this doctrine, receive him not into your house, neither bid him God speed: for he that biddeth him God speed is **partaker** of his evil deeds.

REVEAL — REVELATION

DILIGENT SEEKERS RECEIVE DEPTHS OF TRUTH

Many people say that they do not understand the Bible so they don't read it. This is a serious mistake, because when we read the Bible, searching for truth, God reveals the depths of these truths to diligent seekers. And the more we read, seeking to know Him, seeking His will and ways, the more wonderful He becomes to us in a personal way.

Those who have become teachers of the Word of God have spent time searching for those depths for clearer understanding. They have discovered the joy of finding hidden treasures, which were there all the time, but not visible until they became exceptionally hungry for more and more knowledge of the Lord.

Deuteronomy 29:29 says, "The secret things belong to the Lord our God, but those things which are revealed belong to us and to our children forever, that we may do all the works of the law." This is speaking of the Israelites, God's people in the Old Testament. God revealed Himself to them, and many promises that were for those who would obey Him. Everything God does and says has an important purpose. He had provided laws for them to live by, as guard rails to define their paths for protection.

So also today as we seek the Lord to worship Him, and to surrender our hearts in obedience, God reveals those treasured nuggets of truth for enrichment of our understanding. No one can take these away from you. It's like the Lord just anchors them into your heart that your joy might be full, and to provide for whatever your future need may be. His truths will be there for you.

In Psalm 25:14, we see something similar: "The secret of the Lord is with those who fear Him, and He will show *(reveal to)* them His covenant." The NIV expresses it this way: "The Lord confides in those who fear Him; He makes His covenant known to them." Anyone who does not have an earnest desire, a deep yearning to know the Lord will never experience this intimacy that belongs to His beloved ones. Perhaps you're thinking, "I don't seem to have that, so there's no hope for me." Please hear the Lord calling you for He desires that special relationship with you. In Isaiah 55:6 and 7 we hear this: "Seek the Lord while He may be found, call upon Him while He is near. Let the wicked forsake his way, and the unrighteous man his thoughts; let him return to the Lord, and He will have mercy on him; and to our God for He will abundantly pardon."

The Holy Spirit of God opens up these special treasures to those who honor Him, and desire to have a close relationship with Him. We can see this truth in I Corinthians 2:9-10: "But as it is written, 'Eye hath not seen, nor have entered into the heart of man the things which God has prepared for those who love Him.' But God has revealed them to us through His Spirit, for the Spirit searches all things, yes, the deep things of God."

Andrew Murray has written many books. Among them he wrote a daily devotional, namely, **God's Best Secrets**.[5] It is marvelous book for ministering to the heart, for God has revealed deep truths to him as he persevered in seeking the Lord and His fullness. He could not have written these secrets of the Lord, except by spending hours in God's Word and in communion with Him. As you read any of his books, you will hear God's heart speaking to you, if you are a determined listener who fervently desires to hear God's personal message for you.

PREPARE YOURSELF
AND YOUR CHILDREN TO LISTEN

As you read the Scriptures with this word "reveal," listen for the Lord's call to teach you. He wants to reveal Himself and His glory; reveal His paths of righteousness; reveal the blessings He stored up for those who sincerely seek Him. The following Scriptures tell of this: Colossians 1:26 and 27 says, "...the mystery which has been hidden from ages and from generations, but now has been revealed to His saints. To them God willed to make known what are the riches of the glory of this mystery among the Gentiles; which is Christ in you, the hope of glory."

Then in 1 Peter 1:13, 20-21 NIV, we read, "Therefore, prepare your minds for action; be self controlled; set your hope fully on the grace to be given you when Jesus Christ is revealed. He was chosen before the creation of the world, but was revealed in these last times for your sake. Through Him you believe in God, who raised Him from the dead and glorified Him, and so your faith and hope are in God." God intends for us to act upon the truths that are revealed to us.

Parents have a special privilege in taking their role as 'trainers for their children', to specify a space of time each day to not just read the Word of God, but also teach and discuss that passage with them, revealing the truths and the important application that God has for their lives. Then consider what action God would have each one to take in response to His Word. At the next family gathering each one could give a report, and share their experiences.

REVEALED TRUTH MAKES GOD'S WORD COME ALIVE

The Word can become more than just history, or something to be read dutifully to fulfill God's demands. It will become real and alive for each child before they stumble along in the teen years, if you pray "That the God of our Lord Jesus Christ, the Father of glory, may give to (our family members) the spirit of wisdom and revelation in the knowledge of Him, the eyes of (our) understanding being enlightened; that (we) may know what is the hope of His calling, what are the riches of the glory of His inheritance in the saints, and what is the exceeding greatness of His power toward us who believe, according to the working of His mighty power." *From Ephesians 1:17-19.* What a tremendous opportunity we have for the Holy Spirit to challenge our hearts and to reveal God's purpose to each one personally. God is not a 'something' far out, but desires closeness in His relationship with His children. Just look what 1 John 3:2 tells us, "Beloved, now we are children of God; and it has not yet been revealed what we shall be, but we know that when He is revealed, we shall be like Him, for we shall see Him as He is." God has fabulous blessings for all His children!

Each Scripture in this book reveals truth, and it all fits together for the greater picture of who God is, what He has done, and has prepared for those who believe on His Son, Jesus Christ. Romans 8:18-19 tell us, "For I consider that the sufferings of this present time are not worthy to be compared with the glory which shall be revealed in us. For the earnest expectation of the creation eagerly waits for the revealing of the sons of God."

Seek the Lord with all your heart and He will reveal Himself to you. Then ask Him the questions that you have in your heart; He will answer your earnest heart's desire to know Him. Knowledge of the Lord will also help you to grow in your faith toward Him, from faith to faith. There is so much more to be revealed; press on with Jesus and His Word, so your joy may become full, and you will no longer yearn for the things of the world that have no eternal value. There is great joy in knowing and serving Jesus!

SCRIPTURES FOR
REVEAL — REVELATION

What God reveals and to whom —-

Deut 29:29 "The secret things belong to the Lord our God, but those things which are **revealed** belong to us and to our children forever, that we may do all the words of this law."

Ps. 25:14 The secret of the Lord is with those who fear Him, and He will show (**reveal** to) them His covenant.

Isa. 65:1 NIV "I **revealed** Myself to those who did not ask for Me; I was found by those who did not seek Me. To a nation that did not call on My name, I said, 'Here I am'.."

Jer. 33:6-7 "'Behold, I will bring it health and healing; I will heal them and **reveal** to them the abundance of peace and truth. And I will cause the captives of Judah and the captives of Israel to return, and will rebuild those places as at the first.'"

Matt. 11:25 At that time Jesus answered and said, "I thank You, Father, Lord of heaven and earth, that You have hidden these things from the wise and prudent and have **revealed** them to babes.

Acts 26:15-16 "So I said, 'Who are You, Lord?' And He said, 'I am Jesus, whom you are persecuting. 'But rise and stand on your feet, for I have appeared to you *(Saul, who became Paul)* for this purpose, to make you a minister and a witness both of the things which you have seen and of the things which I will yet **reveal** to you.'"

Rom. 8:18-19 For I consider that the sufferings of this present time are not worthy to be compared with the glory which shall be **revealed** in us. For the earnest expectation of the creation eagerly waits for the **revealing** of the sons of God.

1 Cor. 2:9-10 But as it is written: "Eye hath not seen, nor have entered into the heart of man the things which God has prepared for those who love Him." But God has **revealed** them to us through His Spirit. For the Spirit searches all things, yes, the deep things of God.

Phil. 3:14-15 I press toward the goal for the prize of the upward call of God in Christ Jesus. Therefore let us, as many as are mature, have this mind; and if in anything you think otherwise, God will **reveal** even this to you.

2 Thess. 2:3-8 Let no one deceive you by any means; for that Day will not come unless the falling away comes first, and the man of sin is **revealed**, the son of perdition, who opposes and exalts himself above all that is called God or that is worshiped so that he sits as God in the temple of God, showing himself that he is God. Do you not remember that when I was still with you, I told you these things? And now you know what is restraining, that he may be **revealed** in his own time. For the mystery of lawlessness is already at work; only He who now restrains will do so until He is taken out of the way. And then the lawless one will be **revealed**, whom the Lord will consume with the breath of His mouth and destroy with the brightness of His coming. *Read this portion of Scripture in the NIV, and other versions.*

1 Peter 1:5 ...who are kept by the power of God through faith for salvation ready to be **revealed** in the last time.

Attributes of God revealed —-

Isa. 40:15 "The glory of the Lord shall be **revealed**, and all flesh shall see it together; for the mouth of the Lord has spoken."

Isa. 43:11-13 NIV "I, even I, am the Lord, and apart from Me there is no savior. I have **revealed** and saved and proclaimed – I, and not some foreign god among you. You are My witnesses," declares the Lord, "that I am God. Yes, and from ancient days I am He. No one can deliver out of My hand, when I act, who can reverse it?"

Isa. 53:1 Who has believed our report? And to whom has the arm of the Lord been **revealed**?"

Isa. 56:1 Thus says the Lord: "Keep justice, and do righteousness, for My salvation is about to come, and My righteousness to be **revealed**."

Rom. 1:17-18 For in it *(the Gospel)* the righteousness of God is **revealed** from faith to faith; as it is written, "The just shall live by faith." For the wrath of God is **revealed** from heaven against all ungodliness and unrighteousness of men, who suppress the truth in unrighteousness.

1 Peter 4:13 But rejoice that you participate in the sufferings of Christ, so that you may be overjoyed when His glory is **revealed**.

Revelation of Jesus and revelation through Jesus—-

Matt. 11:27 All things have been delivered to Me by My Father, and no one knows the Son except the Father. Nor does anyone know the Father except the Son, and the one to whom the Son wills to **reveal** Him.

Luke 17:30 Even so will it be in the day when the Son of Man is **revealed**.

John 17:6 NIV "I have **revealed** You to those whom You gave Me out of the world. They were Yours, You gave them to Me and they have obeyed Your Word."

Romans 16:25-27 NIV Now to Him who is able to establish you by my gospel and the proclamation of Jesus Christ, according to the **revelation** of the mystery hidden for long ages past, but now

revealed and made known through the prophetic writings by the command of the eternal God, so that all nations might believe and obey Him— to the only wise God be glory forever through Jesus Christ!

Gal. 1:15-16 But when it pleased God, who separated me from my mother's womb and called me through His grace, to **reveal** His Son in me, that I might preach Him among the Gentiles, I did not immediately confer with flesh and blood.

Eph. 3:1-7 For this reason I, Paul, the prisoner of Christ Jesus for you Gentiles – if indeed you have heard of the dispensation of the grace of God which was given to me for you, how that by **revelation** He made known to me the mystery (as I have briefly written already, by which, when you read, you may understand my knowledge in the mystery of Christ), which in other ages was not made known to the sons of men, as it has now been **revealed** by the Spirit to His holy apostles and prophets: that the Gentiles should be fellow heirs, of the same body, and partakers of His promise in Christ through the gospel, of which I became a minister according to the gift of the grace of God given to me by the effective working of His power.

Col. 1:26-27 ...the mystery which has been hidden from ages and from generations, but now has been **revealed** to His saints. To them God willed to make known what are the riches of the glory of this mystery among the Gentiles: which is Christ in you, the hope of glory.

2 Thess. 1:7-8 ...and to give you who are troubled rest with us when the Lord Jesus is **revealed** from heaven with His mighty angels, in flaming fire taking vengeance on those who do not know God, and on those who do not obey the gospel of our Lord Jesus Christ.

1 Peter 1:13, 20 NIV Therefore, prepare your minds for action; be self controlled; set your hope fully on the grace to be given you when Jesus Christ is **revealed**. He was chosen before the creation

of the world, but was **revealed** in these last times for your sake.

1 John 3:2 Beloved, now we are children of God; and it has not yet been **revealed** what we shall be, but we know that when He is **revealed**, we shall be like Him, for we shall see Him as He is.

GLORY — GLORIOUS

THE GLORY OF GOD IS POWERFUL

The glory of God! What a tremendous subject to study! I experienced the glory of God in a wonderful way while researching these accompanying Scriptures. While typing them I had to take time out, for His glorious presence was so overwhelming in my heart. It is my prayer that you will also experience God's presence in an awesome way while meditating on them.

No imitation of God can manifest such glory and refreshment to your inner being for they are imaginary beings; they have no life for giving love, mercy, or blessings of any kind. How wonderful to belong to the great God, the Creator, Savior and Lord. He is glorious in power and greatness; glorious in holiness; even His name is glorious for He is the King of glory. His right hand is glorious in power, able to dash the enemy in pieces. Over and over again He has shown His glory, His power, and greatness. Moses observed it several times; more often than the Scriptures given on these pages. In fact, Moses was evidently privileged to see God's glory more than all others.

God's glory is not only brightness; it is His presence with greatness and power! His holiness is glorious illumination; so pure and holy. We can't see its fullness, however the Holy Spirit provides a measure of understanding in the hearts of all who genuinely seek to know Him with a committed spirit. *See Jeremiah 9:24 and 24:7; Psalm 27:4, 8; 1 Corinthians 2:6-16.*

GOD'S GLORY IN THE HEAVENS

The people observed His glory in a different manner in Old Testament times, for His glory would appear in a cloud. For example, in Exodus 24:16-17, we read that "the glory of the Lord rested on Mount Sinai, and the cloud covered it six days. And on the seventh day He called to Moses out of the midst of the cloud. The sight of the glory of the Lord was like a consuming fire on the top of the mountain in the eyes of the children of Israel."

Another time, found in Exodus 33:9-11, "the cloud descended and stood at the door of the tabernacle, and the Lord talked with Moses. All the people saw the pillar of cloud standing at the tabernacle door, and all the people rose and worshiped, each man in his tent door. So the Lord spoke to Moses face to face, as a man speaks to his friend." This is so awesome! Then in Exodus 40:34, "the cloud covered the tabernacle meeting, and the glory of the Lord filled the tabernacle." God appeared so many times in this manner, that it seems to me the people would all be horrified to disobey Him; the One who loved them so much, meeting them at their place of worship, and also providing for them in wondrous ways. Instead, they seem to take God's blessings for granted.

As you read the Ezekiel passages, you also sense the majesty of God in the brightness of His glory. It is so tremendous! And then in Habakkuk 3:3- 4, we read, "God came from Teman, the Holy One from Mount Paran. His glory covered the heavens, and the earth was full of His praise. His brightness was like the light; He had rays flashing from His hand, and there His power was hidden." The awesome glory of Almighty God is revealed again and again. How can there be any question as to who God is? As we read the Word we can find Him there. This has been my experience in the deepest trials I've had to go through in my developing years *(Actually I'm still in them)*.

Our Scriptures also tell us that there are times when God's glory shall appear in the future. God has appointed times when He will appear to reveal Himself among His people. It is very well possible that each of these times is not recorded, for we read in John 21:25 that "there are also many other things that Jesus did, which if they were written one by one, I suppose that even the world itself could not contain the books that would be written. Amen." That would surely include the life of Jesus between age 12 until His ascension at age 33, which is approximately 21 years. Quite obviously then, the Old Testament happenings, covering approximately 4,000 years, could not be recorded in their entirety. But, we have adequate revelation to show us God's nature, His will, His ways, and purposes, so we might be able to comprehend and apply these truths for daily living.

GOD'S GLORY REVEALED IN HIS CREATION

The Word tells us that "The heavens declare the glory of God; and the firmament shows His handiwork," in Psalm 19:1. My husband and I were greatly impressed of this in a spectacular way in the Fall of 1978, when we were traveling west on the major highway in Canada just above the Great Lakes. I was reading from the beginning of the Psalms, and when I came to Psalm 19, I felt airborne. These words brought music to the beauty of the heavens and God's creation all around us. The huge colorful rocks were like flower gardens among the trees, which were magnificently and brilliantly dressed for autumn. No man could have created these; it couldn't just happen; only an intelligent God could have created that majestic grandeur! It seemed as though we would be able to see Him out among the trees. He wasn't visibly walking out there, but His presence was very real in what we experienced in our hearts.

There are numerous places on this earth, and numberless times that this is repeated! You have most probably observed God's glorious creativity on some of your travels; and many of you don't have to go very far from your home. Often the heavens reveal some of the most fabulous paintings; many of them appear as though the Lord used angel wings for His vast brush strokes, while other times He has made a variety of interesting and striking designs in the sky.

One of the most spectacular formations, that I've ever seen, was of a huge black bear standing up to a great white horse. There was a storm in the distance, with thunder rolling and lightening flashing beyond the horse, which was reared up toward the bear as if both were ready for battle. It was an awesome reminder of prophecies given in the book of Revelation. God has so many ways of revealing Himself, and revealing what He is able to bring into being at His appointed time. Romans 1:20 tells us, "For since the creation of the world His invisible attributes are clearly seen, being understood by the things that are made, even His eternal power and Godhead, so that they are without excuse."

THE GLORY OF GOD ON JESUS

Although the Lord may not have revealed Himself to you in a cloud of His glory, He has sent His own Son to reveal Himself to us. In Jesus we see His glory manifested among the people of His day. His birth was even heralded by the presence of the "glory of God shining around the shepherds living out in the fields keeping watch over their flock by night." *See Luke 2:8-14*. As you meditate on the Scriptures, you will find this to be very significant, for God highlighted major events with His glorious presence.

Matthew 3:16-17 tell of Jesus' baptism with these words, "when He had been baptized, Jesus came up immediately from the water; and behold, the heavens were opened to Him and He saw the Spirit of God descending like a dove and alighting upon Him. And suddenly a voice came from heaven, saying, 'This is My beloved Son, in whom I am well pleased.'" Even though this is not expressed in terms of 'the glory of the Lord', we know that the glory of God must have appeared in dazzling array across the heavens, accentuating this major event in Jesus' life.

Another outstanding event in Jesus' lifetime on this earth was on the mountain, where He was transfigured before the disciples: Peter, James and John. In Matthew 17:2 we read, "His face shone like the sun, and His clothes became as white as the light." Then suddenly Moses and Elijah appeared and talked with Jesus. This whole scene was so awesome, that it appears like Peter couldn't contain His natural readiness to say what was on his mind. This was way beyond him, yet he felt he had to say something. The other two may have gone into shock, unable to speak. However it's not over yet, while Peter was suggesting that they should build three tabernacles, one for each of them, God's voice comes from out of the cloud, saying, "This is My beloved Son, in whom I am well pleased. Hear Him!" and the disciples all fell on their faces with great fear, a holy reverence. What do you think your response would have been? Can you visualize it? This was truly a very special occasion for Jesus and His inner circle of disciples!

It is hard for me to imagine that Jesus, in His intimate prayer to His Father so short a time before His death, knowing that He had to die, was so composed about the glory that was His. He said in John 17:1, "Father, the hour has come. Glorify Your Son, that Your Son also may glorify You." And in verse 24 He says: "Father, I desire that they also whom You gave Me may be with Me where I am, that they may behold My glory which You have given Me..." We have the tendency to ask, "How can anyone be glorified by a death on the cross? How can that look good, no matter what way you look at it? Doesn't it look like Satan is the winner?"

WE ARE TO LIVE TO THE PRAISE OF HIS GLORY

Only God can bring glory out of the most tragic things that happen in our lives. Think of some of the major people and events in the Word, and observe how God brought victory and showed His glory through it. These people are not the only ones whom God uses for glorious experiences. Isaiah 43:7 says, "Everyone who is called by My name, whom I have created for My glory; I have formed him, yes, I have made him."

The Lord has blessed me to meet Jan Eckles who has gone through the very difficult experiences of becoming blind when her 3 boys were still young, and later losing her youngest son when he was stabbed to death. Through these trials she found the sweetness of God's love and His enabling power in the fullness of the Holy Spirit. Her heart flows with praises to God, giving Him the glory for blessing her so richly. She has written Trials of Today, Treasures for Tomorrow—Overcoming Adversities in Life.[6] She shares how the glory of God shining on His beloved ones, is reflected back to Him through our daily living.

In Ephesians 1:5-6 we find this truth expressed—"adopted as sons by Jesus Christ to Himself, according to the good pleasure of His will to the praise of the glory of His grace, by which He made us accepted in the Beloved." Two more times—in verses 12 and 14, it expresses that we are to live "to the praise of His glory." This is a wonderful picture to have before our eyes, our living "to the praise of His glory." We are not our own, to do as we please; but to live for His pleasure, to delight ourselves in Him, to bring glory to Him.

Do you realize that when you are ministering to others in whatever way that may be; feeding the hungry, clothing the naked, laying hands on the sick, ministering to prisoners, teaching the Word to children, discipling people with the Word, telephone ministry, or wherever the Lord has placed you, you are glorifying the Lord? In Matthew 25:31-40 we have quite a list of ways that we bless Jesus when we do them for those living around us who have needs. When our hearts are right, and we're not looking for personal gain or praise, Jesus is honored and glorified. Praise His name!

This brings our daily living to a much higher level than we normally think. In fact, Romans 8:29-30 tells the story from God's foreknowledge, through the process of predestination, the calling, justification, and then it says: "these He also glorified." Another Scripture that sheds light on this is 2 Corinthians 3:18: "But we all, with unveiled face beholding as in a mirror the glory of the Lord, are being transformed into the same image from glory to glory, just as by the Spirit of the Lord." And Colossians 1:27, where it says: "To them God willed to make known what are the riches of the glory of this mystery among the Gentiles: which is Christ in you, the hope of glory." Glory to God for His unspeakable gifts! It's time to shout, "Hallelujah!"

We have a magnificent example of God's pleasure in those who have fully surrendered themselves to Him, when Jesus received Stephen into His glorious presence in Heaven; "Stephen, being full of the Holy Spirit, gazed in heaven and saw the glory of God, and Jesus standing at the right hand of God." What an entrance into heaven! What glory that will be, when we shall see Him face to face, and enjoy Him forever and forever!

SCRIPTURES FOR
GLORY — GLORIOUS

God is glorious in power and greatness – King of Glory –

Ex. 15:6 "Your right hand O Lord, has become **glorious** in power; Your right hand, O Lord, has dashed the enemy in pieces."

Deut. 5:24 "And you said: "Surely the Lord our God has shown us His **glory** and His greatness, and we have heard His voice from the midst of the fire. We have seen this day that God speaks with man; yet he still lives."

1 Chron. 29:11 "Yours, O Lord, is the greatness, the power and the **glory**; the victory and the majesty; for all that is in heaven and in earth is Yours; Yours is the kingdom, O Lord, and You are exalted as head over all."

Ps. 145:5, 10-12 I will meditate on the **glorious** splendor of Your majesty, and on Your wondrous works. ....All Your works shall praise You, O Lord, and Your saints shall bless You, they shall speak of the **glory** of Your kingdom, and talk of Your power, to make known to the sons of men His mighty acts, and the **glorious** majesty of His kingdom.

1 Tim. 1:17 Now to the King eternal, immortal, invisible, to God who alone is wise, be honor and **glory** forever and ever. Amen.

Glorious in holiness —

Ex. 15:11 "Who is like You, O Lord, among the gods? Who is like You **glorious** in holiness, fearful in praises, doing wonders?"

Isa. 6:1-3 In the year that King Uzziah died, I saw the Lord sitting on a throne, high and lifted up, and the train of His robe filled the temple. Above it stood seraphim; each one had six wings: with two he covered his face, and with two he covered his feet, and with two he flew. And one cried to another and said: "Holy, holy, holy is the Lord of hosts; the whole earth is full of His **glory**!"

His glorious name —

Ps. 24:7-10 Lift up your heads, O you gates! And be lifted up, you everlasting doors! And the **King of glory** shall come in. Who is this **King of glory**? The Lord strong and mighty, the Lord mighty in battle. Lift up your heads, O you gates! Lift up, you everlasting doors! And the **King of glory** shall come in. Who is this **King of glory**? The Lord of hosts, He is the **King of glory**.

Ps. 72:18-19 Blessed be the Lord God, the God of Israel, who only does wondrous things! And blessed be His **glorious** name forever! And let the whole earth be filled with His **glory**. Amen and Amen.

Ps. 105:3 **Glory** in His Holy name; let the hearts of those rejoice who seek the Lord!

Ps. 115:1 Not unto us, O Lord, not unto us, but to Your name give **glory**; because of Your mercy, because of Your truth.

His glory appeared —

Ex. 16:10 Now it came to pass, as Aaron spoke to the whole congregation of the children of Israel, that they looked toward the wilderness, and behold, the **glory** of the Lord appeared in the cloud.

Ex. 24:16-18 Now the **glory** of the Lord rested on Mt. Sinai, and the cloud covered it six days. And on the seventh day He called to Moses out of the midst of the cloud. The sight of the **glory** of the Lord was like a consuming fire on the top of the mountain in the eyes of the children of Israel. So Moses went into the midst of the cloud and went up into the mountain. And Moses was on the mountain forty days and forty nights

Ex. 33:17-23 So the Lord said to Moses, "I will also do this thing that you have spoken; for you have found grace in My sight, and I know you by name." And he said, "Please, show me Your **glory**. Then He said, "I will make all My **goodness** pass before you, and I will proclaim the name of the Lord before you. I will be gracious to whom I will be gracious, and I will have compassion on whom I will have compassion." But He said, "You cannot see My face; for no man shall see Me, and live." And the Lord said, "Here is a place by Me, and you shall stand on the rock. So it shall be, while My **glory** passes by, that I will put you in the cleft of the rock, and will cover you with My hand while I pass by. Then I will take away My hand, and you shall see My back; but My face shall not be seen."

Ex. 40:34 Then the cloud covered the tabernacle of meeting, and the **glory** of the Lord filled the tabernacle.

Lev. 9:22-24 Then Aaron lifted his hand toward the people, blessed them, and came down from offering the sin offering, the burnt offering, and peace offerings. And Moses and Aaron went into the tabernacle of meeting, and came out and blessed the people. Then the **glory** of the Lord appeared to all the people, and fire came out from before the Lord and consumed the burnt offering and the fat on the altar. When all the people saw it, they shouted and fell on their faces.

Ps. 113:4 The Lord is high above all nations, His **glory** above the heavens.

Ezek. 10:4 Then the **glory** of the Lord went up from the cherub, and paused over the threshold of the temple; and the house was filled with the cloud, and the court was full of the brightness of the Lord's **glory.**

Ezek. 11:22-24 So the cherubim lifted up their wings, with the wheels beside them, and the **glory** of the God of Israel was high above them. And the **glory** of the Lord went up from the midst of the city and stood on the mountain, which is on the east side of the city. Then the Spirit took me up and brought me a vision by the Spirit of God into Chaldea, to those in captivity. And the vision that I had seen went up from me.

Ezek. 44:4 Also He brought me by way of the north gate to the front of the temple; so I looked, and behold, the **glory** of the Lord filled the house of the Lord; and I fell on my face.

Hab. 3:3-4 God came from Teman, the Holy One from Mount Paran. His **glory** covered the heavens, and the earth was full of His praise. His brightness was like the light; He had rays flashing from His hand, and there His power was hidden.

Luke 2:8-14 Now there were in the same country shepherds living out in the fields, keeping watch over their flock by night. And behold, an angel of the Lord stood before them, and the **glory** of the Lord shone around them, and they were greatly afraid. Then the angel said to them, "Do not be afraid, for behold, I bring you good tidings of great joy which will be to all people. For there is born to you this day in the city of David a Savior, who is Christ the Lord. And this will be the sign to you: You will find a Babe wrapped in swaddling cloths, lying in a manger." And suddenly there was with the angel a multitude of the heavenly host praising God and saying: "**Glory** to God in the highest, and on earth peace, goodwill toward men!"

His glory shall appear—

Num. 14:20-21 Then the Lord said: "I have pardoned, according to your word; but truly, as I live, all the earth shall be filled with the **glory** of the Lord—"

Isa. 58:8-9 NIV "Then your light will break forth like the dawn, and your healing will quickly appear; then your righteousness will go before you and the **glory** of the Lord will be your rear guard. Then you will call, and the Lord will answer; you will cry for help, and He will say: Here am I."

Hab.2:14 For the earth will be filled with the knowledge of the **glory** of the Lord as the waters cover the sea.

Luke 21:27 "Then they will see the Son of Man coming in a cloud with power and great **glory**.

His glory declared—

Ps. 19:1 The heavens declare the **glory** of God; and the firmament shows His handiwork.

Isa. 66:18-19 "For I know their works and their thoughts. It shall be that I will gather all nations and tongues; and they shall come and see My **glory**. I will set a sign among them; and those among them who escape I will send to the nations; to Tarshish and Pul and Lud, who draw the bow and Tubal and Javan, to the coastlands afar off who have not heard My fame nor seen My **glory**. And they shall declare My **glory** among the Gentiles."

The glory of the Son of God – the Son of Man, Jesus—

Matt. 16:27 "For the Son of Man will come in the **glory** of His Father with His angels, and then He will reward each according to his works."

Matt. 17:1-2, 5 Now after six days Jesus took Peter, James, and John his brother, led them up on a high mountain by themselves; and He was transfigured before them. His face shone (*gloriously*) like the sun, and His clothes became as white as the light. ....While he (*Peter*) was still speaking, behold, a bright cloud (***God's glory***) overshadowed them; and suddenly a voice came out of the cloud saying, "This is My beloved Son, in whom I am well pleased. Hear Him!" *Also Luke 9:29-32*

Luke 9:26 "For whoever is ashamed of Me and My words, of him the Son of Man will be ashamed when He comes in His own **glory**, and in His Father's, and of the holy angels."

Luke 19:37-38 Then as He was now drawing near the descent of the Mount of Olives, the whole multitude of the disciples began to rejoice and praise God with a loud voice for all the mighty works they had seen, saying: "Blessed is the King who comes in the name of the Lord! Peace in heaven and **glory** in the highest!"

Luke 24:25-26 Then He said to them, "O foolish ones, and slow of heart to believe in all that the prophets have spoken! Ought not the Christ to have suffered these things and to enter into His **glory**?"

John 1:14 And the Word became flesh and dwelt among us, and we beheld His **glory**, the **glory** as of the only begotten of the Father, full of grace and truth.

John 2:11 This beginning of signs Jesus did in Cana of Galilee, and manifested His **glory**; and His disciples believed in Him.

John 11:4 When Jesus heard that, He said, "This sickness is not unto death, but for the **glory** of God, that the Son of God may be **glorified** through it."

John 14:13-14 "And whatever you ask in My name, that I will do, that the Father may be **glorified** in the Son. If you ask anything in My name, I will do it."

John 17:1, 4-5 Jesus spoke these words, lifted up His eyes to heaven, and said: "Father, the hour has come. **Glorify** Your Son, that Your Son also may **glorify** You. ....I have **glorified** You on the earth. I have finished the work which You have given Me to do. And now, O Father, **glorify** Me together with Yourself, with the **glory** which I had with You before the world was."

John 17:24 *Part of Jesus' prayer*—- "Father, I desire that they also whom You gave Me may be with Me where I am, that they may behold My **glory** which You have given Me; for You loved Me before the foundation of the world."

Acts 7:55 But he *(Stephen)*, being full of the Holy Spirit, gazed in heaven and saw the **glory** of God, and Jesus standing at the right hand of God.

Rom. 11:36 For of Him *(Jesus)* and through Him and to Him are all things, to whom be **glory** forever. Amen.

2 Cor. 4:3-6 But even if our gospel is veiled, it is veiled to those who are perishing, whose minds the god of this age has blinded, who do not believe, lest the light of the gospel of the **glory** of Christ, who is the image of God, should shine on them. For we do not preach ourselves, but Christ Jesus the Lord, and ourselves Your bondservants for Jesus' sake. For it is the God who commanded light to shine out of darkness, who has shone in our hearts to give the light of the knowledge of the **glory** of God in the face of Jesus Christ.

Heb. 1:3 Who being the brightness of His **glory** and the express image of His person, and upholding all things by the word of His power, when He had by Himself purged our sins, sat down at the right hand of the Majesty on high.

Titus 2:13 Looking for the blessed hope and **glorious** appearing of our great God and Savior Jesus Christ.

The glory of the Lord in relation to His people—

Isa. 43:7 "Everyone who is called by My name, whom I have created for My **glory**; I have formed him, yes, I have made him."

Isa. 60:1-2 Arise, shine; for your light has come! And the **glory** of the Lord is risen upon you. For behold, the darkness shall cover the earth, and deep darkness the people; but the Lord will arise over you, and His **glory** will be seen upon you.

John 17:10, 20-22 *Jesus is in prayer—-* "And all Mine are Yours, and Yours are Mine, and I am **glorified** in them. ...I do not pray for these alone, but also for those who will believe in Me through their word; that they all may be one, as You, Father, are in Me, and I in You; that they also may be one in Us, that the world may believe that You sent Me. And the **glory** which You gave Me I have given to them, that they may be one just as We are one."

Rom. 5:1-2 Therefore, having been justified by faith, we have peace with God through our Lord Jesus Christ, through whom also we have access by faith into this grace in which we stand, and rejoice in hope of the **glory** of God.

Rom. 8:16-18 The Spirit Himself bears witness with our spirit that we are children of God and joint heirs with Christ, if indeed we suffer with Him, that we may also be **glorified** together. For I consider that the sufferings of this present time are not worthy to be compared with the **glory** which shall be revealed in us.

Rom 8:21 ....because the creation itself also will be delivered from the bondage of corruption into the **glorious** liberty of the children of God.

Rom. 8:29-30 For whom He foreknew, He also predestined to be conformed to the image of His Son, that He might be the firstborn among many brethren. Moreover whom He predestined, these He also called; whom He called, these He also justified; and whom He justified, these He also **glorified.**

Rom. 15:17 Therefore I have reason to **glory** in Christ Jesus in the things which pertain to God.

2 Cor. 3:18 But we all, with unveiled face beholding as in a mirror the **glory** of the Lord, are being transformed into the same image from **glory to glory**, just as by the Spirit of the Lord.

Eph. 1:5-6, 12, 14 ...having predestined us to adoption as sons by Jesus Christ to Himself, according to the good pleasure of His will to the praise of the **glory** of His grace, by which He made us accepted in the Beloved. ...that we who first trusted in Christ should be to the praise of His **glory**. ...who is the guarantee of our inheritance until the redemption of the purchased possession, to the praise of His **glory**.

Eph. 1:16b-18 ....making mention of you in my prayers: that the God of our Lord Jesus Christ, the Father of **glory**, may give to you the spirit of wisdom and revelation in the knowledge of Him, the eyes of your understanding being enlightened; that you may know what is the hope of His calling, what are the riches of the **glory** of His inheritance in the saints...

Eph. 3:16 ....that He would grant you, according to the riches of His **glory**, to be strengthened with might through His Spirit in the inner man...

Phil. 4:19 And my God shall supply all your needs according to His riches in **glory** by Christ Jesus.

Col. 1:27-28 To them God willed to make known what are the riches of the **glory** of this mystery among the Gentiles: which is Christ in you, the hope of **glory**. Him we preach, warning every man and teaching every man in all wisdom, that we may present every man perfect in Christ Jesus.

Col. 3:4 When Christ who is our life appears, then you also will appear with Him in **glory**.

2 Thess. 2:13-14 But we are bound to give thanks to God always for you, brethren beloved by the Lord, because God from the beginning chose you for salvation through sanctification by the Spirit and belief in the truth, to which he called you by our gospel, for the obtaining of the **glory** of our Lord Jesus Christ.

2 Tim. 2:10 Therefore I endure all things for the sake of the elect, that they also may obtain the salvation which is in Christ Jesus with eternal **glory**.

1 Peter 1:6-9 In this you greatly rejoice, though now for a little while, if need be, you have been grieved by various trials, that the genuineness of your faith, being much more precious than gold that perishes, though it is tested by fire, may be found to praise, honor and **glory** at the revelation of Jesus Christ, whom having not seen you love, though now you do not see Him, yet believing, you rejoice with joy inexpressible and full of **glory**, receiving the end of your faith–the salvation of your souls.

To God be the glory—

Ps. 29:1-4 Give unto the Lord, O you mighty ones, give unto the Lord **glory** and strength. Give unto the Lord the **glory** due to His name; worship the Lord in the beauty of holiness. The voice of the Lord is over the waters; the God of **glory** thunders; the Lord is over many waters. The voice of the Lord is powerful; the voice of the Lord is full of majesty.

Luke 17:15-18 And one of them (*the ten lepers*), when he saw that he was healed, returned, and with a loud voice **glorified** God, and fell down on his face at His feet; giving Him thanks. And he was a Samaritan. So Jesus answered and said, "Were there not ten cleansed? But where are the nine? Were there not any found who returned to give **glory** to God except this foreigner?"

Rom. 4:20-21 He, Abraham, did not waver at the promise of God through unbelief, but was strengthened in faith, giving **glory** to God and being fully convinced that what He had promised He was also able to perform.

1 Cor. 6:20 For you were bought at a price; therefore **glorify** God in your body and in your spirit; which are God's.

1 Cor. 10:31 Therefore, whether you eat or drink, or whatever you do, do all to the **glory** of God.

KINGDOM

KINGDOMS AND THEIR KING

Every kingdom has a ruler who governs his specific territory. He is the king, the sovereign authority, and has no one to whom he must report, or that he is required to consult about various matters. He possesses the highest rank of power as he reigns in his kingdom. In some countries, where there are kings today, they are still addressed as Your Excellent Highness. People do not greet them as another fellow citizen, or on friendly terms. They are not available as an ordinary citizen. He is carefully protected by armed guards.

Earthly kingdoms are all temporary, lasting according to the physical ability of the ruler and ending with his death. In the Old Testament we read about many kings, one following another in the family line of sons. Pharaoh was king of Egypt; in fact, all their kings were named Pharaoh. We first read of them in Genesis 12:15 and other kings are listed in Genesis 14:1.

Saul was the first king over Israel; David followed him, then his son Solomon, and so on. There is much that can be said of the kingdoms of the earth, however we want to especially focus on God's Kingdom, His kingship and what this means to us.

In the spiritual realm there are two kingdoms, and we must make a definite choice, if we would live in accordance with the ruler-ship that God has set forth in His Word. When we do not choose His authority, then we are subject to Satan's kingdom, for there is no in between.

The kingdom of self belongs to the latter one. This is a hard fact, but is clearly defined in the Word, particularly when Jesus told the religious leaders of His day: "You are of your father the devil, and the desires of your father you want to do. He was a murderer from the beginning, and does not stand in the truth, because there is no truth in him. When he speaks a lie, he speaks from his own resources, for he is a liar and the father of it." Read John 8:31-59, where Jesus discusses the whole issue of either being one of His disciples, or in contrast one of those who chose to not recognize Jesus as the Son of God. He pointed out that their desire to kill Him showed that they could not be children of God, for they would surely love Him. He plainly tells them *(vs.44)* that their father is the devil.

GOD IS HOLY AND REIGNS SUPREMELY

God's kingdom pertains to holiness, truth, righteousness, honor and blessings. His kingdom is eternal; He is forever King of Kings and Lord of Lords. There is no higher authority; He is Sovereign God, Creator of the heavens and the earth, and all that dwells therein; there can be none higher; no other God. All the kingdoms of the earth are under Him. He reigns supremely forever, no replacements, for He is eternal.

King David tells of His tremendous attributes in 1 Chronicles 29:10-13: Therefore David blessed the Lord before all the assembly; and David said: "Blessed are You, Lord God of Israel, our Father, forever and ever, Yours, O Lord, is the greatness, the power and the glory, the victory and the majesty; for all that is in heaven and in earth is Yours; Yours is the kingdom, O Lord, and You are exalted as head over all. Both riches and honor come from You, and You reign over all. In Your hand is power and might; in Your hand it is to make great and to give strength to all. Now therefore, our God, we thank You and praise Your glorious name."

Here are a couple more scriptures that tell of the greatness of God and that His kingdom is eternal—Psalm 45:6 says, "Your throne, O God, is forever and ever; a scepter of righteousness is the scepter of Your kingdom." A scepter is a symbol of authority. Earthly kings held a rod, or staff, decorated with beautiful ornaments, including jewels, to show their sovereignty. However, God's scepter is 'righteousness'. Just thinking about His righteousness and holiness holds one in an aura of His majesty, His awesome greatness. How can we help but worship and praise Him? How can we help but love Him? I pray that as you read about God's greatness and His kingdom, you will experience the same rejoicing in your heart.

Psalm 145:10-13 also tell of His greatness—"All Your works shall praise You, O Lord, and Your saints shall bless You. They shall speak of the glory of Your kingdom, and talk of Your power, to make known to the sons of men His mighty acts, and the glorious majesty of His kingdom. Your kingdom is an everlasting kingdom and Your dominion endures throughout all generations." Isn't that magnificent! Could you want to belong to any other kingdom, when you come to have this knowledge of the King of kings, Almighty God, the Sovereign Lord?

When we think of all the evil that is going on in the world today; of wicked rulers with such strong determination to please self and destroy all that is good; we become more keenly aware how imperative it is to know the Creator God! We need to hear what His Word tells us about His kingdom, for there is security in this knowledge. Even in the Old Testament, those who became kings over God's people were not necessarily godly men. Many were so evil and led the people into evil during their reign as king that you can hardly believe that they were part of the nation of Israel, God's chosen people.

This is also true today in what we want to recognize as 'Christian America'. Not all our leaders have been godly men. We must know the rules and commands of Almighty God, obey them and live for Him above all else. One of His rules tells us to pray for those in authority over us. Since we know that prayer is powerful, it should be very important to us to obey this command; and watch for results because we know that our God hears and answers the prayers of those who 'trust and obey' Him. 2 Chronicles 16:9 says: "The eyes of the Lord run to and fro throughout the whole earth, to show Himself strong on behalf of those whose heart is loyal to Him."

JESUS PRESENTED THE GOSPEL OF GOD'S KINGDOM

Let's take a look at what was taught in the New Testament, let's look at Matthew 3:1-2, where we read about John the Baptist preaching in the wilderness of Judea. His message was, "Repent, for the kingdom of heaven is at hand!" Jesus brought the reality of God's kingdom to us. He presented a new message, called 'The Gospel of the Kingdom'. We never heard of casting out devils and healing all kinds of sickness and diseases in the Old Testament. There were some healings in the Old Testament times, but not like those we see in the ministry of Jesus and thereafter.

The kingdom of God is so different from the kingdoms of this earth that you can hardly recognize any similarity. Jesus came to reveal God's kingdom which ministers to people with amazing grace and boundless love. He calls us and draws us into His kingdom so that we might have eternal life. He offers a life of incredible blessings which could never be earned. They are gifts through the Lord Jesus Christ.

John the Baptist introduced Jesus, who during His ministry brought fresh manna of truth about the kingdom of God, which is the kingdom of heaven. Jesus had just begun ministering a short time when John was imprisoned, and then he sent two of his disciples to ask Jesus, "Are You the coming One, or do we look for another?" Jesus' answer is very interesting; His proof is in what He does. He says, as recorded in Matthew 11:2-6, "Go tell John the things which you hear and see: The blind see and the lame walk; the lepers are cleansed and the deaf hear; the dead are raised up and the poor have the gospel preached to them. And blessed is he who is not offended because of Me."

This list is almost identical to those we find in Matthew 10:7-8, when Jesus was sending out the twelve disciples to minister. He told them, "And as you go, preach, saying, 'The kingdom of heaven is at hand.' Heal the sick, cleanse the lepers, raise the dead, cast out demons. Freely you have received, freely give." This shows us what the kingdom of God brought to the people at that time in history, and His kingdom has not departed.

ONLY ONE WAY INTO GOD'S KINGDOM

Jesus preached a great deal about this kingdom in the Sermon on the Mount and throughout His ministry. Possibly you are familiar with John 3:3, where Jesus said to Nicodemus, "Most assuredly,

I say to you, unless one is born again, he cannot see the kingdom of God," and in verse 5, "Unless one is born of water and of the Spirit he cannot enter the kingdom of God." Since Jesus put re-birth and our obedience to God as absolute requirements for entering the kingdom, we need to take some time with this truth. Why would it be so important? Many people think there are a number of ways to God, and they declare that they feel comfortable with their choice. They worship the way that pleases them, and think that God should be pleased with their efforts.

However, this Scripture, and others, reveal their beliefs to be false and their end will be destruction, not rejoicing in heaven as they expected. One of these is Matthew 7:21-23, where Jesus is saying, "Not everyone who says to Me, 'Lord, Lord,' shall enter the kingdom of heaven, but he who does the will of My Father in heaven. Many will say to Me in that day, 'Lord, Lord, have we not prophesied in Your name, cast out demons in Your name, and done many wonders in Your name?' And then I will declare to them, 'I never knew you; depart from Me, you who practice lawlessness!'"

And another is Matthew 25:11-12, "Afterward the other virgins came also, saying, 'Lord, Lord, open to us!' But he answered and said, 'Assuredly, I say to you, I do not know you.'" We must know God's plan of salvation. The King of kings and Lord of lords is in charge of His kingdom, so we cannot take for granted that heaven is our reward for good deeds. It makes me realize the extreme urgency to know God and to know His requirements so each one, who desires to spend eternity with the Lord Jesus, might be counted worthy to enter the kingdom of heaven.

You may be asking what 'born-again' actually means. Our natural birth is a physical birth; however a second birth is a spiritual one. With the natural birth the physical system begins its new life, independent from the mother, as the baby breathes, makes sounds, opens its eyes and hears sounds. The brain is functioning in a new capacity with new freedom for movements according to how healthy the brain, heart, lungs, nervous system, the limbs, and so forth are at birth.

The spiritual birth is an awakening in our inner being, as we receive the Holy Spirit, in the name of Jesus, into our hearts. He makes us aware of our becoming children of the Living God. As we gain more thorough knowledge of Him, we realize the importance of humbling ourselves to worship and serve the mighty God, our Creator. Many little children have learned about the Lord Jesus through others who are mature in their knowledge, but many do not become born again until they are able to understand the true meaning of believing on the Lord Jesus Christ for salvation after becoming adults.

Jesus came to this earth to manifest His Father, as well as to die on the cross for us. When we truly believe on Jesus and His sacrificial death on our behalf, our spiritual eyes are opened to see the kingdom of God, and Jesus' Spirit gives us spiritual life as He comes to live in the believer's heart. Our ears begin to hear God's Word with new understanding of truth, and we become hungry for more of His Word, which is our spiritual food.

In John 3:5, it says that we are to be re-born of water and the Spirit. The Spirit of Jesus, Who comes to live in us is the Breath of Life, and the water is God's Word. John 15:3 says, "You are already clean because of the word which I have spoken to you." And in Ephesians 5:26 we read, "that He might sanctify and cleanse her with the washing of water by the word." And another one, 1 Peter 1:22-23 says it so beautifully: "Since you have purified your souls in obeying the truth through the Spirit in sincere love of the brethren, love one another fervently with a pure heart, having been born again, not of corruptible seed but incorruptible, through the word of God which lives and abides forever." In each one of these, the water is the Word cleansing, purifying, and it is the incorruptible seed that brings about the re-birth.

GOD'S WORD PRODUCES SPIRITUAL LIFE

Can you see how the Word of God produces the birth through the knowledge of God, which enlightens our eyes, and our spiritual being comes alive as we eat and drink the Word for spiritual food? It reveals our sinful nature and informs us of the need to repent of our sins, so we might be forgiven and cleansed of all our sins. It also reveals that Jesus' blood was the purchase price to redeem the lost, and provided the way for all who believe on the Lord Jesus

Christ to enter into His kingdom, "of righteousness and peace and joy in the Holy Spirit." *Romans 14:17.*

Today you have an opportunity to believe that Jesus made the way for your redemption, and to believe that God wants you to be "rescued from the darkness and gloom of Satan's kingdom and brought into the Kingdom of His dear Son, who bought our freedom with His blood and forgave us all our sins," according to Colossians 1:13-14, NLT. Take time to read some of the other word studies in this book, and surrender your will, your future, all that you are and have to Him, so you might enjoy the blessings of His love, peace and inexpressible joy in your heart.

Read the Scriptures for this subject over and over again. Meditate on them, and seek the Lord's blessing to open your spiritual eyes to see and know the truths contained in them. The Holy Spirit will give you understanding and the ability to apply them to your life's situations and needs. Make sure you enter His eternal Kingdom!

SCRIPTURES FOR
KINGDOM

Kingdom of God and Kingdom of heaven—-

Everlasting Kingdom—

Ps. 45:6 **Your throne**, O God, **is forever and ever**; a scepter of righteousness is the scepter of **Your kingdom.**

Ps. 145:10-13 All Your works shall praise You, O Lord, and Your saints shall bless You. They shall speak of the glory of **Your kingdom**, and talk of Your power, to make known to the sons of men His mighty acts, and the glorious majesty of **His kingdom. Your kingdom** is an **everlasting kingdom** and Your dominion endures throughout all generations.

Daniel 7:27 NIV "'Then the sovereignty, power and greatness of the **kingdoms** under the whole heaven will be handed over to the saints, the people of the Most High. **His kingdom** will be an **everlasting kingdom**, and all rulers will worship and obey Him.'"

Rev. 11:15 Then the seventh angel sounded: and there were loud voices in heaven, saying, "The **kingdoms** of this world have become the **kingdoms of our Lord and of His Christ,** and He shall reign **forever and ever!**"

What the kingdom of God is not and is—-

Rom. 14:16-17 Therefore do not let your good be spoken of as evil; for the **kingdom of God** is not eating and drinking, but righteousness and peace and joy in the Holy Spirit.

1 Cor. 4:20 For the **kingdom of God** is not in word but in power.

The kingdom of heaven is at hand —-

Matt. 3:1-2 In those days John the Baptist came preaching in the wilderness of Judea, and saying, "Repent, for the **kingdom of heaven** is at hand!"

Matt. 4:17, 23 From that time Jesus began to preach and to say, "Repent, for the **kingdom of heaven** is at hand." *Also Mark 1:15.* ....And Jesus went about all Galilee, teaching in their synagogues, preaching the gospel of the **kingdom**, and healing all kinds of sickness and all kinds of disease among the people.

Matt. 10:7-8 "And as you go, preach, saying, 'The **kingdom of heaven** is at hand.' Heal the sick, cleanse the lepers, raise the dead, cast out demons. Freely you have received, freely give."

Who will enter, and who will not enter—

Matt. 5:3, 10, 20 "Blessed are the poor in spirit, for theirs is the **kingdom of heaven**. ...Blessed are those who are persecuted for righteousness' sake, for theirs is the **kingdom of heaven**. ...For I say to you, that unless your righteousness exceeds the righteousness of the scribes and Pharisees, you will by no means enter the **kingdom of heaven**."

Matt. 7:21 "Not everyone who says to Me, 'Lord, Lord', shall enter the **kingdom of heaven**, but he who does the will of My Father in heaven."

Matt. 13:37-38 He answered and said to them: "He who sows the good seed is the Son of Man. The field is the world, the good seeds are the sons of the **kingdom**, but the tares are the sons of the wicked one."

Matt. 21:31b-32 Jesus said to them *(chief priests and elders)*, "Assuredly, I say to you that tax collectors and harlots enter the

kingdom of God before you. For John came to you in the way of righteousness, and you did not believe him; but tax collectors and harlots believed him; and when you saw it, you did not afterward relent and believe him."

Mark 10:14-15 But when Jesus saw it, He was greatly displeased and said to them, "Let the little children come to Me, and do not forbid them; for of such is the **kingdom of God**. Assuredly I say to you, whoever does not receive the **kingdom of God** as a little child will by no means enter it." *Also Matt. 19:14.*

Mark 10:23-25 Then Jesus looked around and said to His disciples, "How hard it is for those who have riches to enter the **kingdom of God!**" *Also Matt, 19:23.* And the disciples were astonished at His words. But Jesus answered again and said to them, "Children, how hard it is for those who trust in riches to enter the **kingdom of God**! It is easier for a camel to go through the eye of a needle than for a rich man to enter the **kingdom of God**."

John 3:3-5 Jesus answered and said to him, "Most assuredly, I say to you, unless one is born again, he cannot see the **kingdom of God**." Nicodemus said to Him, "How can a man be born when he is old? Can he enter a second time into his mother's womb and be born?" Jesus answered, "Most assuredly, I say to you, unless one is born of water and the Spirit, he cannot enter the **kingdom of God**."

Acts 14:21-22 And when they had preached the gospel to that city and made many disciples, they returned to Lystra, Iconium, and Antioch, strengthening the souls of the disciples, exhorting them to continue in the faith, saying, "We must through many tribulations enter the **kingdom of God**."

2 Tim. 4:17-18 But the Lord stood with me and strengthened me, so that the message might be preached fully through me, and that all the Gentiles might hear. Also I was delivered out of the mouth of the lion. And the Lord will deliver me from every evil work and

preserve me for **His heavenly kingdom.** To Him be glory forever and ever. Amen!

James 2:5 Listen, my beloved brethren: Has God not chosen the poor of this world to be rich in faith and heirs of the **kingdom** which He promised to those who love Him?

Least or great in the kingdom of heaven—

Matt. 5:19 "Whoever therefore breaks one of the least of these commandments, and teaches men so, shall be called least in the **kingdom of heaven**; but whoever does and teaches them, he shall be called great in the **kingdom of heaven**."

Matt. 11:11 "Assuredly, I say to you, among those born of women there has not risen one greater than John the Baptist; but he who is least in the **kingdom of heaven** is greater than he.

Matt. 18:1-5 At that time the disciples came to Jesus, saying, "Who then is greatest in the **kingdom of heaven**?" Then Jesus called a little child to Him, set him in the midst of them, and said, "Assuredly, I say to you, unless you are converted and become as little children, you will by no means enter the **kingdom of heaven**. Therefore whoever humbles himself as this little child is the greatest in the **kingdom of heaven**. Whoever receives one little child like this in My name receives Me."

The kingdom of heaven is like—

Matt. 13:24 Another parable He *(Jesus)* put forth to them, saying: "The **kingdom of heaven** is like a man who sowed good seed in his field...."

Matt. 13:31 Another parable He put forth to them, saying: "The **kingdom of heaven** is like a mustard seed, which a man took and sowed in his field...."

Matt. 13:33 Another parable He spoke to them: "The **kingdom of heaven** is like leaven, which a woman took and hid in three measures of meal till it was all leavened."

Matt. 13:44 "Again the **kingdom of heaven** is like treasure hidden in a field, which a man found and hid; and for joy over it he goes and sells all that he has and buys that field."

Matt. 13:45-46 "Again, the **kingdom of heaven** is like a merchant seeking beautiful pearls, who, when he had found one pearl of great price, went and sold all that he had and bought it."

Matt. 13:47-48 "Again, the **kingdom of heaven** is like a dragnet that was cast into the sea and gathered some of every kind, which, when it was full, they drew to shore; and they sat down and gathered the good into vessels, but threw the bad away."

Matt. 18:23 "Therefore the **kingdom of heaven** is like a certain king who wanted to settle accounts with his servants."

Matt. 20:1, 16 "For the **kingdom of heaven** is like a landowner who went out early in the morning to hire laborers for his vineyard... So the last will be first, and the first last. For many are called, but few chosen."

Matt. 22:2-3 "The **kingdom of heaven** is like a certain king who arranged a marriage for his son, and sent out his servants to call those who were invited to the wedding; and they were not willing to come."

Matt. 25:14-15 "For the **kingdom of heaven** is like a man traveling to a far country, who called his own servants and delivered his goods to them. And to one he gave five talents, to another one two, and to another one, to each according to his own ability; and immediately he went on a journey."

Further knowledge and observations about His kingdom—

Ps. 103:19 The Lord has established His throne in heaven, and **His kingdom** rules over all.

Matt. 6:9-10, 13b "In this manner, therefore, pray: Our Father in heaven, hallowed be Your name. Your **kingdom** come. Your will be done on earth as it is in heaven. ...For yours is the **kingdom** and the power and the glory forever. Amen."

Matt. 6:33 "Seek first the **kingdom of God** and His righteousness, and all these things shall be added to you."

Matt. 9:35 Then Jesus went about all the cities and villages, teaching in their synagogues, preaching the gospel of the **kingdom** and healing every sickness and every disease among the people.

Matt. 12:25-28 But Jesus knew their thoughts, and said to them: "Every **kingdom** divided against itself is brought to desolation, and every city or house divided against itself will not stand. If Satan casts out Satan, he is divided against himself. How then will his **kingdom** stand? And if I cast out demons by Beelzebub, by whom do your sons cast them out? Therefore they shall be your judges. But if I cast out demons by the Spirit of God, surely the **kingdom of God** has come upon you."

Matt. 13:10-11 And the disciples came and said to Him, "Why do You speak to them in parables?" He answered and said to them, "Because it has been given to you to know the mysteries of the **kingdom of heaven**, but to them it has not been given."

Matt. 13:18-19 "Therefore hear the parable of the sower; when anyone hears the word of the **kingdom**, and does not understand it, then the wicked one comes and snatches away what was sown in his heart. This is he who received seed by the wayside."

Matt. 13:41-43 "The Son of Man will send out His angels, and they will gather out of **His kingdom** all things that offend, and those who practice lawlessness, and will cast them into the furnace of fire. There will be wailing and gnashing of teeth. Then the righteous will shine forth as the sun in the **kingdom of their Father**. He who has ears to hear, let him hear!"

Matt. 16:18-19 "And I say to you that you are Peter, and on this rock I will build My church, and the gates of Hades shall not prevail against it. And I will give you the keys of the **kingdom of heaven**, and whatever you bind on earth will be bound in heaven, and whatever you loose on earth will be loosed in heaven."

Matt. 21:43 Therefore I say to you, the **kingdom of God** will be taken from you *(the chief priests and the elders of the temple—see verse 23)* and given to a nation bearing the fruits of it.

Matt. 24:14 "And this gospel of the **kingdom** will be preached in all world as a witness to all the nations, and then the end will come."

Matt. 26:29 "But I say to you, I will not drink of this fruit of the vine from now on until that day when I drink it new with you in **My Father's kingdom**."

Luke 17:20-21 Now when He was asked by the Pharisees when the **kingdom of God** would come He answered them and said, "The **kingdom of God** does not come with observation; nor will they say, 'See here!' or 'See there!' For indeed, the **kingdom of God** is within you."

Luke 19:11 Now as they *(apparently His disciples)* heard these things, He spoke another parable, because He was near Jerusalem and because they thought the **kingdom of God** would appear immediately.

Luke 21:29-32 Then He spoke to them a parable: "Look at the fig tree, and all the trees. When they are already budding, you see and know for yourselves that summer is now near. So you also, when you see these things happening, that the **kingdom of God** is near. Assuredly, I say to you, this generation will by no means pass away till all things take place."

1 Thess. 2:11-12 As you know how we exhorted, and comforted, and charged every one of you, as a father does his own children, that you would walk worthy of God who calls you into **His own kingdom** and glory.

2 Thess. 1:3-5 We are bound to thank God always for you, brethren, as it is fitting, because your faith grows exceedingly, and the love of everyone of you all abounds toward each other, so that we ourselves boast of you among the churches of God for your patience and faith in all your persecutions and tribulations that you endure, which is manifest evidence of the righteous judgment of God, that you may be counted worthy of the **kingdom of God**, for which you also suffer.

Rev. 12:10-11 Then I heard a loud voice saying in heaven, "Now salvation, and strength, and the **kingdom of God**, and the power of His Christ have come, for the accuser of our brethren, who accused them before our God day and night, has been cast down. And they overcame him by the blood of the Lamb and by the word of their testimony, and they did not love their lives to the death."

Throne: This word is in many Scripture verses, so it could have it's own place in the book, however, since God is on the throne of His kingdom, I would like to include these few verses from Revelation 22:1-5 at this point—-

"And he *(an angel—see Rev. 21:9)* showed me a pure river of water of life, clear as crystal, proceeding from the **throne of God and of the Lamb**. In the middle of its street, and on either side of the river, was the tree of life, which bore twelve fruits, each tree yielding its fruit every month. The leaves of the tree were for the healing of the nations. And there shall be no more curse, but the **throne of God and of the Lamb** shall be in it, and His servants shall serve Him. They shall see His face, and His name shall be on their foreheads. There shall be no night there: They need no lamp nor light of the sun, for the Lord God gives them light. And they shall reign forever and ever."

Christ's kingdom—

Matt. 16:28 "Assuredly, I say to you, there are some standing here who shall not taste death till they see the Son of Man coming in **His kingdom.**

Matt. 20:21 And He said to her, "What do you wish?" She said to Him, "Grant that these two sons of mine may sit, one on Your right hand and the other on the left, in **Your kingdom.**"

Luke 22:28-30 "But you are those who have continued with Me in My trials. And I bestow upon you a **kingdom**, just as My Father bestowed one upon Me, that you may eat and drink at My table in **My kingdom**, and sit on thrones judging the twelve tribes of Israel."

Luke 23:40-43 But the other *(criminal on the cross next to Jesus)*, answering, rebuked him, saying, "Do you not even fear God, seeing you are under the same condemnation? And we indeed justly, for we receive the due reward of our deeds; but this Man has done nothing wrong." Then he said to Jesus, "Lord, remember me when You come into **Your kingdom.**" And Jesus said to him, "Assuredly, I say to you, today you will be with Me in Paradise."

John 18:36 Jesus answered, "**My kingdom** is not of this world. If **My kingdom** were of this world, My servants would fight, so that I should not be delivered to the Jews; but now **My kingdom** is not from here."

1 Cor. 15:23-25 But each one in his own order: Christ the firstfruits, afterward those who are Christ's at His coming. Then comes the end, when He delivers the **kingdom to God the Father**, when He puts an end to all rule and all authority and power. For He must

reign till He has put all enemies under His feet.

Col. 1:11-17 TLB We are praying, too, that you will be filled with His mighty, glorious strength so that you can keep going no matter what happens—always full of the joy of the Lord, and always thankful to the Father who has made us fit to share all the wonderful things that belong to those who live in the **Kingdom of light**. For He has rescued us out of the darkness and gloom of Satan's **kingdom** and brought us into the **Kingdom of His dear Son**, who bought our freedom with His blood and forgave us all our sins. Christ is the exact likeness of the unseen God. He existed before God made anything at all, and, in fact, Christ Himself is the Creator who made everything in heaven and earth, the things we can see and the things we can't; the spirit world with its **kings and kingdoms**, its rulers and authorities, all were made by Christ for His own use and glory. He was before all else began and it is His power that holds everything together.

2 Peter 1:10-11 Therefore, brethren, be even more diligent to make your call and election sure, for if you do these things you will never stumble; for so an entrance will be supplied to you abundantly into the **everlasting kingdom of our Lord and Savior Jesus Christ**.

Kingdoms of the earth—-

Isa. 37:15-16, 20 Then Hezekiah prayed to the Lord, saying, "O Lord of hosts, the One who dwells between the cherubim, You are God, You alone, of all the **kingdoms of the earth**. You have made heaven and earth. Now therefore, O Lord our God, save us from his hand *(Sennacherib)*, that all the **kingdoms of the earth** may know that You are the Lord, You alone."

Matt. 24:7 For nation will rise against nation, and **kingdom** against **kingdom**. And there will be famines, pestilences, and earthquakes in various places. *Also in Mark 13:8 and Luke 21:10, 11.*

Rev. 11:15 Then the seventh angel sounded: and there were loud voices in heaven, saying, "The **kingdoms of this world** have become the **kingdoms of our Lord and of His Christ**, and He shall reign forever and ever!"

Kingdom of Satan —-

Matt. 12:25-26 But Jesus knew their thoughts, and said to them: "Every **kingdom** divided against itself is brought to desolation, and every city or house divided against itself will not stand. If Satan cast out Satan, he is divided against himself. How then will **his kingdom** stand?

Col. 1:13-14 NLT For He has rescued us out of the darkness and gloom of **Satan's kingdom** and brought us into the **Kingdom of His dear Son**, who bought our freedom with His blood and forgave us all our sins.

Rev. 16:10-11 Then the fifth angel poured out his bowl on the throne of the beast, and **his kingdom** became full of darkness; and they gnawed their tongues because of the pain. They blasphemed the God of heaven because of their pains and their sores, and did not repent of their deeds.

JUDGMENT

GOD'S RIGHTEOUS JUDGMENT

This word oftentimes brings up dark thoughts of condemnation. However, there is another side of judgment that is from God's deep concern for His people. It's a warning for our protection. It makes us more keenly aware of the need for discernment to know what is acceptable before God, what is righteous, and what is unrighteous in God's eyes. We need to judge a place to go; an acceptable concert, party, or movie to attend; whether companionship with a person is good. It is especially important to judge whether it is wise to make an alliance with certain people in business transactions, or to be partners in business.

During the Old Testament times, Moses set up judges to handle their everyday affairs. *See Deuteronomy 1:16-17.* They were to judge righteously, for they were not to judge according to man's wisdom, or with partiality, but as servants of God. They had to take their complaints and disagreements before the Lord, and wait upon Him for righteous judgments.

We also read of Jehoshaphat setting up judges throughout the land, with clear instructions about judging with the "fear of the Lord upon them." They were to remember that "there is no iniquity with the Lord our God, no partiality, nor taking of bribes." *II Chronicles 19:5-7.* How is it that we recognize these words so well? Can it be that we are well aware of unrighteous judgments being made every day? There are prejudices against color of skin; also ethnic and religious prejudices are strongly expressed.

Preferences may be considered natural and acceptable, but intolerance or hatred for certain people groups is serious sin!

Ultimately God is the judge and deals justly with all mankind. No one is outside the perimeter of His view or His knowledge. He is able to assess and to handle any situation. His judgments are true and entirely righteous as we're told clearly in the Psalms. He is observing and judging continuously; judging the thoughts and actions, and even the intentions of mankind. Jeremiah 11:20 tells us, "the Lord tests the mind and the heart." He is well able to judge whether we truly love Him, or just give lip-service at convenient times. We may be very quiet about our opinions, but God knows what is stirring around in our thoughts. If we would pray the prayer of Psalm 19:14, "Let the words of my mouth and the meditation of my heart be acceptable in Your sight, O Lord, my strength and my Redeemer," we would be victorious over the temptation to hide sins in our hearts.

Although Jesus was given the authority to execute judgment, He did not seek His own will, but the will of His Father. Also, Jesus did not come for the purpose of judging and condemning, rather, "He came to seek and to save the lost," and give eternal life to all who would believe in Him, trusting what He was teaching day by day as He walked among them. *See John 3:17, 12:47-48, Luke 19:10.*

MANKIND JUDGING ONE ANOTHER

Our Scriptures cover all kinds of judging, and give us a great deal of wise counsel. But there is an area of judgment that you may still find confusing: Are we, or aren't we to judge others? The answer is two fold: yes and no. Let us take the 'no' first, especially the last verse of Romans 1 and the first six verses of chapter 2 where it warns about judging others. As you read these verses you can feel the hardheartedness and harshness of someone not only pointing their fingers at others, but demanding full payment: "an eye for an eye and a tooth for a tooth." There is no forgiveness, no grace, as though the one judging had never sinned or wronged anyone. The Word tells us that such a person is "treasuring up wrath for himself in the day of wrath," and that "God will give to each one according to his deeds." This is severe judgment. However, God is God! He is wise in everything He says and does! There can be no argument.

Maybe you haven't audibly expressed animosity or hatred, but your heart may have become hardened toward certain individuals. Be willing to observe your silent judgments and what God's will is in your day by day affairs and relationships. Jesus said in Matthew 7:1-2, "Judge not, that you be not judged. For with what judgment you judge, you will be judged; and with the measure you use, it will be measured back to you." It often appears that when someone is very critical of another person in regard to a specific sin and wants it to be dealt with; he is covering up his own involvement in the same kind of sin, or something similar. You see then how it fits— "judge not, that you be not judged." Beware!

Now to address the 'Yes' answer. In 1 Corinthians 6:1-7 we read about some serious things that came up between the families of the Church. There were some folks bringing others to court to settle their problems. Here Paul is writing that such matters should be judged by a wise man in the Church, and not to go before unbelievers in court. Each Christian has to evaluate what types of things belong to this category so that they might approach the governing body of their Church to become involved.

LET GOD BE THE JUDGE—HE IS WISE

How quickly we can get 'all bent out of shape.' I've experienced this. No, I would not take them to court, but I became deeply disturbed. I could not understand why a very simple plan that was agreed upon wasn't fulfilled as planned. Why didn't I foresee the possible turmoil and exasperating difficulties in connection with particular services that were to be rendered? This was one of my troubling questions.

However, I soon came to an understanding that when we give it all over to the Lord, He does a much better job of resolving the problems. He sees all and knows all. He is so wise in all His judgments. He strongly, yet lovingly instructed me in the way I should deal with the situation. This enabled me to let go, and let God be the Judge. Who knows how much more trouble I could have gotten into, if I had gone to court, or if I had gone to his Church to settle the issues? Forgiveness, rather than judgment, has freed me from Satan's torments.

As important as it seemed to me at the time, and to others who were concerned for us, that something very valuable should have been returned to us, God's peace came to my heart when I just released it all to the Lord, choosing mercy instead of a demand. *See James 2:12-13.* It caused my heart to praise the Lord, instead of carrying unforgiveness and the feeling that I wanted what belonged to me, and that it should be returned right away. It's wonderful to be free! Has Satan brought it to my attention since then? Oh yes, often for a while, but I let him know that it's all under the blood of Jesus, forgiven and cleansed from my heart. So since I was set free, I have no more pain when I recall this situation.

In closing, let me give the words of Paul in 2 Corinthians 5:10: "For we must all appear before the judgment seat of Christ, that each one may receive the things done in the body, according to what he has done, whether good or bad." God is righteous in all things, and leads us on righteous paths. Are you walking on that path with Him?

SCRIPTURES FOR
JUDGMENT

The Lord God is judge—-

Deut. 32:36 For the Lord will **judge** His people and have compassion on His servants, when He sees that their power is gone, and there is no one remaining bond or free.

Ps. 7:11 God is a just **judge**, and God is angry with the wicked every day.

Ps. 9:7-8 But the Lord shall endure forever; He has prepared His throne for judgment. He shall **judge** the world in righteousness, and He shall administer **judgment** for the peoples in uprightness.

Ps. 19:9 The fear of the Lord is clean *(pure)*, enduring forever; the **judgments** of the Lord are true and righteous altogether.

Ps. 96:13 For He is coming, for He is coming to **judge** the earth. He shall **judge** the world with righteousness, and the peoples with His truth.

Ps. 97:8-9 Zion hears and is glad, and the daughters of Judah rejoice because of your **judgments**, O Lord. For You, Lord, are most high above all the earth; You are exalted far above all gods.

Isa. 33:22 For the Lord is our **Judge**, the Lord is our Lawgiver, the Lord is our King; He will save us.

Jer. 11:20 But, O Lord of hosts, You who **judge** righteously, testing the mind and the heart, let me see Your vengeance on them, for to You I have revealed my cause.

Luke 18:6-8 NIV And the Lord said, "Listen to what the **unjust judge** says. And will not God bring justice for His chosen ones, who cry out to Him day and night? Will He keep putting them off? I tell you, He will see that they get justice, and quickly. However, when the Son of Man comes, will He find faith on the earth?"

John 5:26-27, 30 *Jesus is speaking*—- "For as the Father has life in Himself, so He has granted the Son to have life in Himself, and has given Him authority to execute **judgment** also, because He is the Son of Man. ...I can of Myself do nothing. As I hear, I **judge**; and My **judgment** is righteous, because I do not seek My own will but the will of the Father who sent Me."

John 12:30-32 Jesus answered and said, "This voice did not come because of Me, but for your sake. Now is the **judgment** of this world; now the ruler of this world will be cast out.

John 12:47-48 *Jesus is speaking*—- "And if anyone hears My words and does not believe, I do not **judge** him; for I did not come to **judge** the world but to save the world. *See also John 3:17*. He who rejects Me, and does not receive My words, has that which **judges** him—the word that I have spoken will **judge** him in the last day."

Rom 1:32—2:6 Who, knowing the righteous **judgment** of God, that those who practice such things are deserving of death, not only do the same but also approve of those who practice them. Therefore you are inexcusable, O man, whoever you are who **judge**, for in whatever you **judge** another you condemn yourself; for you who **judge** practice the same things. But we know that the **judgment** of God is according to truth against those who practice such things. And do you think this, O man, you who **judge** those practicing such things, and doing the same, that you will escape the **judgment** of God? Or do you despise the riches of His goodness, forbearance, and longsuffering, not knowing that the goodness of God leads you to repentance? But in accordance with your harness and your impenitent heart you are treasuring up for yourself wrath in the day of wrath and revelation of the righteous **judgment** of God, who "will render to each one according to his deeds." *Paul was quoting Psalm 62:12.*

Rom 5:16, 18 And the gift is not like that which came through the one who sinned. For the **judgment** which came from one offense, resulted in condemnation, but the free gift which came from many offenses resulted in justification. ...Therefore, as through one man's offense **judgment** came to all men, resulting in condemnation, even so through one Man's righteous act the free gift came to all men, resulting in justification of life.

Rom. 11:33 Oh, the depth of the riches both of the wisdom and knowledge of God! How unsearchable are His **judgments** and His ways past finding out!

Instructions for properly judging —-

Deut. 1:16-17 "Then I *(Moses)* commanded your **judges** at that time, saying, 'Hear the cases between your brethren, and **judge** righteously between a man and his brother or the stranger who is with him. You shall not show partiality in **judgment**; you shall hear the small as well as the great; you shall not be afraid in any man's presence, for the **judgment** is God's. The case that is too hard for you, bring to me, and I will hear it.'"

2 Chron. 19:5-7 Then he *(Jehoshaphat)* set **judges** in the land throughout all the fortified cities of Judah, city by city, and said to the **judges**, "Take heed to what you are doing, for you do not **judge** for man but for the Lord, who is with you in the **judgment**. Now therefore, let the fear of the Lord be upon you; take care to do it, for there is no iniquity with the Lord our God, no partiality, nor taking of bribes."

1 Cor. 6:1-7 Dare any of you, having a matter against another, go to law before the unrighteous, and not before the saints? Do you not know that the saints will **judge** the world? And if the world will be **judged** by you, are you unworthy to **judge** the smallest matters? Do you not know that we shall **judge** angels? How much more, things that pertain to this life? If then you have **judgments** concerning

things pertaining to this life, do you appoint those who are least esteemed by the church to **judge**? I say this to your shame. Is it so, that there is not a wise man among you, not even one, who will be able to **judge** between his brethren? But brother goes to law against brother, and that before unbelievers! Now therefore, it is already an utter failure for you that you go to law against one another. Why do you not rather accept wrong? Why do you not rather let yourselves be cheated? *See the entire chapter.*

1 Cor. 11:28-32 *This reference is part of the instructions for partaking of the Lord's Supper*—- But let a man examine himself, and so let him eat of the bread and drink of the cup. For he who eats and drinks in an unworthy manner eats and drinks **judgment** to himself, not discerning the Lord's body. For this reason many are weak and sick among you, and many sleep. For if we would **judge** ourselves, we would not be **judged**. But when we are **judged**, we are chastened by the Lord, that we may not be condemned with the world.

Judging one another—-

Matt. 7:1-2 *Jesus is speaking*—- "**Judge** not, that you be not **judged**. For with what **judgment** you **judge**, you will be **judged**; and with the measure you use, it will be measured back to you." *Also in Luke 6:37.*

Rom. 2:1 Therefore you are inexcusable, O man, whoever you are who **judge**, for in whatever you **judge** another you condemn yourself; for you who **judge** practice the same things.

Rom. 14:3-4 Let not him who eats despise him who does not eat, and let him who does not eat **judge** him who eats; for God has received him. Who are you to **judge** another's servant? To his own master he stands or falls. Indeed, he will be made to stand, for God is able to make him stand.

Rom. 14:10-13 But why do you **judge** your brother? Or why do you show contempt for your brother? For we shall all stand before the

judgment seat of Christ. For it is written: "As I live, says the Lord, every knee shall bow to Me, and every tongue shall confess to God." So then each of us shall give account of himself to God. Therefore, let us not **judge** one another anymore, but rather resolve this, not to put a stumbling block or a cause to fall in our brother's way.

1 Cor. 2:14-15 The natural man does not receive the things of the Spirit of God, for they are foolishness to him; nor can he know them, because they are spiritually discerned. But he who is spiritual **judges** all things, yet he himself is rightly **judged** by no one.

1 Cor. 4:1-5 Let a man so consider us as servants of Christ and stewards of the mysteries of God. Moreover, it is required in stewards that one be found faithful. But with me it is a very small thing that I should be **judged** by you or by a human court, In fact, I do not even **judge** myself. For I know of nothing against myself, yet I am not justified by this; but He who **judges** me is the Lord. Therefore **judge** nothing before the time, until the Lord comes, who will both bring to light the hidden things of darkness and reveal the counsels of the hearts. Then each one's praise will come from God.

1 Cor. 10:28-29 But if anyone says to you, "This was offered to idols," do not eat it for the sake of the one who told you, and for conscience' sake; for "the earth is the Lord's, and all its fullness." "Conscience," I say, not your own, but that of the other. For why is my liberty **judged** by another man's conscience?

The final Judgment Day—-

Matt. 5:21-22a *Jesus is speaking*—- "You have heard that it was said to those of old, 'You shall not murder, and whoever murders will be in danger of the **judgment**.' But I say to you that whoever is angry with his brother without a cause shall be in danger of **judgment**."

Matt. 12:35-37 *Jesus is speaking*—- "A good man out of the good treasure of his heart brings forth good things, and an evil man out of the evil treasure brings forth evil things. But I say to you that for every idle word men may speak, they will give account of it in the Day of **Judgment**. For by your words you will be justified, and by your words you will be condemned."

2 Cor. 5:9-10 Therefore we make it our aim, whether present or absent, to be well pleasing to Him. For we must all appear before the **judgment** seat of Christ, that each one may receive the things done in the body, according to what he has done, whether good or bad.

Heb. 9:27 And as it is appointed for men to die once, but after this the **judgment**...

James 2:13-14 So speak and so do as those who will be **judged** by the law of liberty. For **judgment** is without mercy to the one who has shown no mercy. Mercy triumphs over **judgment**.

2 Peter 2:3 By covetousness they *(the false prophets)* will exploit you with deceptive words; for a long time their **judgment** has not been idle, and their destruction does not slumber.

Jude vs6 And the angels who did not keep their proper domain, but left their own abode, He has reserved in everlasting chains under darkness for the **judgment** of the great day.

Jude 14-15 Now Enoch, the seventh from Adam, prophesied about these men also, saying, "Behold, the Lord comes with ten thousands of His saints, "to execute **judgment** on all, to convict all who are ungodly among them of all their ungodly deeds which they have committed in an ungodly way, and of all the harsh things which ungodly sinners have spoken against Him."

Rev. 19:1-2 After these things I heard a loud voice of a great multitude in heaven, saying, "Alleluia! Salvation and glory and honor and power belong to the Lord our God! For true and righteous are His **judgments**, because He has **judged** the great harlot, who corrupted the earth with her fornication; and He has avenged on her the blood of His servants shed by her.

COME

COME, LET US REASON TOGETHER

We all like invitations, especially if it's an invitation to enjoy dinner together. How about a day at their cottage, including a boat ride? Not many get a call to come along for a paid vacation, traveling to exotic places, or an invitation to fulfill a personal deep desire! Would you like an invitation to an exciting celebration? Today I am invited out. She said, "Come, let's go out for lunch." It will be a pleasure to be with this dear friend, so I quickly accepted!

However, what could be more blessed than to hear the Lord say, "Come!" As I read these Scriptures, my heart leaps with joy. When I hear His invitation to come– "Come to worship and glorify Him, come to sing, come to sing joyfully to the Rock of our salvation," I can't help but rejoice in the tremendous blessings the Lord has provided for us, especially since it's my privilege to accept His invitations!

In Isaiah 1:18, we hear the Lord say, "Come, let us reason together. Though your sins are like scarlet they shall be as white as snow; though they be red like crimson, they shall be as wool." You may still be living in a sin that causes extreme pain, but you just don't know how to get unhooked, or untangled from its life squeezing tentacles. You know that God can't be pleased, but it's too hard to even pray. It seems to you, like God wouldn't listen if you prayed. Basically God is saying, "Come to Me, let's talk about it. You can't make the changes without Me. All you can do is humbly confess your sin, then I will cleanse your heart. I will give you the strength to refuse sin. Don't keep running, but come to Me and I will bless you."

Possibly you feel like something is weighing you down, holding you back from answering His call to come. In Matthew 11:28, we hear Jesus saying, "Come to Me, all you who labor and are heavy laden, and I will give you rest." Jesus wants you to cast all your burdens upon Him. He's the greatest solver of the things that cause confusion and frustration. When you surrender your all to the Lord it's really like giving up a string of rusty tin cans, loaded with mud, stones and garbage. You know they've been bouncing into the air, coming down on your head and banging against your back. And they just bounce up and hit you again and again.

COME FOR A NEW LIFE—IN CHRIST

God has a wonderful replacement, better than silver and gold– a new life in Christ—eternal life! You already know that the old ways don't work at all: the fears, doubts, questioning God's fairness or His ability to help you. Some of your sins may seem so small and too insignificant to bother about, but they have put you in bondage just the same. They will keep you bound and hinder you from experiencing the fullness of joy that Jesus gives. Can you see the rebellion and disobedience? Remember that it's "the little foxes that spoil the vine," as we read in Song of Solomon 2:15.

What God has for you is much more than earthly goods, or food that temporarily satisfies your taste buds and stomach. What He offers, releases you from the demands of the flesh, and provides satisfaction through blessings on a much higher level. In Isaiah 55:1, we hear the call– "Come everyone who is thirsty, come to the waters. You have no money? Come buy and eat; buy without money and without price." And Jesus is calling out to you in John 6:35 and 37–"I am the bread of life. He who comes to Me shall never hunger, and he who believes in Me shall never thirst. ...All that the Father gives Me will come to Me, and the one who comes to Me I will by no means cast out."

We deserve nothing with our good deeds. We couldn't even earn enough with over-time, or credits for any number of good works; credits for intelligence, or by giving large gifts to the Church, or a charity. There is no way that anyone could earn their way to be worthy of God's love gifts. Many are trying to do this by good works, and are wearing themselves out by using a wrong method. No one else can offer us the peace and rest that Jesus can give. No one! And when you grasp hold of these truths, you'll be ready to surrender your all to Him more quickly, and with understanding. He will not resist those who humbly come to Him, no matter how ugly your sins, nor how many years you have lived in sin.

Jesus knew His mission before He came to this earth. In Matthew 9:12-13 we find one of those purposes: "Those who are well have no need of a physician, but those who are sick. But go and learn what this means; 'I desire mercy and not sacrifice,' For I did not come to call the righteous, but sinners, to repentance." As you read the other chapters you discover all that goes with repentance and forgiveness. Jesus paid the full price for our salvation.

God's Word is full of wonderful truths, such as these—Jesus is "able to save to the uttermost all those who come to God through Him." *Heb.7:25* Jesus said—"I am the way, the truth and the life. No one comes to the Father except through Me." *John 14:6* Jesus wants to fellowship with you. He offers comfort and healing. Through Him, God becomes your Father in heaven, then you can freely go to Him in prayer, asking for things you need. He wants to give you wisdom, insights, understanding and much more, which you'll discover as you study His Word.

What could hold you back from fully trusting Him and fully giving up on yourself? When you really surrender to the Lord Jesus, you'll be so grateful that you gave all your past striving and stumbling around in despair to Him. You'll find that true rest, true hope and genuine soul satisfaction will come into your heart as you accept the Lord's invitation to "Come, follow Me."

COME AND RECEIVE WONDERFUL BLESSINGS

If you come to Jesus as a repentant sinner, and accept the cleansing of His blood, then you can know the joy of His unfailing love and the tremendous blessings that come as you are worshiping

Him. He will enable you to trust Him and obey Him. Obedience to His will protects us from many snares that the devil has set up for catching us unawares. Obedience also opens doors to new opportunities for success and prosperity.

Jesus also pointed out another tremendous blessing in coming to Him; it is in Luke 6:47-48, "Whoever comes to Me, and hears My sayings and does them, I will show you whom he is like: He is like a man building a house, who dug deep and laid the foundation on the rock. And when the flood arose, the stream beat vehemently against that house, and could not shake it, for it was founded on the rock." This is saying that when you have tough things to deal with in life, you won't be knocked down. Jesus' life within you gives sustaining strength. He can lead you to solutions and provide unlimited guidance in so many helpful ways.

Every promise of God is for those who "believe on the Lord Jesus Christ," and when you believe, you can hear the Holy Spirit whisper words like these to you, "Come, and receive these blessings that I offer you by faith in Jesus." There is not a more wonderful, glorious and peaceful way to live. When you grow in your faith and love for the Lord, you will want to "shout for joy to the Lord." You will desire to "worship Him with gladness and with joyful songs."

There is also a large group of Scriptures attached to this chapter under the heading, "The Master is coming, be watchful as you wait." These Scriptures are projecting the time that Jesus comes for His own. Jesus has made everything so clear about the importance of an absolute commitment to Him, so if you are merely committed to a Church, or a Pastor, or a religion, the door will be shut tightly, and no man can open it. However, if you are a true worshiper, you "will worship the Father in spirit and truth; for the Father is seeking such to worship Him. God is Spirit, and those who worship Him must worship in spirit and truth." *John 4:23-24.*

This is a heart worshiping in response to the truths of God's Word, not just on an intellectual level, or worshiping in a way that pleases self; rather it is the kind of worship that comes from the spirit which has come alive with the Spirit of Jesus living within. There arises a desire to glorify Him; exalting the name of Jesus. Honor and glory and praise flows from the heart of those who truly love the Lord!

I invite you to hear the call of Psalm 95, where it says, "Oh come, let us sing to the Lord! Let us shout joyfully to the Rock of our salvation. Let us come before His presence with thanksgiving; let us shout joyfully to Him with psalms. ...O come, let us worship and bow down; let us kneel before the Lord our Maker. For He is our God, and we are the people of His pasture, and the sheep of His hand."

As the song says it– "O come let us adore Him, Christ the Lord." The more you adore the Lord, and worship Him from the depths of your heart; your joy will rise higher and higher!

SCRIPTURES FOR
C O M E

Come to worship and sing—

Ps. 86:9 All nations whom You have made shall **come** and worship.

Ps. 95:1-2, 6-7 O **come**, let us sing to the Lord! Let us shout joyfully to the Rock of our salvation. Let us **come** before His presence with thanksgiving; let us shout joyfully to Him with psalms. ....O **come**, let us worship and bow down; let us kneel before the Lord our Maker. For He is our God, and we are the people of His pasture, and the sheep of His hand.

Ps. 100:1-2 NIV Shout for joy to the Lord, all the earth. Worship the Lord with gladness; **come** before Him with joyful songs.

John 4:21, 23-24 Jesus said to her, "Woman, believe Me, the hour is **coming** when you will neither on this mountain, nor in Jerusalem, worship the Father. ...But the hour is **coming** and now is, when the true worshipers will worship the Father in spirit and truth; for the Father is seeking such to worship Him. God is Spirit, and those who worship Him must worship in spirit and truth."

Heb. 11:6 But without faith it is impossible to please Him, for he who **comes** to God must believe that He is and that He is a rewarder of those who diligently seek Him.

Come for God's blessings—

Ps. 62:1 Truly my soul waits for God; from Him **comes** my salvation.

Prov. 9:3b-6 She *(wisdom)* cries out from the highest places of the city, "Whoever is simple, let him turn in here!" As for him who lacks understanding, she says to him; "**Come** eat of my bread and drink of the wine I have mixed. Forsake foolishness and live, and go in the way of understanding."

Isa. 1:18-20 "**Come** now, and let us reason together," says the Lord. "Though your sins are like scarlet, they shall be as white as snow; though they be red like crimson, they shall be as wool. If you are willing and obedient, you shall eat the good of the land; but if you refuse and rebel, you shall be devoured by the sword; for the mouth of the Lord has spoken.

Isa. 55:1 "Ho! Everyone who thirsts, **come** to the waters; and you who have no money, **come**; buy and eat. Yes, **come**, buy wine and milk without money and without price."

Some reasons why Jesus had to come to the earth—

Matt. 8:7 And Jesus said to him, "I will **come** and heal him."

Matt. 9:12-13 When Jesus heard that, He said to them, "Those who are well have no need of a physician, but those who are sick. But go and learn what this means; 'I desire mercy and not sacrifice.' For I did not **come** to call the righteous, but sinners, to repentance" *Also see Luke 15, the parables of the Lost Sheep, the Lost Coin and the Lost Son; all referring to how much God cares for those who are yet sinners, who need to be found. Jesus died for them too.*

Matt. 11:28 *Jesus was speaking—* "**Come** to Me, all you who labor and are heavy laden, and I will give you rest."

Mark 1:38 But He said to them, "Let us go into the next towns, that I may preach there also, because for this purpose I have come forth."

Luke 19:9-10 And Jesus said to him, "Today salvation has **come** to this house, because he also is a son of Abraham; for the Son of Man has **come** to seek and to save that which was lost."

John 1:6-8 There was a man sent from God, whose name was John. This man **came** for a witness, to bear witness of the Light, that all through him might believe. He was not that Light, but was sent to bear witness of that Light.

John 1:11-15 He *(Jesus)* **came** to His own, and His own did not receive Him. But as many as received Him, to them He gave the right to become children of God. To those who believe in His name: who were born, not of blood, nor of the will of the flesh, or of the will of man, but of God. And the Word became flesh and dwelt among us, and we beheld His glory, the glory of the Father, full of grace and truth. John bore witness of Him and cried out, saying, "This was He of whom I said, 'He who **comes** after me is preferred before me, for He was before me.'"

John 1:29-30 The next day John saw Jesus **coming** toward him, and said, "Behold! The Lamb of God who takes away the sin of the world! "This is He of whom I said, 'After me **comes** a Man who is preferred before me, for He was before me.'"

John 5:24 "Most assuredly, I say to you, he who hears My word and believes in Him who sent Me has everlasting life, and shall **not come** into judgment, but has passed from death into life."

John 6:32-33 Then Jesus said to them, "Most assuredly, I say to you, Moses did not give you the bread from heaven, but My Father gives you the true bread from heaven. For the bread of God is He who **comes** down from heaven and gives life to the world."

John 6:48-51 "I am the bread of life. Your fathers ate the manna in the wilderness, and are dead. This is the bread which **comes** down from heaven, that one may eat of it and not die. I am the living bread which **came** down from heaven. If anyone eats of this bread, he will live forever; and the bread that I shall give is my flesh, which I shall give for the life of the world."

John 11:23-27, 34, 43-44 Jesus said to her, "Your brother will rise again." Martha said to Him, "I know that he will rise again in the resurrection at the last day." Jesus said to her, "I am the resurrection and the life. He who believes in Me, though he may die, he shall live. And whoever lives and believes in Me shall never die. Do you believe this?" She said to Him, "Yes, Lord, I believe that You are the Christ, the Son of God, who is to **come** into the world." ...And He said, "Where have you laid him?" They said to Him, "Lord, **come** and see." ...Now when He had said these things, He cried with a loud voice, "Lazarus **come** forth!" And he who had died came out bound hand and foot with grave-clothes, and his face was wrapped with a cloth. Jesus said to them, "Loose him, and let him go."

Heb. 7:25 Therefore He is also able to save to the uttermost those who **come** to God through Him, since He always lives to make intercession for them.

Heb. 10:8-10 Previously saying, "Sacrifice and offering, burnt offerings, and offerings for sin You did not desire, nor had pleasure in them" (which are offered according to the law), then He said, "Behold, I have **come** to do Your will, O God." He takes away the first that He may establish the second. By that will we have been sanctified through the offering of the body of Jesus Christ once for all.

Come to Jesus; hear Him, believe Him, receive Him, follow Him—

Matt. 4:19-20 NIV **"Come**, follow Me," Jesus said, "and I will make you fishers of men." At once they *(Simon Peter and his brother Andrew)* left their nets and followed Him. *Also see Mark 1:16-18, John 1:35-39.*

Matt. 14:28-29 And Peter answered Him and said, "Lord, if it is You, command me to **come** to You on the water." So He said, "**Come**." And when Peter had **come** down out of the boat, he walked on the water to go to Jesus.

Mark 10:21 Then Jesus, looking at him *(the man called 'Rich Young Ruler')*. "One thing you lack: Go your way, sell whatever you have and give to the poor, and you will have treasure in heaven; and **come**, take up the cross, and follow Me."

Luke 6:47-48 "Whoever **comes** to Me, and hears My sayings and does them, I will show you whom he is like: He is like a man building a house, who dug deep and laid the foundation on the rock. And when the flood arose, the stream beat vehemently against that house, and could not shake it, for it was founded on the rock."

Luke 9:23 Then He said to them all, "If anyone desires to **come** after Me, let him deny himself, and take up his cross daily and follow Me."

John 3:20-21, 31 *Jesus is speaking—* "For everyone practicing evil hates the light and does **not come** to the light, lest his deeds should be exposed, but he who does the truth **comes** to the light, that his deeds may be clearly seen, that they have been done in God." ...*John the Baptist is speaking—* "He who **comes** from above is above all; he who is of the earth is earthly and speaks of the earth. He who **comes** from heaven is above all."

John 5:43-44 "I have **come** in My Father's name, and you do not receive Me; if another **comes** in his own name, him you will receive. How can you believe, who receive honor from one another, and do not seek the honor that **comes** from the only God?"

John 6:35-38 And Jesus said to them, "I am the bread of life. He who **comes** to Me shall never hunger, and he who believes in Me shall never thirst. But I say to you that you have seen Me and yet do not believe. All that the Father gives Me will **come** to Me, and the one who **comes** to Me I will by no means cast out. For I have **come** down from heaven, not to do My own will, but the will of Him who sent Me."

John 6:43-45 Jesus therefore answered and said to them, "Do not murmur among yourselves. No one can **come** to Me unless the

Father who sent Me draws him; and I will raise him up at the last day. It is written in the prophets, 'And they shall all be taught by God!' Therefore everyone who has heard and learned from the Father **comes** to Me."

John 7:28-31 Then Jesus cried out, as He taught in the temple, saying, "You both know Me, and you know where I am from; and I have **not come** of Myself, but He who sent Me is true, whom you do not know. But I know Him, for I am from Him, and He sent Me." Therefore they sought to take Him; but no one laid a hand on Him, because His hour had **not yet come**. And many of the people believed in Him, and said, "When the Christ **comes**, will He do more signs than these which this Man has done?"

John 7: 33-34 Then Jesus said to them, "I shall be with you a little while longer, and then I go to Him who sent Me. You will seek Me and not find Me, and where I am you **cannot come.**

John 7:37-39 On the last day, that great day of the feast, Jesus stood and cried out saying, "If anyone thirsts, let him **come** to Me and drink. He who believes in Me, as the Scripture has said, out of his heart will flow rivers of living water." But this He spoke concerning the Spirit, whom those believing in Him would receive; for the Holy Spirit was not yet given, because Jesus was not yet glorified.

After Jesus' resurrection, "Come and see"—

Matt. 28:5-6 NIV The angel said to the women, "Do not be afraid, for I know that you are looking for Jesus, who was crucified. He is not here; He has risen, just as He said. **Come** and see the place where He lay.

Matt. 28:9 NIV Suddenly Jesus met them. "Greetings," He said. They came to Him, clasped His feet and worshiped Him.

The Master is coming, be watchful as you wait—

The following references are a part of Jesus' teaching about His second coming—-

Matt. 16:27-28 "For the Son of Man will **come** in the glory of His Father with His angels, and then He will reward each according to his works. Assuredly, I say to you, there are some standing here who shall not taste death till they see the Son of Man **coming** in His kingdom."

Matt. 23:39 NIV "For I tell you, you will not see Me again until you say, 'Blessed is He who **comes** in the name of the Lord.'"

Matt. 24:4-6 NIV Jesus answered: "Watch out that no one deceives you. For many will **come** in My name, claiming, 'I am the Christ,' and will deceive many. You will hear of wars and rumors of wars, but see to it that you are not alarmed. Such things must happen, but the end is still to **come**."

Matt. 24:12-14 NIV "Because of the increase of wickedness, the love of most will grow cold, but he who stands firm to the end will be saved. And this gospel of the kingdom will be preached in the whole world as a testimony to all nations, and then the end will **come**."

Matt. 25:6 NIV "At midnight the cry rang out: 'Here's the bridegroom! **Come** out to meet him!'"

Matt. 25:21 NIV *This is in the Parable of the Talents—-* "His master replied, 'Well done, good and faithful servant! You have been faithful with a few things; I will put you in charge of many things. **Come** and share your master's happiness!'" *This was also the master's response to the man who had doubled his 2 talents in verse 23.*

Matt. 25:34-36 NIV "Then the King will say to those on his right, '**Come**, you who are blessed by my Father; take your inheritance, the kingdom prepared for you since the creation of the world. For I was hungry and you gave me something to eat, I was thirsty and you gave me something to drink, I was a stranger and you invited me in, I needed clothes and you clothed me, I was sick and you looked after me, I was in prison and you came to visit me.'"

Matt. 26:64 NIV "Yes, it is as you say," Jesus replied. "But I say to all of you: In the future you will see the Son of Man sitting at the right hand of the Mighty One and **coming** on the clouds of heaven."

Mark 8:38 NIV "If anyone is ashamed of Me and My words in this adulterous and sinful generation, the Son of Man will be ashamed of him when He **comes** in His Father's glory with the holy angels."

Luke 12:35-40 NIV "Be dressed ready for service and keep your lamps burning, like men waiting for their master to return from a wedding banquet, so that when he **come** and knocks they can immediately open the door for him. It will be good for those servants whose master finds them watching when he **comes**. I tell you the truth, he will dress himself to serve, will have them recline at the table and will **come** and wait on them. It will be good for those servants whose master finds them ready, even if he **comes** in the second or third watch of the night. But understand this: If the owner of the house had known at what hour the thief was **coming**, he would not have let his house be broken into. You also must be ready, because the Son of Man will **come** at an hour when you do not expect Him."

Luke 18:6-8 NIV And the Lord said, "Listen to what the unjust judge says. And will not God bring about justice for His chosen ones, who cry out to Him day and night? Will He keep putting them off? I tell you, He will see that they get justice, and quickly. However, when the Son of Man **comes**, will He find faith on the earth?"

Acts 1:11 NIV "Men of Galilee, they said, "why do you stand here looking into the sky? This same Jesus, who has been taken from you into heaven, will **come** back in the same way you have seen Him go into heaven."

Rev. 1:7-8 Behold, He is **coming** with clouds, and every eye will see Him, even they who pierced Him, and all the tribes of the earth will mourn because of Him. Even so, Amen. "I am the Alpha and the Omega, the Beginning and the End," says the Lord, "who is and who was and who is to **come**, the Almighty."

Rev. 22:16-17 "I, Jesus, have sent My angel to testify to you these things in the churches. I am the Root and the Off-spring of David, the Bright and Morning Star." And the Spirit and the bride say, "**Come!**" And let him who hears say, "**Come!**" And let him who thirsts **come**. Whoever desires, let him take the water of life freely.

Rev. 22:20-21 He who testifies to these things says, "Surely I am **coming** quickly." The grace of our Lord Jesus Christ be with you all. Amen

LISTEN

LISTENING IS SERIOUS BUSINESS

In counseling training there is a class especially for learning to listen. They have to become good listeners in order to counsel others. But this is not actually new to anyone, for we've heard this at home and in school through the years, "Listen to me!" Actually, in every training class, music lessons, in sports, seminars, conferences, and the list could go on, because in order to learn, we have to LISTEN!

Listening, or not listening, can be a very critical issue. Perhaps you have had a very serious situation in your life. Inability to hear may cause many kinds of serious problems, such as an accident with an emergency vehicle, or a lack of hearing a warning signal of another kind. Also, not really listening carefully may cause one to miss their plane, or miss taking medications at the proper time. Even hearing one number wrong for making an essential phone call can be serious. Many undesirable consequences can result from not listening.

Some people have had to submit to surgeries because they did not listen to the warnings about their diet. We have been taught about healthful exercise and the need to only eat live foods, such as fruits, vegetables, and whole grains, along with good meats, which can make a huge difference in preventing many serious physical problems. Yet we excuse ourselves so easily for eating dead substances, called junk food, and drink fluids that are deteriorating our health, then laugh it off, but if we won't listen, the catching up will cause us painful times of sickness, or diseases. Also, when we eat and drink the wrong things, it affects our actions; we may become hyper, experience brain fog, become cranky, or even more severe behavior problems.

Adults and children alike are struggling with these difficulties, and the whole family suffers. We can make very bad decisions, and say things that we would not have said if we were able to control ourselves mentally and emotionally. There's a huge price to pay for not listening, and recognizing our real need to love and respect one another, so that we would make the necessary changes – right now, today!

LISTENING TO GOD IS VERY IMPORTANT

Listening to God's voice is very important! Just think of the Deuteronomy 30:19 reference, where God said, "This day I call heaven and earth as witnesses against you that I have set before you life and death, blessings and curses. Now choose life, so that you and your children may live and that you may love the Lord your God, listen to His voice and hold fast to Him. For the Lord is your life." This is a word from God that we can't afford to ignore or even to procrastinate with our decision to choose life. This is an 'every day' decision.

Psalm 81 is an appeal for Israel's repentance. These words from verses 8 and 11-14 are surely applicable to our nation today. "Hear, O My people, and I will admonish you! O Israel, if you will listen to Me! ...But my people would not heed My voice, and Israel would have none of Me. So I gave them over to their own stubborn heart, to walk in their own counsels. Oh, that My people would listen to Me, that Israel would walk in My ways! I would soon subdue their enemies, and turn My hand against their adversaries." The blessings of God do not just automatically flow in our direction. We must continuously listen to the counsel of God's Word in order to walk a path of righteousness and peace.

In the New Testament, James 1:22 NIV says, "Do not merely listen to the Word, and so deceive yourselves. Do what it says." It is very possible that you and I have read wonderful passages from God's Word, and read many books about great subjects of the Word, enjoying every minute of the time spent, but never asked the Lord if that Word we heard had some significance for His instructions for that day. Sometimes we just kind of roll along in our reading without really listening. I've had times when I've had to re-read and re-read again one or more paragraphs because I hadn't really heard what the author was conveying. So many other thoughts can bombard our minds, and we have to take time to pray for the Holy Spirit to bring back our ability to listen and then to follow up with obedience.

Remember that every choice we make either pleases God, or displeases Him. Can it be any other way? He has created us for His pleasure, to serve Him in righteousness, and for His glory. Not as a slave driver, but as Almighty God, whose wisdom and holy purposes bring us to higher levels than we could ever reach with our human wisdom or mental skills. He has given us the instructions and guidance that we need in His Word; also a blue print to follow for our protection, and the greatest blessings of love, peace and joy. However, we must listen!

LISTEN FOR GOD'S WISDOM

Proverbs is a book that describes who the righteous are, and the blessings God has prepared for them, in contrast with the wicked and the consequences for ignoring God. Listening to these words of wisdom is of utmost importance. Several verses in Proverbs emphasize listening as we can hear God speaking: "Let the wise listen;" "Listen, my son;" "My son, pay attention to my wisdom, listen well to my words;" "Listen to my instruction and be wise;" "The way of a fool seems right to him, but a wise man listens to advice." We may think of ourselves to be wise, but it is crucial to seek God's wisdom, His instructions, and even corrections, remembering that His ways are not like ours, and His thoughts are not down on our level. *See Isaiah 55:8-9.* He is perfect in all His thoughts and in His ways.

God's 'Majors and Generals' along the years of history would have totally bombed out if they had not been listening for distinct directions. Think of Noah, Abraham, Moses, Samuel, David, Isaiah and Jeremiah, along with God's leaders in the New Testament. There would have been a very sad closing to their lives, as there was for others around them. Many failed to listen to God. Consider Samson, King Saul, and many other kings of Israel and of Judah, who just ignored God as though He didn't exist. Jonah almost lost out, but God's patience and mercy were at work to preserve him, and saved the city of Nineveh from total destruction.

God chose each man for a special purpose. He already knew everything about each one of them, and knew what they could become when He anointed them and prepared them for special services through the process of their 'listening to His voice.' In John 10:27 NIV we read, "My sheep listen to My voice; I know them, and they follow Me." That gives me a strong incentive to listen more carefully, and to heed His voice. I don't want to miss doing what He has for me to do, or any part of His plan for my life. Do you see the importance for you to hear Him and obey too?

I've had some awesome experiences when I needed explicit instructions for finding a house, or a specific highway. One day I received a phone call for help on the crisis line. After I listened carefully and wrote down pertinent information, I hurried to the young lady. I had never met her, but since I had the right address and I told her what my van looked like, it would work out just fine. She had retreated to her sister's house in another area of the city due to marital problems. When I was near the right street, which was about 12 miles from my home *(city driving)*, I couldn't find the paper with the correct address on it. So I prayed for the Lord to lead me. I was quite sure that I remembered the correct street where she was staying; but what was that house number? I drove slowly for a couple blocks, praying all the way, and then felt led to stop in front of a particular house. Before I could get out of the car, she came from that exact house. The Lord led me right there. He has tested my listening skills many other times; He's been the faithful One to graciously help me each time.

LISTEN TO GOD'S WORD

Make listening to His Word top priority. As you hear any other voice, make sure that the message harmonizes with God's Word, and comes to you with peace as your discerning factor. Satan has set snares to distract our attention, and he even tells us that the godly thing you were intending to do is not really important, especially not right now. He may give a long lingo about your unimportance, and that no one would listen to you anyway. He'll have lots to say to discourage you from doing what God has instructed.

In 1 Samuel 3 we read about Samuel's experiences while growing up in the tabernacle in Shiloh, under the guidance of Eli the priest. One night Samuel heard someone call him by name, and he went to Eli to see what he wanted. Eli said that he hadn't called him so he should go back to bed. This happened two more times. The third time Eli realized that the Lord was calling, so he told Samuel that he should go back and lie down, but when God calls again say this: "Speak, Lord, for your servant is listening."

Samuel did as he was instructed. Then 1 Samuel 3:10 is such an awesome verse, listen to this: "Now the Lord came and stood and called as at other times, "Samuel! Samuel!" And Samuel answered, "Speak, for Your servant hears." Then the Lord revealed to him the plans he had for punishing Eli's two sons for they continued to make themselves contemptible in God's sight. Another important verse I want to show you is verse 19 NIV: "The Lord was with Samuel as he grew up, and he let none of His words fall to the ground." The awesomeness of these verses reminds me of Psalm 46:10, "Be still and know that I am God; I will be exalted among the nations, I will be exalted in the earth!"

As you learn God's rules for living, your desire for listening to Him will grow, and the things of this world will become less and less attractive, and even undesirable. God listens to fervent prayers of those whose hearts are attuned to Him; those who truly seek to please Him in every area of their lives. In fact, He is also looking for those who want to live for him. This Old Testament Scripture from 2 Chronicles 16:9 says, "For the eyes of the Lord run to and fro throughout the whole earth, to show Himself strong on behalf of those whose heart is loyal to Him." God is always watching and ready to bless those who desire to please Him.

GOD HEARS THE REPENTANT HEART

Even the one living deep in sin, who wants to know Him and obey Him, who repents and pleads for God's forgiveness, will be heard, and God will respond with compassionate love and mercy. The repentant thief on the cross is a prime example. Every person who has ever come to the Lord, was a sinner needing the cleansing blood of Jesus. The only way to be saved is by God's grace, through faith in the Lord Jesus Christ. *Galatians 2:8-10.* And 1 John 1:7 and 9 tell us about confessing our sins—"If we walk in the light as He is in the light, we have fellowship with one another, and the blood of Jesus Christ His Son cleanses us from all sin. ...If we confess our sins, He is faithful and just to forgive us our sins and to cleanse us from all unrighteousness." This is reason to praise the Lord with our whole heart!

If you have not read Pat Robertson's book Six Steps to Spiritual Revival,[7] you will want get a copy. It is just a little book, but exceptionally powerful as it gives a path to revival in an orderly form, step by step. He has taught the Word over several decades and has learned to listen to God's voice in the midst of overwhelming circumstances. He shares some awesome experiences from his own life where the power of God intervened in God's exact timing. There are also several victorious experiences written in the book that other people have encountered. His life is an amazing example of humble service to the Lord and in ministry to people everywhere, who want to see God meet their needs.

Can you see how important it is to listen to God's Word and His voice so that you can follow His instructions and experience His blessings? As you continue to seek the Lord, and listen to His voice, He multiplies opportunities that will broaden the possibilities of what you can do. He will give directions for improving the skills He planted in you and provide opportunities to use the gifts that are given to you for fulfilling His purposes in your life. You are very important to Him. He wants to increase your blessings!

Read the attached Scriptures very carefully, and listen for the Lord's personal instructions as the Holy Spirit will respond to your seeking heart. Circle the Scriptures that you know you should begin working with right away. Consider this, you can lose out if you put off for tomorrow, which usually becomes 'much later' or never, what should be done today. God's greatest gifts of love and peace always follow obedience!

SCRIPTURES FOR
L I S T E N

Listen to the Lord, to His Word, Jesus—-

Deut. 30:19-20 NIV This day I call heaven and earth as witnesses against you that I have set before you life and death, blessings and curses. Now choose life, so that you and your children may live and that you may love the Lord your God, **listen** to His voice and hold fast to Him. For the Lord is your life.

1 Sam. 3:8b-10 NIV Then Eli realized that the Lord was calling the boy. So Eli told Samuel, "Go and lie down, and if He calls you, say, "Speak, Lord, for your servant is **listening**." So Samuel went and lay down in his place. The Lord came and stood there, calling as at the other times. "Samuel! Samuel!" Then Samuel said, "Speak, for your servant is **listening**."

Neh. 8:2-3 NIV So on the first day of the seventh month Ezra the priest brought the Law before the assembly, which was made up of the men and women and all who were able to understand. He read it aloud from daybreak till noon as he faced the square before the Water Gate in the presence of men, women and others who could understand. And all the people **listened** attentively to the Book of the Law.

Ps. 81:8, 13-14 "Hear, O My people, and I will admonish you! O Israel, if you will **listen** to Me! ...Oh, that My people would **listen** to Me, that Israel would walk in My ways! I would soon subdue their enemies, and turn my hand against their adversaries."

Mark 9:7 NIV Then a cloud appeared and enveloped them, and a voice came from the cloud: "This is My Son, whom I love, **listen** to Him!"

John 8:42-43 Jesus said to them, "If God were your Father, you would love Me, for I proceeded forth and came from God; nor have I come of Myself, but He sent Me. "Why do you not understand My speech? Because you are not able to **listen** to My word."

John 10:27-28 NIV "My sheep **listen** to my voice; I know them, and they follow Me. I give them eternal life and they shall never perish; no one can snatch them out of My hand."

Listen to His servants—-

Deut. 18:15, 18b-19 NIV "The Lord your God will raise up for you a Prophet like me *(Moses)* from among your own brothers. You must **listen** to him." ..."I will put My words in his mouth, and he will tell them everything I command him. If anyone does not **listen** to My words that the Prophet speaks in My name, I Myself will call him to account." *Also Acts 3:22, 23.*

Is. 51:1 NIV "**Listen** to me, you who pursue righteousness and who seek the Lord: Look to the Rock from which you were cut and to the quarry from which you were hewn."

Isa. 55:2 NIV Why spend money on what is not bread, and your labor on what does not satisfy? **Listen, listen** to me, and eat what is good, and your soul will delight in the richest of fare.

Mark 6:10-13 NIV *Jesus was instructing the twelve—-* "Whenever you enter a house, stay there until you leave that town. And if any place will not welcome you or **listen** to you, shake the dust off your feet when you leave, as a testimony against them." They went out and preached that people should repent. They drove out many demons and anointed many sick people with oil and healed them.

Luke 10:16 NIV "He who **listens** to you, **listens** to Me; he who rejects you rejects Me, but he who rejects Me rejects Him who sent Me."

Acts 13:14-16 But when they departed from Perga, they came to Antioch in Pisidia, and went into the synagogue on the Sabbath day and sat down. And after the reading of the Law and the Prophets, the rulers of the synagogue sent to them, saying, "Men and brethren, if you have any word of exhortation for the people, say on." Then Paul stood up, and motioning with his hand said, "Men of Israel, and you who fear God, **listen**: ..."

1 John 4:4-6 You, dear children, are from God and have overcome them, because the One who is in you is greater than the one who is in the world. They are from the world and therefore speak from the viewpoint of the world, and the world **listens** to them. We are from God, and whoever knows God **listens** to us; but whoever is not from God does not **listen** to us. This is how we recognize the Spirit of truth and the spirit of falsehood.

Listen and submit to wisdom and guidance—-

Prov. 1:5, 6, 32-33 NIV Let the wise **listen** and add to their learning, and let the discerning get guidance—for understanding proverbs and parables, the sayings and riddles of the wise. ...."For the waywardness of the simple will kill them, and the complacency of fools will destroy them; but whoever **listens** to me will live in safety and be at ease, without fear of harm."

Prov. 4:1, 20 NIV **Listen**, my sons, to a father's instruction; pay attention and gain understanding. ...My son, pay attention to what I say; **listen** closely to my words.

Prov. 5:1-2, 7 NIV My son, pay attention to my wisdom, **listen** well to my words of insight, that you may maintain discretion and your lips may preserve knowledge. ....Now then, my sons, **listen** to me; do not turn aside from what I say.

Prov. 8:12, 33-35 NIV "I, wisdom, dwell together with prudence; I possess knowledge and discretion. ...**Listen** to my instruction and be wise; do not ignore it. Blessed is the man who **listens** to me, watching daily at my doors, waiting at my doorway. For whoever finds me, finds life and receives favor from the Lord."

Prov. 12:15 NIV The way of a fool seems right to him, but a wise man **listens** to advice.

Prov. 18:13 NIV He who answers before **listening**—that is folly and his shame.

Prov. 22:17-19 NIV Pay attention and **listen** to the sayings of the wise; apply your heart to what I teach, for it is pleasing when you keep them in your heart and have all of them ready on your lips. So that your trust may be in the Lord, I teach you today, even you.

Prov. 23:19-22 NIV **Listen**, my son, and be wise, and keep your heart on the right path. ....**Listen** to your father, who gave you life, and do not despise your mother when she is old.

Matt. 15:10-11 NIV Jesus called the crowd to Him and said, "**Listen** and understand. What goes into a man's mouth does not make him 'unclean', but what comes out of his mouth, that is what makes him 'unclean'."

James 1:19-20, 22-24 NIV My dear brothers, take note of this: Everyone should be quick to **listen**, slow to speak and slow to become angry, for man's anger does not bring about the righteous life that God desires. ....Do not merely **listen** to the word, and so deceive yourselves. Do what it says. Anyone who **listens** to the word but does not do what it says is like a man who looks at his face in a mirror, and after looking at himself, goes away and immediately forgets what he looks like.

Crying out to God—-

Daniel 9:18-19 NIV Give ear, O God, and hear, open your eyes and see the desolation of the city that bears Your name. We do not make requests of You because we are righteous, but because of Your mercy, O Lord, **listen**! O Lord, forgive! O Lord, hear and act! For Your sake, O my God, do not delay, because Your people bear Your Name."

Some listeners did not acknowledge Jesus as the Son of God—-

John 10:19-21 Therefore there was a division again among the Jews because of these sayings. And many of them said, "He has a demon and is mad. Why do you **listen** to Him?" Others said, "These are not the words of one who has a demon. Can a demon open the eyes of the blind?"

SEEK THE LORD

MANY HAVE TRIED THE WRONG WAY

This request of the Lord has value way beyond our first view of it. To 'seek the Lord' requires discipline and purpose, and they both require significant basic knowledge. So it helps to ask some questions. Who is He? Why should I seek Him? How do I go about this? What difference will it make?

Perhaps you have a 'void' in your life, like a big emptiness within your heart. You may have wondered what caused it, but at the same time tried to satisfy that emptiness in one way or another. Here are some of the ways that people have worked at it: planned more trips; bought a larger home, or a new vehicle; began a fitness program; decided to jog or run marathons; played more golf; possibly added alcohol or drugs to help them cope, or a variety of other available choices. Many have found some enjoyment for a while, but then discovered it didn't really give them lasting satisfaction after all.

There are others who just knew it was of spiritual origin, and began a search for the right spiritual entity that would fill this void. After choosing a religious path, here again, there may have been a feeling of something good happening, but not completely; there's still something wrong. There are many 'religions', which sound so much like the Truth, but just don't fully agree and harmonize with God's Word, the Bible. Remember this: All Truth is from the Lord, our Creator, the eternal God. Truth always harmonizes with God's Word. It will not be in addition to His Word, like a brand new revelation beyond the Word.

Some of you may have even found Christianity, and tried to live by the rules, but lacked fulfillment in the spiritual sense. You are hungry for more knowledge of the truth.

The preaching of the Word, may seem like an addition. However, it should be a study of and observation of the Word, an exposition of the Word and application of the Word of God. Along with this, we must realize that God's Word usually has one or more Scriptures which verify and interpret each specific or foundational truth, each basic doctrine, or principle set forth in His Word. Also, the Holy Spirit is to interpret His Word for us.

OBEDIENCE TO HIS COMMAND BRINGS JOY

Our Scriptures all speak of seeking the Lord as a command. But, you may still ask, "How can I go about seeking Him?" As I approached this dilemma several decades ago, I was led to study His Word. I was so sure that He would reveal Himself in His Word, and I was right. This led me to think of all the attributes, or characteristics, that I could possibly think of Him. I put those words on separate sheets, and then looked for them in the concordances of several Bibles. As I became better acquainted with what I was looking for, I'd see those attributes in the Scriptures while I was reading, and quickly put those references on the proper sheets. Gradually, I wrote out those verses in spiral notebooks, and eventually typed them up.

Truly, as I sought to know the Lord, He became so real to me, and His Word came alive in my heart! It was the most joyful way to seek Him! It became natural to experience His presence as I went to His Word to fellowship with Him. I want to encourage you to do this too. Your spiritual life can take some exciting leaps as you anticipate those glorious experiences with the Lord. This will release you from the bondage of trying hard to obey rules, because your heart will yearn to do God's will, and the Holy Spirit will enable you to follow through.

In the Old Testament, people had to obey the Ten Commandments as a way to live holy lives. God was establishing a way of holiness for a people who were also born in sin, as we are, but had no written Word. The natural way of the sin nature was strong within them. There were no 'churches' to go to, for hearing the Word of God even on a weekly basis. They had to live by the rules given by God's choice servant for daily living, in their worship and in offering sacrifices for their sins. God had anointed their leaders with the Holy Spirit, but all the people did not experience this wonderful blessing.

David sang about it in 1 Chronicles 16. Verse 1 says "Seek the Lord and His strength; seek His face." And in 1 Chronicles 22:19, when he was speaking to the leaders of Israel he commanded them this way, "Now set your heart and your soul to seek the Lord your God." This shows the necessity of our being determined and then to follow it up with discipline. We have an enemy that is not pleased that we shut him out as we choose God's ways for our lives. So it requires an unswerving focus on the Lord Jesus Christ!

You can see why it is easier for us! Jesus has come! He died on the cross for our sins for which we could never pay. He arose again, ascended to Heaven, and is now seated at the right hand of God, the Father, where He intercedes for us. The Holy Spirit has come to live in the hearts of those who believe in Him. We have the complete Written Word. Our worship services are a time for coming together as the body of Christ, to worship and praise Him, to hear His Word, to pray together and fellowship with Him and with one another. What blessed opportunities we have to 'seek the Lord' in the beauty of His holiness and in the fullness of truth!

SEEKING TO PLEASE HIM

In seeking the Lord, we are to seek to please Him. Our hearts should yearn to know what would please Him most, and by the power of the Holy Spirit we are able to serve Him. Our wants and wishes will be changed from our fleshly desires to seeking His pleasure. As Psalm 37:4 says, "Delight yourself also in the Lord, and He shall give you the desires of your heart." So as we wholeheartedly seek to please the Lord, delighting to do His will, we can find joyous fulfillment in Him, and the world becomes less alluring.

We also need to seek the Lord about decisions we make in our lives, even those that we think are insignificant. Our decisions may bring us into blessings, or take us into an independence that leaves

God out, and therefore, into big trouble. It only takes a little veering off the track that can take you miles away from your desired destination. Just consider how this can affect you in many areas of life for years to come.

In fact, take a sheet of paper and list some of your recent decisions. Did you talk to the Lord about them, and then wait for Him to give you an answer? Maybe this is all new to you, so you can begin this new venture today. If Jesus is the Lord of your life, then you will be so grateful that He wants to really be the Lord, and protect you from many pitfalls that can become very costly!

Many strange things can happen to the most faithful, devoted Christian. Praise the Lord that we can go running to Him, seeking His wisdom and guidance for what we are to do in those difficult circumstances we encounter. Remember, God sees everything, and knows everything there is to know – eternity past through eternity future. He's waiting for us to approach Him humbly for the knowledge and wisdom that only He can give. You see, seeking the Lord covers a very broad scope. You can't be too educated for Him to understand you; He's out there way beyond the highest education and wisdom of man. Any knowledge, or wisdom, that has valuable substance, originated with Him. We can only grasp and absorb a small portion, for man is a finite creature. We cannot envision or understand, or contain all the wisdom and knowledge of God, who is infinite.

SEEKING THE LORD WHOLEHEARTEDLY

Seeking the knowledge God has for us, and His wisdom for applying that knowledge changes the way we see life, and surely changes the path we want to take. According to God's Word, this brings many blessings instead of hardships that can be avoided. In the Old Testament, Psalm 119:1-2 says, "Blessed are the undefiled in the way, who walk in the law of the Lord! Blessed are those who keep His testimonies, who seek Him with the whole heart!" And a New Testament correlation is in Matthew 6:33, "But seek first the kingdom of God and His righteousness, and all these things shall be added to you." The last phrase is referring to the previous verses. We have the tendency to worry about how we can manage to obtain a pleasurable supply without first seeking God's kingdom and His righteousness. That requires much harder work on our part, for God's blessing is not on it. This helps us to realize that the more we seek the Lord, and His will for our lives, we'll also learn the powerful blessing of contentment as Paul did *(Phil. 4:11)*, and much less desire to chase after things of the world. *See 1 John 2:15-17.* The Lord becomes the center of our attention. He brings peace that passes understanding and becomes the joy of our lives, and the people who love Him become our dearest friends.

At this point I'm seeing that most of the Scriptures for this word are in the Old Testament. In the New Testament, except for the Matthew 6:33 text, our verses tell us about seeking Jesus. Since Jesus is the divine Son of God, and He is the Lord Jesus, seeking Him is a way of seeking God. The book of Hebrews especially reveals this truth in Hebrews 1:1-4, "God, who at various times and in various ways spoke in time past to the fathers by the prophets, has in these last days spoken to us by His Son, whom He has appointed heir of all things, through whom also He made the worlds; who being the brightness of His glory and the express image of His person, and upholding all things by the word of His power, when He had by Himself purged our sins, sat down at the right hand of the Majesty on high, having become so much better than the angels, as He has by inheritance obtained a more excellent name than they."

Then in I John 2 the author is telling us who Jesus is in relationship to us, and how essential it is to follow His ways. Verses 5 and 6 say, "But whoever keeps His word, truly the love of God is perfected in him. By this we know that we are in Him. He who says he abides in Him ought himself also to walk just as He walked."

In closing, my heart's desire is that you will follow the call of Psalm 105:3 and 4, "Glory in His holy name; let the hearts of those rejoice who seek the Lord! Seek the Lord and His strength; seek His face evermore!"

SCRIPTURES FOR
SEEK THE LORD

They were commanded to—

Deut. 4:29-31 *Moses is commanding obedience to Israel–* "But from there you will **seek the Lord your God**, and you will find Him if you **seek Him** with all your heart and with all your soul. When you are in distress, and all these things come upon you in the latter days, when you turn to the Lord your God and obey His voice (for the Lord your God is a merciful God), He will not forsake you nor destroy you, nor forget the covenant of your fathers which He swore to them."

1 Chron. 16:10-11 *This is part of David's song of thanksgiving–* Glory in His holy name; let the hearts of those rejoice who **seek the Lord**! **Seek the Lord** and His strength; **seek His face** evermore!

1 Chron. 22:19 *David is speaking to the leaders of Israel–* "Now set your heart and your soul to **seek the Lord your God.** Therefore arise and build the sanctuary of the Lord God, to bring the ark of the covenant of the Lord and the holy articles of God into the house that is to be built for the name of the Lord."

Psalm 105:1-4 Oh, give thanks to the Lord! Call upon His name; make known His deeds among the peoples! Sing to Him, sing psalms to Him; talk of all His wondrous works! Glory in His holy name; let the hearts of those rejoice who **seek the Lord**! **Seek the Lord and His strength; seek His face** evermore!

Isa. 55:6-9 **Seek the Lord** while He may be found, call upon Him while He is near. Let the wicked forsake his way, and the unrighteous man his thoughts; let him return to the Lord, and He will have mercy on him; and to our God, for He will abundantly pardon. For My thoughts are not your thoughts, nor are your ways My ways," says the Lord. For as the heavens are higher than the earth, so are My ways higher than your ways, and My thoughts than your thoughts.

Instructions regarding seeking the Lord—

1 Chron. 28:9 "As for you, my son Solomon, know the God of your father, and serve Him with a loyal heart and with a willing mind; for the Lord searches all hearts and understands all the intent of the thoughts. If you **seek Him**; He will be found by you; but if you forsake Him, He will cast you off forever."

2 Chron. 15:1-4 Now the Spirit of God came upon Azariah the son of Obed. And he went out to meet Asa and said to him: "Hear me, Asa, and all Judah and Benjamin. The Lord is with you while you are with Him. If you **seek Him**, He will be found by you; but if you forsake Him, He will forsake you. For a long time Israel has been without the true God, without a teaching priest, and without law; but when in their trouble they turned to the Lord God of Israel, and **sought Him;** He was found by them."
Isa. 51:1 "Listen to Me, you who follow after righteousness, you who **seek the Lord**: Look to the rock from which you were hewn, and to the hole of the pit from which you were dug."

Hosea 10:12 Sow for yourselves righteousness; reap in mercy; break up your fallow ground, for it is time to **seek the Lord**, till He comes and rains righteousness on you.

Zeph. 2:3 **Seek the Lord**, all you meek of the earth, who have upheld His justice. **Seek righteousness, seek humility**. It may be that you will be hidden in the day of the Lord's anger.

Matt. 6:33-34 "But **seek first the kingdom of God** and **His righteousness**, and all these things shall be added to you. Therefore do not worry about tomorrow, for tomorrow will worry about its own things. Sufficient for the day is its own trouble." *Also Luke 12:31*.

God responds with blessings—

2 Chron. 7:12-15 Then the Lord appeared to Solomon by night, and said to him: "I have heard your prayer, and have chosen this place for Myself as a house of sacrifice. When I shut up heaven and there is no rain, or command the locusts to devour the land, or send pestilence among My people, if My people who are called by My name will humble themselves, and pray and **seek My face**, and turn from their wicked ways, then I will hear from heaven, and will forgive their sin and heal their land. Now My eyes will be open and My ears attentive to prayer made in this place.

2 Chron. 31:20-21 Thus Hezekiah did throughout all Judah, and he did what was good and right and true before the Lord his God. And in every work that he began in the service of the house of God, in the law and in the commandment, to **seek his God**, he did it with all his heart. So he prospered.

Ps. 9:9-10 The Lord also will be a refuge for the oppressed, a refuge in times of trouble. And those who know Your name will put their trust in You; for You, Lord, have not forsaken those who **seek You**.

Ps. 22:26-28 The poor shall eat and be satisfied; those who **seek Him** will praise the Lord. Let your heart live forever! All the ends of the world shall remember and turn to the Lord, and all the families of the nations shall worship before You. For the kingdom is the Lord's, and He rules over the nations.

Ps. 34:10 The young lions lack and suffer hunger; but those who **seek the Lord** shall not lack any good thing.

Ps. 69:32 The humble shall see this and be glad; and you who **seek God**, your hearts shall live.

Ps. 119:1-2 Blessed are the undefiled in the way, who walk in the law of the Lord! Blessed are those who keep His testimonies, who **seek Him** with the whole heart!

Prov. 28:5 Evil men do not understand justice, but those who **seek the Lord** understand all.

Jer. 29:11-13 For I know the thoughts that I think toward you, says the Lord, thoughts of peace and not of evil, to give you a future and a hope. Then you will call upon Me and go and pray to Me, and I will listen to you. And you will **seek Me** and find Me, when you **search for me** with all your heart.

Lam. 3:25-27 The Lord is good to those who wait for Him, to the soul who **seeks Him**. It is good that one should hope and wait quietly for the salvation of the Lord. It is good for a man to bear the yoke in his youth.

These set their heart to seek Him—

2 Chron. 11:16,-7 And after the Levites left those from all the tribes of Israel, such as **set their heart to seek the Lord God** of Israel, came to Jerusalem to sacrifice to the Lord God of their fathers. So they strengthened the kingdom of Judah, and made Rehoboam the son of Solomon, strong for three years, because they walked in the way of David and Solomon for three years.

Ezra 6:21 Then the children of Israel who had returned from the captivity ate together with all who had separated themselves from the filth of the nations of the land in order to **seek the Lord God** of Israel.

Ps. 27:4, 8 One thing I have desired of the Lord, that will I **seek**: that I may dwell in the house of the Lord all the days of my life, to **behold the beauty of the Lord**, and to inquire in His temple. ....When You said "**Seek My face**," My heart said to You, "**Your face, Lord, I will seek**."

Ps. 63:1 O God, You are my God; early will **I seek You**; my soul thirsts for You in a dry and thirsty land where there is no water.

Zech. 8:20-22 "Thus says the Lord of hosts: 'Peoples shall yet come, inhabitants of many cities; the inhabitants of one city shall go to another, saying, "Let us continue to go and pray before the Lord, and **seek the Lord of hosts**. I myself will go also." Yes, many people and strong nations shall come to **seek the Lord of hosts** in Jerusalem, and to pray before the Lord.'"

Prayers—

Ps. 40:16 Let all those who **seek you** rejoice and be glad in You; let such as love Your salvation say continually, "The Lord be magnified!" *Also Psalm 70:4.*

Ps. 83:1-2, 16, 18 Do not keep silent, O God! Do not hold Your peace, and do not be still, O God! For behold, Your enemies make a tumult; and those who hate You have lifted up their head. ....Fill their faces with shame, that they may **seek Your name, O Lord**. ....That they may know that You, whose name alone is the Lord, are the Most High over all the earth.

Isa. 26:7-9 The way of the just is uprightness; O Most Upright, You weigh the path of the just. Yes, in the way of Your judgments, O Lord, we have waited for You; the desire of our soul is for Your name and for the remembrance of You. With my soul I have desired You in the night, yes, by my spirit within me I will **seek You** early; for when Your judgments are in the earth, the inhabitants of the world will learn righteousness.

True repentance—

Jer. 50:4 "In those days and in that time," says the Lord, "The children of Israel shall come, they and the children of Judah together with continued weeping they shall come, and **seek the Lord their God**. They shall ask the way to Zion, with their faces toward it, saying, Come let us join ourselves to the Lord in a perpetual covenant that will not be forgotten."

Hosea 3:4-5 For the children of Israel shall abide many days without king or prince, without sacrifice or sacred pillar, without ephod or teraphim. Afterward the children of Israel shall return and **seek the Lord** their God and David, their king. They shall fear the Lord and His goodness in the latter days.

Hosea 5:14-15 "For I will be like a lion to Ephraim, and like a young lion to the house of Judah. I, even I, will tear them and go away; I will take them away, and no one shall rescue. I will return again to My place till they acknowledge their offense. Then they will **seek My face**. In their affliction they will earnestly **seek Me**."

Warnings—-

2 Chron 12:14 And he *(Rehoboam)* did evil, because he did not prepare his heart to **seek the Lord**. *Read all of Chapter 12.*

Amos 5:4, 6-7, 14 For thus says the Lord to the house of Israel: **"Seek Me** and live; ....**Seek the Lord** and live, lest He break out like fire in the house of Joseph, and devour it, with no one to quench it in Bethel— you who turn justice to wormwood, and lay righteousness to rest in the earth!" ....Seek good and not evil, that you may live; so the Lord God of hosts will be with you, as you have spoken."

Amos 8:11-12 "Behold, the days are coming," says the Lord God, "that I will send a famine on the land, not a famine of bread, nor a thirst for water, but of hearing the words of the Lord. They shall wander from sea to sea, and from north to east; they shall run to and fro, **seeking the word of the Lord**, but shall not find it."

Seeking the Lord Jesus—

Mal. 3:1 "Behold, I send My messenger, and he will prepare the way before Me. And **the Lord, whom you seek**, will suddenly come to His temple, even the Messenger of the covenant, in whom you delight. Behold, He is coming," says the Lord of hosts.

Mark 1:35-38 Now in the morning, having risen a long while before daylight, He *(Jesus)* went out and departed to a solitary place; and there He prayed. And Simon and those who were with Him **searched for Him**. When they found Him, they said to Him, "Everyone is looking for You." *(KJV: All men **seek for thee**.)* But He said to them, "Let us go into the next towns, that I may preach there also, because for this purpose I have come forth."

John 6:24, 26-27 When the people therefore saw that Jesus was not there, nor His disciples, they also got into boats and came to Capernaum, **seeking Jesus**. ....Jesus answered them and said, "Most assuredly, I say to you, you **seek me**, not because you saw the signs, but because you ate of the loaves and were filled. Do not labor for the food which perishes, but for the food which endures to everlasting life, which the Son of Man will give you, because God the Father has set His seal on Him."

John 7:32-34 The Pharisees heard the crowd murmuring these things concerning Him and the Pharisees and the chief priests sent officers to take Him. Then Jesus said to them, "I shall be with you a little while longer, and then I will go to Him who sent Me. You will **seek Me** and not find Me, and where I am you cannot come. *Also see John 8:21 and John 13:33.*

Matt. 28:5-6 But the angel answered and said to the women, "Do not be afraid, for I know that you **seek Jesus** who was crucified. He is not here; for He is risen, as He said. Come, see the place where the Lord lay." *Also in Mark 16:6.*

NEW

SURPRISED BY NEW THINGS AND NEW WAYS

There was a time in my younger years, probably around age nine to eleven, when I thought that life was extremely dull. We lived on a small farm just outside of a little village in Michigan, 'Lamont on the Grand' (River), and it seemed like nothing new ever happened. In the 30s and the 40s things were very, very different. There were mostly dirt roads, few paved highways, and no super-highways, as we know them today. In the country everything seemed old, for most homes were not even painted with bright colors. Our driveways were just dirt. We didn't even have loads of gravel brought in to keep the dust down.

We lacked many of today's conveniences. We had to pump our water. Fortunately the pump was in the garage, rather than a long distance from the house. But we possessed the most humiliating out-house behind the house, which was especially a miserable state of affairs in the winter's cold snowy weather, even for a child. Lawn mowers had no power, except what your muscles put to it. Father plowed with the horse drawn metal plow, which he had to direct into the ground and all along the way for straight furrows. The big pot belly stove in the living room had to be fed some coal, wood and waste paper for our heat, then had to be cleaned properly before the next load was put in. I've probably painted enough of the picture to impress you with my difficulty to think there could possibly be anything new. It was always the 'same ole, same ole' hardships year after year.

Well, you can tell that I had a lot to learn as new things came into being, and continued to develop way beyond our imaginations. Electricity brought limitless new things. We could not have imagined radio, TV, telephones, let alone the tape players and discs of various types, computers, satellite dishes, and all that each of these provide for our lives. The building of automobiles and planes were barely beginning to reveal their potential. And there are so many more things that are newly developed, too numerous to mention.

We can have such a hard time putting things all together in our day by day living, and struggling with how to personally fit in. The truth is: we don't always accept new things, particularly if we haven't been asked to participate in the planning of it, or we weren't given an opportunity to give our speech about what we thought of it. Possibly the proposed change was just too big a surprise, requiring too great an adjustment. In some kinds of situations, we are too pleased with our long followed routine, our way of doing things. These are strong hindrances which may keep us from going forward when God calls us to further our education, or other ways of preparing for new fields, new ventures and new challenges which would open doors to greater possibilities.

GOD'S WORD IS FULL OF REFRESHING NEWNESS

God's word is full of new things, in fact, there are many Scriptures using this word. I wonder if you will be as surprised as I was that this word is used so often. Let's begin with a new song. My heart leaps into rejoicing as I read about the new song we are urged to sing. And Psalm 40:3 is particularly great as we read that the Lord put a new song in David's mouth. He had been in a "horrible pit" *(can you identify?)*, but after the Lord set his "feet upon a rock and established his steps" He put a new song in his mouth!

Then in Psalm 98:1, we have another new song—- "Oh, sing to the Lord a new song! For He has done marvelous things; His right hand and His holy arm have gained Him the victory." Here I am reminded of 1 Corinthians 15:57, "But thanks be to God, who gives us the victory through our Lord Jesus Christ." This is really exciting! These few verses are like a hydraulic lift when you feel discouraged, because the new song brings great joy with it. God does marvelous things! He surely does! Many of God's new things were recorded in the Old Testament; however, they are still being fulfilled. Many of the prophecies which we have seen fulfilled are repeated in other generations, according to those who are speaking about the prophetic realm.

The Scriptures listed from the book of Isaiah tell us about many new things. Isaiah 42:9 and 43:18 and 19 are similar. Here they are: "Behold, the former things have come to pass, and new things I declare; before they spring forth I tell you of them." "...Do not remember the former things, nor consider the things of old. Behold, I will do a new thing, now it shall spring forth; shall you not know it? I will even make a road in the wilderness and rivers in the desert." There are many times in our lives when we need to get out of our little box, and allow FAITH IN GOD to swing open doors to new horizons so we might live "to the praise of His glory."

GOD'S WORD IS ALIVE WITH WONDERS

We have to learn to follow new instructions, no matter where we are: at home, in school all the way through higher education. It's the same story on any job: as a plumber, electrician, banker, auto mechanic, engineer, construction worker, and any other kind of service. We all know how important it is to follow exact instructions in the various branches of the armed services. However, God's instructions are always the most important to follow, and we can save ourselves from a multitude of difficulties if we pay attention. The above verses tell us that the old things have been fulfilled, and should not even be remembered. Reading the surrounding verses will provide clearer understanding. There are always new things, and God uses new methods whenever He chooses, even though His nature does not change.

Another problem that often hinders us in following God's instructions is in limiting God. One of Morris Cerullo's numerous books is entitled How to Take the Limits Off God.[8] His books are power packed. They help us to understand how we are blocking God from doing all He desires to do in our lives. He has experienced the awesome power of God throughout his life, in ways that would seem absolutely impossible for anyone to experience.

Do you remember that in Acts 4:29-30 Peter and John and fellow

Christians were together praying for God to give them boldness to speak His word, asking also that God would stretch out His hand to heal, and that signs and wonders might be done through the name of His holy Servant Jesus? The place where they were together praying was shaken, and they were all filled with the Holy Spirit. They received from the Lord all that they asked for. God's signs and wonders are always new things! He is not confined to our limited vision or understanding, nor is He limited to any way He has chosen to do things in the past. God has revealed this before hundreds of thousands of people in many nations, on numerous occasions, where Morris Cerullo and His workers have ministered as God's servants.

God's word is so alive, full of wonders beyond our imagination. I often marvel how God brings new things into being, many times 'suddenly'; when least expected. No wonder we are instructed in Colossians 4:2 (NIV) to: "Devote yourselves to prayer, being watchful and thankful." If we are not prayerful and watchful, spiritually awake, we can miss hearing God's voice and miss great opportunities for serving the Lord in guiding others into His kingdom. In the natural, we cannot fathom how God can use us, but if we set our minds on things of the Spirit and live according to the Spirit, He will guide and provide.

GOD'S NEW COVENANT BROUGHT CHANGES

In Jeremiah 31:31, we read, "Behold, the days are coming, says the Lord, when I will make a new covenant with the house of Israel and with the house of Judah..." This is quoted in Hebrews 8:8. Further along in Hebrews 9:13-15 we read a central truth: "For if the blood of bulls and goats and the ashes of a heifer, sprinkling the unclean, sanctifies for the purifying of the flesh, how much more shall the blood of Christ, who through the eternal Spirit offered Himself without spot to God, cleanse your conscience from dead works to serve the living God? And for this reason He is the Mediator of the new covenant, by means of death, for the redemption of the transgressions under the first covenant, that those who are called may receive the promise of the eternal inheritance."

Did you hear the tremendous blessing attached to God's new covenant? Jesus is the Mediator of the new covenant; He made it possible to make this great change from the old, namely, sacrificing bulls and goats and other animals, to the complete sacrifice of Himself as the Lamb of God, bringing in the new covenant. In Hebrews 8:6-7 and 13 we read: "But now He has obtained a more excellent ministry, inasmuch as He is also Mediator of a better covenant, which was established on better promises. For if that first covenant had been faultless, then no place would have been sought for a second. ...In that He says, 'A new covenant,' He has made the first obsolete. Now what is becoming obsolete and growing old is ready to vanish." It is so important to read all of Hebrews 8, 9 and 10 in order to better understand the change from the old covenant to the new.

Let's go back to Matthew 26:27-28, where Jesus is sharing about the new covenant with His disciples at the Passover Supper, just before giving His life on the cross: "Then He took the cup, and gave thanks, and gave it to them, saying, 'Drink from it, all of you. For this is my blood of the new covenant, which is shed for many for the remission of sins.'" Everything that Jesus said and did during His ministry was preparing His disciples for putting away the old, and receiving the new. Christ's ultimate sacrifice was replacing the old covenant that God had made with His people. From that point people had to make a choice, to stay with God's temporary plan of the Old Testament, or accept Jesus as the perfect sacrifice for our sins, which makes the greatest change for the rest of our lives.

As you read the other Scriptures you will see how many rituals had to change as the new covenant took effect. They add a great deal of light to this subject; such as a change from circumcision to believers' baptism, which is a part of becoming new creatures in Christ Jesus and experiencing the process of being born again. There's deliverance from bondage to the law of sin and death, to living by God's grace with a new Spirit of life in our hearts, rather than the oldness of the letter of the law. *See Romans 8:1-17.* We are to put off the old and put on the new man: "that you put off, concerning your former conduct, the old man which grows corrupt according to the deceitful lusts, and be renewed in the spirit of your mind, and that you put on the new man which was created according to God, in true righteousness and holiness." *Ephesians 4:22-24.* In the Colossians Scripture we find a list of things that have to be put off in verses 5-9, then, "and have put on the new man who is renewed in knowledge according to the image of Him who created him." *Colossians 3:10.*

Even our day of worship has been changed from the Sabbath, which is associated with the burden of the law, to the first day of the week, as a response to continually celebrating the day of Jesus' resurrection and our newness of life. Romans 6:4-6 gives us a picture of how His death and resurrection are symbolized in baptism: "Therefore we were buried with Him through baptism into death, that just as Christ was raised from the dead by the glory of the Father, even so we also should walk in newness of life. For if we have been united together in the likeness of His death, certainly we also shall be in the likeness of His resurrection, knowing this, that our old man was crucified with Him, that the body of sin might be done away with, that we should no longer be slaves of sin." It takes time to grasp the full meaning of this, but it is essential for rejoicing in the greatness of what Jesus has done on our behalf. Galatians 2:20 is Paul's testimony of the change in his life which came because of his experience with this truth.

In the book of Galatians, chapters 3-5, there are many things spelled out about the freedom from the bondages of the old covenant. In Galatians 4:21-31 we are told about Hagar, representing Mount Sinai and bondage, and corresponding to the present Jerusalem. Then it says in verses 26 and 31: "but the Jerusalem above is free, which is the mother of us all. ...So then, brethren, we are not children of the bondwoman but of the free." And Galatians 5:1 says, "Stand fast therefore in the liberty by which Christ has made us free, and do not be entangled again with a yoke of bondage."

This brings us to a whole new territory that cannot be treated with the extensive research and presentation that it should have. While I have given references to the New Covenant, I urge you to further study other writers who have thoroughly studied the Scriptures on this subject.

NEW COMMANDMENT—LOVE AS JESUS LOVED

We also hear about the new commandment to love one another as Jesus had loved them with compassion and forgiveness. Previously the command was to love one another as we love ourselves. Jesus updated it to a much higher level as He was preparing the disciples for His walk toward death on the cross for our sins. In John 15:12-13 we read: "This is My commandment, that you love one another as I have loved you. Greater love has no one than this, than to lay down one's life for his friends." This seems impossible to follow, but it is a command that Jesus issued. This is what the disciples were to teach the new believers after Jesus went on to heaven. There are Christians in other countries who understand this to the fullest extent. To love as Jesus loved requires living in a close relationship with Him, being aware of His presence within our hearts, and living in obedience to the Lord, desiring to know His will and to please Him. Galatians 5:13 tells us, "For you, brethren, have been called to liberty; only do not use liberty as an opportunity for the flesh, but through love serve one another."

Then there's the matter of speaking with new tongues, and that we are to walk in newness of life. Also, we are given a new name, and there will be a new Jerusalem. You will find all of these in the attached concordance.

Let me close with 2 Corinthians 5:17: "Therefore, if anyone is in Christ, he is a new creation; old things have passed away; behold, all things have become new." This is so tremendous, so powerful, so blessed and joyous. Jesus came to this earth to provide the "all things new" for us. If you haven't accepted Him as your Savior and Lord, I pray that these Scriptures help you to understand the greatness of what Jesus has accomplished on your behalf. Only Jesus can provide salvation for all mankind, for we were all born as sinners. We all stand in need of the Lord Jesus Christ. Don't wait! His love is waiting to embrace you. He can make all things new for you, incredibly true—all things new for you!

I urge you to pray this prayer: "Oh Lord God, I now see what You have done for me. I am a sinner in need of what Jesus has done as He shed His blood on the cross to pay the huge price for my sins. I repent! Please forgive me and cleanse me of all my sins. Come into my heart and make me a new creature in Christ Jesus. I really need all things to become new. I want to live for You. Amen!" If you prayed that prayer, watch for the changes that will come, providing you with new vibrancy, with the abundant life that is in Jesus!

SCRIPTURES FOR
N E W

New songs—

Ps. 33:1-3 Rejoice in the Lord, O you righteous! For praise from the upright is beautiful. Praise the Lord with the harp; make melody to Him with an instrument of ten strings. Sing to Him a **new song**; play skillfully with a shout of joy.

Ps. 40:3 He has put a **new song** in my mouth—- Praise to God; many will see it and fear, and will trust in the Lord.

Ps. 96:1-2 O sing to the Lord a **new song**! Sing to the Lord, all the earth. Sing to the Lord, bless His name; proclaim the good news of His salvation from day to day.

Ps. 98:1 Oh, sing to the Lord a **new song**! For He has done marvelous things; His right hand and His holy arm have gained Him the victory.

Isa. 42:10-12 Sing to the Lord a **new song**, and His praise from the ends of the earth, you who go down to the sea, and all that is in it, you coastlands and you inhabitants of them! Let the wilderness and its cities **lift up their voice**, the villages that Kedar inhabits, let the inhabitants of Sela sing, let them shout from the top of the mountains. Let them give glory to the Lord, and declare His praise in the coastland.

Rev. 5:9-10 And they sang a **new song**, saying: "You are worthy to take the scroll, and to open its seals; for You were slain, and have redeemed us to God by Your blood out of every tribe and tongue and people and nation, and have made us kings and priests to our God; and we shall reign on the earth."

New things—-

Isa. 42:9 Behold, the former things have come to pass, and **new things** I declare; before they spring forth I tell you of them.

Isa. 43:19 Behold, I will do a **new thing**, now it shall spring forth; shall you not know it? I will even make a road in the wilderness and rivers in the desert.

Isa. 45:18-19 Do not remember the former things, nor consider the things of old. Behold, I will do a **new thing**, now it shall spring forth; shall you not know it? I will even make a road in the wilderness and rivers in the desert.

Isa, 48:6 "You have heard; see all this. And you will not declare it? I have made you **hear new things** from this time, even hidden things, and you did not know them."

Rev. 21:5 Then He who sat on the throne said, "Behold, I make **all things new**." And He said to me, "Write, for these words are true and faithful."

New name—-

Isa. 62:2 The Gentiles shall see your righteousness, and all kings your glory. You shall be called by a **new name**, which the mouth of the Lord will name.

Rev. 2:17 "He who has an ear, let him hear what the Spirit says to the Churches. To him who overcomes I will give some of the hidden manna to eat. And I will give him a white stone, and on the stone a **new name** written which no man knows except him who receives it."

Rev. 3:11-13 " Behold, I am coming quickly! Hold fast what you have, that no one may take your crown. He who overcomes, I will make him a pillar in the temple of God, and he shall go out no more. I will write on him **the name of My God and the name of the city of My God, the New Jerusalem**, which comes down out of heaven from My God. And I will write on him **My new name**. He who has an ear, let him hear what the Spirit says to the Churches."

New heavens and new earth—-

Isa. 65:17 "For behold, I create **new heavens and a new earth**; and the former shall not be remembered or come to mind."

Isa. 66:22-23 "For as the **new heavens and the new earth** which I will make shall remain before Me," says the Lord, "So shall your descendants and your name remain. And it shall come to pass that from one **New Moon** to another, all flesh shall come to worship before Me," says the Lord.

Rev. 21:1, 5 Now I saw a **new heaven and a new earth**, for the first heaven and the first earth had passed away. Also there was no more sea. Then He who sat on the throne said, "Behold, I make all things **new**." And He said to me, "Write, for these words are true and faithful."

New covenant—-

Jer. 31:31 "Behold, the days are coming, says the Lord, when I will make a **new covenant** with the house of Israel and with the house of Judah—- " *Quoted in Hebrews 8:8; see verses 7-13 and 9:15.*

Matt. 26:27-28 Then He *(Jesus)* took the cup, and gave thanks, and gave it to them, saying, "Drink from it, all of you. For this is my blood of the **new covenant**, which is shed for many for the remission of sins." *Also see Luke 22:20, and 1 Corinthians 11:25.*

Heb. 8:13 In that He says, "A **new covenant**," He has made the first obsolete. Now what is becoming obsolete and growing old is ready to vanish away.

Heb. 9:15 And for this reason He is the Mediator of the **new covenant**, by means of death, for the redemption of the transgressions under the first covenant, that those who are called may receive the promise of the eternal inheritance.

Heb. 12:24 ...to Jesus the Mediator of the **new covenant**, and to the blood of sprinkling that speaks better things than that of Abel.

The Lord's mercy and compassion—-

Lam. 3:22, 23 Through the Lord's mercies we are not consumed, because His compassions fail not. **They are new** every morning; great is Your faithfulness.

Zeph. 3:5 NIV The Lord within her is righteous; He does no wrong. Morning by morning He dispenses His justice and every **new day** He does not fail, yet the unrighteous know no shame.

New heart and new spirit—-

Ezek. 11:19-20 Then I will give them **one heart**, and I will put a **new spirit** within them, and take the stony heart out of their flesh, and give them a heart of flesh, that they may walk in My statutes and keep My judgments and do them; and they shall be My people, and I will be their God.

Ezek. 18:31a Cast away from you all the transgressions, which you have committed, and get yourselves **a new heart and a new spirit**.

Ezek. 36:26-27 I will give you **a new heart and put a new spirit** within you; I will take the heart of stone out of your flesh and give you a heart of flesh. I will put My Spirit within you and cause you to walk in My statutes, and you will keep My judgments and do them.

New tongues—-

Mark 16:17 And these signs will follow those who believe: In My name they will cast out demons; they will speak with **new tongues**.

Acts 2:1-4 When the Day of Pentecost had fully come, they were all with one accord in one place. And suddenly there came a sound from heaven, as of a rushing mighty wind, and it filled the whole house where they were sitting. Then there appeared to them divided tongues, as of fire, and one sat upon each of them. And they were all filled with the Holy Spirit and began to speak with **other** *(new) tongues*, as the Spirit gave them utterance. *See also Acts 2:5-11.*

Acts 10:44-47 While Peter was still speaking these words, the Holy Spirit fell upon all those who heard the word. And those of the circumcision who believed were astonished, as many as came with Peter, because the gift of the Holy Spirit had been poured out on the Gentiles also. For **they heard them speak with tongues**, and magnify God. Then Peter answered, "Can anyone forbid water, that these should not be baptized who have received the Holy Spirit just as we have?

Acts 19:6 And when Paul had laid hands on them, the Holy Spirit came upon them, and they spoke with *(new)* **tongues** and prophesied.

New wine—-

Luke 5:36-39 Then He spoke a parable to them: "No one puts a piece from a **new garment** on an old one; otherwise the **new** makes a tear, and also the piece that was taken out of the **new** does not match the old. And no one puts **new wine** into old wineskins; or else the **new wine** will burst the wineskins and be spilled, and the wineskins will be ruined. But **new wine** must be put into **new wineskins**, and both are preserved. And no one, having drunk old wine, immediately desires **new**; for he says, 'The old is better.'"

New commandment—-

John 13:34-35 "A **new commandment** I give to you, that you love one another; as I have loved you, that you also love one another. By this all will know that you are My disciples, if you have love for one another."

1 John 2:8 Again, a **new commandment** I write to you, which thing is true in Him and in you, because the darkness is passing away, and the true light is already shining.

New life, new creation—-

Rom. 6:4 Therefore we were buried with Him through baptism into death, that just as Christ was raised from the dead by the glory of the Father, even so we also should walk in **newness of life**.

Rom. 7:6 But now we have been delivered from the law, having died to what we were held by, so that we should serve in the **newness of the Spirit** and not in the oldness of the letter.

2 Cor. 5:17 Therefore, if anyone is in Christ, he is a **new creation**; old things have passed away; behold, **all things** have become **new**.

Gal. 6:15 For in Christ Jesus neither circumcision nor uncircumcision avails anything, but a **new creation**.

Eph. 4:23-24 And be renewed in the spirit of your mind, and that you put on the **new man** which was created according to God, in true righteousness and holiness.

Col. 3:9-10 Do not lie to one another, since you have put off the old man with his deeds, and have put on the **new man** who is renewed in knowledge according to the image of Him who created him.

Heb. 10:19-21 Therefore, brethren, having boldness to enter the Holiest by the blood of Jesus, by a **new** and **living** way which He consecrated for us, through the veil, that is, His flesh, and having a High Priest over the house of God...

1 Peter 1:3 NIV Praise be to the God and Father of our Lord Jesus

Christ! In His great mercy He has given us **new birth** into a living hope through the resurrection of Jesus Christ from the dead.

1 Peter 2:1-3 Therefore, laying aside all malice, all deceit, hypocrisy, envy, and all evil speaking, as **newborn** babes, desire the pure milk of the word that you may grow thereby, if indeed you have tasted that the Lord is gracious.

BELIEVE

WE SET STANDARDS FOR WHAT WE BELIEVE

There are certain standards that we have formed in the course of living which cause us to believe a certain way about almost anything you can think of. Have you ever taken time to consider why you believe exactly as you do? Are there things you remember your parents telling you that you hold to very firmly? Did you have a teacher that impressed you with certain profound statements? Have you been influenced by a Pastor, Conference speakers, or read books that changed your life in a major way? Have you had a painful experience by way of health issues, being physically attacked, a broken relationship, or another type of traumatic event? These are all powerful influences. There are many other possibilities of things we've heard or seen, and other types of experiences that have shaped what we believe, covering the many facets of life.

GOD'S WORD OUR FOUNDATION

The spiritual realm is not a matter of believing according to our personality, religious ideas, ethnic culture, or other kinds of preferences. Rather it is a matter of seeking to know the true God, and learning what His plan is for you and me personally. He created us for particular purposes to be fulfilled in His kingdom. We are given a perfect guidebook, known as the Bible, which reveals all we need to know about Him, His will and His ways.

As you read through the Scriptures for this word, you can see that there are a great number of them telling us what to believe, what to not believe, and the dangers of not believing the truths of the Word of God. This is a very important subject for every person on the earth. It is a serious error to believe in a dead religion. Anything that is a religious system of rules and regulations, put together by man, or a group of people, cannot be from God, even if they say they have been to heaven and back again. Those who have had a 'heaven' experience are totally supporting the truths of the Bible, for the true God in heaven refers them to His book of truth.

Our spiritual foundation has to come from the Creator God, given to us by His Spirit, and will give Him all the glory. Only the true God can provide forgiveness for our sinful condition and the reconciliation of mankind to Him. Any one man, though he may have a large following, cannot rightly put together a religious system, and then claim to be a special Prophet of God, or even Deity. That is as far out, as if I wrote a book on scientific data, which is not my field of expertise. It would be possible for me to gather a little data from here, and some from over there, and add some lengthy sophisticated terminology to glue everything together to prove my authenticity. I purposefully used the word 'glued', for it would be as ridiculous as that sounds. What we believe about spiritual things strongly influences the way we live in every aspect of life, and determines where we will be after the body dies; either in heaven, or in hell for all eternity.

BELIEVE THE TEACHINGS
OF THE LORD JESUS CHRIST

The New Testament begins a new era of time. In the first chapter of Matthew we read the genealogy of Jesus Christ, the Son of God. In Matthew 3:17, at the time of Jesus' baptism there was a heavenly announcement of this fact: "...suddenly a voice came from heaven, saying, "This is My beloved Son, in whom I am well pleased." The coming of Jesus changed dates from B.C. (before Christ) to A.D. (Anno Domini, the year of the Lord). Everything hinges on whether or not we believe on the Lord Jesus Christ. Those who believe in Jesus have found a new life of love and joy and peace that passes understanding. Just before Jesus went to the cross, He was instructing His disciples about things to come. In

John 14:27-29 we read, "Peace I leave with you, My peace I give to you; not as the world gives do I give to you. Let not your heart be troubled, neither let it be afraid. You have heard Me say to you, 'I am going away and coming back to you.' If you loved Me, you would rejoice because I said, 'I am going to the Father,' for My Father is greater than I. And now I have told you before it comes, that when it does come to pass, you may believe." This is the Good News which is given throughout the four gospels.

What Jesus taught, laid a foundation for what people were and are to continue to believe, for it is a matter of life and death. John 3:16-17 expresses this: "For God so loved the world that He gave His only begotten Son, that whoever believes in Him should not perish but have everlasting life. For God did not send His Son into the world to condemn the world, but that the world through Him might be saved." This is the Good News which is given throughout the four gospels. In Mark 16:15-16 Jesus was giving the disciples instructions about this; "Go into all the world and preach the gospel to every creature. He who believes and is baptized will be save; but he who does not believe will be condemned."

God is very much concerned about what each individual believes. That is why this word is used so often in the Bible, and why Jesus especially emphasized it. He came to reveal the Father and His will to all people, and to reveal what we needed to know in order to live in a way that pleases Him. In John 12:44-46 we read, "Then Jesus cried out and said: "He who believes in Me, believes not in Me but in Him who sent Me. And he who sees Me sees Him who sent Me. I have come as a light into the world, that whoever believes in Me should not abide in darkness." You know how hard it is to 'be in the dark' about anything, you keep on wondering what's going on. We work in the light of day, or we turn on lights so we might see clearly. Light, or enlightenment, gives understanding.

BELIEVE IN JESUS FOR ETERNAL LIFE

Jesus continually taught the disciples and crowds of people the way to believe so that they might enjoy the blessings of being born again, and to be filled with His Spirit. When His Spirit lives in our hearts, we have a strong desire to obey Him, and are empowered to do what pleases God. The tremendous result will be everlasting life in heaven where His glory is the light and where there is no night. The gift of everlasting life is a sure reward to those who believe on Jesus. Jesus was speaking in John 5:24: "Most assuredly, I say to you, he who hears My word and believes in Him who sent Me has everlasting life, and shall not come into judgment, but has passed from death into life." Jesus was also speaking in John 6:40: "And this is the will of Him who sent Me, that everyone who sees the Son and believes in Him may have everlasting life; and I will raise him up at the last day."

If your basis of faith rests on anyone other than the Lord Jesus Christ, you will not be in God's loving presence after you die. In Romans 8:11 we read, "But if the Spirit of Him who raised Jesus from the dead dwells in you, He who raised Christ from the dead will also give life to your mortal bodies through His Spirit who dwells in you." Jesus came to save people from their sins. Rebellion against God in any one of a multitude of ways, we are saying that we prefer our own way of handling things in our lives. The only way to be set free is to believe on the Lord Jesus Christ as your personal Savior and let Him be your Lord.

We must repent, turn from self and our selfish ways of living. Peter was preaching to a crowd of people after Jesus had ascended to heaven, and the Holy Spirit descended upon the believers. At the close of the sermon, many people asked what they should do. Peter's reply is given in Acts 2:38 and 39: "Repent, and let every one of you be baptized in the name of Jesus Christ for the remission of sins; and you shall receive the gift of the Holy Spirit. For the promise is to you and to your children, and to all who are afar off, as many as the Lord our God will call." We must believe what God's Word tells us, and choose to surrender ourselves to His Lordship.

RECEIVE JESUS AND BECOME A CHILD OF GOD

One of the great privileges of believing on Jesus is given in John 1:12-13: "But as many as received Him, to them He gave the right to become children of God, to those who believe in His name: who were born, not of blood, nor of the will of the flesh, nor of the will of man, but of God." In 2 Corinthians 6:17-18 we have another reference to being God's children: Therefore "Come out from among them and be separate, says the Lord. Do not touch what is unclean, and I will receive you. I will be a Father to you, and you shall be My sons and daughters, says the Lord Almighty."

Romans 8 tells more about becoming children of God and about living according to the Spirit. It's a great chapter! It begins with, "There is therefore now no condemnation to those who are in Christ Jesus, who do not walk according to the flesh, but according to the Spirit." Then verses 14-17 tell further about being children of God, "For as many as are led by the Spirit of God, these are sons of God. For you did not receive the spirit of bondage again to fear, but you received the Spirit of adoption by whom we cry out, 'Abba, Father.' The Spirit Himself bears witness with our spirit that we are children of God, and if children, then heirs—heirs of God and joint heirs with Christ, if indeed we suffer with Him, that we may also be glorified together." These Scriptures tell the wonderful story of being in the 'family of God'. Here are a few more references that you may want to look up: Gal. 4:4-6, Phil 2:15, Heb. 2:11 and 1 John 3:10.

HEALING REQUIRES BELIEVING

Although I won't go into a study on healing, I urge you to study further about the marvelous healings that Jesus performed. Take note of Jesus referring to the words 'faith' and believe'. You will also find the Apostles continued to do as Jesus taught them and had sent them out anointed to do, which are the works that Jesus did. Mark 3:14-15 says this: "Then He appointed twelve, that they might be with Him and that He might send them out to preach, and to have power to heal sicknesses and to cast out demons," then the verses following reveals the names of the twelve.

In Matthew 10:1 it says, "And when He had called His twelve disciples to Him, He gave them power over unclean spirits, to cast them out, and to heal all kinds of sickness and all kinds of disease." Luke 9:1-2 give similar words, then in Luke 10, Jesus is sending out seventy others to also perform the same works of the Lord. In Luke 10:16 Jesus is expressing the seriousness of anyone refusing to believe: "He who hears you hears Me, he who rejects you rejects Me, and he who rejects Me rejects Him who sent Me."

I do want to point out that Jesus is our Healer as well as Savior. When Jesus was at Peter's house and healed his mother-in-law, He also healed many people who were brought to Him. The story is in Matthew 8:14-17. Verse 17 says, "that it might be fulfilled which was spoken by Isaiah the prophet, saying: "He Himself took our infirmities and bore our sicknesses." *A quote from Isaiah 53:5.* Peter also tells us in 1 Peter 2:24—"by whose stripes you were healed." This is a powerful Scripture that puts a great light on all the other times that Jesus was healing.

Everywhere that Jesus went, He was teaching, preaching, casting out demons and healing people from all kinds of afflictions and diseases. That was His work while here on the earth. Jesus introduced the Kingdom of God, as is found in Matthew 10:7-8: "And as you go, preach, saying, 'The kingdom of heaven is at hand.' Heal the sick, cleanse the lepers, raise the dead, cast out demons. Freely you have received, freely give." All of these miracles and healings are a part of God's Kingdom blessings.

As you read the accompanying Scriptures, you will find many tremendous truths to believe. It is always very helpful when studying the Word, to take notes as you discover the greatness of the truths that are contained in them. I urge you to make lists, of all the wonderful truths given in these Scriptures. As the song says, "Count your blessings, name them one by one, and it will surprise you what the Lord has done." In the same way, you will be greatly surprised as you take time to do a more thorough study.

If you need healing, call the Oral Roberts prayer line,[9] or the Morris Cerullo Helpline.[10]

God bless you abundantly as you study His Word and find Jesus to be the fulfillment and joy that you had been missing!

SCRIPTURES FOR
B E L I E V E

Believe the Living God and His Son Jesus Christ—

Isa. 43:10 "You are my witnesses," says the Lord, "And my servant whom I have chosen, that you may know and **believe** Me, and understand that I am He. Before Me there was no God formed, nor shall there be after Me." *See verses 8-13*

John 1:6-7 There was a man sent from God, whose name was John. This man came for a witness, to bear witness of the Light, that all through him might **believe.**

John 3:16-17 For God so loved the world that He gave His only begotten Son, that whoever **believes** in Him should not perish but have everlasting life. For God did not send His Son into the world to condemn the world, but that the world through Him might be saved.

John 4:42 Then they said to the woman, "Now we **believe**, not because of what you said, for we ourselves have heard Him and we know that this is indeed the Christ, the Savior of the world."

John 6:28-29 Then they said to Him *(Jesus),* "What shall we do, that we may work the works of God?" Jesus answered and said to them, "This is the work of God, that you **believe** in Him whom He sent."

John 9:35-38 Jesus heard that they had cast him *(man born blind)* out; and when He had found him, He said to him, "Do you **believe** in the Son of God?" He answered and said, "Who is He, Lord, that I may **believe** in Him?" And Jesus said to him, "You have both seen Him and it is He who is talking with you." Then he said, "Lord, I believe!" And he worshiped Him.

John 11:25-27 NIV Jesus said to her *(Martha),* "I am the resurrection and the life. He who **believes** in Me will live, even though he dies; and whoever lives and **believes** in Me will never die. Do you believe this?" "Yes, Lord," she told Him, "I **believe** that You are the Christ, the Son of God, who was to come into the world"

John 11:40-42 NIV *At Lazarus' tomb—-* Then Jesus said, "Did I not tell you that if you **believed**, you would see the glory of God?" So they took away the stone. Then Jesus looked up and said, "Father, I thank You that You have heard Me. I knew that You always hear Me, but I said this for the benefit of the people standing here, that they may **believe** that You sent Me."

John 14:11 "**Believe** Me that I am in the Father and the Father in Me, or else **believe** Me for the sake of the works themselves."

Rom. 4:3, 11 For what does the Scripture say? "Abraham **believed** God, and it was accounted to him for righteousness." *(Also Gal. 3:6; James 2:23)* .....And he *(Abraham)* received the sign of circumcision, a seal of the righteousness of the faith which he had while still uncircumcised, that he might be the father of all those who **believe**, though they are uncircumcised, that righteousness might be imputed to them also.

1 Tim. 3:16 NIV Beyond all question, the mystery of godliness is great: He *(Jesus)* appeared in a body, was vindicated by the Spirit, was seen by angels, was preached among the nations, was **believed** on in the world, was taken up in glory.

1 Tim. 4:9-10 NIV This is a trustworthy saying that deserves full acceptance (and for this we labor and strive), that we have put our hope in the living God, who is the Savior of all men, and especially of those who **believe**.

Heb. 11:6 But without faith it is impossible to please Him, for he who comes to God must **believe** that He is, and that He is a rewarder of those who diligently seek Him.

1 John 3:23 NIV And this is His command: to **believe** in the name of His Son, Jesus Christ, and to love one another as He commanded us.

1 John 5:5 Who is he who overcomes the world, but he who **believes** that Jesus is the Son of God?

Believers and baptism—

Mark 16:15-16 Go into all the world and preach the gospel to every creature. He who **believes** and is **baptized** will be saved; but he who **does not believe** will be condemned.

Acts 2:41 Then those who gladly received *(believed)* his word were **baptized**; and that day about three thousand souls were added to them.

Acts 8:12-13 But when they **believed** Philip as he preached the things concerning the kingdom of God and the name of Jesus Christ, both men and women were **baptized**. Then Simon himself also **believed**; and when he was **baptized** he continued with Philip, and was amazed, seeing the miracles and signs which were done.

Acts. 8:36-37 Now as they *(Philip and the Eunuch of Ethiopia)* went down the road, they came to some water. And the eunuch said, "See, here is water, what hinders me from being **baptized**?" Then Philip said, "If you **believe** with all your heart, you may." And he answered and said, "I **believe** that Jesus Christ is the Son of God."

Acts 10:45-48 And those of the circumcision who **believed** were astonished, as many as came with Peter, because the gift of the Holy Spirit had been poured out on the Gentiles also. For they heard them speak with tongues and magnify God. Then Peter answered, "Can anyone forbid water, that these should not be **baptized** who have received the Holy Spirit just as we have?" And he commanded them to be **baptized** in the name of the Lord. Then they asked him to stay a few days.

Acts 16:30-34 And he *(the Philippian jailer)* brought them out and said, "Sirs, what must I do to be saved?" So they *(Paul and Silas)* said, "**Believe** on the Lord Jesus Christ, and you will be saved, you and your household." Then they spoke the word of the Lord to him and to all who were in his house. And he took them the same hour of the night and washed their stripes. And immediately he and all his family were **baptized**. Now when he had brought them into his house, he set food before them; and he rejoiced, having **believed** in God with all his household.

Acts 18:8 Then Crispus, the ruler of the synagogue, **believed** on the Lord with all his household. And many of the Corinthians, hearing, **believed** and were **baptized**.

Acts 19:2-5 And finding some disciples he *(Paul)* said to them, "Did you receive the Holy Spirit when you **believed**?" So they said to him, "We have not so much as heard whether there is a Holy Spirit." And he said to them, "Into what then were you **baptized**" So they said, "Into John's **baptism**." Then Paul said, "John indeed **baptized** with a **baptism** of repentance, saying to the people that they should **believe** on Him who would come after him, that is, on Christ Jesus."

When they heard this, they were **baptized** in the name of the Lord Jesus.

Blessings and privileges for believers—

2 Chron. 20:20 So they rose early in the morning and went out into the Wilderness of Tekoa; and as they went out, Jehoshaphat stood and said, "Hear me, O Judah and you inhabitants of Jerusalem: **Believe** in the Lord your God and you shall be established; **believe** his prophets, and you shall prosper."

Ps. 27:13 I would have lost heart, unless I had **believed** that I would see the goodness of the Lord in the land of the living.

Matt. 9:28-29 And when He had come into the house, the blind men came to Him. And Jesus said to them, "Do you **believe** that I am able to do this?" They said to Him, "Yes, Lord." Then He touched their eyes, saying, "According to your faith let it be to you."

Matt. 21:22 "And whatever things you ask in prayer, **believing**, you will receive."

Mark 9:23 Jesus said to him, "If you can **believe**, all things are possible to him who **believes**."

Mark 11:22-24 So Jesus answered and said to them, "Have faith in God. For assuredly, I say to you, whoever says to this mountain, 'Be removed and be cast into the sea,' and does not doubt in his heart, but **believes** that those things he says will be done, he will have whatever he says. Therefore I say to you, whatever things you ask when you pray, **believe** that you receive them, and you will have them."

Mark 16:17-18 "And these signs will follow those who **believe**: In My name they will cast out demons; they will speak with new tongues; they will take up serpents; and if they drink anything deadly, it will by no means hurt them; they will lay hands on the sick, and they will recover."

John 1:12-13 But as many as received Him, to them He gave the right to become children of God, to those who **believe** in His name: who were born, not of blood, nor of the will of the flesh, nor of the will of man, but of God.

John 5:24 "Most assuredly, I say to you, he who hears My word and **believes** in Him who sent Me has everlasting life, and shall not come into judgment, but has passed from death into life."

John 6:40 "And this is the will of Him who sent Me, that everyone who sees the Son and **believes** in Him may have everlasting life; and I will raise him up at the last day."

John 7:37-39 On the last day, that great day of the feast, Jesus stood and cried out, saying, "If anyone thirsts, let him come to Me and drink. He who **believes** in Me, as the Scripture has said, out of his heart will flow rivers of living water." But this He spoke concerning the Spirit, whom those **believing** in Him would receive; for the Holy Spirit was not yet given, because Jesus was not yet glorified.

John 12:44-46 Then Jesus cried out and said, "He who **believes** in Me, **believes** not in Me, but in Him who sent Me. And he who sees Me sees Him who sent Me. I have come as a light into the world, that whoever **believes** in Me should not abide in darkness."

John 13:19-20 "Now I *(Jesus)* tell you before it comes, that when it does come to pass, you may **believe** that I am He. Most assuredly, I say to you, he who receives whomever I send receives Me; and he who receives Me receives Him who sent Me."

John 14:12 "Most assuredly I *(Jesus)* say to you, he who **believes** in Me, the works that I do he will do also; and greater works than these he will do, because I go to My Father."

John 16:26-27 In that day you will ask in My name, and I do not say to you that I shall pray the Father for you; for the Father Himself loves you, because you have loved Me, and have **believed** that I came forth from God.

John 17:20-21 "I do not pray for these alone, but also for those who will **believe** in Me through their word; that they all may be one, as You, Father, are in Me, and I in You; that they also may be one in Us, that the world may **believe** that You sent Me."

John 20:28-31 And Thomas answered and said to Him, "My Lord and my God!" Jesus said to him, "Thomas because you have seen Me, you have **believed**. Blessed are those who have not seen and yet have **believed**."

Acts 5:14-16 And **believers** were increasingly added to the Lord, multitudes of both men and women, so that they brought the sick out into the streets and laid them on beds and couches, that at least the shadow of Peter passing by might fall on some of them. Also a multitude gathered from the surrounding cities to Jerusalem, bringing sick people and those who were tormented by unclean spirits, and they were all healed.

Acts 10:43-44 "To Him *(Jesus)* all the prophets witness that, through His name, whoever **believes** in Him will receive remission of sins." While Peter was still speaking these words, the Holy Spirit fell upon all those who heard the word."

Rom. 4:20-25 He *(Abraham)* did not waver at the promise of God through **unbelief**, but was strengthened in faith, giving glory to God, and being fully convinced that what He had promised He was also able to perform. And therefore "it was accounted to him for righteousness." Now it was not written for his sake alone that it was imputed to him, but also for us. It shall be imputed to us who **believe** in Him who raised up Jesus our Lord from the dead, who was delivered up because of our offenses, and was raised because of our justification.

Rom. 15:13 Now may the God of hope fill you with all joy and peace in **believing**, that you may abound in hope by the power of the Holy Spirit.

1 Cor. 1:21 For since, in the wisdom of God, the world through wisdom did not know God, it pleased God through the foolishness of the message preached to save those who **believe**.

Eph. 1:13-14 In Him you also trusted, after you heard the word of truth, the gospel of your salvation; in whom also, having **believed**, you were sealed with the Holy Spirit of promise, who is the guarantee of our inheritance until the redemption of the purchased possession, to the praise of His glory.

1 Thess. 2:13 For this reason we also thank God without ceasing, because when you received the word of God which you heard from

us, you welcomed it not as the word of men, but as it is in truth, the word of God, which also effectively works in you who **believe**.

Those who believe through the preaching of God's servants—

Acts 4:4 ...many of those who heard the word **believed**; and the number of the men came to be about five thousand.

Acts 9:40, 42 But Peter put them all out, and knelt down and prayed. And turning to the body he said, "Tabitha, arise." And she opened her eyes, and when she saw Peter she sat up. ...And it became known throughout all Joppa, and many **believed** on the Lord.

Acts 11:21 And the hand of the Lord was with them and a great number **believed** and turned to the Lord.

Rom. 10:14-17 How then shall they call on Him in whom they have **not believed**? And how shall they **believe** in Him of whom they have not heard? And how shall they hear without a preacher? And how shall they preach unless they are sent? As it is written: "How beautiful are the feet of those who preach the gospel of peace, who bring glad tidings of good things!"

Unbelief—

Mark 9:24 Immediately the father of the child cried out and said with tears, "Lord, I **believe**; help my **unbelief**!"

Mark 16:11 NIV When they *(the disciples)* heard that Jesus was alive and that she (Mary Magdalene) had seen Him, they **did not believe** it. *Also Luke 24:11*

Luke 1:20 NIV And now you *(Zachariah)* will be silent and not able to speak until the day this happens, because you **did not believe** my words, which will come true at their proper time.

Luke 8:13 "But the ones on the rock are those who, when they hear, receive the Word with joy; and these have no root, who **believe for a while** and in time of temptation fall away."

Luke 22:67 NIV "If you are the Christ," they said, "tell us." Jesus answered, "If I tell you, you will **not believe** Me."

Luke 24:13-15, 25 Now behold, two of them *(we only know one name-Cleopas)* were traveling that same day to a village called Emmaus, which was seven miles from Jerusalem. And they talked together of all these things which had happened. So it was, while they conversed and reasoned, that Jesus Himself drew near and went with them. ... Then He said to them, "O foolish ones, and **slow of heart to believe** in all that the prophets have spoken!"

John 5:37-38, 44-47 "And the Father Himself, who sent Me, has testified of Me. You have neither heard His voice at any time, nor seen His form. But you do not have His word abiding in you, because whom He sent, Him you **do not believe**. ....How can you **believe**, who receive honor from one another, and do not seek the honor that comes from the only God? Do not think that I shall accuse you to the Father; there is one who accuses you–Moses, in whom you trust. For if you **believed** Moses, you would **believe** Me; for he wrote about Me. But if you **do not believe** his writings, how will you **believe** My words?"

James 1:6-8 NIV But when he asks, he must **believe and not doubt**, because he who doubts is like a wave of the sea, blown and tossed by the wind. That man should not think he will receive anything from the Lord; he is a double-minded man, unstable in all he does.

1 Peter 2:7-8 Therefore, to you who **believe**, He is precious; but to those who are disobedient, "The stone which the builders rejected has become the chief cornerstone," and "A stone of stumbling and a rock of offense." They stumble, being disobedient to the word, to which they also were appointed.

1 John 5:10 He who **believes** in the Son of God has the witness in himself; he who **does not believe** has made Him a liar, because he **has not believed** the testimony that God has given of His Son.

Warnings—

Matt. 18:6 "But whoever causes one of these little ones who **believe** in Me to sin, it would be better for him if a millstone were hung around his neck, and he were drowned in the depth of the sea." *Also Mark 9:42.*

Matt. 21:24-25 *Jesus is responding to the chief priests and elders in the temple when He is speaking in these verses— —-* But Jesus answered and said to them, "I also will ask you one thing, which if you tell Me, I likewise will tell you by what authority I do these things: The baptism of John – where was it from? From heaven or from men?" And they reasoned among themselves, saying, "If we say, 'From heaven,' He will say to us, 'Why then did you **not believe** Him?'

Mark 5:35-36 While Jesus was still speaking, some came from the ruler of the synagogue's house *(Jairus)* who said, "Your daughter is dead. Why trouble the Teacher any further? As soon as Jesus heard the word that was spoken, He said to the ruler of the synagogue, "Do not be afraid; only **believe**." *Also see Luke 8:50.*

Mark 16:16b "....but he who **does not believe** will be condemned."

John 3:18 He who **believes** in Him is not condemned; but he who does **not believe** is condemned already, because he **has not believed** in the name of the only begotten Son of God.

John 8:24 "Therefore I said to you that you will die in your sins; for if you **do not believe** that I am He, you will die in your sins."

James 2:19- 20, 26 You **believe** that there is one God. Good! Even the demons **believe** that–and shudder. You foolish man, do you want evidence that faith without deeds is useless? ....As the body without the spirit is dead, so faith without deeds is dead.

1 John 4:1, 3 Beloved, **do not believe** every spirit, but test the spirits, whether they are of God; because many false prophets have gone out into the world. ....and every spirit that does not confess that Jesus Christ has come in the flesh is not of God. And this is the spirit of the Antichrist, which you have heard was coming, and is now already in the world.

FOLLOW

DO NOT TURN ASIDE FROM FOLLOWING THE LORD

Have you ever stood in a line, expecting to see a certain person, and after an hour discover that you're in the wrong line? Or, followed a long line of cars, and when it was too late, you discovered you were heading up a ramp onto a highway? Oops! Not your choice! There are even worse scenarios than those. Let's talk about it.

The words of Leviticus 18:1-4 are foundational for a godly life, God's basic instructions to follow for blessings and happiness. You may think, "It sounds too tough, I don't like the word MUST!" Consider the importance of the sides on a bridge. They are obviously there to protect people from falling to their death in water, or onto a train track below, or into something as steep and deep as a canyon. God's Word is powerful and is like a searchlight for the same purpose of protecting us from serious dangers and catastrophes.

Wisdom tells us to find out what God's directions are, and then follow them exactly. In 1 Samuel 12:20 we read, "Do not turn aside from following the Lord, but serve the Lord with all your heart." Even as you're driving, you have to make a choice what streets, or highways, you will take. It's a wholehearted choice to follow that route; half of you can't be going another direction in the same vehicle. Now if you make another choice, then your goal has changed. Do you see the point? We need to know what God has for us to do, learn how He wants it done, and wholeheartedly follow Him.

JESUS SAID, "FOLLOW ME"

There are many Old Testament Scriptures for this word, but it's most important to observe the words of Jesus and the Apostles' writings for this word study.

When Jesus was calling certain men as disciples, He appears to say to each of them something like this, "Follow Me, and I will make you fishers of men." There were others who expressed their desire to follow Jesus, but His answer was, "Foxes have holes and birds of the air have nests, but the Son of Man has nowhere to lay His head." So Jesus was essentially telling them to follow Him as He preached, taught and healed the sick, so they could learn the message that He had for their lives.

Jesus' way was going to be very different than anything they had ever known. He brought the new Way to live righteously. We are to repent of our sins and experience the new birth by the washing of the water of God's Word and by His Spirit. *See John 3:5, John 15:3-5, Ephesians 5:25-27, Romans 8:9-11.* We are no longer to live by Old Testament regulations and traditions, but in accordance to the teachings of Jesus.

Jesus emphasizes this during His Sermon on the Mount. Several times He says, "You have heard....," or "Furthermore it has been said......," and then He adds, "But I say to you....." He does not cancel out what was spoken in the laws of the Old Testament, but shows them the necessity of going beyond the "Thou shalt nots" and other rules set forth in those days. If you would desire to learn a new process at work, just learning what not to do is not enough. God is calling us to a life of loving as Jesus loves. So we are not to look for what we can get by with, but look for ways that we can be the instruments and the messengers of God's love and grace.

Jesus came to serve. In everything He did, He was not earning plaques, rewards, this world's goods or applause. He came to give His all for us in a very humble walk with the poorest of humanity. His feet may have been bleeding and His body exhausted, but He continued to minister to all the needs of the multitudes of men, women and children who followed Him.

In His entire ministry, His entire ministry, His life was an example for godly living. We are to follow Jesus in humble service, compelled by His love within us. Franklin Graham, Billy Graham's son, is such an example. In his book, Living Beyond the Limits,[11] you can learn what true humble service is, and find out how to really live beyond the limits. If you read this book you will find that it is so enlightening and encouraging to dare to step out and surrender to serving the Lord in far greater capacities than you realized were available. There are so many opportunities to express God's love, and help bring in the harvest in these last days.

THERE IS SAFETY IN GOD'S LOVE FORMULA

I Corinthians 13:4-8a gives a beautiful description of true love. "Love suffers long and is kind; love does not envy; love does not parade itself, is not puffed up; does not behave rudely, does not seek its own, is not provoked, thinks no evil; does not rejoice in iniquity, but rejoices in the truth; bears all things, believes all things, hopes all things, endures all things. Love never fails."

You probably noticed that this formula does include what love is not. Can you see that there are many situations where you need to know 'what not to do' first, so you can get a clearer picture of what is wise and appropriate; what is the more perfect path to follow? For example, you need to know who the leader is going to be. Is he/she honest? Is this person safe to follow? Is the person in this for selfish ends, which could mean that I might be dumped at the next curve? Are there just dollar signs drawing us this direction? Can I please God if I take these steps forward? Where is this leading me and my family? You can consider other questions you need to ask before taking steps to follow any person or something that requires your signature.

Jesus' disciple, John, came to him quite upset one day as he said, "Teacher, we saw someone who does not follow us, casting out demons in Your name, and we forbade him because he does not follow us." But Jesus said, "Do not forbid him, for no one who works a miracle in My name can soon afterward speak evil of Me." We are so prone to think that if someone doesn't do things the way we do, they must not be Christians. There is an example of this in Mark 9:38-41 where it says, "Now John answered Him, saying, 'Teacher, we saw someone who does not follow us casting out demons in Your name, and we forbade him because he does not follow us.' But Jesus said, 'Do not forbid him, for no one who works a miracle in My name can soon afterward speak evil of Me. For he who is not against us is on our side. For whoever gives you a cup of water to drink in My name, because you belong to Christ, assuredly, I say to you, he will by no means lose his reward.'"

I see the above Scripture revealing a very important point to us, and Jesus is the one who spoke these words. They are not a 'take it or leave it.' So the question is, do we really want to know God's will in all things, and follow Him, or can we just set up rules that suit our ideas and doctrines, thinking that God ought to be pleased with us for however many reasons we can point out? The parable of the ten virgins comes to my mind.

THE TRUE FOLLOWERS OF JESUS

The ten virgins have something in common; they are all waiting for the bridegroom. This would categorize them at least as 'Church goers', because the bridegroom is Jesus, and they are all waiting for the bridegroom to come. The ten virgins are anticipating a special occasion with him. But the rendition of this in Matthew 25:1-13, shows the seriousness of how the ten virgins were living during the time that they were waiting for the bridegroom's return. They all had lamps, they all slumbered and slept while waiting, but five of them are called foolish because they did not have enough oil in their lamps. The foolish five went out to buy oil when the bridegroom came, and we find that the bridegroom did not wait for them. He took the five wise virgins in with him to the wedding; and the door was shut. What finality that reveals to us! The bridegroom made the choice, no other possibility.

But my heart goes 'bang'. Couldn't there be an opportunity to discuss things, and give them some time to buy the oil they needed for their lamps? Evidently not! This shows that these five virgins were not living according to the standards established in God's Word. They were following what they perceived to be good enough, as though God ought to be pleased and surely would not refuse to take them to heaven. Maybe they were involved in good works, but rarely prayed or studied the Bible. Maybe they mixed religious stuff from other organizations with truth, thinking they were compatible. There are many organizations like that, they are religious, but are not in harmony with God's Word. Remember, Satan used Scriptures when alluring Jesus in the wilderness. It is probably better stated, "He miss-used" the Written Word of God. Most likely they never had a personal relationship with the Lord. What could have prevented them from being accepted? The door was shut. When they called, "Lord, Lord, open to us!" He answered and said, "Assuredly, I say to you, I do not know you." Then Jesus gives this warning: "Watch therefore, for you know neither the day nor the hour in which the Son of Man is coming."

I don't know what beliefs you follow, but I need to ask this question, "What is the Lord saying to you about this? There are many interpretations as to what the oil in this passage represents. As I read the Word, I dare not make up my own conclusions or interpretations. Just as you write a letter to someone, who can best interpret what you mean with the words you use? You know exactly what your words mean. So it is with God's Word, which is inspired by the Holy Spirit. We must go to Him to seek His interpretation in order to follow truth.

Observe these Scriptures. Exodus 28:41 speaks of the anointing to be for consecration and to sanctify. In 1 Samuel 16:3-13 we read about Samuel hearing from God which son of Jesse he was to anoint to become the future king. In verses 12 and 13 we see that David was God's choice so He told Samuel to anoint him. Samuel took the horn of oil and anointed him, and then we read that from that day on the Spirit of the Lord was on David in power.

When Jesus was baptized, the Holy Spirit came upon Him. You can read this account in Matthew 3:16-17 and in Luke 3:21-22. Then when the 120 were baptized with the Holy Spirit, recorded in Acts 2:1-4, there were tongues of fire above each one of their heads. In Matthew 3:11 John the Baptist foretold that Jesus would baptize with the Holy Spirit and fire. Luke 3:16 says the same. After Jesus had been baptized He was led by the Spirit of God into the wilderness. In Luke 4:1 it says, "Then Jesus, being filled with the Holy Spirit, returned from the Jordan and was led by the Spirit into the wilderness."

In Acts 4:31 we read, "And when they had prayed, the place where they were assembled together was shaken; and they were all filled with the Holy Spirit, and they spoke the word of God with boldness." They had already been baptized with the Holy Spirit as recorded in Acts 2:1-4. However, in the account given in Acts 4:23-31, while they were together, after being threatened to not speak the name of Jesus, they cried out to God in prayer. They asked Him to give them boldness to speak His word, and that He would stretch out His hand to heal, and that signs and wonders may be done through the name of His holy Servant Jesus. Suddenly the power of God shook the place where they were meeting and it is saying that they were all filled with the Holy Spirit. Can you see clearly what it means to have enough oil in our lamps so that we might be accepted by the Bridegroom, Jesus, when He comes? I pray that as you re-examine all of these Scriptures, that you will be praying for the Holy Spirit to guide you and quicken your understanding with what the Lord wants you to see and know assuredly about having enough oil in your lamp, so the door will not be shut before you. God has a purpose for giving this parable in the exact place He put it in His Word.

ABIDING IN GOD'S LOVE

Early in the Gospels Jesus is saying, "Follow Me." And the Apostle John says in 1 John 2:6, "He who says he abides in Him *(Jesus)* ought himself also to walk just as He walked." One important part of Jesus' walk was that He perfectly obeyed His Father. John 6:37-38 says, "All that the Father gives Me will come to Me, and the one who comes to Me I will by no means cast out. For I have come down from heaven, not to do My own will, but the will of Him who sent Me." When Jesus was carrying out His Father's will, He was living out His love for Him. This is a powerful truth, and is basic to the message that Jesus is conveying to His followers.

In John 14:10-11, as Jesus is preparing His disciples for the time that He would be leaving this earth, He said, "If you keep My commandments, you will abide in My love, just as I have kept My Father's commandments and abide in His love. These things I have spoken to you, that My joy may remain in you, and that your joy may be full."

So it follows, if we love Jesus, we will also love Father God. As we keep His commandments, we will abide in His love, and our joy will be full. There's no question about the fact that peace will abide in our hearts too. Romans 14:17 says, "For the kingdom of God is not eating and drinking, but righteousness and peace and joy in the Holy Spirit." That brings in the Holy Spirit too, for He is the Spirit of God.

The above study cannot possibly give everything there is to know on this subject, especially since there are many truths that hinge onto nearly every verse. I am recommending two books which cover a part of this subject more thoroughly. As we follow Jesus, He wants us to walk in the fullness of what He has provided for us. If we don't, we will be losers of tremendous blessings and will be ill equipped to serve Him. One is Claim Your Inheritance, by Richard Roberts[12] and the other is Heirs of the Promise, from the Potter's House.[13] As you read the other Scriptures, make lists for yourself. It will greatly benefit your understanding of how to follow God's ways. These are some of the additional treasures you can fish for.

Here are some comforting words that Jesus gives in John 10. Here are verses 4, 10b and 14—"And when he brings out his own sheep, he goes before them; and the sheep follow him, for they know his voice. ... I have come that they may have life, and that they may have it more abundantly. ...I am the good shepherd; and I know My sheep, and am known by My own." The only safe place is to be close to the Good Shepherd, Jesus, following in His footsteps!

SCRIPTURES FOR
FOLLOW

Following the Lord – or not –

Lev. 18:1-4 The Lord said to Moses, "Speak to the Israelites and say to them: 'I am the Lord your God. You must not do as they do in Egypt, where you used to live, and you must not do as they do in the land of Canaan, where I am bringing you. Do not **follow** their practices. You must obey my laws and be careful to follow my decrees. I am the Lord your God."

Deut. 1:35-36 ...except Caleb the son of Jephunneh; he shall see it, and to him and his children I am giving the land on which he walked, because he wholly **followed** the Lord.

Josh. 22:16-18, 23, 29 "Thus says the whole congregation of the Lord: 'What treachery is this that you have committed against the God of Israel, to turn away this day from **following** the Lord, in that you have built for yourselves an altar, that you might rebel this day against the Lord? Is the iniquity of Peor not enough for us, from which we are not cleansed till this day, although there was a plague in the congregation of the Lord, but that you must turn away this day from **following** the Lord? And it shall be, if you rebel today against the Lord, that tomorrow He will be angry with the whole congregation of Israel.'" .... "If we have built ourselves an altar, to turn from **following** the Lord, or if to offer on it burnt offerings or grain offerings, or if to offer peace offerings on it, let the Lord Himself require an account." ...."Far be it from us that we should rebel against the Lord, and turn from **following** the Lord this day, to build an altar for burnt offerings, for grain offerings, or for sacrifices, besides the altar of the Lord our God which is before His tabernacle."

1 Sam. 12:20, 23-24 Then Samuel said to the people, "Do not fear.

You have done all this wickedness; yet do not turn aside from **following** the Lord, but serve the Lord with all your heart. ....Moreover, as for me, far be it from me that I should sin against the Lord in ceasing to pray for you; but I will teach you the good and the right way. Only fear the Lord, and serve Him in truth with all your heart; for consider what great things He has done for you."

1 Kings 9:6-7 "But if you or your sons at all turn from **following** Me, and do not keep My commandments and My statutes which I have set before you, but go and serve other gods and worship them, then I will cut off Israel from the land which I have given them; and this house which I have consecrated for My name I will cast out of My sight. Israel will be a proverb and a byword among all peoples."

1 Kings 11:4, 6, 9-11 For it was so, when Solomon was old, that his wives turned his heart after other gods; and his heart was not loyal to the Lord his God, as was the heart of his father David. ....Solomon did evil in the sight of the Lord, and did not fully **follow** the Lord, as did his father David. ....So the Lord became angry with Solomon, because his heart had turned from the Lord God of Israel, who had appeared to him twice, and had commanded him concerning this thing, that he should not go after other gods; but he did not keep what the Lord had commanded. Therefore the Lord said to Solomon, "Because you have done this, and have not kept My covenant and My statutes, which I have commanded you, I will surely tear the kingdom away from you and give it to your servant."

2 Chron. 34:33 Thus Josiah removed all the abominations from all the country that belonged to the children of Israel, and made all who were present in Israel diligently serve the Lord their God. All his days they did not depart from **following** the Lord God of their fathers.

Following godly qualities—

Deut. 16:20 You shall **follow** what is altogether just, that you may live and inherit the land which the Lord your God is giving you.

Prov. 15:9 The way of the wicked is an abomination to the Lord, but He loves him who **follows** righteousness.

Prov. 21:21 He who **follows** righteousness and mercy finds life, righteousness and honor.

Isa. 51:1 Listen to Me, you who **follow** after righteousness; you who seek the Lord: Look to the rock from which you were hewn, and to the hole of the pit from which you were dug.

2 Thess. 3:7-10 For you yourselves know how you ought to **follow** us, for we were not disorderly among you; nor did we eat anyone's bread free of charge, but worked with labor and toil night and day, that we might not be a burden to any of you. Not because we do not have authority, but to make ourselves an example of how you should **follow** us. For even when we were with you, we commanded you this: If anyone will not work, neither shall he eat.

1 Tim. 4:6 If you instruct the brethren in these things, you will be a good minister of Jesus Christ, nourished in the words of faith and of the good doctrine which you have carefully **followed**.

Following Jesus – or not –

Matt. 4:19 Then He said to them (Peter & Andrew), "**Follow** Me, and I will make you fishers of men." *Also Mk 1:17*

Matt. 8:19-22 Then a certain scribe came and said to Him, "Teacher, I will **follow** you wherever you go." And Jesus said to him, "Foxes have holes and birds of the air have nests, but the Son of Man has nowhere to lay His head." Then another of His disciples said to Him, "Lord, let me first go and bury my father." But Jesus said to him, "**Follow** Me, and let the dead bury their own dead."

Matt. 9:9 As Jesus passed on from there, He saw a man named Matthew sitting at the tax office. And He said to him, "**Follow** Me."

So he arose & **followed** Him.

Matt. 10:38 And he who does not take his cross and **follow** after Me is not worthy of Me.

Matt. 16:24 Then Jesus said to His disciples, "If anyone desires to come after Me, let him deny himself, and take up his cross and **follow** Me." *Also Mk 8:34; Lu. 9:23*

Matt. 19:21 Jesus said to him *(The rich young ruler)*, "If you want to be perfect, go, sell what you have and give to the poor, and you will have treasure in heaven; and come, **follow me**."

Matt. 19:27 Then Peter answered and said to Him, "See, we have left all and **followed** You. Therefore what shall we have?"

Matt. 20:34 So Jesus had compassion and touched their eyes. And immediately their eyes received sight and they **followed** Him.

Mark 3:7 But Jesus withdrew with His disciples to the sea. And a great multitude from Galilee **followed** Him, and from Judea and Jerusalem and Idumea and beyond the Jordan; and those from Tyre and Sidon, a great multitude, when they heard how many things He was doing, came to Him.

Mark 5:35-37 While He *(Jesus)* was still speaking, some came from the ruler of the synagogue's house who said, "Your daughter is dead. Why trouble the Teacher any further?" As soon as Jesus heard the word that was spoken, He said to the ruler of the synagogue, "Do not be afraid, only believe." And He permitted no one to **follow** him except Peter, James, and John the brother of James.

Mark 9:38-39 Now John answered Him saying, "Teacher, we saw someone who does not **follow** us casting out demons in Your name, and we forbade him because he does not follow us." But Jesus said, "Do not forbid him, for no one who works a miracle in My name can soon afterward speak evil of Me."

John 10:4-5, 14 *Jesus is speaking* — "And when he brings out his own sheep, he goes before them; and the sheep **follow** him, for they know his voice. Yet they will by no means **follow** a stranger, but will flee from him, for they do not know the voice of strangers." ...."I am the good shepherd; and I know My sheep, and am known by My own."

1 Cor. 10:31–11:1 NIV So whether you eat or drink or whatever you do, do it all for the glory of God. Do not cause anyone to stumble, whether Jews, Greeks or the church of God– even as I try to please everybody in every way. For I am not seeking my own good but the good of many, so that they may be saved. **Follow** my example, as I **follow** the example of Christ.

1 Cor. 13:13–14:1 NIV And now these three remain: faith, hope, love. But the greatest of these is love. **Follow** the way of love and eagerly desire spiritual gifts, especially the gift of prophecy.

1 Peter 2:21 For to this you were called, because Christ also suffered for us, leaving us an example, that you should **follow** His steps.

Blessings on those who, by faith, follow the Lord's ways—

Ps. 23:6 Surely goodness and mercy shall **follow** me all the days of my life; and I will dwell in the house of the Lord forever.

Matt. 19:28 So Jesus said to them, "Assuredly I say to you, that in the regeneration, when the Son of Man sits on the throne of His glory, you who have **followed** Me will also sit on twelve thrones, judging the twelve tribes of Israel."

John 8:12 Then Jesus spoke to them again, saying, "I am the light of the world. He who **follows** Me shall not walk in darkness, but have the light of life."

John 12:26 "If anyone serves Me, let him **follow** Me; and where I am, there My servant will be also. If anyone serves Me, him My Father will honor."

Rev. 14:4, 13 These are the ones who were not defiled with women, for they are virgins. These are the ones who **follow** the Lamb wherever He goes. These were redeemed from among men, being firstfruits to God and to the Lamb. ....Then I heard a voice from heaven saying to me, "Write: 'Blessed are the dead who die in the Lord from now on.'" "Yes," says the Spirit, "that they may rest from their labors, and their works **follow** them."

ACKNOWLEDGE

ACKNOWLEDGE GOD IN ALL YOUR WAYS

Although you most probably know this word, and how to use it, the dictionary provides some interesting thoughts, which make our well-known Scriptures more meaningful. The dictionary says—"to admit to be true; to recognize the authority or claims of; to give recognition by response; expressing thanks to show receipt of some kind of a gift." Does this help you to think of ways that you have acknowledged the Lord's goodness, or the thoughtfulness of a person, whom the Lord has used for bringing a blessing to you?

There is one outstanding Scripture, where the word 'acknowledge' is truly significant. It seems to be God's strong counsel for many a situation. Those of you who know the word may well have guessed that it's Proverbs 3:5 and 6. "Trust in the Lord with all your heart, and lean not on your own understanding; in all your ways acknowledge Him, and He shall direct your paths." This basic text sums up many other Scriptures from the Old and New Testaments. It is so powerful for application over and over again.

We have to start with 'trusting in the Lord' with our whole being. It's not a matter of saving a few ideas that we could try, just in case. There is no plan B, because we are not to lean on our limited view and understanding. God's view is into eternity. No wonder we are to walk by faith and not by sight. Our scope of knowing and observing is restricted by many human limitations. What a blessing to realize that God is unlimited in every way we can approach our circumstances and the people involved. So, as we choose to obey His Word, and just trust Him, acknowledging His wisdom and understanding, we won't even attempt to instruct Him how to handle our problems. He has promised to direct our paths.

Joseph, the son of Jacob, comes to mind here. You may know the story from Genesis 37 to 47. These chapters hold some very interesting history of the Israelites. Joseph was an important key to where they became established as a family, and then as a nation. If you know anything about Joseph's brothers trying to get rid of him, and selling him to the Ishmaelites, also called Midianite Traders, then you can understand just a little bit what Joseph experienced as he is taken as a slave by total strangers from his familiar family and territory. He had no Bible to instruct him in God's ways. He had no Sunday School training, however, surely the stories of God's grace and amazing delivering power had come down from his great-grandfather Abraham, then through Grandpa Isaac and his father. I can imagine that in his home there were times of rehearsing their experiences that revealed the greatness of God.

Now, en route toward the unknown he is desperate to trust the God that has been his father's companion through many fierce circumstances. I wonder if he relived one episode after another to keep from being overcome by wild tormenting thoughts. This requires acknowledging God as One who is far greater than all the universe that He created. He would have surely acknowledged God as One of superior wisdom and understanding for taking care of him in such a dreadfully painful situation.

I recently met the author of a very interesting book, The Seven Robes of Joseph, by Lydia Chorpening.[14] Most probably few of us could imagine Joseph having seven robes. You will need to read her book to discover what she found during her study of Joseph's life.

TO ACKNOWLEDGE HIM WE MUST KNOW HIM

Acknowledging the Lord really requires more than just knowing about His attributes, we need to know Him! This will cause us to turn to Him quickly, rather than waiting until we're caught between the 'rock and a hard place'. Knowing His awesomeness and compassion from personal encounters reveals His faithfulness in doing exactly what He has promised in His Word. We have the tendency to respond according to the manner that our emotions dictate.

In Isaiah 33:13 we find these instructions, "Hear, you who are afar off, what I have done; and you who are near, acknowledge My might." How extremely important these instructions are, not only for them, but for our lives too. God's might, His power, is at work on our behalf, and is working in us to do His will. *See Phil. 1:6 and 2:13.* It is just one of His absolute characteristics. Remember this, He never changes. We might not experience all the blessings He wants to pour out upon us, because those blessings are attached to His conditions.

We can find many Scriptures that show the disobedience of God's children. We don't even have to look at the heathen, those who have never acknowledged the Lord as their God. In the book of Jeremiah, we learn so much about God's people going their own way, ignoring the Lord. Here are a few verses, chapter 7:23-27: "But this is what I commanded them, saying, 'Obey My voice, and I will be your God, and you shall be My people. And walk in all the ways that I have commanded you, that it may be well with you.' Yet they did not obey or incline their ear *(did not acknowledge Him)*, but followed the counsels and the dictates of their evil hearts, and went backward and not forward. Since the day that your fathers came out of the land of Egypt until this day, I have even sent to you all My servants the prophets, daily rising up early and sending them. Yet they did not obey Me or incline their ear, but stiffened their neck. They did worse than their fathers. Therefore you shall speak all these words to them, but they will not obey you. You shall also call to them, but they will not answer you."

God already knew what their response would be, and they suffered for it, but in chapter 33 we read some awesome blessings. There He promises healing, rebuilding, cleansing and pardon. And in verse 9 we read, "Then it shall be to Me a name of joy, a praise, and an honor before all nations of the earth, who shall hear all the good that I do to them; they shall fear and tremble for all the goodness and all the prosperity that I provide for it."

In the book of Hosea, there are many examples of how Israel rejected God's will for them, and they also suffered greatly for their choices. It's so important to observe whether or not we're trying to make up for our failures and wrong doings by appeasing God with some kind of sacrifice. He sees it all, for He knows our thoughts and intentions, just as clearly as He knows our speech and actions. In these Old Testament books we find that God continuously calls them back to obedience, so they could experience the love of His heart, and to live in the luxurious plans that He had for them.

If you read all of Jeremiah and all of Hosea, you will hear how much God still loved His people, even though they sinned grievously. His heart was yearning for His people to acknowledge Him as the One who constantly and wisely watched over them, providing their every need along their journey of life. But when life was going along smoothly, they forgot Him, worshiping other gods again. It doesn't seem possible does it?

Do you know what it is like to experience rejection from your children? Do they by words, or actions, tell you that they are far wiser than you? Do they ignore your pleas about things that are important for health and safety, or family harmony and unity? Have they let you down through lack of communication? If you have experienced any disappointments with your children, then you surely can feel God's heart-cry in the above scriptures. People who think of God as just some 'higher power', or 'something way out there beyond the blue', or even 'the man upstairs' have no conception of the true God, the great 'I Am', the eternal Holy God, Creator of the universe, and the giver of life!

God is not just a 'power force', but experiences emotions, which are expressed in His mercy, compassion and lovingkindnesses. He calls us into a love relationship with Himself. He sent His own Son, Jesus, to redeem us and provide reconciliation. When Jesus came to this earth, one major purpose was to reveal His Father's nature, so we could know Him—see John 1:1-5, John 17 and Hebrews—chapters 1-3, just to name a few.

Can you think of ways that you daily acknowledge God as the Most High God, and as your Father in heaven? How about ways that you often forget to acknowledge Him in your daily journey? Are you aware of acknowledging God when you go to Church to worship Him, singing praises, fervently praying for His kingdom to come and His will to be done in your life, as well as throughout the earth? Or are you just 'attending Church', which doesn't require very much?

DAVID GLORIOUSLY ACKNOWLEDGED GOD

One of the most glorious acknowledgments of God, is David's prayer in 1 Chronicles 29:10-14-NIV: "Praise be to You, O Lord, God of our father Israel, from everlasting to everlasting. Yours, O Lord is the greatness and the power and the glory and the majesty and the splendor, for everything in heaven and earth is Yours. Yours, O Lord, is the kingdom, You are exalted as head over all. Wealth and honor come from You, You are the ruler of all things. In Your hands are strength and power to exalt and give strength to all. Now, our God, we give You thanks, and praise Your glorious name. But who am I, and who are my people, that we should be able to give as generously as this? Everything comes from You, and we have given You only what comes from Your hand."

As we observe each phrase in this prayer, and really hear the honor and praise that David is expressing, it can take you right from the place where you may be sitting and lift you to spiritual heights. Can you feel that? Do you feel the transforming power? This really helps us to understand that there is nothing too hard for God to figure out. We can trust God with the smallest issue all the way to the most earthshaking, heartrending situations that we could encounter. We don't expect those kinds of trials, and surely don't ask for them, but life brings us many things that are way beyond us. But God, if we acknowledge Him properly as God, will guide us and give us directions to the solutions.

We had an embarrassing experience when my husband was to preach at a Church in Indiana a few decades ago. He had already preached at the morning service and we had dinner with a number of families who stayed at Church for the day. As we were finishing a snack before the evening service, my husband went to get his evening message to familiarize himself with his notes. That door was locked, and no one could find the key, since the Pastor, who was out of town, was the only one who knew where it was. They just had no need for that key during their many years in the building. Actually, our sons (ages 9 & 11) were guilty, for they had changed clothes in that room, and the door was in a locked mode when they left the room.

Praise God, one of the elders suggested that we women pray while the men searched. About fifteen minutes later, the keys were found in a most unusual place in a box on a top shelf. They sincerely believed that those keys would not have been found if we weren't humbling ourselves before the Lord in prayer. In this way we acknowledged the Lord's awareness of where it was, and He honored that.

It seemed impossible, but we were experiencing this again in a threatening situation at home two days later. My husband was a Supervisor at the Post Office and held keys for locks that no one else had. He was due to leave the house in a half hour, and they were not in their usual place. We were frantic at first, then we decided to pray. I prayed aloud, praising the Lord that He knew right where those keys were, so we would take care of the other necessities, and trust that by the time Wayne had to leave for work, he'd have the keys. While eating breakfast, I realized that I had forgotten to call our daughter for school. The thought came to me to put the shades up as I called her, so it would be easier for her to recognize morning had arrived. As I raised the shades, there were the keys on the dresser. One of our sons had strangely laid them there, thinking that they were her keys. It shows how things can happen so out of character, or without explanation. However, when we simply, but trustingly acknowledge God, He will tell us the solution, or lead us right to it, sometimes in the most amazing ways!

SUGGESTIONS FOR ACKNOWLEDGING GOD

We are created beings, and truly need to acknowledge the God who created all things, which we read about in Genesis 1 and 2. There are many other places in God's Word, especially in the Psalms and in Isaiah, where they again speak of His tremendous power in creating the universe and the inhabitants. We will never outgrow our need to acknowledge Him and proclaim His praise with deepest gratitude and joy! Let me give some suggestions for acknowledging God on a daily basis—-

—Acknowledge Him when you awaken by saying a similar prayer as this, "Good morning Father, You are so great and greatly to be praised! Thank you for the night of rest. Keep me close to You today. I want to honor You in everything I do and say! Lead me in Your paths, so I will be where You want me to be, saying what You want me to say, fulfilling Your purposes for my life. Thank you for being here for me today. I love You and praise the name of Jesus!"

—Acknowledge any sin that may be hindering a blessed relationship with the Lord. You may even be getting twinges of pain in your heart sometimes as God reminds you of that sin and it is hindering your prayers.

—Acknowledge Him in every circumstance, and in every decision you make.

—Acknowledge Him as the One who has the solution to your problems, even in organizing your schedule, finding your keys, instructing the children, or where you placed those important papers.

—Acknowledge Him as the giver of all good and perfect gifts. That includes each family member, friends, your Pastor and Church family, especially His Word of knowledge, instructions, wonderful promises, protection, mercy, compassion and all that these mean to you; the sunshine and rain, health, food, clothing, shelter, car, and many other blessings that surround us from day to day. Besides these: lakes, breezes, even the clouds in the sky protecting from excess heat, or seen as gorgeous displays of His unsurpassed creativity; also our ability to see, to hear, speak, use our hands and feet, to work and play, ability to enjoy God's magnificent handiwork in endless ways, and in the realm of His abundant grace.

Let me ask you some pertinent questions—-

Was this word 'acknowledge' a familiar word to you? Did you know Proverbs 3:5 and 6 by heart? List some of the times that you did not follow the instructions of this major Scripture, and discovered later that you didn't act wisely. Tell about the outcome. Did your experience send you to God's Word for help? By each situation, write the Scripture that gave you the truth that you needed. Also write some experiences in your life when you did acknowledge the Lord, and add the way that the Lord showed you the path to take which brought the right results, and possibly even great victory.

In all of God's Word, there are so many instructions about acknowledging Him without necessarily using this word. I urge you to research some Scriptures. This is so valuable and enriching for spiritual growth. God bless you as you acknowledge Him with a strong assurance that He will answer your earnest prayers. Then lift your voice with highest, glorious praise to the Lord God Almighty, for He is worthy!

SCRIPTURES FOR
ACKNOWLEDGE

Acknowledging the Lord—-

Ps. 91:14-16 "Because he loves Me," says the Lord, "I will rescue him; I will protect him, for he **acknowledges** My name. He will call upon Me, and I will answer him; I will be with him in trouble, I will deliver him and honor him. With long life will I satisfy him and show him My salvation."

Prov. 3:5-6 Trust in the Lord with all your heart, and lean not on your own understanding; in all your ways **acknowledge** Him, and He shall direct your paths.

Isa. 33:13 "Hear, you who are afar off, what I have done; and you who are near, **acknowledge** My might."

Jer. 10:23-25a NIV "I know, O Lord, that a man's life is not his own; it is not for man to direct his steps. Correct me Lord, but only with justice—not in your anger, lest you reduce me to nothing. Pour out your wrath on the nations that do not **acknowledge** You, on the peoples who do not call on Your name."

Hosea 6:1-3, 6 NIV "Come, let us return to the Lord, He has torn us to pieces but He will heal us; He has injured us but He will bind up our wounds. After two days He will revive us; on the third day He will restore us, that we may live in His Presence. Let us **acknowledge** the Lord; let us press on to **acknowledge** Him. As surely as the sun rises, He will appear; He will come to us like the winter rains; like the spring rains that water the earth." ... "For I desire mercy, not sacrifice, and **acknowledgment** of God rather than burnt offerings."

Hosea 8:2-3 NIV "Israel cries out to Me, 'O our God, we **acknowl-**

edge You!' But Israel has rejected what is good; an enemy will pursue him."

Hosea 13:4-6 NIV "...But I am the Lord your God, who brought you out of Egypt. You shall **acknowledge** no God but Me, no Savior except Me. I cared for you in the desert, in the land of burning heat. When I fed them, they were satisfied; when they were satisfied, they became proud; then they forgot Me." *See Psalm 106 and 107.*

Luke 7:29-30 NIV (All the people, even the tax collectors, when they heard Jesus' words, **acknowledged** that God's way was right, because they had been baptized by John. But the Pharisees and experts in the law *(Sadducees)* rejected God's purpose for themselves, because they had not been baptized by John.)

Col. 2:1-3 KJV For I would that ye knew what great conflict I have for you, and for them at Laodicea, and for as many as have not seen my face in the flesh; that their hearts might be comforted, being knit together in love, and unto all riches of the full assurance of understanding, to the **acknowledgment** of the mystery of God, and of the Father, and of Christ; in whom are hid all the treasures of wisdom and knowledge.

Acknowledgment of sin—-

Ps. 32:5 I **acknowledged** my sin to You, and my iniquity I have not hidden. I said, "I will confess my transgressions to the Lord, and you forgave the iniquity of my sin.

Ps. 51:3-4 For I **acknowledge** my transgressions, and my sin is always before me. Against You, You only, have I sinned, and done this evil in Your sight—that You may be found just when You speak, and blameless when You judge.

Jer. 3:11-13 Then the Lord said to me, "Backsliding Israel has shown herself more righteous than treacherous Judah. Go and proclaim these words toward the north, and say: 'Return, backsliding Israel,' says the Lord; 'I will not remain angry forever. Only **acknowledge** your iniquity, that you have transgressed against the Lord your God, and have scattered your charms to alien deities under every green tree, and you have not obeyed My voice,' says the Lord."

Jer. 14:20 We **acknowledge**, O Lord, our wickedness and the iniquity of our fathers, for we have sinned against You.

Hosea 4:1 NIV Hear the word of the Lord, you Israelites, because the Lord has a charge to bring against you who live in the land; "There is no faithfulness, no love, no **acknowledgment** of God in the land."

Hosea 5:15 "I will return again to My place till they **acknowledge** their offense *(guilt NIV)*. Then they will seek My face; in their affliction they will earnestly seek Me."

Acknowledgment of Jesus—-

Matt. 10:32-33 NIV "Whoever **acknowledges** Me *(Jesus)* before men, I will also **acknowledge** him before My Father in heaven. But whoever disowns Me before men, I will disown him before My Father in heaven." *Also Luke 12:8*

Phlm. vss4-6 I thank my God, making mention of you always in my prayers, hearing of your love and faith which you have toward the Lord Jesus and toward all the saints, that the sharing of your faith may become effective by the **acknowledgment** of every good thing which is in you in Christ Jesus.

1 John 2:23 Whoever denies the Son does not have the Father either; he who **acknowledges** the Son has the Father also.

I John 4:2, 3 NIV This is how we can recognize the Spirit of God: Every spirit that **acknowledges** that Jesus Christ has come in the flesh is from God, but every spirit that does not **acknowledge** Jesus is not from God. This is the spirit of the Antichrist, which you have heard is coming and even now is already in the world.

I John 4:13-15 NIV We know that we live in Him and He in us, because He has given us of His Spirit. And we have seen and testify that the Father has sent His Son to be the Savior of the world. If anyone **acknowledges** that Jesus is the Son of God, God lives in Him and He in God.

2 John vs.7 NIV Many deceivers who do not **acknowledge** Jesus Christ as coming in the flesh, have gone out into the world. Any such person is the deceiver and the Antichrist.

The Lord Acknowledges—-

Ex. 2:24, 25 So God heard their groaning, and God remembered His covenant with Abraham, with Isaac, and with Jacob. And God looked upon the children of Israel, and God **acknowledged** them.

Jer. 24:5-7 "Thus says the Lord, the God of Israel: 'Like these good figs, so will I **acknowledge** those who are carried away captive from Judah, whom I have sent out of this place for their own good, into the land of the Chaldeans. For I will set My eyes on them for good, and I will bring them back to this land; I will build them and not pull them down, and I will plant them and not pluck them up. Then I will give them a heart to know Me, that I am the Lord; and they shall be My people, and I will be their God, for they shall return to Me with their whole heart.'"

Other acknowledgments—-

I Cor. 14:37 If anyone thinks himself to be a prophet or spiritual, let him **acknowledge** that the things which I write to you are the commandments of the Lord.

I Cor. 16:17-18 I am glad about the coming of Stephanas, Fortunatus, and Achaicus, for what was lacking on your part they supplied. For they refreshed my spirit and yours. Therefore

acknowledge such men.

Titus 1:1-2 Paul, a bondservant of God and an apostle of Jesus Christ, according to the faith of God's elect and the **acknowledgment** of the truth which accords *(leads to NIV)* with godliness, in hope of eternal life which God, who cannot lie, promised before time began...

UNDERSTANDING

KNOWLEDGE AND UNDERSTANDING GO TOGETHER

Having knowledge and understanding are essential, and even crucial in so many spheres of life. It's a tremendous blessing to have unity and harmony in your home. It takes understanding hearts for patient, caring relationships. That is also true for any group of people working together on a project, in an office complex, or with a team playing a game, even in understanding and agreeing on the rules. We all gain a measure of understanding as we experience life. Sometimes it's because we have discovered a path to blessings and other times it comes through our consequences from failures. It's obvious that our understanding has to grow, and will grow in accordance with our personal experiences, particularly in association with various disciplines we exercise. In the field of education, or in preparation for a specific job, there are numerous requirements to fully understand. In other types of training, such as, bodybuilding for a sport, for the armed services, for being a police officer or fireman, the same important factors apply.

With all of that in mind, how much more important it truly is to understand God, our Creator, and what our responsibility is in a relationship to Him. Consider for a moment what happens when there is a lack of understanding in your family, in a major situation at church, or at work. Oftentimes, the misunderstandings in any area of life relate to a lack of understanding the basic truths God has provided for us in His Word. We can not quickly absorb those truths. We can only understand through studying and meditating on

His Word, and asking the Holy Spirit to quicken our understanding.

We have all gone through the stage of believing that we are at our peak of knowledge and understanding around the age of seventeen or eighteen. We couldn't imagine why anyone questioned our ability to understand most of the things that we would encounter in life. Surely we don't need anyone to assist or counsel us. Isaiah 28:9-10 says it perfectly—"Whom will he teach knowledge? And whom will he make to understand the message? Those just weaned from milk? Those just drawn from the breasts? For precept must be upon precept, precept upon precept, line upon line, line upon line, here a little, there a little." God's Word is so full of wisdom and knowledge to provide understanding for those who yearn for God's will and ways, to sit at His feet drinking in all we can absorb.

We have often heard of a child saying to the parents, "You don't understand." And the parents will respond, "No, you don't understand." Obviously there is a serious lack of understanding between them, and this is very difficult in our daily interactions with one another. While it is understandable that the parent has a far higher level of understanding, yet there is always the area of respect in listening carefully to the child's heart, to hear how our decisions affect them.

PATIENCE AND MERCY ARE ESSENTIAL

Training includes the manner in which we deal with the problems of life. What are they learning from us about handling those who disagree with them? Is there room for grace and mercy, even as our Father in heaven is so gracious and merciful with us? Can we help the child, the teen, to grow in the presence of difficult situations? This may be a turning point for them in an area of understanding, and for the adults too. Each of these difficult moments can provide a platform for teaching and guiding, if we see it in that light. There is always room for each person to grow in their understanding of one another.

This certainly holds true for husbands and wives, and in other relationships too, be it at work, or any group working together on some type of a project, large or small, simple or with major significance. Understanding one another is as important as understanding the details and scope of what you are about to undertake. Oftentimes we feel the greater burden lies with accomplishing our projected goal, without recognizing the importance of the people involved, even a child.

Considering those last statements, my heart is so grateful that we can turn to God, our Father in heaven, who knows all there is to know—way beyond our knowledge. Isn't it really amazing that He is so patient, merciful and understanding with us! He has made the provision for us to seek counsel in His Word, and through prayer. He does not need to be instructed by man, although we sometimes pray as though He needs our knowledge and wisdom in order to understand how to answer our requests. We have a tendency to treat God the same way our children treat us. But He is limitless in all wisdom, knowledge, understanding, insight, and discernment. What a blessing to know that!

There are many places in the Word that make this clear; Isaiah 40 is one of them. Verses 13-14 and 28 provide some humbling questions. Listen— "Who has directed the Spirit of the Lord, or as His counselor has taught Him? With whom did He take counsel, and who instructed Him, and taught Him in the path of justice? Who taught Him knowledge, and showed Him the way of understanding? ...Have you not known? Have you not heard? The everlasting God, the Lord, the Creator of the ends of the earth, neither faints nor is weary. His understanding is unsearchable."

APPLYING GOD'S WISDOM AND UNDERSTANDING

Obviously, we have so much to learn! Psalm 14:2 says, "The Lord looks down from heaven upon the children of men, to see if there are any who understand, who seek God." Then in Proverbs 2:1-11, we have God's instructions concerning this whole area of life. We can't afford to ignore them. "My son, if you receive my words, and treasure my commands within you, so that you incline your ear to wisdom, and apply your heart to understanding; yes, if you cry out for discernment, and lift up your voice for understanding, if you seek her as silver, and search for her as for hidden treasures; then you will understand the fear of the Lord, and find the knowledge of God. For the Lord gives wisdom; from His mouth come knowledge and understanding; He stores up sound wisdom for the upright; He guards the paths of justice, and preserves the way of His saints. Then you will understand righteousness and justice, equity and every good path. When wisdom enters your heart, and knowledge is pleasant to your soul, discretion will preserve you; understanding will keep you."

We need to pray that the Lord will cause us to desire greater understanding of His Word, and to apply those words to our daily lives. All of Psalm 119 especially, contains conversations with God. It appears to me that they may be a collection of statements and requests to the Lord. Verse 27 is really a cry: "Make me understand the way of Your precepts; so shall I meditate on Your wonderful works." And verses 34-35 are similar: "Give me understanding, and I shall keep Your law; indeed, I shall observe it with my whole heart. Make me walk in the path of Your commandments, for I delight in it."

In the New Testament, we have Paul's prayers for the saints in Ephesus and for the Colossian Christians. The prayer in Colossians 1:9-10 is given in the attached Scriptures, so I'll give the one in Ephesians 1:17-19 here: "...that the God of our Lord Jesus Christ, the Father of glory, may give to you the spirit of wisdom, and revelation in the knowledge of Him, the eyes of your understanding being enlightened; that you may know what is the hope of His calling, what are the riches of the glory of His inheritance in the saints, and what is the exceeding greatness of His power toward us who believe, according to the working of His mighty power..." You will most probably want to continue reading all of the book of Ephesians.

TAKE TIME TO STUDY THE WORD OF GOD

These Scriptures help us to realize that there is much more to understand. Unless we diligently study the Word of God, we can become complacent and easily satisfied with ourselves where we are at. This makes us ignorant of some of the most important things that God wants to teach us. Have you noticed that the first part of the word – ignorant – is ignore?

While observing our need, it should cause us to be more conscientious about working at understanding one another in our homes and teaching the children principles from God's Word. Remember that God is our Father in heaven. How far does He bend over with a caring, merciful heart to help us understand the issues of life on our level? I have found my heavenly Father to be extremely gracious toward me, even when I've made huge blunders.

In closing, here are some foundational Scriptures for this major area of our lives:

"O Lord, You have searched me and known me. You know my sitting down and my rising up; You understand my thoughts afar off." Psalm 139:1-2

" The entrance of Your words gives light; it gives understanding to the simple." Psalm 119:13

"Yes, if you cry out for discernment, and lift up your voice for understanding, if you seek her as silver, and search for her as for hidden treasures; then you will understand the fear of the Lord, and find the knowledge of God." Proverbs 2:3-5

"Trust in the Lord with all your heart, and lean not on your own understanding; in all your ways acknowledge Him, and He shall direct your paths." Proverbs 3:5-6

"See then that you walk circumspectly (*with caution and prudence*), not as fools but as wise, redeeming the time, because the days are evil. Therefore do not be unwise, but understand what the will of the Lord is." Ephesians 5:15-17

May the Lord bless you immensely with His Word today! I pray that as you increase your understanding, it will bring humbleness to your heart. Since He has expressed His faithfulness in giving His truths to bless you, and as He has shown that He loves you so dearly, may you rejoice with joy unspeakable, giving glory to His name!

SCRIPTURES FOR
UNDERSTANDING

Wisdom, understanding and knowledge come from God—

1 Chron. 22:12 "Only may the Lord give you wisdom and **understanding**, and give you (Solomon) charge concerning Israel, that you may keep the law of the Lord your God."

Ps. 119:13 The entrance of Your words gives light; it gives **understanding** to the simple.

Ps. 139:1-2 O Lord, You have searched me and known me. You know my sitting down and my rising up; You **understand** my thoughts afar off.

Ps. 147:5 Great is our Lord, and mighty in power; His **understanding** is infinite.

Prov. 3:5-6 Trust in the Lord with all your heart, and lean not on your own **understanding**; in all your ways acknowledge Him, and He shall direct your paths.

Prov. 3:19 The Lord by wisdom founded the earth; by **understanding** He established the heavens.

Prov. 21:30 There is no wisdom or **understanding** or counsel against the Lord.

Isa. 11:1-2 There shall come forth a Rod from the stem of Jesse, and a Branch shall grow out of his roots. The Spirit of God shall rest upon Him, the Spirit of wisdom and **understanding**, the Spirit of counsel and might, the Spirit of knowledge and of the fear of the Lord. *A prophecy about the coming of Jesus, the Messiah.*

Isa. 28:9-10 "Whom will he teach knowledge? And whom will he make to **understand** the message? Those just weaned from milk? Those just drawn from the breasts? For precept must be upon precept, precept upon precept, line upon line, line upon line, here a little, there a little."

Isa. 40:13-14, 28 Who has directed the Spirit of the Lord, or as His counselor has taught Him? With whom did He take counsel, and who instructed Him, and taught Him in the path of justice? Who taught Him knowledge, and showed Him the way of **understanding**? ....Have you not known? Have you not heard? The everlasting God, the Lord, the Creator of the ends of the earth, neither faints nor is weary. His **understanding** is unsearchable.

Isa. 43:10-11 "You are my witnesses," says the Lord, "and My servant whom I have chosen, that you may know and believe Me, and **understand** that I am He, before Me there was no God formed, nor shall there be after Me. I, even I, am the Lord, and besides Me there is no savior."

Jer. 51:15 He has made the earth by His power; He has established the world by His wisdom, and stretched out the heaven by His **understanding**.

Luke 2:45-47 So when they *(Jesus' parents)* did not find Him, they returned to Jerusalem, seeking Him. Now so it was that after three days they found Him in the temple, sitting in the midst of the teachers, both listening to them and asking them questions. And all who heard Him were astonished at His **understanding** and answers.

Luke 4:44-45 Then He *(Jesus)* said to them, "These are the words which I spoke to you while I was still with you, that all things must be fulfilled which were written in the law of Moses and the Prophets and the Psalms concerning Me." And He opened their **understanding**, that they might comprehend the Scriptures.

Eph. 1:16-19 ....do not cease to give thanks for you, making mention of you in my prayers: that the God of our Lord Jesus Christ, the Father of glory, may give to you the spirit of wisdom and revelation in the knowledge of Him, the eyes of your **understanding** being enlightened; that you may know what is the hope of His calling, what are the riches of the glory of His inheritance in the saints, and what is the exceeding greatness of His power toward us who believe, according to the working of His mighty power....

2 Tim. 2:7 Consider what I say, and may the Lord give you **understanding** in all things.

We must choose understanding—

Ps. 14:2 The Lord looks down from heaven upon the children of men, to see if there are any who **understand**, who seek God. *Also Ps. 53:2.*

Prov. 2:1-11 My son, if you receive my words, and treasure my commands within you, so that you incline your ear to wisdom, and apply your heart to **understanding**; yes, if you cry out for discernment, and lift up your voice for **understanding**, if you seek her as silver, and search for her as for hidden treasures; then you will **understand** the fear of the Lord, and find the knowledge of God. For the Lord gives wisdom; from His mouth come knowledge and **understanding**; He stores up sound wisdom for the upright; He guards the paths of justice, and preserves the way of His saints. Then you will **understand** righteousness and justice, equity and every good path. When wisdom enters your heart, and knowledge is pleasant to your soul, discretion will preserve you; **understanding** will keep you.

Prov. 4:5-8 Get wisdom! Get **understanding**! Do not forget, nor turn away from the words of my mouth. Do not forsake her, and she will preserve you; love her, and she will keep you. Wisdom is the principle thing; therefore get wisdom. And in all your getting, get **understanding**. Exalt her, and she will promote you; she will bring you honor, when you embrace her.

Prov. 8:12-14, 17 I, wisdom, dwell with prudence, and find out knowledge and discretion. The fear of the Lord is to hate evil; pride and arrogance and the evil way and the perverse mouth I hate. Counsel is mine, and sound wisdom; I am **understanding**, I have strength. ....I love those who love me, and those who seek me diligently will find me.

Prov. 9:10 The fear of the Lord is the beginning of wisdom, and the knowledge of the Holy One is **understanding**.

Jer. 9:24 But let him that glories glory in this, that he **understands** and knows Me, that I am the Lord, exercising lovingkindness, judgment, and righteousness in the earth. For in these I delight," says the Lord.

Matt. 13:18-19, 23 "Therefore hear the parable of the sower: when anyone hears the word of the kingdom and does not **understand** it, then the wicked one comes and snatches away what was sown in his heart. This is he who received seed by the wayside. ....But he who received seed on the good ground is he who hears the word and **understands** it, who indeed bears fruit and produces: some a hundred-fold, some sixty, some thirty."

Matt. 15:10-11 When He called the multitude to Himself, He said to them, "Hear and **understand**: not what goes into the mouth defiles a man; but what comes out of the mouth, this defiles a man." *Also see verses 16, 17.*

Fervent prayers for understanding—

1 Kings 3:7-12 "Now, O Lord my God, You have made Your servant king instead of my father David, but I am a little child; I do not know how to go out or come in. And Your servant is in the midst of Your people whom You have chosen, a great people, too numerous to be numbered or counted. Therefore give to Your servant an **understanding** heart to judge Your people, that I may discern between good and evil. For who is able to judge this great

people of Yours?" The speech pleased the Lord, that Solomon had asked this thing. Then God said to him: "Because you have asked this thing, and have not asked long life for yourself, nor have asked riches for yourself, nor have asked the life of your enemies, but have asked for yourself **understanding** to discern justice, behold, I have done according to your words; see, I have given you a wise and **understanding** heart, so that there has not been anyone like you before you, nor shall any like you arise after you."

Ps. 119:27 Make me **understand** the way of Your precepts; so shall I meditate on Your wonderful works.

Ps. 119:34 Give me **understanding**, and I shall keep Your law; indeed, I shall observe it with my whole heart.

Col. 1:9-12 For this reason we also, since the day we heard it, do not cease to pray for you, and ask that you may be filled with the knowledge of His will in all wisdom and spiritual **understanding**; that you may walk worthy of the Lord, fully pleasing Him, being fruitful in every good work and increasing in the knowledge of God; strengthened with all might, according to His glorious power, for all patience and longsuffering with joy; giving thanks to the Father who has qualified us to be partakers of the inheritance of the saints in the light. *Also see Ephesians 1:17-20.*

Blessings accompany understanding—

Ps. 107:43 Whoever is wise will observe these things, and will **understand** the lovingkindness of the Lord.

Ps. 111:10 The fear of the Lord is the beginning of wisdom; a good **understanding** have all those who do His commandments. His praise endures forever.

Prov. 3:13-15 Happy is the man who finds wisdom, and the man who gains **understanding**; for her proceeds are better than the profits of silver, and her gain than fine gold; She is more precious than rubies, and all the things you may desire cannot compare with her. *Also Proverbs 16:16.*

Prov. 13:15 Good **understanding** gains favor, but the way of the unfaithful is hard.

Prov. 14:6 A scoffer seeks wisdom and does not find it, but knowledge is easy to him who **understands**.

Prov. 16:22 **Understanding** is a wellspring of life to him who has it. But the correction of fools is folly.

Dan. 10:10-14 Suddenly, a hand touched me, which made me tremble on my knees and on the palms of my hands. And he said to me, "O Daniel, man greatly beloved, **understand** the words that I speak to you, and stand upright, for I have now been sent to you." While he was speaking this word to me, I stood trembling. Then he said to me, "Do not fear, Daniel, for from the first day that you set your heart to **understand**, and to humble yourself before your God, your words were heard; and I have come because of your words. But the prince of the kingdom of Persia withstood me twenty-one days; and behold, Michael, one of the chief princes, came to help me, for I had been left alone there with the kings of Persia. Now I have come to make you **understand** what will happen to your people in the latter days, for the vision refers to many days yet to come."

Col. 2:1-3 For I want you to know what a great conflict I have for you and those in Laodicea, and for as many as have not seen my face in the flesh, that their hearts may be encouraged being knit together in love, and attaining to all riches of the full assurance of **understanding** to the knowledge of the mystery of God, both of the Father and of Christ, in whom are hidden all the treasure of wisdom and knowledge.

1 John 5:20 And we know that the Son of God has come and has given us an **understanding**, that we may know Him who is true; and we are in Him who is true, in His Son Jesus Christ. This is the

true God and eternal life.

Qualities of the one who has understanding—

Prov. 10:13 Wisdom is found on the lips of him who has **understanding**, but a rod is for the back of him who is devoid of **understanding**.

Prov. 10:23 To do evil is like sport to a fool, but a man of **understanding** has wisdom.

Prov. 11:12 He who is devoid of wisdom despises his neighbor, but a man of **understanding** holds his peace.

Prov. 14:29 He who is slow to wrath is great in **understanding**, but he who is impulsive exalts folly.

Prov. 15:14 The heart of him who has **understanding** seeks knowledge, but the mouth of fools feeds on foolishness.

Prov. 15:21 Folly is joy to him who is destitute of discernment, but a man of **understanding** walks uprightly.

Prov. 15:32 He who disdains instruction despises his own soul, but he who heeds rebuke gets **understanding**.

Prov. 17:27 He who has knowledge spares his words, and a man of **understanding** is of a calm spirit.

Prov. 28:5 Evil men do not **understand** justice, but those who seek the Lord **understand** all.

Heb. 11:3 By faith we **understand** that the worlds were framed by the Word of God, so that the things which are seen were not made of things which are visible.

These lack understanding—

Ps. 32:9 Do not be like the horse or like the mule, which have no **understanding**, which must be harnessed with bit and bridle, else they will not come near you.

Matt. 13:13-15 "Therefore, I *(Jesus)* speak to them in parables, because seeing they do not see, and hearing they do not hear, nor do they **understand**. And in them the prophecy of Isaiah (6:9, 10) is fulfilled, which says: 'Hearing you will hear and not **understand**, and seeing you will see and not perceive; for the hearts of this people have grown dull. Their ears are hard of hearing and their eyes they have closed, lest they should see with their eyes and hear with their ears, lest they should **understand** with their hearts and turn, so that I should heal them.'" *Mark 4:11-12; Luke 8:10; John 12:37-41 and Acts 28:25-27.*

Matt. 16:8-12 But Jesus, being aware of it, said to them, "O you of little faith, why do you reason among yourselves because you have brought no bread? Do you not yet **understand**, or remember the five loaves of the five thousand and how many baskets you took up? Nor the seven loaves of the four thousand and how many large baskets you took up? How is it you do not **understand** that I did not speak to you concerning bread? – but to beware of the leaven of the Pharisees and Sadducees." Then they **understood** that He did not tell them to beware of the leaven of bread, but of the doctrine of the Pharisees and Sadducees. *Also Mark 8:17-21.*

John 12: 16 His disciples did not **understand** these things at first; but when Jesus was glorified, then they remembered that these things were written about Him and that they had done these things to Him.

Acts 7:25 "For he *(Moses)* supposed that his brethren would have **understood** that God would deliver them by his hand, but they did not **understand**."

Acts 8:30-31 So Philip ran to him *(the eunuch of Ethiopia),* and heard him reading the prophet Isaiah, and said, "Do you **understand** what you are reading?" And he said, "How can I, unless someone guides me?" And he asked Philip to come up and sit with him.

Rom. 3:10-11 As it is written: "There is none righteous, no, not one; there is none who **understands**; there is none who seeks after God."

1 Tim. 1:5-7 Now the purpose of the commandment is love from a pure heart, from a good conscience, and from sincere faith, from which some, having strayed, have turned aside to idle talk, desiring to be teachers of the law, **understanding** neither what they say nor the things which they affirm.

2 Peter 3:16 ....as also in all his epistles, speaking in them of these things, in which are some things hard to **understand**, which untaught and unstable people twist to their own destruction, as they do also the rest of the Scriptures.

Warnings—

John 8:42-43 Jesus said to them, "If God were your Father, you would love Me, for I proceeded forth and came from God; nor have I come of Myself, but He sent Me. Why do you not **understand** My speech? Because you are not able to listen to My word."

Rom. 1:20 For since the creation of the world His invisible attributes are clearly seen, being **understood** by the things that are made, even His eternal power and Godhead, so that they are without excuse.

1 Cor. 13:2 And though I have the gift of prophecy, and **understand** all mysteries and all knowledge, and though I have all faith, so that I could remove mountains, but have not love, I am nothing.

Eph. 4:17-18 This I say, therefore, and testify in the Lord, that you should no longer walk as the rest of the Gentiles walk, in the futility of their mind, having their **understanding** darkened, being alienated from the life of God, because of the ignorance that is in them, because of the blindness of their heart....

Eph. 5:15-17 See then that you walk circumspectly *(with caution and prudence),* not as fools but as wise, redeeming the time, because the days are evil. Therefore do not be unwise, but **understand** what the will of the Lord is.

Phil. 4:6-7 Be anxious for nothing, but in everything by prayer and supplication, with thanksgiving, let your requests be made known to God; and the peace of God which surpasses all **understanding**, will guard your hearts and minds through Christ Jesus.

2 Peter 2:12 But these, like natural brute beasts made to be caught and destroyed, speak evil of the things they do not **understand**, and will utterly perish in their own corruption.

TRUST

TRUST GOD ABOVE ALL ELSE

When we think of the word TRUST today, it seems that we immediately have the questions arise in our minds, "Trust whom?" and "Trust what?" I have, and you most probably have also unwisely trusted people, and things. We've lost lots of time, energy and money while expecting the promised goods to be worth it all. Then the truth became very clear, that there is nothing in this whole deal that can be trusted. We had put far too much trust in the person who promised that our investment would give us years of satisfaction, even providing substantially during our retirement years.

The Scriptures give us wise instructions in Psalm 118:8-9, "It is better to trust in the Lord than to put confidence in man. It is better to trust in the Lord than to put confidence in princes." How different our experiences might have been if we took enough time to seek the Lord, and wait upon Him for His directions, thereby 'setting our trust in Him' before making a decision.

We find this word almost exclusively in the Old Testament, especially urging us to put our trust in God. Putting our trust in God cannot leave us stranded. If we conscientiously read the fine print in the Word of God, we will learn to trust Him even more, and His response is positive in so many wonderful ways.

We need to pursue that thought. What does God's Word really teach us? Can we trust too much? 2 Samuel 22:31 says, "As for God His way is perfect; the word of the Lord is proven; He is a shield to all who trust in Him." This word is so important to remember, that it is repeated in Psalm 18:30. We can find numerous situations all over the Old Testament when people were in desperate circumstances because of their wickedness. They were stricken with sickness and diseases, abandonment, heavy burdens, nearly losing all they possessed, including their lives. God delivered them when they repented and planted their trust in the Lord! When we trust the Lord totally, letting go of the whole situation, He can become our defense and deliverer. Applying this to what you may dealing with right now, can you believe that He knows how?

This is one of the most joyous words as we see what God has done. Listen to what Psalm 5:11-12 tells us, "But let all those rejoice who put their trust in You; let them ever shout for joy, because you defend them; let those also who love Your name be joyful in You. For You, O Lord, will bless the righteous; with favor You will surround him as with a shield." Do you hear that? — The righteous can "rejoice" and "shout for joy," because He defends us in the midst of our trials and hardships. Many times we feel like giving up, but when we trust the Lord, He shows us unopened doors to brand new possibilities and solutions that we couldn't even imagine before.

Isn't that what happened with Jehoshaphat, as we read that account in II Chronicles 20:1-30? Jehoshaphat was told that the people of Moab, the Ammonites and others were coming against him. He was overwhelmed with fear, but didn't try to solve this by himself. He set himself to seek the Lord, and also proclaimed a fast throughout all of Judah. When the people came together, Jehoshaphat stood up and prayed. Part of his prayer was: "O Lord God of our fathers, are You not God in heaven, and do You not rule over all the kingdoms of the nations, and in Your hand is there not power and might, so that no one is able to withstand You?"

Can you hear that Jehoshaphat has a solid relationship with God? It's like he reminds God of who He is and His attributes which make Him very capable to take charge of those who think they can outsmart God's people. It's good to read the whole passage, for his prayer may give you insight as to why God answered this prayer so quickly. Of course, it's not just the words he uses, but the confidence and trust that he had in Almighty God. Isn't Jehoshaphat's prayer the one we need to pray over our nation?

WE LEARN TO TRUST THROUGH EXPERIENCES

We can learn so much from these Old Testament Scriptures! We need to just immerse ourselves in the Word, soak up and absorb deeply the truths of how God blessed those who 'set their face like a flint' in their steadfastness as they trusted in Him. Those who wrote those powerful truths about God had experienced the absolute trustworthiness of what God had promised. They proved His Word to be true. They stayed anchored to the Rock of truth, which is revealed in the New Testament to be Jesus.

There were periods of time that large numbers of God's children just trusted their own cleverness, their resourcefulness and strength, as though they didn't need God. Every time, they walked right into disasters of all kinds. Their enemies overtook them, thousands were slaughtered, while others became captives, and lived under a cloud of extremely harsh treatment with no end in sight. How foolish!

But, would the Lord want to open our eyes to see how often we do the similar things, only with slightly different modern (up-to-date) variations? It is worth taking time to seek the Lord's observation in regard to how much we trust Him, and how we go about making decisions in our lives. How many strong ideas control your thinking, so that trusting God is really too-far-out? Your 'control center' may well be saying, "I can't wait that long, it's too risky, I need an answer NOW!" Watch out for the disasters that quite likely will follow.

JOB GREW IN HIS RELATIONSHIP TO GOD

Although we may not understand everything that God wanted to change in Job's philosophy of life, and what he understood about God's will and ways, we surely can learn much from the manner in which God humbled him by confronting him with some astounding questions. Let's consider the questions presented in Job 38:1-11: "Then the Lord answered Job out of the whirlwind, and said: "Who is this who darkens counsel by words without knowledge? Now prepare yourself like a man; I will question you, and you shall answer Me. Where were you when I laid the foundations of the earth? Tell Me, if you have understanding. Who determined its measurements? Surely you know! Or who stretched the line upon it? To what were its foundations fastened? Or who laid its cornerstone, when the morning stars sang together, and all the sons of God shouted for joy? Or who shut in the sea with doors, when it burst forth and issued from the womb; when I made the clouds its garment, and thick darkness its swaddling band; when I fixed My limit for it, and set bars and doors; when I said, 'This far you may come, but no farther, and here your proud waves must stop!'"

In Job 39, the Lord continued to question Job, and here are just a few, verses 9-12: "Will the wild ox be willing to serve you? Will he bed by your manger? Can you bind the wild ox in the furrow with ropes? Or will he plow the valleys behind you? Will you trust him because His strength is great? Or will you leave your labor to him? Will you trust to him to bring home your grain, and gather it to your threshing floor?"

As God is questioning Job, we can observe many of His attributes. God is pointing out how limited the knowledge and understanding of all mankind is. How can we put our trust in anyone, or anything, above our trust in God? Why do we have the tendency to have so much confidence in our ability to calculate with all our accumulated knowledge, which may add up to a thimble full, or more like a few grains of sand, in comparison to God's infinite view of all things, with understanding of all the universe which He created. Yet we imagine that we are so intelligent in vast regions of available knowledge. The Word of God reveals that we cannot wisely place our trust in anybody or in anything without the guidance of the Holy Spirit, and that requires time to test our understanding of the guidance He is giving to us.

God's Word gives lots of warnings in the Old Testament, which need to be understood in today's language, because many of the references apply to their time of existence. They will have another application for today, such as in Isaiah 31:1: "Woe to those who go down to Egypt for help, and rely on horses, who trust in chariots because they are many, and in horsemen because they are very strong, but who do not look to the Holy One of Israel, nor seek the Lord!" Obviously our trust is placed in entirely different things that speak of intelligence, wisdom and strength for provision or deliverance, but will bring that same 'woe' upon us, if we misplace our trust in earthly means for wisdom or deliverance.

GOD PROMISES BLESSINGS
TO THOSE WHO TRUST IN HIM

In the following Scriptures we are given some contrasts: Isaiah 57:13 says, "When you cry out, let your collection of idols deliver you. But the wind will carry them all away, a breath will take them. But he who puts his trust in Me shall possess the land, and shall inherit My holy mountain." Also in Jeremiah 17:7-8—"Blessed is the man who trusts in the Lord, and whose hope is the Lord. For he shall be like a tree planted by the waters, which spreads out its roots by the river, and will not fear when heat comes; but its leaf will be green, and will not be anxious in the year of drought, nor will cease from yielding fruit." And in Jeremiah 39:17-18—"But I will deliver you in that day," says the Lord, "and you shall not be given into the hand of men of whom you are afraid. For I will surely deliver you, and you shall not fall by the sword; but your life shall be as a prize to you, <u>because you have put your trust in Me</u>." These contrasts give us a clear picture of how different the results are when we choose to move along on our own agenda, or choose to acknowledge God as our Father in heaven, and as the Lord of our lives.

Let me ask you a few questions to ponder—

Name some situations when you should have trusted the Lord, but did things your way, using your own limited understanding. What kinds of trouble did you experience with each one? What did it take to discover how you were the cause of your problems? And even some tragic mistakes? Has He delivered you from further agony? If not, what is it that the Lord requires of you to do? Have you learned to really trust the Lord, or are you having difficulty putting your life into God's hands, allowing Him to make choices for you according to His wisdom and the tremendous love He has for you? List the Scriptures that are coming to mean the most to you. Add to each one—why they have become meaningful.

My blessing to you is contained in the following Scriptures— "Oh, taste and see that the Lord is good; blessed is the man who trusts in Him! ...The Lord redeems the soul of His servants, and none of those who trust in Him shall be condemned." *Psalm 34:8, 22.*

SCRIPTURES FOR
T R U S T

Those who trust in God are blessed —-

2 Sam. 22:1-3, 31 Then David spoke to the Lord the words of this song, on the day when the Lord had delivered him from the hand of all his enemies, and from the hand of Saul. And he said: "The Lord is my rock and my fortress and my deliverer; the God of my strength, in whom I will **trust**; my shield and the horn of my salvation, my stronghold and my refuge; my Savior, You save me from violence." "...As for God His way is perfect; the word of the Lord is proven; He is a shield to all who **trust** in Him." *Also see Psalm 18:1-2, 30.*

2 Kings 18:5-7a He *(King Hezekiah)* **trusted** in the Lord God of Israel, so that after him was none like him among all the kings of Judah, nor who were before him. For he held fast to the Lord; he did not depart from following Him, but kept His commandments, which the Lord had commanded Moses. The Lord was with him; he prospered wherever he went.

1 Chron. 5:19-20 They *(The sons of Reuben, the Gadites, and the half tribe of Manasseh)* made war with the Hagrites, Jetur, Naphish, and Nadab. And they were helped against them, and the Hagrites were delivered into their hand, and all who were with them, for they *(God's people)* cried out to God in the battle. He heeded their prayer, because they put their **trust** in Him.

Ps. 5:11-12 But let all those rejoice who put their **trust** in You; let them ever shout for joy, because you defend them; let those also who love Your name be joyful in You. For You, O Lord, will bless the righteous; with favor You will surround him as with a shield.

Ps. 9:9-10 The Lord also will be a refuge for the oppressed, a refuge in times of trouble. And those who know Your name will put their **trust** in You; for You, Lord, have not forsaken those who seek You.

Ps. 13:5-6 But I have **trusted** in Your mercy; my heart shall rejoice in Your salvation. I will sing to the Lord, because He has dealt bountifully with me.

Ps. 22:4-5 Our fathers **trusted** in You; they **trusted**, and You delivered them. They cried to You, and were delivered; they **trusted** in You, and were not ashamed.

Ps. 33:21-22 For our heart shall rejoice in Him, because we have **trusted** in His holy name. Let Your mercy; O Lord, be upon us, just as we hope in You.

Ps. 34:8, 22 Oh, taste and see that the Lord is good; blessed is the man who **trusts** in Him! ....The Lord redeems the soul of His servants, and none of those who **trust** in Him shall be condemned.

Ps. 36:7 How precious is Your lovingkindness, O God! Therefore the children of men put their **trust** under the shadow of Your wings.

Ps. 37:39-40 But the salvation of the righteous is from the Lord; He is their strength in the time of trouble. And the Lord shall help them and deliver them; He shall deliver them from the wicked, and save them, because they **trust** in Him.

Ps. 40:3-4 He has put a new song in my mouth—praise to our God; many will see it and fear, and will **trust** in the Lord. Blessed is that man who makes the Lord His **trust**, and does not respect the proud, nor such as turn aside to lies.

Ps. 64:10 The righteous shall be glad in the Lord, and **trust** in Him. And all the upright in heart shall glory.

Ps. 73:28 But it is good for me to draw near to God; I have put my **trust** in the Lord God, that I may declare all Your works.

Ps. 84:11-12 For the Lord God is a sun and shield; the Lord will give grace and glory; no good thing will He withhold from those who walk uprightly. O Lord of hosts, blessed is the man who **trusts** in You!

Ps. 125:1 Those who **trust** in the Lord are like Mount Zion, which cannot be moved, but abides forever.

Prov. 28:25 He who is of a proud heart stirs up strife, but he who **trusts** in the Lord will be prospered.

Prov. 29:25 The fear of man brings a snare, but whoever **trusts** in the Lord shall be safe.

Prov. 30:5 Every word of God is pure; He is a shield to those who put their **trust** in Him.

Isa. 26:3-4 You will keep him in perfect peace, whose mind is stayed on You, because he **trusts** in You. **Trust** in the Lord forever, for in Yah *(Jehovah)*, the Lord, is everlasting strength.

Jer. 17:7-8 *Thus saith the Lord: ....*"Blessed is the man who **trusts** in the Lord, and whose hope is the Lord. For he shall be like a tree planted by the waters, which spreads out its roots by the river, and will not fear when heat comes; but its leaf will be green, and will not be anxious in the year of drought, nor will cease from yielding fruit.

Jer. 39:17-18 "But I will deliver you in that day," says the Lord, "and you shall not be given into the hand of men of whom you are afraid. For I will surely deliver you, and you shall not fall by the sword; but your life shall be as a prize to you, because you have put your **trust** in Me," says the Lord.

Nahum 1:7 The Lord is good, a stronghold in the day of trouble; and He knows those who **trust** in Him.

Rom. 15:13 NIV May the God of hope fill you with all joy and peace as you **trust** in Him, so that you may overflow with hope by the power of the Holy Spirit.

Eph. 1:12-14 …that we who first **trusted** in Christ should be to the praise of His glory. In Him you also **trusted**, after you heard the word of truth, the gospel of your salvation; in whom also, having believed, you were sealed with the Holy Spirit of promise, who is the guarantee of our inheritance until the redemption of the purchased possession, to the praise of His glory.

These have made a declaration to trust the Lord—-

Ps. 7:1-2 O Lord my God, in You I put my **trust**; save me from all those who persecute me; and deliver me, lest they tear me like a lion, rending me in pieces, while there is none to deliver.

Ps. 25:1-2, 20 To You, O Lord, I lift up my soul. O my God, I **trust** in You; let me not be ashamed; let not my enemies triumph over me. ….Keep my soul, and deliver me; let me not be ashamed, for I put my **trust** in You.

Ps. 52:8 But I am like a green olive tree in the house of God; I **trust** in the mercy of God forever and ever.

Ps. 56:3-4 Whenever I am afraid, I will **trust** in You. In God (I will praise His word), in God I have put my **trust**; I will not fear. What can flesh do to me?

Ps. 61:3-4 For You have been a shelter for me, a strong tower from the enemy. I will abide in Your tabernacle forever; I will **trust** in the shelter of Your wings.

Ps. 91:2 I will say of the Lord, "He is my refuge and my fortress; my God, in Him I will **trust**."

Ps. 119:41-42 Let Your mercies come also to me, O Lord—Your salvation according to Your Word. So shall I have an answer for him who reproaches me, for I **trust** in Your Word.

Isa. 12:1-2 And in that day you will say: "O Lord, I will praise You; though You were angry with me, Your anger is turned away and You comfort me. Behold, God is my salvation, I will **trust** and not be afraid; 'for Yah, the Lord, is my strength and song, He also has become my salvation.'"

2 Cor. 1:9-11 Yes, we had the sentence of death in ourselves, that we should not **trust** in ourselves but in God who raises the dead, who delivered us from so great a death, and does deliver us; in whom we **trust** that He will still deliver us, you also helping together in prayer for us, that thanks may be given by many persons on our behalf for the gift granted to us through many.

1 Tim. 4:10 For to this end we both labor and suffer reproach, because we **trust** in the living God, who is the Savior of all men, especially of those who believe.

Instructed and encouraged to put our trust in the Lord —-

Ps. 4:5 Offer the sacrifices of righteousness, and put your **trust** in the Lord.

Ps. 37:3-6 **Trust** in the Lord, and do good; dwell in the land, and feed on His faithfulness. Delight yourself also in the Lord, and He shall give you the desires of your heart. Commit your way to the Lord, **trust** also in Him and He shall bring it to pass. He shall bring forth your righteousness as the light and your justice as the noonday.

Ps. 62:7-8 In God is my salvation and my glory; the rock of my strength, and my refuge, is in God. **Trust** in Him at all times, you people; pour out your heart before Him; God is a refuge for us.

Ps. 118:8-9 It is better to **trust** in the Lord than to put confidence in man. It is better to **trust** in the Lord than to put confidence in princes.

Prov. 3:5-6 **Trust** in the Lord with all your heart and lean not on your own understanding; in all your ways acknowledge Him, and He shall direct your paths.

Isa. 50:10 "Who among you fears the Lord? Who obeys the voice of His Servant? Who walks in darkness and has no light? Let him **trust** in the name of the Lord and rely upon His God.

Isa. 57:13 "When you cry out, let your collection of idols deliver you. But the wind will carry them all away, a breath will take them. But he who puts his **trust** in Me shall possess the land, and shall inherit My holy mountain."

1 Tim. 6:17 Command those who are rich in this present age not to be haughty, nor to **trust** in uncertain riches, but in the living God, who gives us richly all things to enjoy.

Beware of putting trust in the wrong things or people—-

Job 38:1, 39:9-12 The Lord answered Job out of the whirlwind, and said:
  "Will the wild ox be willing to serve you? Will he bed by your manger? Can you bind the wild ox in the furrow with ropes? Or will he plow the valleys behind you? Will you **trust** him because his strength is great? Or will you leave your labor to him? Will you **trust** him to bring home your grain, and gather it to your threshing floor?"

Ps. 20:7-8 Some **trust** in chariots, and some in horses; but we will remember the name of the Lord our God. They have bowed down and fallen; but we have risen and stand upright.

Ps. 49:6-7 Those who **trust** in their wealth and boast in the multitude of their riches, none of them can by any means redeem his brother, nor give to God a ransom for him—.

Ps. 146:3-4 Do not put your **trust** in princes, nor in a son of man, in whom there is no help. His spirit departs, he returns to his earth; in that very day his plans perish.

Isa. 31:1 Woe to those who go down to Egypt for help, and rely on horses, who **trust** in chariots because they are many, and in horsemen because they are very strong, but who do not look to the Holy One of Israel, nor seek the Lord!

Jer. 17:5-6 Thus says the Lord: "Cursed is the man who **trusts** in man, and makes flesh his strength, whose heart departs from the Lord. For he shall be like a shrub in the desert, and shall not see when good comes, but shall inhabit the parched places in the wilderness, in a salt land which is not inhabited."

Mark 10:24 And the disciples were astonished at His words. But Jesus answered again and said to them, "Children, how hard it is for those who **trust** in riches to enter the kingdom of God!"

Luke 16:11 "Therefore if you have not been faithful in the unrighteous mammon, who will commit to your **trust** the true riches?"

Luke 18:9 Also He spoke this parable to some who **trusted** in themselves that they were righteous, and despised others: *The NIV says this—-"To some who were confident of their own righteousness and looked down on everybody else, Jesus told this parable."*

ABIDE

ABIDING IN GOD'S WORD AND IN HIM

Do you use this word? Most of us don't. However, you can probably think of at least two hymns that speak about abiding. In my mind there's a peacefulness attached to abiding, especially in connection with reading about the importance of His Word abiding in us, and that we are to abide in Him. We cannot experience a relationship with Him and enjoy His blessings unless He abides in us. Christians are the temple of the Holy Spirit, His abiding place, according to 1 Corinthians 3:16 and 2 Corinthians 6:16. Our Scriptures give us so many wonderful insights in regard to abiding.

In Psalm 15:1, David is asking, "Lord, who may abide in Your tabernacle? Who may abide in Your holy hill?" The tabernacle of the Lord is a holy place, so it appears that he is wondering how anyone would be able to abide there. In verse two the answer begins with: "He who walks uprightly, and works righteousness, and speaks the truth in his heart;" then the rest of the chapter tells what the upright person will not do. There is much for us to learn from this Psalm. It is worth considering the message for our lives today, since believers are the temple of the Holy Spirit, in contrast to a building in the Old Testament times.

To abide in His tabernacle, is to dwell in Him, Christ Jesus, who is the Life, the Truth, and the Way. Since Jesus is the Word, abiding in God's Word is synonymous with abiding in Him, as we also commune with Him. John 15 gives a wonderful view of abiding in Jesus as a branch attached to the vine. The branch draws life from the vine so it can produce fruit. We cannot live our lives as the world lives and still bear good fruit. When we receive Jesus into our hearts, He abides in us, and His life within us is for our spiritual growth and empowering because He is Eternal Life.

Without His life in us, we do not have eternal life, therefore could not live in heaven. *See 1 John 5:11-13, 20.* As we receive the knowledge of God, we are enabled to truly know Him and live with Him eternally. It is possible to ignore Him, and just bypass the requirements for His children for a period of time. In fact, that is how Christians become spiritually weak and cannot handle the difficulties in life. It's like going without food. When we neglect reading God's Word and communing with the Lord in prayer we hurt ourselves immensely. Attending worship services provides nourishment for our souls, but is also a matter of obedience, for the Lord understands our need for fellowshipping with other Christians as well as to be spiritually fed. If we ignore these needs, we will suffer in many areas of our lives. It is the same as neglecting to eat nourishing food, or try to live without eating.

Producing fruit means to fulfill what God has called each of us to do, including winning souls for Christ Jesus. We are the body of Christ, and the life of Christ in us gives us the ability to do as Jesus was doing when He was abiding here on the earth. But there is no way that we can do this unless we are also abiding in the Word of God, which is our major source of spiritual food.

ABIDING IS DAY BY DAY LIVING

Abiding refers to our day by day living. It implies steadfastness in seeking God's perfect will in His Word, which also brings enlightenment to His perfect design for us as His children. It will help us to not be moved by opinions, or pushed by whims and emotions; not swayed by personal interpretations and imaginations of men. A branch abiding in the vine will receive life giving properties, called nutrients, which gives strength to stay through the storms, and without this, the branch cannot live. A branch that is not abiding in the vine will die; it will be pruned off and thrown in a pile to be disposed. Jesus is comparing us to the vine and the branch for an example of what would happen to us if we do not heed God's instructions day by day.

It's hard to think that God would do that, but this warning is in His Word to protect us from failing to grow in knowledge and faith, which He has provided for us. We cannot afford to be complacent about what God intends for us to hear. Obedience is a requirement, not an option.

There are special privileges for those who abide in Him. John 15:7-8 says, "If you abide in Me, and My words abide in you, you will ask what you desire, and it shall be done for you. By this my Father is glorified, that you bear much fruit; so you will be My disciples." In subsequent verses we're told that as we obey His commandments, we would be able to abide in the Father's love and experience fullness of His joy. It takes time to focus on these truths before you can grasp all that the Lord has provided for those who abide in Him.

ABIDING IN THE SECRET PLACE

In Psalm 91:1 we learn that "those who dwell in the secret place of the Most High, shall abide under the shadow of the Almighty." Or it may be said, "Those who abide under the shadow of the Almighty, shall dwell in the secret place of the Most High." Isn't that wonderful! It's a personal decision. You can live with the joy, or the sorrow, of your decision. But, you cannot make it for a spouse, your children, relatives or friends. Prayer can make a difference, but we can't make their decisions for them.

The word 'abide' also has a restful connotation for me; not hurried, not anxious, but feeling safe and secure right there. I find this rest when I take up the Word and sit with the Lord to talk with Him. In that quietness I can hear His voice more clearly. Since it's a sacred time with the Lord, I recommend not allowing the telephone to interrupt you, and even asking others to not disturb your special tryst with the Lord. All kinds of thoughts want to barge in; it takes strong determination to put them out of the way. At times we need to wait upon the Lord for clarity of His Word, so we can understand His interpretation. We need this special time for enlightenment to make wise decisions in the multitude of our daily responsibilities, even in the little things.

Abiding in His presence is the most delightful period of time. It is refreshing to the body as well as the spirit and soul. It is a peaceful time; a time for 'blessed quietness, holy quietness,' as the song says. It's like sitting under a holy mist, being cleansed of worries and cares, as the Word instructs us, and draws one into a closer fellowship with Him. This is dwelling under the shadow of the Almighty, in His secret place, experiencing the flow of peace from the glory of His awesome holiness.

In 1 John 2:5 we read, "Whoever keeps His Word, truly the love of God is perfected in him. By this we know that we are in Him." This is a powerful statement about the blessings of abiding in Him. Even way back in the Old Testament, in Psalm 125:1, those who trusted in the Lord were likened to Mount Zion, which abides forever. It just cannot be moved. This is especially true of those who abide in Christ Jesus, for His very life abides in the believer, strengthening and stabilizing him. This reminds me of those who are able to stand strong for Jesus, even when they are threatened with torture, or slowly destroying a family member. There is something that the Lord gives to them, which is totally unexplainable, yet they are able to resist renouncing the Lord. May this give us reason to examine ourselves to see how easily we are swayed from making certain commitments because of the cost it would be to us.

A REWARD AWAITS THOSE WHOSE WORK STAND THE TESTS

"Every man's work shall be made manifest, for the day shall declare it, because it shall be revealed by fire; and the fire shall try every man's work of what sort it is. If any man's work abide which he hath built thereupon, he shall receive a reward" *I Corinthians 3:13, 14 KJV.* I believe this is refining fire. We begin in life with a selfish spirit, so God allows certain kinds of experiences to refine our hearts, removing the dross, the impurities. We'll experience a refining fire more than once along the way. It's not a pleasure to go through a refining time; but afterward one can be so thankful for the changes that came in our engraved patterns of thinking.

God says, "If any man's work abide," in other words: whatever you have done in service to the Lord, it goes through God's refining process before it can be acceptable to the Lord. If you are following God's call without the personal concern for greatness; if souls are saved unto eternal life; if your services bear fruit to the glory of God, then for this you will be rewarded. When you sense God's pleasure as you are serving Him, your faith grows stronger, and you will be greatly motivated to praise and glorify the Lord more and more. Your whole being will be stirred to express praise and honor to the Lord, the Holy One, for He is the Great I Am! To abide in Him, is to enjoy His presence, and to desire to seek Him to glorify Him. Abiding in Jesus is so wonderful!

It's very important to test how genuine your relationship is with the Lord. Those who abide in Jesus will reflect His Spirit, His merciful heart, His compassionate concern for others; and they rejoice freely at every opportunity to tell of His blessings and the miracles that He has done in their lives. 1 John 2:6 says, "He who says he abides in Him ought himself also to walk just as Jesus walked."

Would you take this short test? Answering these questions honestly will help you see where you need to grow.

What do other people see in you?

Would they easily recognize that God's Spirit dwells in you?

Are you experiencing the blessings of having Jesus abide in you?

Could you give a testimony of your security in His abiding presence?

Are you in Worship Services regularly for spiritual nourishment?

Have you ever brought someone else along with you, so they may receive Jesus too?

Will you make Psalm 61:1-4 your heart cry today?

"Hear my cry, O God; attend to my prayer. From the end of the earth I will cry to You, when my heart is overwhelmed; lead me to the Rock that is higher than I. For You have been a shelter for me, a strong tower from the enemy. I will abide in Your tabernacle forever; I will trust in the shelter of Your wings."

Remember, God hears the prayers of the sincere and humble hearts. Have you discovered this truth in God's Word? Searching for those Scriptures will be a refreshing blessing!

SCRIPTURES FOR
ABIDE — DWELL

Who may abide with the Lord—

Psalm 15:1-5 Lord, who may **abide** in Your tabernacle? Who may **dwell** in Your holy hill? He who walks uprightly, and works righteousness, and speaks the truth in his heart; He who does not backbite with his tongue, nor does evil to his neighbor nor does he take up a reproach against his friend; in whose eyes a vile person is despised, but he honors those who fear the Lord; He who swears to his own hurt and does not change; He who does not put out his money at usury, nor does he take a bribe against the innocent. He who does these things shall never be moved.

Ps. 125:1 Those who trust in the Lord are like Mount Zion, which cannot be moved, but **abides** forever.

Luke 19:3-6 And he *(Zacchaeus)* sought to see who Jesus was, but could not because of the crowd, for he was of short stature. So he ran ahead and climbed up into a sycamore tree to see Him, for He was going to pass that way. And when Jesus came to the place, He looked up and saw him, and said to him, "Zacchaeus, make haste and come down; for today I must stay *(abide)* at your house." So he made haste and came down, and received Him joyfully.

John 14:15-20 "If you love Me, keep My commandments. And I will pray the Father, and He will give you another Helper (comforter) that He may **abide** with you forever– the Spirit of truth, whom the world cannot receive, because it neither sees Him nor knows Him; but you know Him, for He **dwells** with you and will be in you. I will not leave you orphans; I will come to you. A little while longer and the world will see Me no more, but you will see Me. Because I live, you will live also. At that day you will know that I am in My Father, and you in Me, and I in you."

2 Tim. 2:11-13 KJV It is a faithful saying: For if we be dead with Christ, we shall also live with Him; if we suffer, we shall also reign with Him; if we deny Him, He also will deny us; if we believe not, yet He **abideth** faithful; He cannot deny Himself.

1 Peter 1:22-23 Since you have purified your souls in obeying the truth through the Spirit in sincere love of the brethren, love one another fervently with a pure heart, having been born again, not of corruptible seed but incorruptible, through the Word of God which lives and **abides** forever.

1 John 2:17 The world is passing away, and the lust of it; but he who does the will of God **abides** forever.

1 John 2:27-28 But the anointing which you have received from Him **abides** in you, and you do not need that anyone teach you; but as the same anointing teaches you concerning all things, and is true, and is not a lie, and just as it has taught you, you shall **abide** in Him, that when He appears, we may have confidence and not be ashamed before Him at His coming.

2 John vs9b He who **abides** in the doctrine of Christ has both the Father and the Son.

How to abide in God's blessings—

Ps. 91:1 He who **dwells** in the secret place of the Most High shall **abide** under the shadow of the Almighty.

Prov. 19:23 The fear of the Lord leads to life, and he who has it will **abide** in satisfaction; he will not be visited with evil.

John 8:31-32 Then Jesus said to those Jews who believed Him, "If you **abide** in My Word, you are My disciples indeed. And you shall know the truth, and the truth shall make you free.

John 8:35-36 "A slave does not **abide** in the house forever, but a son **abides** forever. Therefore, if the Son makes you free, you shall be free indeed."

John 12:46 I *(Jesus)* have come as a light into the world, that whoever believes in Me should not **abide** in darkness.

1 Cor. 3:13-14 JKV Every man's work shall be made manifest, for the day shall declare it, because it shall be revealed by fire; and the fire shall try every man's work of what sort it is. If a man's work **abide** which he hath built thereupon, he shall receive a reward.

1 Cor. 13:13 And now **abide** faith, hope, love, these three; but the greatest of these is love.

2 Tim. 1:14 That good thing which was committed to you, keep by the Holy Spirit who **dwells** in us.

1 John 2:10 He who loves his brother *(family and believers)* **abides** in the light, and there is no cause for stumbling in him.

1 John 2:14 I have written to you, fathers, because you have known Him who is from the beginning. I have written to you, young men, because you are strong, and the Word of God **abides** in you, and you have overcome the wicked one.

1 John 3:5-6 And you know that He was manifested to take away our sins, and in Him there is no sin. Whoever **abides** in Him does not sin. Whoever sins has neither seen Him nor known Him.

Missing God's blessings—

Mark 6:10-11 KJV And He *(Jesus)* said unto them, "In what place soever ye enter into an house, there **abide** till ye depart from that place. And whosoever shall not receive you, nor hear you, when ye depart thence, shake off the dust under your feet for a testimony against them. Verily I say unto you, it shall be more tolerable for

Sodom and Gomorrha in the day of judgment, than for that city." *Also Luke 9:4-5*

John 3:36 He who believes in the Son has everlasting life; and he who does not believe the Son shall not see life, but the wrath of God **abides** on him.

John 5:38 But you do not have His Word **abiding** in you, because whom He sent, Him you do not believe.

1 John 3:14b-17 He who does not love his brother **abides** in death. Whoever hates his brother is a murderer, and you know that no murderer has eternal life **abiding** in him. By this we know love, because He laid down His life for us. And we also ought to lay down our lives for the brethren *(believers)*. But whoever has this world's goods, and sees his brother in need, and shuts up his heart from him, how does the love of God **abide** in Him?

2 John vs9a Whoever transgresses and <u>does not</u> **abide** in the doctrine of Christ <u>does not</u> have God.

Abiding unity of the Father, Son, the Holy Spirit and faithful believers —

John 14:10-11 Do you not believe that I am in the Father, and the Father in Me? The words that I speak to you I do not speak on My own authority; but the Father who **dwells** in Me does the works. Believe Me that I am in the Father and the Father in Me, or else believe Me for the sake of the works themselves.

John 14:23 Jesus answered and said to him, "If anyone loves Me, he will keep My Word; and My Father will love him, and We will come to him and make Our home *(abiding place)* with him." *Also see John 17:16-26*

John 15:1, 4-7 "I *(Jesus)* am the true vine, and my Father is the vinedresser. **Abide** in Me, and I in you. As the branch cannot bear fruit of itself, unless it **abides** in the vine, neither can you, unless you **abide** in Me. I am the vine, you are the branches. He who **abides** in Me, and I in him, bears much fruit; for without Me you can do nothing. If anyone does not **abide** in Me, he is cast out as a branch and is withered; and they gather them and throw them into the fire, and they are burned. If you **abide** in Me, and My words **abide** in you, you will ask what you desire, and it shall be done for you."

John 15:9-10 "As the Father loved Me, I also have loved you; **abide** in My love. If you keep My commandments, you will **abide** in My love, just as I have kept My Father's commandments and **abide** in His love."

1 Cor. 3:16 Do you not know that you are the temple of God and that the Spirit of God **dwells** in you?

2 Cor. 6:16 And what agreement has the temple of God with idols? For you are the temple of the living God. As God has said: "I will **dwell** in them and walk among them. I will be their God, and they shall be My people." *See Lev. 26:11, 12; Ex. 29:45*

1 John 2:5-6 Whoever keeps His Word, truly the love of God is perfected in him. By this we know that we are in Him. He who says he **abides** in Him ought himself also to walk just as Jesus walked.

1 John 2:24-25 Therefore let that **abide** in you which you heard from the beginning. If what you heard from the beginning **abides** in you, you also will **abide** in the Son and in the Father. And this is the promise that He has promised us – eternal life.

1 John 3:24 Now he who keeps His commandments **abides** in Him, and He in him. And by this we know that He **abides** in us, by the Spirit whom He has given us.

1 John 4:12-13 No one has seen God at any time. If we love one another, God **abides** in us, and His love has been perfected in us.

By this we know that we **abide** in Him, and He in us, because He has given us of His Spirit.

1 John 4:15-16 Whoever confesses that Jesus is the Son of God, God **abides** in him, and he in God. And we have known and believed the love that God has for us. God is love, and he who **abides** in love **abides** in God, and God in him.

A prayer, I will abide—

Ps. 61:1-4 Hear my cry, O God; attend to my prayer. From the end of the earth I will cry to You, when my heart is overwhelmed; lead me to the Rock that is higher than I. For You have been a shelter for me, a strong tower from the enemy. I will **abide** in Your tabernacle forever; I will trust in the shelter of Your wings.

WALK

WALKING WITH GOD

Walk is a familiar word. Most of us take our ability to walk for granted. Have you observed how many times you might have thanked the Lord for that ability to move around so easily? Does it take more than one hand to count? Anyone who does not have the ability to walk, for whatever the reason, strongly desires the privilege. Temporary immobility does not impress us in regard to our privilege as much as it does for someone who has had to rely on help from others to move from one place to another due to long term paralysis.

Since the word implies moving around, it seemed good to begin with that consideration, however, when we see that word in the Scriptures it has to do with the choices we make in life, choosing to walk in God's ways or our own desires. So when we even read about Enoch and Noah walking with God, it is truly saying that they lived according to as much as they knew about God and what His will was for them. During their life times, living years apart, sin was unrestrained. Both Enoch and Noah evidently lived unto the Lord, separated from involvement with others who lived in sin, for God's will to be accomplished. It could not have been easy. Not at all!

Abram's father and forefathers were not godly men according to Joshua 24:2 and 14-15, even though his family was in the lineage of Noah's son Seth. So the Lord told him to leave his father's house and to get out of that country; He would bring him to a new land and make him a great nation with tremendous blessings. Obviously this was to be a drastic change for Abram, who later became Abraham. His story begins in Genesis 11 where Shem's descendants are listed, down to Abram the son of Terah. His father left Ur of the Chaldeans to go to the land of Canaan, and dwelt in Haran. He had taken Abram and Sarai and Lot with him. This also included all their servants and possessions.

This is where the Lord came to Abram with instructions of what he was to do, but he had no idea where the Lord was leading him. *See Genesis 12.* That took faith in a huge measure. No wonder he is called "the father of faith." Further enlightenment can be found in Romans 4 and Galatians 3. These are exciting chapters to examine and study. Everything that God did with Abram, later named Abraham, required faith. He was 'set apart' by God to birth a people who were to be set apart unto God. They became a nation, called Jews, who were dealt with as a special people.

Already much had happened in Abram's life before our text in Genesis 17:1-2 takes place. Here God says to him, "I am Almighty God; walk before Me and be blameless. And I will make My covenant between Me and you, and will multiply you exceedingly." This was a strong command, along with outstanding promises. We find that Abram 'believed God and it was accounted for righteousness'. He walked by faith, believing that God was trustworthy in all that He would require of him, and God never failed him. God never fails those who walk by faith.

That word 'exceedingly' is an extraordinary word. It expresses something that far surpasses what we ordinarily have experienced, seen or known. As you walk through the Scriptures given in this book, take note of all the tremendous blessings the Lord promises to those who are obedient to His Word. This is a bit of homework for you.

WALKING ACCORDING TO THE SPIRIT OF GOD

In the Old Testament Scriptures we hear much about God's commandments, statutes and precepts. These words are not used as often today, however Jesus gave an up-date on the commandments while He was preaching and teaching. The Sermon on the Mount gives us several. It's true that we are not under the law, but it doesn't mean that we may become lawless people. When you think of the Ten Commandments, is there any one of them that we don't have to live by today? The New Testament broadens the meaning and fulfillment of them through Jesus. So as we examine Romans 8:1-5 we can understand that better— "There is therefore now no condemnation to those who are in Christ Jesus, who do not walk according to the flesh, but according to the Spirit. For the law of the Spirit of life in Christ Jesus has made me free from the law of sin and death. For what the law could not do in that it was weak through the flesh, God did by sending His own Son in the likeness of sinful flesh, on account of sin: He condemned sin in the flesh, that the righteous requirement of the law might be fulfilled in us who do not walk according to the flesh but according to the Spirit. For those who live according to the flesh set their minds on the things of the flesh, but those who live *(walk)* according to the Spirit, the things of the Spirit." Take note of verse 2, where it says, "For the law of the Spirit of life in Christ Jesus has made me free from the law of sin and death. This is the real difference for us today: 'the law of the Spirit of life in Christ Jesus'. It is wise to read through that whole chapter, in fact, begin with chapter 3 or 4, and read through chapter 8. It is very enjoyable as well as enlightening.

It is my prayer that you have fallen in love with the Lord and His Word by now. It would be especially wonderful if you already had that exuberant love before you began this book!

Some of you may have walked through tunnels of darkness. You may be having difficulty overcoming some of the dark thoughts that torment you. I have two books to recommend to you. The authors are in harmony, but their books have a little different approach. The one is Victory Over the Darkness, by Neil Anderson[15] and also has a separate Study Guide. The other is Reclaiming Surrendered Ground by Jim Logan,[16] which has a separate workbook. Actually, all Christians should have at least one of them, and even find out where there may be a group study.

WALKING WITH WISDOM FROM THE WORD
As we look at the Old Testament Scriptures that tell about walking in God's ways, there is still so much for us to obey. God hasn't

changed. We live under a new covenant since Jesus came, but there are many guidelines that still apply, and we'll be far happier if we follow them. Paul said in Romans 4:23-25: "Now it was not written for his sake alone that it was imputed to him, but also for us. It shall be imputed to us who believe in Him who raised up Jesus our Lord from the dead, who was delivered up because of our offenses, and was raised because of our justification."

Then in Romans 15:4 we find— "For whatever things were written before were written for our learning, that we through the patience and comfort of the Scriptures might have hope." And in 1 Corinthians 10:1-12 it speaks of the Old Testament examples. Quoting from verse 11: "Now all these things happened to them as examples, and they were written for our admonition, upon whom the ends of the ages have come." If we overlook the truths laid down for us in the Old Testament, we'll also wonder why we're having many of the problems we have instead of the blessings that God, our Father, desires for us to have. Notice how these still apply—"He who walks with integrity walks securely, but he who perverts his ways will become known," and another, "He who walks with wise men will be wise, but the companion of fools will be destroyed."

Romans 6:4 is a foundational Scripture for our new life in Christ—"Therefore we were buried with Him through baptism into death, that just as Christ was raised from the dead by the glory of the Father, even so we also should walk in the newness of life." Jesus provided the new life, and our New Testament Scriptures give us many instructions about walking in accordance with the Holy Spirit, in the name of Jesus. *See John 14:26.*

WALKING BY FAITH IN ALL OF GOD'S WORD

We are to walk by faith, not by sight, according to 2 Corinthians 5:7. That is exactly what Abraham had to do too, and look at the overflowing blessings that the Lord brought to him. It didn't mean that he never had to have tests, trials and suffering, but all of these kinds of things could make him stronger in his 'faith walk', and in ours too! Romans 8:28, which you probably already know, is such a comfort as it gives us purpose for trusting God through thick and thin; good times and discomforts, so we can keep on walking as

Jesus walked. Colossians 2:6-7 help us to see this too—"As you therefore have received Christ Jesus the Lord, so walk in Him, rooted and built up in Him and established in the faith, as you have been taught, abounding in it with thanksgiving."

In 1 Thessalonians 4:1-2 we hear about the commandments that came through Jesus Christ, which showed them how they should walk to please God. Then in 2 John vs6, we read—"This is love, that we walk according to His commandments. This is the commandment, that as you have heard from the beginning, you should walk in it." That is interesting, isn't it? Oh, I just remembered another Scripture found in 1 John 3:21-24—"Beloved, if our heart does not condemn us, we have confidence toward God. And whatever we ask we receive from Him, because we keep His commandments and do those things that are pleasing in His sight. And this is His commandment: that we should believe on the name of His Son Jesus Christ and love one another, as He gave us commandment. Now he who keeps His commandments abides in Him, and He in him. And by this we know that He abides in us, by the Spirit whom He has given us." What tremendously important instructions God is giving here for our walk with Him—a walk that comes from our abiding in Christ Jesus, and He in us. *Also see John 15, about the vine and branches.*

I would love to hear of more healings today. When Jesus was here, he healed all who were brought to Him, without filling out a questionnaire to qualify for the healing. Then he taught the disciples, the 12 *(Matt. 10 and Luke 9)* and the 70 *(Luke 10)*, so they would be able to carry on the work of Jesus after He ascended to heaven. I've written more about this under the title Miracles-Miraculous, which will be in a coming book.

In Mark 16:15-20, Mark is giving Jesus' dissertation just before He ascended to heaven. Jesus said that those who believe will lay hands on the sick, in His name, and they will recover. And, in verse 20 it says, "And they went out and preached everywhere, the Lord working with them and confirming the word through the accompanying signs." Recognizing that faith involves expectancy, then there should always be room for God's confirmation on what has been spoken by demonstrating His presence through His power.

Paul makes an interesting statement in 1 Corinthians 2:4-5 NIV—"And my speech and my preaching were not with persuasive words of human wisdom, but in demonstration of the Spirit and of power, that your faith should not be in the wisdom of men but in the power of God."

These Scriptures really speak for themselves. We need more of the demonstration of the power of the Holy Spirit, since the Lord confirmed the Word through the accompanying signs and wonders. *See Acts 2:43; 4:29-33; 6:8; Romans 15:18-19; Hebrews 2:1-4.* Waiting on the Holy Spirit to demonstrate His power is an important part of WALKING IN THE POWER OF THE HOLY SPIRIT AND IN THE WILL OF GOD in our worship services!

God bless you as you grow in His truth, so you may walk uprightly!

SCRIPTURES FOR
WALK

God walked with man—

Gen. 3:8 And they heard the sound of the Lord God **walking** in the garden in the cool of the day, and Adam and his wife hid themselves from the presence of the Lord God among the trees of the garden.

Gen. 5:22 After he begot Methuselah, Enoch **walked** with God three hundred years, and had sons and daughters.

Gen. 6:9 This is the genealogy of Noah, Noah was a just man, perfect in his generations. Noah **walked** with God.

Deut. 23:14 "For the Lord your God **walks** in the midst of your camp, to deliver you and give your enemies over to you; therefore your camp shall be holy, that He may see no unclean thing among you, and turn away from you."

God commands how to walk—with blessings—

Gen. 17:1-2 When Abram was ninety-nine years old, the Lord appeared to Abram and said to him, "I am Almighty God; **walk** before Me and be blameless. And I will make My covenant between Me and you, and will multiply you exceedingly."

Lev. 26:3-4, 12-13 "If you **walk** in My statutes and keep My commandments, and perform them, then I will give you rain in its season, the land shall yield its produce, and the trees of the field shall yield their fruit. ...I will **walk** among you and be your God, and you shall be My people. I am the Lord your God, who brought you out of the land of Egypt, that you should not be slaves; I have broken the bands of your yoke and made you **walk** upright."

Deut. 5:33 "You shall **walk** in all the ways which the Lord your God has commanded you, that you may live and that it may be well with you, and that you may prolong your days in the land which you shall possess."

Deut. 8:6-7 "Therefore you shall keep the commandments of the Lord your God, to **walk** in His ways and to fear Him. For the Lord your God is bringing you into a good land, a land of brooks of water, of fountains and springs, that flow out of valleys and hills..."

Deut. 11:22-23 "For if you carefully keep all these commandments which I command you to do—to love the Lord your God, to **walk** in all His ways, and to hold fast to Him—then the Lord will drive out all these nations from before you, and you will dispossess greater and mightier nations than yourselves."

Deut. 28:9 "The Lord will establish you as a holy people to Himself, just as He has sworn to you, if you keep the commandments of the Lord your God and **walk** in His ways. Then all peoples of the earth shall see that you are called by the name of the Lord, and they shall be afraid of you."

Ps. 1:1-2 Blessed is the man who **walks not** in the counsel of the ungodly, nor stands in the path of sinners, nor sits in the seat of the scornful; but his delight is in the law of the Lord, and in His law he meditates day and night.

Deut. 4:11-12 I have taught you in the way of wisdom; I have led you in right paths. When you **walk**, your steps will not be hindered, and when you run, you will not stumble.

Isa. 30:21, 23 Your ears shall hear a word behind you, saying, "This is the way **walk** in it." Whenever you turn to the right hand or whenever you turn to the left. ...Then He will give the rain for your seed with which you sow the ground, and bread of the increase of the earth; it will be fat and plentiful. In that day your cattle will feed in large pastures.

God's presence is with them—

Ex. 18:19-20 *Jethro speaking to Moses—* "Listen now to my voice; I will give you counsel, and God will be with you: Stand before God for the people so that you may bring the difficulties to God. And you shall teach them the statutes and the laws, and show them the way in which they must **walk** and the work they must do."

Ps. 23:4 Yea, though I **walk** through the valley of the shadow of death, I will fear no evil; for You are with me; Your rod and Your staff, they comfort me.

Ps. 89:15-16 Blessed are the people who know the joyful sound! They **walk**, O Lord, in the light of Your countenance. In Your name they rejoice all day long, and in Your righteousness they are exalted.

Ps. 138:7 Though I **walk** in the midst of trouble, You will revive me; You will stretch out Your hand against the wrath of my enemies, and Your right hand will save me.

Walking in righteousness—

Gen. 48:15 And he *(Jacob)* blessed Joseph, and said: "God, before whom my fathers Abraham and Isaac **walked**, the God who has fed me all my life long to this day..."

Ps. 15:1-2 Lord, who may abide in Your tabernacle? Who may dwell in Your holy hill? He who **walks** uprightly, and works righteousness, and speaks the truth in his heart, He who does not backbite with his tongue, nor does evil to his neighbor, nor does he take up a reproach against his friend.

Ps. 84:11 For the Lord God is a sun and shield; the Lord will give grace and glory; no good thing will He withhold from those who **walk** uprightly.

Ps. 119:1-3 Blessed are the undefiled in the way, who **walk** in the law of the Lord! Blessed are those who keep His testimonies, who seek Him with the whole heart! They also do no iniquity; they **walk** in His ways.

Prov. 2:7 He stores up sound wisdom for the upright; He is a shield to those who **walk** uprightly.

Prov. 10:9 He who **walks** with integrity **walks** securely, but he who perverts his ways will become known.

Prov. 13:20 He who **walks** with wise men will be wise, but the companion of fools will be destroyed.

Mic. 6:8 He has shown you, O man, what is good; and what does the Lord require of you but to do justly, to love mercy, and to **walk** humbly with your God?

Matt. 14:28-29 And Peter answered Him and said, "Lord, if it is You, command me to come to You on the water." So He said, "Come." And when Peter has come down out of the boat, he **walked** on the water to go to Jesus.

Rom. 4:3, 9, 12 For what does the Scripture say? "Abraham believed God, and it was accounted to him for righteousness." ...Does this blessedness then come upon the circumcised only, or upon the uncircumcised also? For we say that faith was accounted to Abraham for righteousness. ...and the father of circumcision to those who not only are of the circumcision, but who also **walk** in the steps of the faith which our father Abraham had while still uncircumcised.

Rom. 6:4 Therefore we were buried with Him through baptism into death, that just as Christ was raised from the dead by the glory of the Father, even so we also should **walk** in the newness of life.

Rom. 8:1, 4 There is therefore now no condemnation to those who are in Christ Jesus, who do not **walk** according to the flesh, but according to the Spirit. ...that the righteous requirement of the law might be fulfilled in us who do not **walk** according to the flesh but according to the Spirit.

Rom. 13:13-14 Let us **walk** properly, as in the day, not in revelry and drunkenness, not in lewdness and lust, not in strife and envy, but put on the Lord Jesus Christ, and make no provision for the flesh, to fulfill its lusts.

Rom. 14:15 Yet if your brother is grieved because of your food, you are no longer **walking** in love. Do not destroy with your food the one for whom Christ died.

2 Cor. 4:1-2 Therefore, since we have this ministry, as we have received mercy, we do not lose heart. But we have renounced the hidden things of shame, **not walking** in craftiness nor handling the word of God deceitfully, but by manifestation of the truth commending ourselves to every man's conscience in the sight of God.

2 Cor. 5:7 For we **walk** by faith, not by sight.

Gal. 5:16 I say then: **Walk** in the Spirit, and you shall not fulfill the lust of the flesh.

Gal. 5:25-26 If we live in the Spirit, let us also **walk** in the Spirit. Let us not become conceited, provoking one another, envying one another.

Eph. 2:1-2, 10 And you He made alive, who were dead in trespasses and sins, in which you once **walked** according to the course of this world, according to the prince of the power of the air, the spirit who now works in the sons of disobedience. ...For we are His workmanship, created in Christ Jesus for good works, which God prepared beforehand that we should **walk** in them.

Eph. 5:1-2, 8-10 Therefore be imitators of God as dear children. And

walk in love, as Christ also has loved us and given Himself for us, an offering and a sacrifice to God for a sweet-smelling aroma. ...For you were once darkness, but now you are light in the Lord. **Walk** as children of light (for the fruit of the Spirit is in all goodness, righteousness, and truth), finding out what is acceptable to the Lord.

Eph. 5:15-17 See then that you **walk** circumspectly *(cautiously)*, not as fools but as wise, redeeming the time, because the days are evil. Therefore do not be unwise, but understand what the will of the Lord is.

Phil. 3:16-18 Nevertheless, to the degree that we have already attained, let us **walk** by the same rule, let us be of the same mind. Brethren, join in following my example, and note those who so **walk**, as you have us for a pattern. For many **walk**, of whom I have told you often, and now tell you even weeping, that they are the enemies of the cross of Christ.

Col. 1:9-12 For this reason we also, since the day we heard it, do not cease to pray for you, and to ask that you may be filled with the knowledge of His will in all wisdom and spiritual understanding; that you may **walk** worthy of the Lord, fully pleasing Him, being fruitful in every good work and increasing in the knowledge of God; strengthened with all might, according to His glorious power, for all patience and longsuffering with joy; giving thanks to the Father who has qualified us to be partakers of the inheritance of the saints in the light.

Col 2:6-7 As you therefore have received Christ Jesus the Lord, so **walk** in Him, rooted and built up in Him and established in the faith, as you have been taught, abounding in it with thanksgiving.

1 Thess. 4:1-2, 12 Finally then, brethren, we urge and exhort in the Lord Jesus that you should abound more and more, just as you received from us how you ought to **walk** to please God; for you know what commandments we gave you through the Lord Jesus. ...that you may **walk** properly toward those who are outside, and

that you may lack nothing.

1 John 1:5-7 This is the message which we have heard from Him and declare to you, that God is light and in Him is no darkness at all. If we say that we have fellowship with Him, and **walk** in darkness, we lie and do not practice the truth. But if we **walk** in the light as He is in the light, we have fellowship with one another, and the blood of Jesus Christ His Son cleanses us from all sin.

1 John 2:5-6 But whoever keeps His Word, truly the love of God is perfected in him. By this we know that we are in Him. He who says he abides in Him ought himself also to **walk** just as He *(Jesus)* **walked**.

2 John vs6 This is love, that we **walk** according to His commandments. This is the commandment, that as you have heard from the beginning, you should **walk** in it.

Rev. 3:4 "You have a few names even in Sardis who have not defiled their garments; and they shall **walk** with Me in white, for they are worthy."

Rev. 21:10-11, 24 And he carried me away in the Spirit to a great and high mountain, and showed me the great city, the holy Jerusalem, descending out of heaven from God, having the glory of God. Her light was like a most precious stone, like a jasper stone, clear as crystal. ...And the nations of those who are saved shall **walk** in its light, and the kings of the earth bring their glory and honor into it.

Healing the lame—

Matt. 9:4-5 But Jesus, knowing their thoughts, said, "Why do you think evil in your hearts? For which is easier, to say, 'Your sins are forgiven you,' or to say, 'Arise and **walk**'?" *Also see Mark 2:8-11 and Luke 5:22-24.*

Matt. 11:4-6 Jesus answered and said to them, "Go and tell John the things which you hear and see: The blind see and the lame **walk**; the lepers are cleansed and the deaf hear; the dead are raised up and the poor have the gospel preached to them. And blessed is he who is not offended because of Me." *Also see Luke 7:22-23.*

John 5:8-13 Jesus said to him, "Rise, take up your bed and **walk**." And immediately the man was made well, took up his bed, and **walked**. And that day was the Sabbath. The Jews therefore said to him who was cured, "It is the Sabbath; it is not lawful for you to carry your bed." He answered them, "He who made me well said to me, 'Take up your bed and **walk**.'" Then they asked him, "Who is the Man who said to you, "Take up your bed and **walk**'?" But the one who was healed did not know who it was, for Jesus had withdrawn, a multitude being in that place.

Acts 3:6-9 Then Peter said, "Silver and gold I do not have, but what I do have I give you: In the name of Jesus Christ of Nazareth, rise up and **walk**. And he took him by the right hand and lifted him up, and immediately his feet and ankle bones received strength. So he, leaping up, stood and **walked** and entered the temple with them— **walking** and **leaping**, and praising God. And all the people saw him **walking** and praising God.

Jesus teaching about their walk—

Matt. 8:12 Then Jesus spoke to them again, saying, "I am the light of the world. He who follows Me shall **not walk** in darkness, but have the light of life.

John 11:9-10 Jesus answered, "Are there not twelve hours in the day? If anyone **walks** in the day, he does not stumble, because he sees the light of this world. But if one **walks** in the night, he stumbles, because the light is not in him."

John 12:35-36a Then Jesus said to them, "A little while longer the light is with you. **Walk** while you have the light, lest darkness overtake you; he who **walks** in darkness does not know where he is going. While you have the light, believe in the light, that you may become sons of light."

Warnings—

Lev. 26:23-24 'And if by these things you are not reformed by Me, but **walk** contrary to Me, then I also will **walk** contrary to you, and I will punish you yet seven times for your sins.'

Deut. 8:19-20 "Then it shall be, if you by any means forget the Lord your God, and follow other gods, and serve them and worship them, I testify against you this day that you shall surely perish. As the nations which the Lord destroys before you, so you shall perish, because you would not be obedient to the voice of the Lord your God."

Prov. 2:11-13 Discretion will preserve you; understanding will keep you, to deliver you from the way of evil, from the man who speaks perverse things, from those who leave the paths of uprightness to **walk** in the ways of darkness.

Prov. 3:21-23 My son, let them not depart from your eyes—keep sound wisdom and discretion; so they will be life to your soul and grace to your neck. Then you will **walk** safely in your way, and your foot will not stumble.

Dan. 4:37 Now I, Nebuchadnezzar, praise and extol and honor the King of heaven, all of whose works are truth, and His ways justice. And those who **walk** in pride He is able to put down.

1 Peter 5:8-9 Be sober, be vigilant; because your adversary the devil **walks** about like a roaring lion, seeking whom he may devour. Resist him, steadfast in the faith, knowing that the same sufferings are experienced by your brotherhood in the world.

STEADFAST

GOD IS UNWAVERING AND FAITHFUL

Steadfast means to be unwavering, faithful, loyal, consistent, firmly fixed, resolute, steady and focused. What a tremendous attribute! This is truly one of God's great attributes. There is no wavering, or unfaithfulness in Him.

When I was visiting a church several years ago, I heard the Pastor say numerous times throughout his message, "God is unpredictable. You just can't depend on what God is going to do. Sometimes He heals, and sometimes He doesn't. Sometimes He blesses, and sometimes He doesn't. He is unpredictable." My heart was hurting when I heard that, for God is always true to His word. The word 'unpredictable' says to me that God is not faithful to His Word. We don't always see and hear what God does, or realize what He would do if we truly trusted Him. We don't even recognize our lack of faith, our vacillating between believing and then wondering what's going on. We are often unstable in what we actually believe about God's will and His ways, however, God is faithful to Himself and to His Word.

As I consider again what 'unpredictable' means, I'm reminded that God's ways are not our ways, and His thoughts are not our thoughts, rather, they are far higher than ours, as we find in Isaiah 55:8 and 9. He is consistent and firmly fixed in all that He has spoken, and this is observable throughout all of the Old Testament history. It is also obvious that God is the same today; He blesses those who fear Him, who walk uprightly and obey Him. He greatly encourages those who desire to walk in His ways. He continuously says that we should not be afraid, not be discouraged, or to despair with worry. All of this is for our protection, for He doesn't want us to fall prey to the enemy of our souls as he cunningly draws us into questioning God's integrity. God does not change His promises or His rules, because His love is steadfast and sure.

Psalm 111:7-8 NIV says to us—"The works of His hands are faithful and just, all His precepts are trustworthy. They are steadfast for ever and ever, done in faithfulness and uprightness." He is unwavering in all He does; His judgments, His plans, His purposes and any other criterion one would choose to examine closely. God's precepts are trustworthy for fulfilling His purposes, for He is God. He is also unchangeable in righteousness and justice.

We often have a tendency to think of God as the highest type of man, on the level of Santa Claus, or the king of some country in the world. Not so. He has never been on man's level; for He is our Creator, which makes us His creation. He came in the form of man in His Son. However, Jesus was not an ordinary man; He was fully God and fully man. Colossians 2:9 says, "In Him dwells all the fullness of the Godhead bodily." We cannot in some way declare His wisdom, or knowledge and understanding as being on the level of ours, nor His righteousness and integrity, for we can only receive a measure from Him through the Holy Spirit. The positive side of this is that we serve a God who is far above us in every possible category of life. Jesus is very God, and is the giver of life, for He is eternal life. He cannot depart from His sovereignty, His purity, or His perfect Divine nature.

JESUS IS STEADFAST

We can see God's faithfulness, and Jesus' too, as we hear John sharing in chapter 3:16—"For God so loved the world that He gave His only begotten Son, that whoever believes in Him should not perish but have everlasting life." He gave His Son at such a great price, remaining steadfast to all His promises, which are found in the Old Testament prophecies foretelling the birth and life of Jesus. You can count on everything He has spoken to be faithful and true.

In Luke 9:51 we read that "Jesus steadfastly set His face to go to Jerusalem." He knew the purpose of His coming to this earth was to pay the debt of our sins. So even though He knew how He would suffer with excruciating pain throughout the whole ordeal of taking our sins upon Himself, He was steadfast all the way. When the fullness of time had come, He deliberately walked to Jerusalem in God's timing for that purpose.

CHRIST IN US MAKES BELIEVERS STEADFAST

In the New Testament, we find that the believers are steadfast in many ways. In a simple every day kind of illustration, I think of a car being faithful in being a car, for thus it was made. When you start the engine and put the vehicle into gear, it goes wherever you choose to steer it, steadfast to its purpose. When we become believers, we receive the Holy Spirit. He enables us to be faithful as believers in Jesus Christ, and as we give Him the controls of our lives, we can be steadfast to fulfill our responsibilities. However, we cannot be steadfast without yielding to the Holy Spirit's leading and His empowerment. Ephesians 1:19 says, "and what is the exceeding greatness of His power toward us who believe, according to the working of His mighty power..."

In Acts 2 we read about the new Christians. They gladly received the message that Peter preached; then they followed his instructions in becoming baptized, and "continued steadfastly in the apostles' doctrine and fellowship, in the breaking of bread, and in prayers." There was a beautiful bonding together as they were obedient to all that God had set forth for them to do. I can sense the joy that flowed in their hearts as they continued steadfastly in accordance with what they were just taught. Anyone who becomes independent and stubborn will encounter many difficulties; relationships are shattered, loneliness sets in like a disease, and it's hard to find your place in the body of Christ.

Steadfastness requires an unselfish spirit as it presses on to fulfill its purpose without wavering. We can't allow doubts to interfere with whatever we know we are called to do "as to the Lord." *Colossians 3:17, 23.* We cannot afford to drag along our past sins, or go floundering along without following the Word of Truth, which may be a form of procrastinating. We have a picture of steadfastness in Philippians 3:13-16 where Paul said, "Brethren, I do not count myself to have apprehended *(captured God's ultimate perfection)*; but one thing I do, forgetting those things which are behind and reaching forward to those things which are ahead, I press toward the goal for the prize of the upward call of God in Christ Jesus. Therefore let us, as many as are mature, have this in mind; and if in anything you think otherwise, God will reveal even this to you. Nevertheless, to the degree that we have already attained, let us walk by the same rule, let us be of the same mind."

STEADFASTNESS IN PRAYER

We are given instructions in Romans 12:10-13 for the way to live a godly life: "Be kindly affectionate to one another with brotherly love, in honor giving preference to one another; not lagging in diligence, fervent in spirit, serving the Lord; rejoicing in hope, patient in tribulation, continuing steadfastly in prayer; distributing to the needs of the saints, given to hospitality." Can you hear what blessings there would be for all who would listen carefully and follow these instructions? Diligence and fervency are absolutely necessary as we go about serving the Lord. Truly we need to continue steadfastly to obey all of God's Word, if we sincerely desire to live in the flow of God's love and peace and joy. That could be our spiritual thermometer. The measure of the joy we have, and being bathed in God's love and peace will show us how close we are to the Lord in fellowship and steadfast in His service.

As we just observed in those verses of Romans 12, living the godly life includes "continuing steadfastly in prayer." I realize that anyone who has to meet deadlines with a job, being at work at a certain time, or other types of time frames, may have difficulty setting a time for prayer. However, it is good to realize that a bowed head, folded hands and closed eyes are not always necessary for proper prayer. It is so freeing to know that as you're on the run, you can breathe your heart's needs to the Lord. While driving to work, to the grocery store, or while on vacation, just pray with your eyes open as you travel along on the street or highway. Praising the Lord is possibly the most important part of prayer and the most powerful kind of prayer! It may become one of your most glorious encounters with the Lord. Do you suppose that if we were steadfast in praising the Lord for a whole week, without asking for anything, the Lord might answer those needs we've presented week after week without seeing answers? I'm going to do just that. There is so much joy in praising the Lord; the joy that gives great strength!

Whatever is troubling you about your life, your family, the Church family, the nation, can freely be expressed in a conversation with the Lord. And while you're praying, remember your Pastor (or Pastors) and all the ministries of your Church; those who are ill, need surgery, are facing death or loss of a loved one. Pray for those who are being persecuted for 'righteousness sake', others who are risking their lives for the sake of spreading the gospel around the world, including missionaries; Christian ministries, television ministries, and those on the radio too. There is no limit to what our outreach can be as ambassadors for the Lord. Oh, it's so good to also close your prayers with praise to Him, for He is worthy of high praises from our hearts all day long!

You probably know the song "What a Friend we have in Jesus." Nearly every line ends with: take it to the Lord in prayer. Believing prayer is taking everything to God in prayer with the assurance that God answers prayer. It is refreshing to the spirit and helps one to become restful in God's love and promises. As we really trust Him, all our anxieties and fears will fall away, and our hearts will begin expressing anticipation and joy.

Continuing steadfastly in prayer is possible for everyone, even children. Years ago I heard about a lady who was moaning and groaning on the phone as she listened to the caller reveal serious problems in her home. This went on for a while, and her four year old little girl interrupted her to say, "Mommy, mommy, why don't we pray? Jesus will fix it!" Tearfully, the mother suggested to the lady on the phone that they could seek the Lord in prayer, and her daughter would pray too. So they did, and within days things turned around.

GOD GIVES THE VICTORY THROUGH JESUS

One of the most precious Scriptures to me is I Corinthians 15:57-58 because God gave this to me in the midst of a very perplexing problem, involving ministering to a caller on the

Christian Lifelines, a crisis line. I was on my way to pick her up from one place to bring her to another, and there was a temptation to be afraid. I had prayed for God's exact guidance and for peace in my heart, which would be a sure sign I had received His instructions. The watch that I had with me, slid off the dashboard as I rounded a corner on that frigid February morning, when the snow was at least three feet high on both sides of the road.

When I picked it up off the floor, it showed 11:57 and immediately changed to 11:58. Since the Lord had given messages to me so often with the numbers on a digital clock, translated into Scripture verses, I quickly saw 1 Corinthians 15:57 and 58. It says: "But THANKS be to GOD, who GIVES US the VICTORY through our LORD JESUS CHRIST. Therefore, my beloved brethren, be steadfast, immovable, always abounding in the work of the Lord, knowing that your labor is not in vain in the Lord." That word from the Lord took away the fear, and released a flow of praise from my heart to the Lord instead. That was more than just peace.

This was a great lesson for me to deeply understand the faithfulness of God to all of His promises, especially when we are serving Him as ambassadors to deliver His truth and love to others, and sometimes even be their deliverer. It helped me also to be more steadfast in prayer, as God gave me something so visible to bring a specific Scripture to my attention. It was like God's voice was powerfully speaking this truth so I wouldn't tremble and lose the faith that He had built into me. He had given me an unusual task and He wanted me to be "steadfast, immovable, always abounding in the work of the Lord," which I enjoyed doing so much in less complicated situations. I must add that "Victory in Jesus" was the outcome.

I pray that you will recognize the importance of being steadfast in the things that God has shown you as you read this message. May your life experience a jump-start to be more steadfast to fulfill God's special call on your life! As the Holy Spirit inspires you, these Scriptures will bless you greatly from this day forward!

SCRIPTURES FOR
STEADFAST-STEADFASTLY

God's attributes—

Ps. 111:7-8 NIV The works of His hands are faithful and just, all His precepts are trustworthy. They are **steadfast** for ever and ever, done in faithfulness and uprightness.

Dan. 6:26 I *(King Darius)* make a decree that in every dominion of my kingdom, men must tremble and fear before the God of Daniel. For He is the living God, and **steadfast** forever; His kingdom is the one which shall not be destroyed, and His dominion shall endure to the end.

David's desire for—

Ps. 51:10 Create in me a clean heart, O God, and renew a **steadfast** spirit within me.

Ps. 57:7 My heart is **steadfast**, O God, my heart is **steadfast**; I will sing and give praise.
See Ps. 108:1.

Blessings related to steadfastness—

Ps. 112:1, 7 NIV Praise the Lord. Blessed is the man who fears the Lord, who finds great delight in His commands. .....He will have no fear of bad news; his heart is **steadfast**, trusting in the Lord.

Isa. 26:3 NIV You will keep in perfect peace him whose mind is **steadfast**, because he trusts in You.

2 Cor. 3:7-8 KJV But if the ministration of death, written and

engraved in stones, was glorious, so that the children of Israel could not **steadfastly** behold the face of Moses for the glory of his countenance; which glory was to be done away: How shall not the ministry of the Spirit be rather glorious?

Jesus sets His face steadfastly —

Lu. 9:51 Now it came to pass, when the time had come for Him *(Jesus)* to be received up, that He **steadfastly** set His face to go to Jerusalem.

Believers in relation to steadfastness —

Acts 1:9-11 Now when He *(Jesus)* had spoken these things, while they watched, He was taken up, and a cloud received Him out of their sight. And while they looked **steadfastly** toward heaven as He went up, behold two men stood by Him in white apparel, who also said, "Men of Galilee, why do you stand gazing up into heaven? This same Jesus, who was taken up from you into heaven, will also come in like manner as you saw Him go into heaven."

Acts 2:41-42 Then those who gladly received his word *(Peter's preaching)* were baptized; and that day about three thousand souls were added to them. And they continued **steadfastly** in the apostles' doctrine and fellowship, in the breaking of bread, and in prayers.

Acts 6:15 And all who sat in the council, looking **steadfastly** at him *(Stephen)*, saw his face as the face of an angel.

Acts 7:54-56 KJV *After Stephen addressed the council and those who were false witnesses, we find these verses —-* When they heard these things they were cut to the heart, and they gnashed on him *(Stephen)* with their teeth. But he, being full of the Holy Ghost, looked up **steadfastly** into heaven, and saw the glory of God, and Jesus standing on the right hand of God, and said, Behold, I see the heavens opened, and the Son of man standing on the right hand of God.

Acts 14:8-10 KJV And there sat a certain man at Lystra, impotent in his feet, being a cripple from his mother's womb, who never had walked: the same heard Paul speak: who **steadfastly** beholding him, and perceiving that he had faith to be healed, said with a loud voice, "Stand upright on thy feet." And he leaped and walked.

Rom. 12:10-13 Be kindly affectionate to one another with brotherly love, in honor giving preference to one another; not lagging in diligence, fervent in spirit, serving the Lord; rejoicing in hope, patient in tribulation, continuing **steadfastly** in prayer; distributing to the needs of the saints, given to hospitality.

2 Cor. 1:7 And our hope for you is **steadfast**, because we know that as you are partakers of the sufferings, so also you will partake of the consolation.

Col. 2:5 For though I am absent in the flesh, yet I am with you in spirit, rejoicing to see your good order and the **steadfastness** of your faith in Christ.

Instructions for believers—

1 Cor. 7:37 Nevertheless he who stands **steadfast** in his heart, having no necessity, but has power over his own will, and has so determined in his heart that he will keep his virgin, does well.

1 Cor. 15:57-58 But thanks be to God, who gives us the victory through our Lord Jesus Christ. Therefore, my beloved brethren, be **steadfast**, immovable, always abounding in the work of the Lord, knowing that your labor is not in vain in the Lord.

Col. 1:21-23 And you, who once were alienated and enemies in your mind by wicked works, yet now He has reconciled in the body of His flesh through death, to present you holy, and blameless, and above reproach in His sight–if indeed you continue in the faith, grounded and **steadfast**, and are not moved away from the hope of the gospel which you heard, which was preached to every creature under heaven, of which I, Paul, became a minister.

Heb. 2:2-4 For if the word spoken through angels proved **steadfast**, and every transgression and disobedience received a just reward, how shall we escape if we neglect so great a salvation, which at the first began to be spoken by the Lord, and was confirmed to us by those who heard Him, God also bearing witness both with signs and wonders, with various miracles, and gifts of the Holy Spirit, according to His own will?

Heb. 3:14 For we have become partakers of Christ if we hold the beginning of our confidence **steadfast** to the end.

Heb. 6:19-20 This hope we have as an anchor of the soul, both sure and **steadfast**, and which enters the Presence behind the veil, where the forerunner has entered for us, even Jesus, having become High Priest forever according to the order of Melchizedek.

1 Peter 5:10-11 NIV And the God of all grace, who called you to His eternal glory in Christ, after you have suffered a little while, will himself restore you, and make you strong, firm and **steadfast**. To Him be the power for ever and ever. Amen.

Compassionately God warns His children—-

Ps. 78:37-38 For their heart was not **steadfast** with Him, nor were they faithful in His covenant. But He, being full of compassion, forgave their iniquity, and did not destroy them. Yes, many a time He turned His anger away, and did not stir up all His wrath...

1 Peter 5:8-9 Be sober, be vigilant, because your adversary the devil walks about like a roaring lion seeking whom he may devour. Resist him, **steadfast** in the faith, knowing that the same sufferings are experienced by your brotherhood in the world.

2 Peter 3:17-18 You therefore, beloved, since you know this beforehand, beware lest you also fall from your own **steadfastness**, being

led away with the error of the wicked; but grow in the grace and knowledge of our Lord and Savior Jesus Christ. To Him be glory both now and forever. Amen.

REFUGE

GOD IS THE ONLY SAFE REFUGE

It is spring as I write this, and while the tulips and daffodils are beginning to show their colorful faces like the glow of sunshine, and there are great expectations for a glorious season, but there are also severe storms around our country, including tornadoes and hurricanes. These storms often present a pressing need for a place of refuge, where there is adequate protection, such as a basement, a church, or a school. It is more difficult to escape to a safe place when the storm is rushing violently toward you.

There are many serious circumstances that people in other countries are more familiar with than we are in North America, such as internal strife, torturing innocent people and massive slaughtering as they please. At the time of this writing, there are refugees scattered across several countries, desperately in need of their basic necessities. They are being cast out of their own homes, forced to leave everything behind. Many husbands and sons are whipped and murdered before the eyes of family members, terrible persecution, with only hateful and vicious intentions. Where is a place of refuge, a place of protection from their enemies? How far will they have to trudge along, losing family members who couldn't go all the way? Who will sacrifice for them?

We don't think of a need for a place of refuge when everything is going well, the family is doing fine, no complaints with the job, and life in general appears to be secure and promising. However, there may be reasons to consider what our place of refuge might be in case of some serious threat to our home or family. What about training young children how to get out in case of a fire? Wouldn't it be wise to teach your children what to do in the consideration of various scenarios that could happen at school, if alone at home, or as they are out somewhere walking or shopping? Not in a way of putting a dark cloud of fear over them, but giving wise information with the comfort of your prayers and God's presence being with them at all times. They need a sure foundation in the Word so they will absolutely know they are secure in the Lord; that He is watching over them and trusting Him provides their need for "refuge and strength in time of trouble."

GOD'S WORD INSTRUCTS US

We find our word in the Old Testament almost exclusively. Times have drastically changed, so the types of situations that send us to the Lord as our refuge differ quite a bit. Having worked for several years on a Crisis-line has shown me some very serious situations in regard to child abuse and spouse abuse. They need a place of refuge, oftentimes - right now! Those who are caught in a trap with sinful habits, such as alcohol or drugs, need a place of refuge where they might be protected from further abuse to themselves and to others. There are even elderly people whose children are abusing them physically, emotionally, and/or with their finances. Please be alerted that there can be abuses going on in the nursing home where your loved one resides. It is important to be very observant, as a family member, or as one ministering there. They too need a place where they will be protected from further abuse.

These examples show us that a refuge is not only a place for you to go when fleeing from an enemy who is overcoming you with destructive armament, but there are many kinds of situations in life that cause us to seek refuge. We've observed that a refuge is a safe place, a shelter—a place for aid or relief, which may be at a neighbor's home. However, there is no one on the earth who can give absolute security through all types of storms. Only Almighty God is completely able to be "a shield for all who take refuge in Him." *Psalm 18:30b.* He is able to give us knowledge and wisdom that no one else has access to. He knows where our enemy is stationed. He knows all of Satan's devious ways and his battle gear for destroying you and me.

The Word of God is so encouraging. Psalm 34:7-8 says, "The angel of the Lord encamps around those who fear Him, and He delivers them. Taste and see that the Lord is good; blessed is the man who takes refuge in Him." And Proverbs 29:25 says, "The fear of man brings a snare, but whoever trusts in the Lord shall be safe." Another special one is Proverbs 18:10: "The name of the Lord is a strong tower; the righteous run to it and are safe." Aren't these tremendous Scriptures! Those who fear the Lord, and trust in Him, are the righteous, who stand in awe of God's greatness and power. They know His love for them, and that He is absolutely trustworthy, therefore they have the courage to remain standing as Ephesians 6:10-18 instructs us to do.

GOD'S LOVE IS OUR PROTECTION

Let's take some verses from the well known Psalm 91, where God is described as a refuge. Verses 1-4: "He who dwells in the shelter of the Most High will rest in the shadow of the Almighty. I will say of the Lord, 'He is my refuge and my fortress, my God, in whom I trust.' Surely He will save you from the fowler's snare and from the deadly pestilence. He will cover you with His feathers, and under His wings you will find refuge; His faithfulness will be your shield and rampart."

Many years ago I was with a group of ladies, seated around a table, and one of them shared about an experience she had a couple years previous to that. She had been shopping, and as she went to her car that evening, a man stepped out from along side of a van demanding her purse. As he pointed a gun toward her, she suddenly pointed her umbrella at him and yelled, "Feathers, feathers." He ran as fast as he could to the get-away car, and off they sped. She had claimed Psalm 91 several years previous to that incident as her psalm for protection, and thought if she ever needed help, she would just recite that psalm. But in the state of panic all she could think of was 'feathers.' It still worked. I believe it had to do with her secure relationship with the Lord, trusting Him for her refuge in time of trouble. The Lord responded with power on her behalf; the enemy became confused and fearful. Praise God for His boundless love and endless ways to protect us!

In the New Testament we have some insight in Romans 8:31-39, where it speaks of God's love being our protective place. In verse 31 it says; "If God is for us, who can be against us?" Then verse 35 says, "Who shall separate us from the love of Christ? Shall trouble or hardship or persecution or famine or nakedness or danger or sword?" Verse 37 gives an answer: "No, in all these things we are more than conquerors through Him who loved us." Paul continues to name other possible causes for becoming separated from the shelter of God's love, but He concludes that "nothing will be able to separate us from the love of God that is in Christ Jesus our Lord." Do you feel embraced in the security of his love? Can you see how God comes to our rescue in ways that we could not even think of?

Maybe some still ask, "How can I find God as my refuge?" Trust Him to be who He claims to be, and trust Him for every promise that He has given to us in His Word, trusting Him with all your heart. When we fear the Lord more than anything else, He is ready to be our refuge and strength. Search His Word for God's character traits, His attributes. As you seek for these golden nuggets of truth, you will gain precious information about who God really is, and your faith will be built up beyond what you could even imagine was possible.

Hide this Scripture from Psalm 62:6-7 in your heart: **"My salvation and my honor depend on God. He is my mighty rock, my refuge. Trust in Him at all times, O people; pour out your hearts to Him, for God is our refuge."**

SCRIPTURES FOR
R E F U G E

Cities for refuge—-

Num. 35:6, 10 "Now among the cities which you will give to the Levites you shall appoint six cities of **refuge**, to which a manslayer may flee. And to these you shall add forty two cities. ….Speak to the children of Israel, and say to them: 'When you cross the Jordan in the land of Canaan, then you shall appoint cities of **refuge** for you, that the manslayer who kills a person accidentally may flee there.'"

The Eternal God, a refuge—-

Deut. 33:27 The eternal God is your **refuge**, and underneath are the everlasting arms; He will thrust out the enemy from before you, and will say, 'Destroy'!

Ps. 9:9-10 NIV The Lord is a **refuge** for the oppressed, a stronghold in times of trouble. Those who know Your name will trust in You, for You, Lord, have never forsaken those who seek You.

Ps. 18:30 NIV As for God, His way is perfect; the word of the Lord is flawless. He is a shield for all who take **refuge** in Him.

Ps. 14:6 NIV You evildoers frustrate the plans of the poor, but the Lord is their **refuge.**

Ps. 34:7-8 NIV The angel of the Lord encamps around those who fear Him, and He delivers them. Taste and see that the Lord is good; blessed is the man who takes **refuge** in Him.

Ps. 36:7-8 NIV How priceless is Your unfailing love! Both high and low among men find **refuge** in the shadow of Your wings. They feast on the abundance of Your house; You give them drink from Your river of delights.

Ps. 46:1 NIV God is our **refuge** and strength, an ever present help in trouble.

Ps. 91:1-4 NIV He who dwells in the shelter of the Most High will rest in the shadow of the Almighty. I will say of the Lord, "He is my **refuge** and my fortress, my God, in whom I trust." Surely He will save you from the fowler's snare and from the deadly pestilence. He will cover you with His feathers, and under His wings you will find **refuge**; His faithfulness will be your shield and rampart.

Prov. 14:26 NIV He who fears the Lord has a secure fortress, for His children it will be a **refuge**.

Prov. 30:5 NIV Every word of God is flawless; He is a shield to those who take **refuge** in Him.

Crying out to God for refuge—-

Ps. 16:1 NIV Keep me safe, O God, for in You I take **refuge**.

Ps. 17:6-8 NIV I call upon You, O God, for You will answer me, give ear to me and hear my prayer. Show the wonder of Your great love, You who save by Your right hand those who take **refuge** in You from their foes. Keep me as the apple of Your eye; hide me in the shadow of Your wings.

Ps. 25:20-21 NIV Guard my life and rescue me; let me not be put to shame, for I take **refuge** in You. May integrity and uprightness protect me, because my hope is in You.

Ps. 31:1-3 NIV In You, O Lord, I have taken **refuge**; let me never be put to shame; deliver me in Your righteousness. Turn Your ear to me, come quickly to my rescue, be my Rock of **refuge**, a strong fortress to save me. Since You are my Rock and my fortress, for the sake of Your name lead and guide me.

Ps. 57:1-3 NIV Have mercy on me, O God, have mercy on me, for in You my soul takes **refuge**. I will take **refuge** in the shadow of Your wings until the disaster has passed. I cry out to God Most High, to God, who fulfills His purpose for me. He sends from heaven and saves me, rebuking those who hotly pursue me; God sends His love and His faithfulness.

Ps. 61:1-4 NIV Hear my cry, O God; listen to my prayer. From the ends of the earth I call to you, I call as my heart grows faint; lead me to the Rock that is higher than I. For You have been my **refuge**, a strong tower against the foe. I long to dwell in Your tent forever and take **refuge** in the shelter of Your wings.

Ps. 71:1-4 NIV In You, O Lord, I have taken **refuge**; let me never be put to shame. Rescue me and deliver me in Your righteousness; turn Your ear to me and save me. Be my rock of **refuge**, to which I can always go; give the command to save me, for You are my rock and my fortress. Deliver me, O my God, from the hand of the wicked, from the grasp of the evil and cruel men.

Ps. 141:8 NIV But my eyes are fixed on You, O Sovereign Lord; in You I take **refuge** – do not give me over to death.

Ps. 142:5 NIV I cry to You, O Lord; I say, "You are my **refuge**, my portion in the land of the living."

Praising the Lord for being their refuge—-

Ps. 5:11 NIV But let all who take **refuge** in You be glad; let them ever sing for joy. Spread Your protection over them, that those who love Your name may rejoice in You.

Ps. 18:1-3 NIV I love You, O Lord, my strength. The Lord is my rock, my fortress and my deliverer; my God is my rock in whom I take **refuge**. He is my shield and the horn of my salvation, my stronghold. I call to the Lord, who is worthy of praise, and I am saved from my enemies.

Ps. 59:16-17 NIV But I will sing to Your strength, in the morning I will sing of Your love; for You are my fortress, my **refuge** in times of trouble. O my Strength, I sing praise to You; You, O God, are my fortress, my loving God.

Ps. 62:7-8 NIV My salvation and my honor depend on God. He is my mighty rock, my **refuge**. Trust in Him at all times, O people; pour out your hearts to Him, for God is our **refuge**.

Ps. 71:7-8 NIV I have become like a portent to many, but You are my strong **refuge**. My mouth is filled with Your praise, declaring Your splendor all day long.

God's promise gives hope and a refuge—-

Heb. 6:17-20 Thus God, determining to show more abundantly to the heirs of promise the immutability of His counsel, confirming it by an oath, that by two immutable things, in which it is impossible for God to lie, we might have strong consolation, who have fled for **refuge** to lay hold of the hope set before us. This hope we have as an anchor of the soul, both sure and steadfast, and which enters the Presence behind the veil, where the forerunner has entered for us, even Jesus, having become High Priest forever according to the order of Melchizedek.

DELIVERANCE

GOD IS THE GREAT DELIVERER

One of the greatest stories of deliverance is when the Israelites fled from Egypt by night. Yes, they had to flee! God was directing everything toward this magnificent escape from their captors. He instructed them every step in their preparation, and continued to guide them through this enormous, heart shaking and earth shaking event to safety. Without God's powerful intervention there would have been no hope! He rolled back the waters of the Red Sea; He withheld the enemy from overtaking them, and then destroyed the Egyptians as they tried to cross the same path that the God had prepared for His people. God was in charge.

The Lord continued to deliver the Israelites throughout Old Testament history when they turned to Him for wisdom and guidance, and obeyed those instructions. As you read the Scriptures, you'll find that no matter who their leader was, and no matter what the circumstances, when they sought the Lord, He heard their plea and overcame their enemies.

Our God lacks nothing! His wisdom far excels man's wisdom. He is able to see into the hearts of men, discerning their evil plans. His mighty power far surpasses man's abilities in any area of life. Man just cannot defeat God. Psalm 97:10 says, "You who love the Lord, hate evil! He preserves the souls of His saints; He delivers them out of the hand of the wicked." Even though we have a part in what is to be done, it is God that makes things right, for He is our Deliverer. That verse says: 'You who love the Lord'. The Israelites would not have been delivered if they did not believe God, trust Him and obey Him. I don't know if they understood a love relationship: it was when God gave the law through Moses, that He said, "Thou shalt love the Lord thy God." Love is a higher level of trusting and obeying. Love will cause us to profusely praise the Lord! Our love for Him will not allow us to be concerned if someone hears us expressing our love and praise to Him!

THERE'S SECURITY IN KNOWING GOD AND HIS WORD

Maybe you're in the midst of a baffling, frustrating situation, when doubts and questions arise. Satan loves to ask questions. We see this in his discourse with Eve in the Garden of Eden in Genesis. Sometimes we question if God really cares about us when we are hurting in the midst of some of the horrible situations that unexpectedly come upon us. We don't have the answers, but God's Word always has the perfect answers for us. Praise the Lord! Praise the Lord!

We desperately need to recognize who God is, and that we can trust Him at all times. In Isaiah 14:24 and 27 NIV, we read: "The Lord Almighty has sworn, 'Surely, as I have planned so it will be, and as I have purposed, so it will stand.' .....For the Lord Almighty has purposed, and who can thwart Him? His hand is stretched out, and who can turn it back?" We must know the Scriptures, and the surety of God's character; then we can quote these truths to the devil, as Jesus did, and he will have to flee! Praise God again, for He is our refuge and our strength, a very present shelter in time of trouble. That shelter is His love, and His love is active, not on a shelf in the closet, or in a lock-box. He is real! He is right there for you today!

Another incredible deliverance is recorded in Daniel 3, where Shadrack, Meshack and Abed-Nego *(Daniel's friends)* bravely tell the king, "O Nebuchadnezzar, we have no need to answer you in this matter. If that is the case, our God whom we serve is able to deliver us from the fiery furnace, and He will deliver us from your hand, O King." And God did deliver them in a miraculous way, sending an angel, possibly Jesus, to protect them in the fire. The heat of that furnace killed those who threw them in, yet these three men of God had no burns whatsoever; did not have singed hair on their bodies; robes were not scorched, nor even smelled like fire, as they came out of the furnace (3:27). This changed the heart of King Nebuchadnezzar to serve God, and then commanded that everyone else must serve Him too.

In Daniel 6 we read of Daniel's protection in the lions' den. From verse 19-23 we read that God had sent an angel to shut the lions' mouths so that he had no wounds on him. As you read the whole story, you hear of Daniel's absolute devotion to God in the way He steadfastly honored and worshiped Him; prayed to the Lord, and praised Him with unwavering trust.

In Psalm 91:14-15 we read of God's unfailing promises for those who love Him: "Because he has set his love upon Me, therefore I will deliver him; I will set him on high, because he has known My name. He shall call upon Me, and I will answer him; I will be with him in trouble; I will deliver him and honor him." This is from God's heart, and this may well have been spoken about Abraham, Moses, Joshua, Nehemiah, Ezra, King Jehosphaphat and many others along through the years, but the Lord may also say this of you, if indeed your heart is fervently in love with Him. Are you turning to Him for all your needs and for His delivering wisdom and power? There is no safer way to go, whether your need is in relationships, in the financial realm, or when your physical health seems to be crumbling.

Perhaps your problem is with a zoning board, a transportation problem, or of much greater magnitude in your marriage, or with a child. Not even one problem is beyond our heavenly Father's eyes, or His ability to hear and answer your prayers. His hand is not short *(Isa. 59:1)*; nothing is too hard for Him *(Jer. 32:17, 27); * nothing is impossible for Him *(Mk. 10:27)*. God's ways are always in accordance with His wisdom, for our best, and with eternity in view. However, along with this let's look at 1 John 5:14-15: "Now this is the confidence that we have in Him, that if we ask anything according to His will, He hears us. And if we know that He hears us, whatever we ask, we know that we have the petitions that we have asked of Him." And I must add this one: Mark 9:23 says: Jesus said to him, "If you can believe, all things are possible to him who believes." What changes can come into your life with the knowledge of what God has already said in His Word?

THE PLACE FOR FULL SURRENDER AND PATIENCE

We must surrender to Him, allowing His choice for deliverance. We don't need to make the choices of 'how, when and where' according to our best understanding. Proverbs 3:5-6 apply so well here: "Trust in the Lord with all your heart and lean not upon your own understanding. In all your ways acknowledge Him, and He shall direct your paths." When we surrender the whole package to Him, all the stuff that instigates fears and anxieties, even worried that we didn't use the right words in our prayers, then you can be sure of this– He is well able to deliver you from whoever your enemy is and whatever your enemy has in mind. Let go! Let go! And He will totally deliver you, for He is able!

We find a wonderful testimony in Psalm 40:1-5 NIV: "I waited patiently for the Lord; He turned to me and heard my cry. He lifted me out of *(delivered me from)* the slimy pit, out of the mud and mire; He set my feet on a rock and gave me a firm place to stand. He put a new song in my mouth, a hymn of praise to our God. Many will see and fear and put their trust in the Lord. Blessed is the man who makes the Lord his trust, who does not look to the proud, to those who turn aside to false gods *(to earthly provisions instead of God)*. Many, O Lord my God, are the wonders You have done. The things You planned for us no one can recount to You; were I to speak and tell of them, they would be too many to declare." Don't miss looking up these Scriptures too—- Psalm 27:1; Psalm 28:6-7 and Psalm 37:7-11.

How often we rush toward just any available person or thing for deliverance in time of need, rather than humbly bowing before the Lord. If we would wait patiently for Him, how different our lives could be. He would give us wisdom, and even orchestrate changes in the situation.

There have been many episodes in my life when I didn't have a clue for getting out of those serious situations in my life. I must say, it took me a long time to really learn how to patiently trust the Lord in the tough, painful experiences, but God was faithful as my

Father, to graciously train me in the midst of these trials. I discovered how easily and quickly He could deal with whatever I fully gave to Him. He tells us in Psalm 55:22 to "Cast your burden on the Lord, and He shall sustain you; He shall never permit the righteous to be moved."

Nothing is too hard for Him. He is absolutely able to take our burdens and deliver us from whatever is about to overtake us. He is able to set a healing process into action, or any other intervention that could be needed at the time. He knows everything about us, and even our body's needs. Sometimes He alerts us to our need for a change in our mind-set, our expectations, which may be more negative than positive, and our daily routine which may well be stuck in the mud. He will reveal the simple changes we should make, such as diet and exercise, better choices in work habits, and the way that we deal with stresses. We may need to observe the way we often push ourselves unmercifully.

Let go! Give it all to Him. He is well able to direct your steps and deliver you to safety. You may not need other kinds of intervention, not even medications, but He will reveal that to you. Remember, with God all things are possible! Deliverance may not come in five minutes, or over night, but He will not ignore you– His unfailing love is too great! Read the scriptures again; listen closely for His voice. He will give you guidance and encouragement. Your joy may be overflowing in the morning, just because He is able!

SCRIPTURES FOR
DELIVERANCE

God is the Deliverer-

Ex. 3:7-8a And the Lord said, "I have surely seen the oppression of My people who are in Egypt, and have heard their cry because of their taskmasters, for I know their sorrows. So I have come down to **deliver** them out of the hand of the Egyptians, and to bring them up from that land to a good and large land, to a land flowing with milk and honey..."

Jdgs 7:2-3a, 7 The Lord said to Gideon, "You have too many men for me to **deliver** Midian into their hands. In order that Israel may not boast against me that her own strength has saved her, announce now to the people, 'Anyone who trembles with fear may turn back and leave Mount Gilead.'" ....The Lord said to Gideon, "With the 300 men that lapped I will save you and give the Midianites into your hands. Let all the other men go, each to his own place."

2 Chron. 20:17 NIV "You will not have to fight this battle. Take up your positions; stand firm and see the **deliverance** the Lord will give you, O Judah and Jerusalem. Do not be afraid; do not be discouraged. Go out to face them tomorrow, and the Lord will be with you."

Ps. 33:18-19 Behold, the eye of the Lord is on those who fear Him, on those who hope in His mercy, to **deliver** their soul from death, and to keep them alive in famine.

Ps. 35:9-10 And my soul shall be joyful in the Lord; it shall rejoice in His salvation. All my bones shall say, "Lord, who is like You, **delivering** the poor from him who is too strong for him. Yes, the poor and the needy from him who plunders him?"

Ps. 37:39-40 The salvation of the righteous comes from the Lord; He is their stronghold in time of trouble. The Lord helps them and **delivers** them; He **delivers** them from the wicked and saves them, because they take refuge in Him.

Ps. 50:14-15 "Offer to God thanksgiving, and pay your vows to the Most High. Call upon Me in the day of trouble; I will **deliver** you, and you shall glorify Me."

Ps. 72:12 NIV For He will **deliver** the needy who cry out, the afflicted who have no one to help.

Ps. 91:14-15 Because he has set his love upon Me, therefore I will **deliver** him; I will set him on high, because he has known My name. He shall call upon Me, and I will answer him; I will be with him in trouble; I will **deliver** him and honor him.

Ps. 97:10 You who love the Lord, hate evil! He preserves the souls of His saints; He **delivers** them out of the hand of the wicked.

Prov. 21:31 The horse is prepared for the day of battle, but **deliverance** is of the Lord.

Isa. 50:2-3 Thus says the Lord; ..."Why, when I came, was there no man? Why, when I called, was there none to answer? Is My hand shortened at all that it cannot redeem? Or have I no power to **deliver**? Indeed with My rebuke I dry up the sea, I make the rivers a wilderness; their fish stink because there is no water, and die of thirst. I clothe the heavens with blackness, and I make sackcloth their covering."

Dan. 6:16 So the king gave the command, and they brought Daniel and cast him into the den of lions. But the king spoke, saying to Daniel, "Your God, whom you serve continually, He will **deliver** you."

Gal. 1:3-4 Grace to you and peace from God the Father and our Lord Jesus Christ, who gave Himself for our sins, that He might

deliver us from this present evil age, according to the will of our God and Father.

Col. 1:12-14 ...giving thanks to the Father who has qualified us to be partakers of the inheritance of the saints in the light. He has **delivered** us from the power of darkness and conveyed us into the kingdom of the Son of His love, in whom we have redemption through His blood, the forgiveness of sins.

1 Thess. 1:10 And to wait for His Son from heaven, whom He raised from the dead, even Jesus who **delivers** us from the wrath to come.

2 Peter 2:6-9 ...and turning the cities of Sodom and Gomorrah into ashes, condemned them to destruction, making them an example to those who afterward would live ungodly; and **delivered** righteous Lot, who was oppressed by the filthy conduct of the wicked (for that righteous man, dwelling among them, tormented his righteous soul from day to day by seeing and hearing their lawless deeds) — then the Lord knows how to **deliver** the godly out of temptations and to reserve the unjust under punishment for the day of judgment.

Jude vs. 5 Though you already know all this, I want to remind you that the Lord **delivered** His people out of Egypt, but later destroyed those who did not believe!

Praying for deliverance —

Ps. 31:1-2 In You, O Lord, I put my trust; let me never be ashamed; **deliver** me in Your righteousness. Bow down Your ear to me, **deliver** me speedily; be my rock of refuge, a fortress of defense to save me.

Ps. 59:1-2 **Deliver** me from my enemies, O my God; defend me from those who rise up against me. **Deliver** me from the workers of iniquity, and save me from bloodthirsty men.

Ps. 71:1-5 In You, O Lord, I put my trust; let me never be put to shame. **Deliver** me in Your righteousness, and cause me to escape; incline Your ear to me, and save me. Be my strong refuge, to which I may resort continually; you have given the commandment to save me, for You are my rock and my fortress. **Deliver** me, O my God, out of the hand of the wicked, out of the hand of the unrighteous and cruel man. For You are my hope, O Lord God; You are my trust from my youth.

Ps. 119:170 Let my supplication come before You; **deliver** me according to Your word.

Matt. 6:13 *Part of the prayer Jesus taught His disciples as a model—*"And do not lead us into temptation, but **deliver** us from the evil one, for Yours is the kingdom and the power and the glory forever. Amen"

Testimonies of deliverance—

1 Sam. 17:36-37 NIV Your servant has killed both the lion and the bear; this uncircumcised Philistine will be like one of them, because he has defied the armies of the living God. The Lord who **delivered** me from the paw of the lion and the paw of the bear will **deliver** me from the hand of this Philistine."

2 Sam. 22:1-3 NIV David sang to the Lord the words of this song when the Lord **delivered** him from the hand of all his enemies and from the hand of Saul. He said: "The Lord is my rock, my fortress and my **deliverer**; my God is my rock, in whom I take refuge, my shield and the horn of my salvation. He is my stronghold, my refuge and my savior– from violent men you save me." *Also Ps. 18:1-3*

Ps. 32:7 You are my hiding place; You shall preserve me from trouble; You shall surround me with songs of **deliverance**.

Ps. 34:4, 7 NIV I sought the Lord, and He answered me, He **delivered** me from all my fears. The angel of the Lord encamps around those who fear Him and He **delivers** them.

Ps. 56:12-13 Vows made to You are binding upon me, O God; I will render praises to You, for You have **delivered** my soul from death. Have You not kept my feet from falling, that I may walk before God in the light of the living?

Jer. 20:13 Sing to the Lord! Praise the Lord! For He has **delivered** the life of the poor from the hand of evildoers.

Dan. 3:16-17 Shadrach, Meshach and Abed-Nego answered and said to the king, "O Nebuchadnezzar, we have no need to answer you in this matter. If that is the case, our God whom we serve is able to **deliver** us from the fiery furnace, and He will **deliver** us from your hand, O king."

2 Cor. 1:9-10 NIV Indeed, in our hearts we felt the sentence of death. But this happened that we might not rely on ourselves but on God, who raises the dead. He has **delivered** us from such a deadly peril and He will **deliver** us. On Him we have set our hope that He will continue to **deliver** us.

Phil. 1:19 For I know this will turn out for my **deliverance** through your prayers and the supply of the Spirit of Jesus Christ.

2 Tim. 4:17-18 But the Lord stood with me and strengthened me, so that the message might be preached fully through me, and that all the Gentiles might hear. Also I was **delivered** out of the mouth of the lion. And the Lord will **deliver** from every evil work and preserve me for His heavenly kingdom. To Him be glory forever and ever. Amen!

Other truths regarding deliverance—

Ps. 41:1 Blessed is he who considers the poor; the Lord will **deliver** him in time of trouble.

Prov. 2:11-13 Discretion will preserve you, understanding will keep you, to **deliver** you from the way of evil, from the man who speaks perverse things, from those who leave the paths of uprightness to walk in the ways of darkness.

Matt. 11:27 *Jesus is speaking—* "All things have been **delivered** to Me by My Father, and no one knows the Son except the Father. Nor does anyone know the Father except the Son, and the one to whom the Son wills to reveal Him."

Luke 4:18-19 KJV *Jesus was speaking in the synagogue in Nazareth—* "The Spirit of the Lord is upon me, because He hath anointed Me to preach the gospel to the poor; He hath sent Me to heal the broken-hearted, to preach **deliverance** to the captives, and recovering of sight to the blind, to set at liberty them that are bruised, to preach the acceptable year of the Lord."

Rom 7:24-25, 8:1 O wretched man that I am! Who will **deliver** me from this body of death? I thank God – through Jesus Christ our Lord! So then, with the mind I myself serve the law of God, but with the flesh the law of sin. There is therefore now no condemnation to those who are in Christ Jesus, who do not walk according to the flesh, but according to the Spirit.

STRENGTH

GOD'S STRENGTH IS
MADE PERFECT IN OUR WEAKNESS

We have all had some bad days without the necessary strength to even figure out how to begin the day. At such a time as this, even a simple thing takes more energy than you have. It is so easy to just give up. It affects everything within us, especially our attitude and behavior which in turn naturally affects everyone around us. We really need help!

It is a tremendous blessing to read the scriptures on strength. God is never lacking it. Also, He is able to give us strength, and He can do for us what He said to Paul in 2 Corinthians 12:9, "My grace is sufficient for you, for My strength is made perfect in weakness." The Lord desires for us to understand His "grace sufficiency" and realize that the truth He is offering to Paul is possible for us too.

On the one hand it is not wise to be caught up with thoughts of how miserable we feel, but there are times that we should reach out for help by calling on someone to pray with us. We are to help the weak, and at times you may be that weak one. Many times our strength disappears because of the pressures in life. Psalm 27:1 and 14 have an answer for us—"The Lord is my light and my salvation; whom shall I fear? The Lord is the strength of my life; of whom shall I be afraid? Wait on the Lord; be of good courage and He shall strengthen your heart; wait I say, on the Lord!"

It is very helpful to put this in a prayer. This is one way to do that: "O Lord, my God, I am so thankful that You are my light and my salvation. You tell me that I should not fear. It is the fear that is so determined to overtake me today, but Your Word tells me not to fear. This helps me to realize that You will help me through these circumstances by being my light so I can see what is really happening. I know that I can trust You all the way. I am assured that You are my salvation and deliverer. I am grateful that You are able to save me from going under by the weight of the burden. You have promise to be the strength of my life. What a promise! Why would I rather be afraid, when You are with us and ready to take the battle from us so we can experience victory instead of defeat? Lord, help me to wait on You, even as You have counseled me in Your Word. I feel the courage and strength coming like a stream of refreshing water. Thank you, Lord, I know that I can wait on You, for You are faithful to Your children. In our weakness, You are always strong on our behalf as we turn to You. Today I will step aside and let You take over. I will praise You with my whole heart! Praise the Lord! Amen."

Psalm 18:32 tells me, "It is God who arms me with strength, and makes my way perfect." Psalm 59:16-17 says, "But I will sing of Your strength, in the morning I will sing of Your love; for You are my fortress, my refuge in times of trouble. O my Strength, I sing praise to You; You, O God, are my fortress, my loving God." These are strong declarations. Can you see how powerful it can be for us to chase the clouds away by declaring the goodness of the Lord, and who He is to each of us in our daily lives? Can you feel strength flowing in?

MANY THINGS CAN DRAIN OUR STRENGTH

There are so many reasons for our strength being low. Possibly you are a care giver, and the extra duties are overwhelming to your mind and body. We need to guard our hearts from falling into depression and search the Word for the exact message that your heart needs. The Scriptures that are attached may be just right, however, there may be some other key words that are more meaningful to you and you can check your Bible's concordance to find additional insights that will minister to you.

Whatever your situation may be, only the Lord can be your help and shield. Psalm 28:7-8 can be your message from the Lord for this very hour. It tells us: "The Lord is my strength and my shield; my heart trusted in Him, and I am helped; therefore my heart greatly rejoices, and with my song I will praise Him. The Lord is their strength, and He is the saving refuge of His anointed." This is David's testimony of God's faithfulness. Isn't that what we need so much to trust God for? If you know the song, then sing Great Is Thy Faithfulness, this will add to the strength of your heart and mind! I've seen it work, and that is because it's so true, God is faithful! When we see what God has done to help us, not only does a song come into our hearts, but this stimulates new strength.

Many times we try to fit too much into one day, and our strength disappears long before the end of the day. One outstanding time in my life which could have drained me like that, was when Dr. Billy Graham came to Indianapolis, Indiana for a crusade in 1980. This was an exciting time for thousands of people, and I was one of them. I signed up as a member of the choir, became a counselor, and after the meetings, I worked at another church building with the response cards. I was also working eight-hour days taking care of a lady, so I realized in advance that I'd need extra strength. As I was praying about this, the Lord informed me that I should go to the Scriptures and find verses that told how we could gain strength. I wrote out several of them, and rehearsed them day by day. I never lacked strength during that time of ministry. It was amazing how God's strength continuously sustained me.

REJOICING AND PRAISING GOD BRINGS STRENGTH

Sometimes it's the mental demand that takes the most from us. Any time we're dealing with situations that put great stress on us, and we try so hard to work everything out to please everyone involved, the pressure will take a toll. Though many people had been in very frightening and disastrous circumstances before Moses, their need for strength is not recorded. Also, there seems to be no record of their giving God glory and praise for the strength He provided. Moses appears to be the first one to bless the Lord for being his strength and adds the word 'song' right with it. I've felt extremely tired at times, and when strength came back, there was a song in my heart too. Have you had that experience? When I'm relieved of pain, songs just start rolling in my heart.

David is one who expresses it often. In 2 Samuel 22 David spoke the words of a song to the Lord, in which He is rejoicing in the God of his strength. There were many times when he had to totally rely on God's strength in battles, and when fleeing from his enemies. That really helps us to see how available God is when our needs push us, or pile up on us. Psalm 46:1 says: "God is our refuge and strength, a very present help in trouble." Isn't that great to know! He's right there. He sees everything, so all we have to do is call out for help, and He'll be there. We may not get the total, instant relief we desire, but we can be confident in knowing that God is responding to fervent, trusting prayers.

In Psalm 68 we find a call to "Ascribe strength to God; His excellence is over Israel, and His strength is in the clouds. O God, You are more awesome than Your holy places. The God of Israel is He who gives strength and power to His people." This is a very encouraging statement, for David had experienced God's strength often, and had seen God's hand in the clouds. He may have seen what we know as hurricanes and tornadoes. They do reveal a power in the clouds, and no man, in his own strength, can stop them. I have heard of Christians with powerful faith who have diverted storms, or have spoken to the storm to lift up, in the name of Jesus, and they obeyed.

Psalm 81 begins with "Sing aloud to God our strength; make a joyful shout to the God of Jacob. Raise a song and strike the timbrel, the pleasant harp with the lute." We should be so ready to give our all to the Lord in song, when we've had the blessing of strength. I started to say 'extra strength', however, just having strength for our tasks is reason to praise the Lord. He is the provider of our strength.

How beautiful Psalm 93:1 is, as it describes the Lord—"The Lord reigns, He is clothed with majesty; the Lord is clothed, He has girded Himself with strength." What a tremendous picture of the beauty and greatness of God! Those who seek to know the Lord in an intimate relationship, by seeking His face and communing with Him in His Word, in worship and praise, sense the truth of this in their spirits. In the time of sweet communion we are strengthened in our hearts, and I can believe that even our cells are rejuvenated as stress falls away.

Many Christians know the truth of Nehemiah 8:10, for the 'joy of the Lord' has been their strength many times along the way. Joy is so uplifting and strengthening, and when we are joyous in our relationship with the Lord, we find lasting strength. It isn't something that lasts only an hour; it tends to carry one for a period of time. Of course, it can make a difference if the joy comes from gratitude. We've probably all heard that 'wisdom is the principle thing', but in certain circumstances 'gratitude is the principle thing', for joy is attached, or is produced by a deeper emotion. Just take some time to observe this in your life.

Since I mentioned above about gratitude, I decided to check on verses with that word in it. Here is an interesting fact: The King James Version doesn't appear to use the word. Then I found just two verses listed in my NIV concordance. So I took the Colossians 3:16 reference, where the KJV says: "Let the word of Christ dwell in you richly in all wisdom; teaching and admonishing one another in psalms and hymns and spiritual songs, singing with <u>grace</u> in your hearts to the Lord." The New Living Translation says: "Let the words of Christ, in all their richness, live in your hearts and make you wise. Use His words to teach and counsel each other. Sing psalms and hymns and spiritual songs to God with <u>thankful</u> hearts." So the words grace and thankful are given in place of grateful. The thankful heart truly generates joy, which in turn produces strength. This is great!

WAITING IN QUIETNESS RENEWS STRENGTH

Isaiah 30:15b is very special, and can bless anyone who needs strength—"In returning and rest you shall be saved; in quietness and confidence shall be your strength."

Returning to the Lord is a place of refuge, a quiet place, the place to drink at the Fountain of Life for every need. He is the place where you can find renewed strength. As Psalm 23:3 says, "He restores my soul." Isaiah 40:31 expresses a similar truth: "But those who wait on the Lord shall renew their strength; they shall mount up with wings like eagles, they shall run and not be weary, they shall walk and not faint." These verses are so encouraging and stabilizing during times when nothing seems to be stable around us. The Lord can bless us 'beyond our asking and thinking' *(See Ephesians 3:20)* as we wait on Him, resting on His truths and His faithfulness to His children. The waiting does not mean to do nothing, but we are to attune our hearts to listen for His instructions, for obedience is more important than any kind of barging ahead on our own limited understanding. We can get terribly messed up trying to fix what only God can fix.

SOME SPECIAL INSTRUCTIONS

We oftentimes have a tendency to place our trust in the wrong thing, just as Psalm 33:16 and 17 show us: "No King is saved by the multitude of an army; a mighty man is not delivered by great strength. A horse is a vain hope for safety; neither shall it deliver any by its great strength." Possibly you can think of other things, or people, that you have trusted, which would be a parallel to an army or a horse. Your situation became futile, but don't be discouraged, just learn from your experience, and run back to the Lord with a repentant heart, remembering Isaiah 41:10 encourages us with "Fear not, for I am with you; be not dismayed, for I am your God. I will strengthen you, yes, I will help you, I will uphold you with My righteous right hand."

We might see others faltering, or stumbling along in their weaknesses. We may even be a little bit proud that we've done better in the same kind of circumstances, and have become critical. We are instructed in Romans 15:1 with: "We then who are strong ought to bear with the scruples of the weak, and not to please ourselves." And Galatians 6:1 is somewhat similar: "Brethren, if a man is overtaken in any trespass, you who are spiritual *(strong)* restore such a one in a spirit of gentleness, considering yourself lest you also be tempted." What a blessing to know that God cares so much for us when we falter and even fail to please Him at a time of definite weakness.

JESUS NEEDED STRENGTH

Even Jesus needed extra strength along the way. Not much is written about them, but one very outstanding time was in the

Garden of Gethsemane. We have a record in Luke 22:41-43, "And He *(Jesus)* was withdrawn from them about a stone's throw, and He knelt down and prayed, saying, 'Father, if it is Your will, take this cup away from Me; nevertheless, not My will, but Yours, be done.' Then an angel appeared from heaven, strengthening Him." In some of the deep valleys that people have gone through, they also needed angels to protect them. Many can testify to God's tremendous compassion and mercy in His sending ministering angels to deliver and strengthen them.

As you read the many other Scriptures, you will find a wealth of enlightenment for your life, along with the greatness of God's love for each one of His children, especially when we turn to Him for wisdom and strength. His eye is on the sparrows, and His Word assures us that He cares for our needs far more than that.

In closing, I pray 1 Thessalonians 3:12-13 over you— "May the Lord make your love increase and overflow for each other and for everyone else, just as ours does for you. May He strengthen your hearts so that you will be blameless and holy in the presence of our God and Father when our Lord Jesus comes with all His holy ones."

SCRIPTURES FOR
S T R E N G T H

God's strength —

Ex. 13:3 And Moses said to the People: "Remember this day in which you went out of Egypt, out of the house of bondage; for by **strength** of hand the Lord brought you out of this place." *Also see Ex. 13:14*

Ex. 15:2 The Lord is my **strength** and song, and He has become my salvation; He is my God, and I will praise Him; my father's God, and I will exalt Him. *See Ps. 118:14 and Isa. 12:2*

Ex. 15:13 You in Your mercy have led forth the people whom You have redeemed; You have guided them in Your **strength** to Your habitation.

2 Sam. 22:1-3 Then David spoke to the Lord the words of this song, on the day when the Lord had delivered him from the hand of all his enemies, and from the hand of Saul. And he said: "The Lord is my rock and my fortress and my deliverer; the God of my **strength**, in whom I will trust; my shield and the horn of my salvation, my **stronghold** and my refuge; my Savior, You save me from violence." *See Ps. 18:1, 2*

1 Chron. 16:7-8, 11, 27 On that day David first delivered this psalm into the hand of Asaph and his brethren, to thank the Lord: Oh, give thanks to the Lord! Call upon His name; make known His deeds among the peoples! ....Seek the Lord and His **strength**; seek His face evermore! ....Honor and majesty are before Him; **strength** and gladness are in His place.

Ps. 68:34-35 Ascribe **strength** to God; His excellence is over Israel, and His **strength** is in the clouds. O God, You are more awesome than Your holy places. The God of Israel is He who gives **strength** and power to His people.

Ps. 74:13 You divided the sea by Your **strength**; You broke the heads of the sea serpents in the waters.

Ps. 81:1 Sing aloud to God our **strength**; make a joyful shout to the God of Jacob. Raise a song and strike the timbrel, the pleasant harp with the lute.

Ps. 93:1 The Lord reigns, He is clothed with majesty; the Lord is clothed, He has girded Himself with **strength**. Surely the world is established, so that it cannot be moved.

Isa. 25:1, 4 O Lord, You are my God. I will exalt You, I will praise Your name, for You have done wonderful things; Your counsels of old are faithfulness and truth. ....For You have been a **strength** to the poor, a **strength** to the needy in his distress, a refuge from the storm, a shade from the heat, for the blast of the terrible ones is as a storm against the wall.

Isa. 40:25-26 "To whom then will you liken Me, or to whom shall I be equal?" says the Holy One. Lift up your eyes on high, and see who has created these things, who brings out their host by number; He calls them all by name, by the greatness of His might and the **strength** of His power; not one is missing.

1 Cor. 1:18, 23-25 For the message of the cross is foolishness to those who are perishing, but to us who are being saved it is the power of God. ....we preach Christ crucified, to the Jews a stumbling block and to the Greeks foolishness, but to those who are called, both Jews and Greeks Christ the power of God and the wisdom of God. Because the foolishness of God is wiser than men, and the weakness of God is **stronger** than men.

Our strength is very small—-

Ps. 71:9 Do not cast me off in the time of old age; do not forsake me when my **strength** fails.

Rom. 5:6 For when we were still without **strength**, in due time Christ died for the ungodly.

2 Cor. 1:8-9 For we do not want you to be ignorant, brethren, of our trouble which came to us in Asia: that we were burdened beyond measure, above **strength**, so that we despaired even of life. Yes, we had the sentence of death in ourselves, that we should not trust in ourselves but in God who raises the dead...

2 Cor. 12:7-10 And lest I should be exalted above measure by the abundance of the revelations, a thorn in the flesh was given to me, a messenger of Satan to buffet me, lest I be exalted above measure. Concerning this thing I pleaded with the Lord three times that it might depart from me. And He said to me, "My grace is sufficient for you, for My **strength** is made perfect in weakness." Therefore most gladly I will rather boast in my infirmities, that the power of Christ may rest upon me. Therefore I take pleasure in infirmities, in reproaches, in needs, in persecutions, in distresses, for Christ's sake. For when I am weak then I am **strong**.

Where we can find strength—

1 Chron. 29:12 Both riches and honor come from You, and You reign over all. In Your hand is power and might; in Your hand it is to make great and to give **strength** to all.

2 Chron. 16:9a "For the eyes of the Lord run to and fro throughout the whole earth, to show Himself **strong** on behalf of those whose heart is loyal to Him."

Neh. 8:10 Then he said to them, "Go your way, eat the fat, drink the sweet, and send portions to those for whom nothing is prepared; for this day is holy to our Lord. Do not sorrow, for the joy of the Lord is your **strength**.

Ps. 18:32 It is God who arms me with **strength**, and makes my way perfect.

Ps. 19:14 Let the words of my mouth and the meditation of my heart be acceptable in Your sight, O Lord, my **strength** and my Redeemer.

Ps. 27:1, 14 The Lord is my light and my salvation; whom shall I fear? The Lord is the **strength** of my life; of whom shall I be afraid? ....Wait on the Lord; be of good courage and He shall **strengthen** your heart; wait I say, on the Lord!

Ps. 28:7-8 The Lord is my **strength** and my shield; my heart trusted in Him, and I am helped; therefore my heart greatly rejoices, and with my song I will praise Him. The Lord is their **strength**, and He is the saving refuge of His anointed.

Ps. 29:11 The Lord will give **strength** to His people; the Lord will bless His people with peace.

Ps. 37:39 But the salvation of the righteous is from the Lord; He is their **strength** in time of trouble.

Ps. 46:1 God is our refuge and **strength**, a very present help in trouble.

Ps. 59:9 NIV O my **Strength**, I watch for You; You, O God, are my fortress, my loving God

Ps. 59:16-17 NIV But I will sing of Your **strength**, in the morning I will sing of Your love; for You are my fortress, my refuge in times of trouble. O my **Strength**, I sing praise to You; You, O God, are my fortress, my loving God.

Ps. 62:7 In God is my salvation and my glory; the rock of my **strength**, and my refuge, is in God.

Ps. 73:26 My flesh and my heart fail; but God is the **strength** of my heart and my portion forever.

Ps. 84:5-7 Blessed is the man whose **strength** is in You, whose heart is set on pilgrimage. As they pass through the Valley of Baca, they make it a spring; the rain also covers it with pools. They go from **strength to strength**; each one appears before God in Zion.

Prov. 24:5 A wise man is **strong**, yes, a man of knowledge increases **strength**.

Isa. 30:15 For thus says the Lord God, the Holy One of Israel: "In returning and rest you shall be saved; in quietness and confidence shall be your **strength.**

Isa. 40:29-31 He gives power to the weak, and to those who have no might He increases **strength**. Even the youths shall faint and be weary, and the young men shall utterly fall, but those who wait on the Lord shall renew their **strength**; they shall mount up with wings like eagles, they shall run and not be weary, they shall walk and not faint.

Hab. 3:19 The Lord God is my **strength**; He will make my feet like deer's feet, and He will make me walk on my high hills.

Zech. 10:6, 12 "I will **strengthen** the house of Judah, and I will save the house of Joseph. I will bring them back, because I have mercy on them. They shall be as though I had not cast them aside; for I am the Lord their God, and I will hear them." ..."So I will **strengthen** them in the Lord, and they shall walk up and down in His name," says the Lord.

Acts 18:21b-23 And he (*Paul*) sailed from Ephesus. And when he had landed at Caesarea, and gone up and greeted the church, he went down to Antioch. After he had spent some time there, he departed and went over the region of Galatia and Phrygia in order, **strengthening** all the disciples.

Eph. 3:14-16 For this reason I bow my knees to the Father of our Lord Jesus Christ, from whom the whole family in heaven and earth is named, that He would grant you, according to the riches of His glory, to be **strengthened** with might through His Spirit in the inner man—

Phil. 4:13 I can do all things through Christ who **strengthens** me.

1 Thess. 3:12-13 NIV May the Lord make your love increase and overflow for each other and for everyone else, just as ours does for you. May He **strengthen** your hearts so that you will be blameless and holy in the presence of our God and Father when our Lord Jesus comes with all His holy ones.

Do not trust these for strength—

Ps. 33:16-17 No king is saved by the multitude of an army; a mighty man is not delivered by great **strength**. A horse is a vain hope for safety; neither shall it deliver any by its great **strength**.

Ps. 52:6-7 The righteous also shall see and fear, and shall laugh at him, saying, "Here is the man who did not make God his **strength**, but trusted in the abundance of his riches, and **strengthened** himself in his wickedness."

Instructions—

Isa. 35:3-4 **Strengthen** the weak hands, and make firm the feeble knees. Say to those who are fearful-hearted, "Be **strong**, do not fear! Behold your God will come with vengeance, with the recompense of God; He will come and save you."

Isa. 40:9 O Zion, you who bring good tidings, get up into the high mountain; O Jerusalem, you who bring good tidings, lift up your voice with **strength**, lift it up, be not afraid; say to the cities of Judah, "Behold your God!"

Isa. 41:10 'Fear not, for I am with you; be not dismayed, for I am your God. I will **strengthen** you, yes, I will help you, I will uphold you with My righteous right hand."

Mark 12:30 'And you shall love the Lord your God with all your heart, with all your soul, with all your mind, and with all your **strength**.'

Eph. 6:10-11 Finally, my brethren, **be strong** in the Lord and in the power of His might. Put on the whole armor of God, that you may be able to stand against the wiles of the devil.

Heb. 12:12-13 Therefore **strengthen** the hands which hang down, and the feeble knees, and make straight paths for your feet, so that what is lame may not be dislocated, but rather be healed.

Warnings—

Prov. 3:7-8 Do not be wise in your own eyes; fear the Lord and depart from evil. It will be health to your flesh and **strength** to your bones.

Isa. 44:9, 12 Those who make an image, all of them are useless, and their precious things shall not profit; they are their own witnesses; they neither see nor know, that they may be ashamed. ....The blacksmith with the tongs works one in the coals, fashions it with hammers, and works it with the **strength** of his arms. Even so, he is hungry, and his **strength** fails; he drinks no water and is faint.

Jer. 9:23-24 NIV This is what the Lord says: "Let not the wise man boast of his wisdom or the **strong** man boast of his **strength** or the rich man boast of his riches, but let him who boasts boast about this; that he understands and knows Me, that I am the Lord who exercises kindness, justice and righteousness on earth, for in these I delight," declares the Lord.

Luke 11:20-23 "But if I cast out demons with the finger of God, surely the kingdom of God has come upon you. When a **strong** man, fully armed, guards his own palace, his goods are in peace. But when a **stronger** than he comes upon him and overcomes him, he takes from him all his armor in which he trusted, and divides his spoils. He who is not with Me is against Me, and he who does not gather with Me scatters."

Luke 22:31-32 And the Lord said, "Simon, Simon! Indeed, Satan has asked for you, that he may sift you as wheat. But I have prayed for you, that your faith should not fail; and when you have returned to Me, **strengthen** your brethren."

Rev. 3:1-2, 8 "And to the angel of the church in Sardis write, 'These things says He who has the seven Spirits of God and the seven stars: "I know your works, that you have a name that you are alive, but you are dead. Be watchful, and **strengthen** the things which remain, that are ready to die, for I have not found your works perfect before God."

Rev. 3:7-8 "And the angel of the church in Philadelphia write, 'These things says He who is holy, He who is true, "He who has the key of David, He who opens and no one shuts, and shuts and no one opens: I know your works. See, I have set before you an open door, and no one can shut it; for you have a little **strength**, have kept my word, and have not denied My name."

Prayers—

Luke 22:41-43 And He *(Jesus)* was withdrawn from them about a stone's throw, and He knelt down and prayed, saying, "Father, if it is Your will, take this cup away from Me; nevertheless, not My will, but Yours, be done." Then an angel appeared to Him from heaven, **strengthening** Him.

Col. 1:9-12 For this reason we also, since the day we heard it, do not cease to pray for you, and to ask that you may be filled with the knowledge of His will in all wisdom and spiritual understanding; that you may walk worthy of the Lord, fully pleasing Him, being fruitful in every good work and increasing in the knowledge of God; **strengthened** with all might, according to His glorious power, for all patience and longsuffering with joy; giving thanks to the Father who has qualified us to be partakers of the inheritance of the saints in the light.

1 Peter 5:10 But may the God of all grace, who called us to His eternal glory by Christ Jesus, after you have suffered a while, perfect, establish, **strengthen** and settle you.

Faith, obedience to the Word of God, and His blessings follow—

Ps. 138:3 In the day when I cried out, You answered me, and made me bold with **strength** in my soul.

Acts 16:5 So the churches were **strengthened** in the faith, and increased in number daily.

Rom. 4:20 He (*Abraham*) did not waver at the promise of God through unbelief, but was **strengthened** in faith, giving glory to God.

1 Cor. 15:56-57 The sting of death is sin, and the **strength** of sin is the law. But thanks be to God, who gives us the victory through the Lord Jesus Christ.

REJOICE

A THANKFUL HEART CAUSES ONE TO REJOICE

Perhaps your heart doesn't feel like rejoicing right now. You may not have had any great experiences for a long time. In fact, things may have been going backward and downward for quite some time, instead of the desired upward and forward. You may have been wondering how much lower your spirit could sink before there's a turn around. You ask, "How long will it be before someone realizes that I'm still here on this earth and really need some love and fellowship?"

Our Scriptures on this word give us many reasons for rejoicing. Most of them have nothing to do with our circumstances; rather it is whether or not our spirit is in fellowship and agreement with the Lord. We can't help but marvel as we read the Word, how God rescued His people from the most horrendous situations, including times when their enemies were about to slaughter them all. God was never baffled, or having a fit over what to do with these enemy nations, as they came after His people with large armies, fully equipped with their armor and battle equipment. God will never need instructions from man on how to handle anyone's problems.

This is one of our great reasons to rejoice. Our God is able to do anything. His ways and thoughts are far above ours. His view is not limited to the here and now, but sees all eternity— the past, present and future are always observable to Him. We cannot comprehend that, but it's true. When we acknowledge and accept that as fact, then we can rejoice that we serve a God who possesses such magnificent attributes, way beyond our imagination. Being in His Word daily gives us the advantage to hear Him and experience His presence consistently. We don't need to crumble under bondages and live in the discouragements of undesirable things that happen in life. Sometimes these are even due to our bad choices and can turn into deep depression, if we allow it.

Our very first Scriptures are from David's song of thanksgiving and praise to God for the return of the ark of the Lord to Jerusalem. He had made an earlier attempt *(1 Chron. 13)*, but failed because he had consulted the people and moved ahead with what seemed 'right in the eyes of the people'. They were caught up in getting the ark moved, but did not ask God how it was to be done. In verse 10 we read: "Then the anger of the Lord was aroused against Uzza, and He struck him because he put his hand to the ark; and he died there before God." This illustrates the serious consequences we will face if we turn to the wisdom of man instead of the Lord. The second time that David was going to move the ark, he consulted the Lord and he prepared a place for it, so all went well. What a marvelous time for rejoicing when the ark was brought back to God's people. "Glory in His holy name; let the hearts of those rejoice who seek the Lord," is part of David's song of thanksgiving to the Lord, which is recorded in 1 Chronicles 16:8-36. It is beautiful!

JOY COMES TO OUR HEARTS WHEN WE RESPOND TO HIS WORD

Oftentimes when we've first experienced some dark days and then the sun shines, we begin to feel refreshed and are able to express great joy. What a contrast for our lives when we gain an understanding of Psalm 89:15-16: "Blessed are the people who know the joyful sound! They walk, O Lord, in the light of Your countenance. In Your name they rejoice all the day long, and in Your righteousness they are exalted."

When we need help in finding reasons to rejoice, the Psalms provide gardens with panoramic music from the praises to God. These flowing praises can lift your spirits higher and higher—-

Psalm 105:1-5 *This is also a part of 1 Chronicles 16* —- "Oh, give thanks to the Lord! Call upon His name; make known His deeds among the peoples! Sing to Him, sing psalms to Him; talk of all His wondrous works! Glory in His holy name; let the hearts of those rejoice who seek the Lord! Seek the Lord and His strength; seek His face evermore! Remember His marvelous works which He has done, His wonders, and the judgments of His mouth."

Psalm 5:11, 12 "But let all those rejoice who put their trust in You; let them ever shout for joy, because You defend them; let those also who love Your name be joyful in You. For You, O Lord, will bless the righteous; with favor You will surround him as with a shield."

Psalm 33:1-3 "Rejoice in the Lord, O you righteous! For praise from the upright is beautiful. Praise the Lord with the harp; make melody to Him with an instrument of ten strings. Sing to Him a new song; play skillfully with a shout of joy."

Psalm 68:3-6 "But let the righteous be glad; let them rejoice before God; yes, let them rejoice exceedingly. Sing to God, sing praises to His name; extol Him who rides on the clouds, by His name Yah, and rejoice before Him. A father of the fatherless, a defender of widows, is God in His holy habitation. God sets the solitary in families; He brings out those who are bound into prosperity; but the rebellious dwell in a dry land."

There are many more in the references that follow, but these will give you a beautiful view of how gracious and merciful God is, and how much He wants to bless His people with His wondrous works and mighty deeds. He wants us to rejoice in all that He does and even in the things that He allows to happen to us which are not exactly pleasing to us, but are part of our spiritual exercises.

REJOICE IN THE LORD ANYWAY

Under the category for rejoicing in sufferings, trials and persecutions, we find the Lord challenging us to rejoice in Him no matter what is happening. Rejoicing can only come from a grateful, trusting heart. The heart of gratitude will produce thanksgiving and praise and worship to the Lord. It will also overflow with thankfulness to the people around us, those who are the Lord's channels of blessing to us, and sometimes are used of the Lord to chide us.

Like Philippians 4:4 says, "Rejoice in the Lord always. Again I will say, rejoice!" And Paul also wrote similar words to the Christians in Thessalonica: "Rejoice always." God is in essence speaking these words through him, "No matter what your circumstances are, just focus your eyes on Me and keep on believing and rejoicing. Even shout aloud with joy in your hearts. When you have chosen to acknowledge Me in those circumstances, you can know that I will bring you victory through the Lord Jesus Christ!"

When our hearts don't feel like rejoicing, it is uplifting to find God's promises that specifically apply to the troubling circumstances and take the opportunity to write the actual words of Scripture in notebooks. It really helps in committing His Word to your heart, and becomes a ready reference when you need them most.

HOLD TO GOD'S WORD AS SPIRITUAL ARMOR

Some of His powerful promises are in Romans 8. According to verses 5 and 6, we must have our mind set on what the Spirit desires, since the mind controlled by the Spirit is life and peace. It is of great value to read this whole chapter as often as it takes to capture those wonderful truths in your spirit. Write down each phrase that expresses some kind of blessing the Lord provides for us. Then begin reading them so often that you will have them committed to your heart. When you do, the enemy cannot steal from you what God has spoken to your heart, especially when you are determined to receive them as His gifts to you. They are really more than gifts; they serve as spiritual armor to stand against the enemy's cunning deceptions.

You can do the same thing with other Scriptures that the Lord leads you to during your devotional time; while you are listening to His Word being taught in a worship service, or another class in Church, on the radio or TV; wherever the Lord chooses to instruct you. The Lord set me on such a path while in a Christian High School. Our Bible teacher expected us to take notes on Sundays during the sermon. Then we had to be ready to share those notes whenever he chose to call on any two or three of the class. I learned to take notes really fast, and found that I usually learned much more that way, because my mind couldn't wander. It was an excellent discipline.

A rejoicing heart is from the Lord, as we spend time with Him, desiring to know Him more perfectly. It doesn't come from any earthly source. You cannot find this blessing in the most enjoyable pleasures this earth has to give to you. Observe carefully in the New Testament Scriptures what reasons are given for rejoicing. It always comes from a heart relationship with the Lord, springing up from communing with Him and enjoying His presence!

As you carefully look at the surrounding circumstances of those who are rejoicing in the Word, you will find that they have gone through tough trials, threatened by those who hated Jesus, and therefore hated them too. They had prayed for their enemies, and asked the Lord for a holy boldness to preach the Good News. Sometimes it seems as though God neglected to take care of them as they still suffered beatings and imprisonment, but that didn't stop the flow of their rejoicing in the Lord! You do not hear of them crying to the Lord, "Why do you allow them to treat us like this?" Instead in the account of Paul and Silas recorded in Acts 16:16-34, after having gone through a beating with rods, and their feet fastened in stocks *(a terribly painful position)*, they are praying and singing hymns to God loudly enough that the other prisoners and guards were able to hear them singing! This turned the heart of the keeper of the prison toward the Lord.

A REJOICING HEART IS A GREAT TESTIMONY TO GOD'S GRACE

What a testimony of God's sustaining grace for those who love Him! What a testimony of God's patience in the presence of the sin of those who are enemies of the gospel. I see God giving an opportunity to show the enemy what power He has to bless His faithful, trusting children in the midst of their suffering. Some have even come to Christ as they observed the manifestation of God's love and power giving courage and upholding strength to His own precious people while being persecuted, as seen in the above record.

Are you rejoicing in the Lord? Can you see now how it comes? Joy is generated while doing what God has called you to do; whether it is to stand strong for truth, right there on the job, or answering His call to service in other ways. When we know, that we know, that God is with us, guiding our foot steps, causing things to work for our good, because we love Him *(Read Psalm 91),* and accept His call to fulfill His purposes *(Romans 8:28)* in our lives, we can rejoice greatly in Him!

Will you take a look over your years, even before receiving Christ Jesus in your heart, and observe the times and ways that the Lord was blessing you and protecting you? Write a testimony about these experiences with Him. See how He changed your path to richer pastures, and gave you living water. See how He carried you when the burdens were too heavy and whispered tender comforting words so you wouldn't feel so alone!

Search the Word for accounts of people who were rejoicing in the Lord. Why were they rejoicing so gloriously? Were they always free from danger? See what God did to change the circumstances in their lives because of their joyful hearts. Then rejoice for His goodness and mercy in your life, without reservations! You will be so blessed! Joy will overflow your heart! You will bless others too, so that they will also believe your God is a great God to serve!

Hallelujah! Let us rejoice together!

SCRIPTURES FOR
R E J O I C E

A call and a command to rejoice—

1 Chron. 16:8-10 O give thanks to the Lord! Call upon His name, make known His deeds among the peoples! Sing to Him, sing psalms to Him; talk of all His wondrous works! Glory in His holy name; let the hearts of those **rejoice** who seek the Lord!

1 Chron 16:31-33 Let the heavens **rejoice**, and let the earth be glad; and let them say among the nations, "The Lord reigns." Let the sea roar, and all its fullness; let the field **rejoice**, and all that is in it. Then the trees of the woods shall **rejoice** before the Lord, for He is coming to judge the earth."

Ps. 5:11-12 But let all those **rejoice** who put their trust in You; let them ever shout for joy, because You defend them; let those also who love Your name be joyful in You. For You, O Lord, will bless the righteous; with favor You will surround him as with a shield.

Ps. 32:11 Be glad in the Lord and **rejoice**, you righteous; and shout for joy, all you upright in heart!

Ps. 33:1-3 **Rejoice** in the Lord, O you righteous! For praise from the upright is beautiful. Praise the Lord with the harp; make melody to Him with an instrument of ten strings. Sing to Him a new song; play skillfully with a shout of joy.

Ps. 68:3-6 But let the righteous be glad; let them **rejoice** before God; yes, let them **rejoice** exceedingly. Sing to God, sing praises to His name; extol Him who rides on the clouds, by His name Yah, and **rejoice** before Him. A father of the fatherless, a defender of widows, is God in His holy habitation. God sets the solitary in families; He brings out those who are bound into prosperity; but the rebellious dwell in a dry land.

Ps. 97:1, 12 The Lord reigns; let the earth **rejoice**; let the multitude of isles be glad! ...**Rejoice** in the Lord, you righteous, and give thanks at the remembrance of His holy name.

Ps. 98:4-6 Shout joyfully to the Lord, all the earth; break forth in song, **rejoice**, and sing praises. Sing to the Lord with the harp, with the harp and the sound of a psalm with trumpets and the sound of a horn; shout joyfully before the Lord, the King.

Ps. 107:22 Let them sacrifice the sacrifices of thanksgiving, and declare His works with **rejoicing**.

Isa. 65:17-19 For behold, I create new heavens and a new earth; and the former shall not be remembered or come to mind. But be glad and **rejoice** forever in what I create; for behold, I create Jerusalem as a **rejoicing**, and her people a joy. I will **rejoice** in Jerusalem and joy in My people; the voice of weeping shall no longer be heard in her, nor the voice of crying.

Phil. 3:1 Finally, my brethren, **rejoice** in the Lord. For me to write the same things to you is not tedious, but for you it is safe.

Phil 4:4 **Rejoice** in the Lord always. Again I will say, **rejoice**!

1 Thess. 5:16-18 **Rejoice** always, pray without ceasing, in everything give thanks; for this is the will of God in Christ Jesus for you.

Special occasions when there was great rejoicing—-

<u>This is part of Solomon's prayer when dedicating the temple</u>:
2 Chron. 6:41 "Now therefore, arise, O Lord God, to Your resting place, you and the ark of Your strength. Let Your priests, O Lord God, be clothed with salvation; and let Your saints **rejoice** in goodness." *See verses 14-42*

<u>This is the day of dedicating the re-built wall of Jerusalem:</u>
Neh. 12:43 Also that day they offered great sacrifices, and **rejoiced**, for God had made them **rejoice** with great joy; the women and the children also **rejoiced**, so that the joy of Jerusalem was heard afar off. *See verses 27-43*

<u>From Mary's song while with Elizabeth, announcing the coming of her son, Jesus.</u>
Luke 1:46-48 And Mary said, "My soul magnifies the Lord, and my spirit has **rejoiced** in God my Savior. For He has regarded the lowly state of His maidservant; for behold, henceforth all generations will call me blessed."

<u>Elizabeth's time of rejoicing:</u>
Luke 1:57-58 Now Elizabeth's full time came for her to be delivered, and she brought forth a son. When her neighbors and relatives heard how the Lord had shown great mercy to her, they **rejoiced** with her.

<u>The lost sheep is found:</u>
Luke 15:3-7 So he *(Jesus)* spoke this parable to them saying: "What man of you, having a hundred sheep, if he loses one of them, does not leave the ninety nine in the wilderness, and go after the one which is lost until he finds it? And when he has found it he lays it on his shoulder, **rejoicing**. And when he comes home, he calls together his friends and neighbors, saying to them, '**Rejoice** with me, for I have found my sheep which was lost!' I say to you that likewise there will be more joy in heaven over one sinner who repents than over ninety nine just persons who need no repentance."

<u>The lost coin is found:</u>
Luke 15:8-10 "Or what woman, having ten silver coins, if she loses one coin, does not light a lamp, sweep the house, and search carefully until she finds it? And when she has found it, she calls her friends and neighbors together, saying, '**Rejoice** with me, for I have found the piece which I lost!' Likewise, I say to you, there is joy in the presence of the angels of God over one sinner who repents."

<u>When viewing the coming Messiah, Abraham rejoiced:</u>
John 8:54-56 Jesus answered, "If I honor Myself, My honor is nothing. It is My Father who honors Me, of whom you say that He is your God. Yet you have not known Him, but I know Him. And if I say, 'I do not know Him,' I shall be a liar like you; but I do know Him and keep His word. Your father Abraham **rejoiced** to see My day, and he saw it and was glad."

<u>The Ethiopian eunuch's baptism:</u>
Acts 8:38-39 So he commanded the chariot to stand still. And both Philip and the eunuch went down into the water, and he baptized him. Now when they came up out of the water, the Spirit of the Lord caught Philip away, so that the eunuch saw him no more; and he went on his way **rejoicing**.

<u>The marriage of the Lamb, Jesus:</u>
Rev. 19:7 "Let us be glad and **rejoice** and give Him glory, for the marriage of the Lamb has come, and His wife has made herself ready."

Many other reasons for rejoicing—-

Ps. 31:7-8 I will be glad and **rejoice** in Your mercy, for You have considered my trouble; You have known my soul in adversities, and have not shut me up into the hand of the enemy; You have set my feet in a wide place.

Ps. 63:6-8 When I remember You on my bed, I meditate on You in the night watches. Because You have been my help, therefore in the shadow of Your wings I will **rejoice**. My soul follows close behind You; Your right hand upholds me.

Ps. 71:23-24 My lips shall greatly **rejoice** when I sing to You, and my soul, which You have redeemed. My tongue also shall talk of Your righteousness all the day long; for they are confounded, for they are brought to shame who seek my hurt.

Ps. 89:15 Blessed are the people who know the joyful sound! They walk, O Lord, in the light of Your countenance. In Your name they **rejoice** all day long, and in Your righteousness they are exalted.

Ps. 96:11-13 Let the heavens **rejoice**, and let the earth be glad; let the sea roar, and all its fullness; let the field be joyful, and all that is in it. Then all the trees of the woods will **rejoice** before the Lord. For He is coming, for He is coming to judge the earth. He shall judge the world with righteousness, and the peoples with His truth.

Ps. 118:15, 24 The voice of **rejoicing** and salvation is in the tents of the righteous; the right hand of the Lord does valiantly. ...This is the day the Lord hath made; we will **rejoice** and be glad in it.

Isa. 61:7, 10 Instead of your shame you shall have double honor, and instead of confusion they shall **rejoice** in their portion. Therefore in their land they shall possess double; everlasting joy shall be theirs. ...I will greatly **rejoice** in the Lord, my soul shall be joyful in my God; for He has clothed me with the garments of salvation, He has covered me with the robe of righteousness, as a bridegroom decks himself with ornaments, and a bride adorns herself with her jewels.

Isa. 66:10-11 "**Rejoice** with Jerusalem, and be glad with her, all you who love her; **rejoice** for joy with her, all you who mourn for her; that you may feed and be satisfied with the consolation of her bosom, that you may drink deeply and be delighted with the abundance of her glory."

Luke 10:20-21 "Nevertheless **do not rejoice** in this, that the spirits are subject to you, but rather **rejoice** because your names are written in heaven." In that hour Jesus **rejoiced** in the Spirit and said, "I thank You, Father, Lord of heaven and earth, that You have hidden these things from the wise and prudent and revealed them to babes. Even so, Father, for so it seemed good in Your sight."

John 14:28 "You have heard Me say to you, 'I am going away and coming back to you.' If you loved Me, you would **rejoice** because I said, 'I am going to the Father,' for My Father is greater than I."

John 16:20-21 "Most assuredly, I say to you that you will weep and lament, but the world will **rejoice**, and you will be sorrowful, but your sorrow will be turned into joy. Therefore you now have sorrow, but I will see you again and your heart will **rejoice**, and your joy no one will take from you."

Rom. 5:1-2 Therefore, having been justified by faith, we have peace with God through our Lord Jesus Christ, through whom also we have access by faith into this grace in which we stand, and **rejoice** in hope of the glory of God.

Rom 5:10-11 For if when we were enemies we were reconciled to God through the death of His Son, much more, having been reconciled, we shall be saved by His life. And not only that, but we also **rejoice** in God through our Lord Jesus Christ, through whom we have now received the reconciliation.

1 Cor. 13:4-6 Love suffers long and is kind; love does not envy; love does not parade itself, is not puffed up; does not behave rudely, does not seek its own, is not provoked, thinks no evil; **does not rejoice** in iniquity, but **rejoices** in the truth.

Phil. 1:18, 25-26 What then? Only that in every way, whether in pretense or in truth Christ is preached, and in this I **rejoice**, yes, and will **rejoice**. ...And being confident of this, I know that I shall remain and continue with you all for your progress and joy of faith, that your **rejoicing** for me may be more abundant in Jesus Christ by my coming to you again.

1 Thess. 2:19-20 For what is our hope, or joy, or crown of **rejoicing**? Is it not even you in the presence of our Lord Jesus Christ at His coming? For you are our glory and joy.

1 Thess. 3:9-11 For what thanks can we render to God for you, for all the joy with which we **rejoice** for your sake before our God,

night and day praying exceedingly that we may see your face and perfect what is lacking in your faith? Now may our God and Father Himself, and our Lord Jesus Christ, direct our way to you.

Heb. 3:4-6 For every house is built by someone, but He who built all things is God. And Moses indeed was faithful in all His house as a servant, for a testimony of those things which would be spoken afterward, but Christ as a Son over His own house, whose house we are if we hold fast the confidence and the **rejoicing** of the hope firm to the end.

Rejoice in suffering, trials and persecutions—-

Matt. 5:11-12 Blessed are you when they revile and persecute you, and say all kinds of evil against you falsely for My sake. **Rejoice** and be exceedingly glad, for great is your reward in heaven, for so they persecuted the prophets who were before you. *Also Luke 6:23*

Acts 5:41 So they departed from the presence of the council, **rejoicing** that they were counted worthy to suffer shame for His name.

Rom 12:14-15 Bless those who persecute you; bless and do not curse. **Rejoice** with those who **rejoice**; and weep with those who weep.

1 Cor. 12:26 And if one member *(of the body of Christ)* suffers, all the members suffer with it; or if one member is honored, all the members **rejoice** with it.

2 Cor. 6:8-10 By honor and dishonor, by evil report and good report, as deceivers, and yet true; as unkown, and yet well known; as dying, and behold we live; as chastened, and yet not killed; as sorrowful, yet always **rejoicing**; as poor, yet making many rich; as having nothing, and yet possessing all things.

Phil. 2:14-18 Do all things without complaining and disputing, that you may become blameless and harmless, children of God without fault in the midst of a crooked and perverse generation, among whom you shine as lights in the world, holding fast the word of life, so that I may **rejoice** in the day of Christ, that I have not run in vain or labored in vain. Yes, and if I am being poured out as a drink offering on the sacrifice and service of your faith, I am glad and **rejoice** with you all. For the same reason you also be glad and **rejoice** with me.

Phil. 2:27-28 For indeed he *(Epaphroditus)* was sick almost unto death; but God had mercy on him, and not only on him but on me also, lest I should have sorrow upon sorrow. Therefore I sent him the more eagerly, that when you see him again you may **rejoice**, and I may be less sorrowful.

Col. 1:24-26 I now **rejoice** in my sufferings for you, and fill up in my flesh what is lacking in the afflictions of Christ, for the sake of His body, which is the church, of which I became a minister according to the stewardship from God which was given to me for you, to fulfill the word of God, the mystery which has been hidden from ages and from generations, but now has been revealed to His saints.

1 Peter 1:6-9 In this you greatly **rejoice**, though now for a little while, if need be, you have been grieved by various trials, that the genuineness of your faith, being much more precious than gold that perishes, though it is tested by fire, may be found to praise, honor and glory at the revelation of Jesus Christ, whom having not seen you love. Though now you do not see Him, yet believing, you **rejoice** with joy inexpressible, and full of glory, receiving the end of your faith—the salvation of your souls.

1 Peter 4:12-13 Beloved, do not think it strange concerning the fiery trial which is to try you, as though some strange thing happened to you; but **rejoice** to the extent that you partake of Christ's sufferings, that when His glory is revealed, you may also be glad with exceeding joy.

WORSHIP

TRUE WORSHIP IS GIVING HIGH HONOR

These Scriptures make us aware of God's sovereignty; that He is the only true God, the great 'I Am'; the holy, holy, holy Lord God Almighty. True worship is to give high honor to God; humbling ourselves before Him, desiring to seek His face and to experience the blessedness of His holiness, His great glory!

As I wrote that first paragraph, I visualized a picture of hundreds of men who were worshiping a false god, which I had seen in a Christian magazine a few days ago. They too were giving honor, as they knelt with their faces to the ground, but their god was not a holy living being. I wonder what they feel as they worship. Could they possibly experience compassionate love for one another, and for people who are not of their religion, when they worship this being? They are truly dedicated, but what is the value? What assurance do they have that their god will bless them? Are they experiencing a flowing peace or joy springing up in their hearts? Are they blessed with physical and emotional healings, and the many other blessings that our Almighty God gives to those who honor Him, or are they governed by fear of those who control them?

Drawing near to the living Lord in worship is a time of devotion that stirs the heart to love, and give, and produces hunger for even greater knowledge of Him, along with His wisdom, for serving Him. We need to give all our attention to Him, without distractions of self or anything else. He must be the object of our wholehearted worship. Many people understand this from the moment they meet Jesus, and discover the power of His love, which delivered them from bondages to alcohol, drugs, or other horrible sins. They immediately feel such a strong devotion to the One who delivered them. There is no hesitation; they're compelled deep in their hearts to praise the Lord and worship Him, not even counting the hours that they spend in His presence, for this precious time is full of gratitude and joy! Absolutely delightful worship time!

ALL WORSHIPERS DO NOT WORSHIP THE SAME

In the Old Testament the people usually traveled great distances to worship the Lord, with God's people coming from all over the area to the tabernacle, and later, the temple. Some of them built an altar right in the area where they had an encounter with God, and entered into a time of worshiping Him. Many times they left other kinds of evidence at the place where God met them in a spectacular way.

Today many people think of worship as a Sunday morning thing, but worship is for anywhere, anytime. What we might call 'devotional time', is also a time for worship with a sincere heart, acknowledging God's wonderful presence, expressing our love for Him, and gratitude for the abundance of His blessings. It's a time to breathe in the breath of His life. Some people include singing to the Lord and even dancing before the Lord in their homes, as their hearts overflow with great joy before Him.

All worshipers do not worship in the same way. Our personalities differ greatly, and our experiences are vastly different too. There is a good example to consider, when Jesus was at the house of Simon, He pointed out that the one who recognizes how much they are forgiven, also loves the most. From Luke 7:47, we read of Jesus saying, "Therefore I say to you, her sins, which are many, are forgiven, for she loved much. But to whom little is forgiven, the same loves little." This rings true in our manner of worship to the Lord. The greater our experience of forgiveness and transformation, the greater our love for the Lord, and naturally more exuberance is expressed in adoration and honor to Him.

This reminds me of David's praise and worship described in 1

Chronicles 29:10-19. Here are the first few verses: "Blessed are You, Lord God of Israel, our Father, forever and ever. Yours, O Lord, is the greatness, the power and the glory, the victory and the majesty; for all that is in heaven and in earth is Yours; Yours is the kingdom, O Lord, and You are exalted as head over all. Both riches and honor come from You, and You reign over all. In Your hand is power and might; in Your hand it is to make great and to give strength to all. Now therefore, our God, we thank You and praise Your glorious name." Can you imagine David expressing these words with a monotone voice? Actually, in verse 9 it says: "Then the people rejoiced, for they had offered willingly, because with a loyal heart they had offered willingly to the Lord; and King David also rejoiced greatly." So this tells it very well. Their hearts were rejoicing, and therefore David lifted his voice to worship and praise the Lord! Can you almost hear their uninhibited shouting and singing hallelujahs to the Lord? Can you hear the sounds of glorious joy?

TRUE WORSHIP CHANGES OUR HEARTS

As I have spent time with each word, my heart has been blessed immensely, but this one is outstanding because of the greatness of what worshiping the Lord does in our spirit, soul and body, as we humble ourselves before Him. Besides experiencing a lift above the earthly pressures, it is absolutely life changing. The more we believe God and absorb the truths of God's Word, and the more we commune with Him, the more we will grow and become transformed into His likeness. There are three words, where this transformation develops from one level to another.

From faith to faith: "For in it the righteousness of God is revealed <u>from faith to faith</u>; as it is written, 'The just shall live by faith.'" *Romans 1:17*

From strength to strength: "Blessed is the man whose strength is in You, whose heart is set on pilgrimage. As they pass through the Valley of Baca, they make it a spring; the rain also covers it with pools. They go <u>from strength to strength</u>; each one appears before God in Zion." *Psalm 84:5-7*

From glory to glory: "But we all, with unveiled face, beholding as in a mirror the glory of the Lord, are being transformed into the same image <u>from glory to glory</u>, just as by the Spirit of the Lord." *2 Corinthians 3:18*

There is another Scripture which I discovered a few days ago which has a double-word in it, not expressing exactly as the three above examples do, but I think it is interesting for you to know about it: from John 1:16, "And of His *(Jesus')* fullness we have all received, and <u>grace for grace</u>."

WORSHIP EXALTS THE LORD AND INCLUDES PRAISE

Worship is a time for singing worshipful songs, drawing close to His awesome presence, but another means of worshiping the Lord is when we bring our tithes, our offerings and gifts to Him. It is an expression of our devotion, our oneness through Jesus Christ, and involvement in our King's business. There's a line in a gospel song that says, "I'm here on business for my King." So as our hearts worship Him, we see Him as our King of kings and Lord of lords. He is Sovereign God, ruler over all the nations, and the joy in our hearts can transcend human language as we focus on who He is! He is real, and desires to communicate with us.

So we see that worship is exalting the Lord our God for who He is, focusing on His divine nature, His attributes. We express to Him the wonders of His Being as we have seen Him in His Word and in His expressions, or other manifestations of Himself. The words of Deuteronomy 10:17 are great—"For the Lord your God is God of gods and Lord of lords, the great God, mighty and awesome." In 2 Samuel 22, we find David's song of praise to Him. Throughout the chapter David is praising and worshiping God. He addressed the Lord by some of His attributes, and then describes ways that the Lord delivered him from enemies of various kinds. He is so overwhelmed with all God is and does, that he just overflows with thanksgiving and praise as he worships the Lord.

The same is true in 1 Chronicles 16:7-36, which is David's song of thanksgiving when the ark of God was placed in the tabernacle. His worship and praise coming from the depths of his heart gives me a mental view of a great outdoor fountain spraying cool water way up in the air. In verse 29 we read, "Give to the Lord the glory due His name; bring an offering, and come before Him. Oh, worship the Lord in the beauty of holiness!"

It appears to me, that there were more exuberant expressions with louder voices in the worship among God's people during these Old Testament times. There's a beautiful example in 2 Chronicles 29:28-30 NIV, "The whole assembly bowed in worship, while the singers sang and the trumpeters played. All this continued until the sacrifice of the burnt offering was completed. When the offerings were finished, the king and everyone present with him knelt down and worshiped. King Hezekiah and his officials ordered the Levites to praise the Lord with the words of David and of Asaph the seer. So they sang praises with gladness and bowed their heads and worshiped."

OFTENTIMES WORSHIP
INCLUDED DANCING AND SHOUTING

Another special time is described in 2 Samuel 6:12-15. The background of this is in the fact that the Philistines had defeated Israel approximately 70 years previous to this time, and they had captured the ark of God. Now Israel defeated the Philistines, so they were able to bring back the ark. *(1 Samuel 4:10, 11; 2 Samuel 5:17- 6:11)* Here we pick up our story in 2 Samuel 6:12-15: "Now it was told King David, saying, "The Lord has blessed the house of Obed-Edom and all that belongs to him, because of the ark of God." So David went and brought up the ark of God from the house of Obed-Edom to the City of David with gladness. And so it was, when those bearing the ark of the Lord had gone six paces, that he sacrificed oxen and fatted sheep. Then <u>David danced before the Lord with all his might</u>; and David was wearing a linen ephod. So David and all the house of Israel brought up the ark of the Lord <u>with shouting and with the sound of the trumpet</u>." Also, in verse 16 we read that King David was seen <u>"leaping and whirling before the Lord</u>." If you read the full record, God was greatly pleased! There may have been many other special occasions, without being recorded, when their worship time overflowed with great joy and gladness before the Lord.

Reading books about praise and worship can greatly enlarge your understanding of how rich and joyous your praise to the Lord could become. There are two books that have been powerful in my life, and I am so thankful that the Lord brought these to my attention. So I count it a privilege to have this opportunity to share the authors and titles with you. The first one, Power in Praise, by Merlin Carothers,[17] I read in the early 70s. Over 15 million of his praise books have been sold. He has done a great work in prisons with his books and is still active! The second one is Empowered by Praise, by Michael Youssef.[18] I've also appreciated his ministry, Leading the Way, on television. God is using him mightily as he teaches the Word of God.

As we consider our failure to give God all the glory due to His name, and observe in contrast the greatness of His mercy and saving grace, there is great reason to learn much more about praising Him in our worship services and every day of the week. How can we really worship God without a glorious feeling in our souls? That glorious feeling comes from gratitude and rejoicing in the heart!

David seems to strongly command himself in Psalm 103:1-2, where he says: "Bless the Lord, O my soul and <u>all that is within me</u>, bless His holy name! Bless the Lord, O my soul, <u>and forget</u> not all His benefits…" "All that is within me" speaks to me of the uninhibited excitement shown at football games, when 'all that is within the fans' is being freely expressed in favor of their team. Who is really worthy of the highest honor we could express? Why are we are so timid in Church? There is little expression of our love for the Lord, perhaps this is why there is so little of the 'joy of the Lord'.

With that in mind, we'll go back to Exodus 32 when Moses had just come down from the mountain where he received the tablets from God, with the Ten Commandments engraved on them. Verses 17-19 say, "And when Joshua heard the noise of the people as they shouted, he said to Moses, "There is a noise of war in the camp." But he said: "It is not the noise of the shout of victory, nor the noise of the cry of defeat, but the sound of singing I hear." So it was, as soon as he came near the camp, that he saw the calf and the dancing. So Moses' anger became hot, and he cast the tablets out of his hands and broke them at the foot of the mountain."

The Israelites were worshiping with loud singing and dancing, but their focus was toward a golden calf. Do we have our 'golden calves' too? They don't look alike, but are they of the same level of preciousness to us, so that we get all excited and give far too much time and devotion to these things?

There is a wonderful song in many hymnbooks. The first lines say, "O worship the King all glorious above and gratefully sing of His power and His love." This is so exhilarating! As our love for the Lord grows, our joy will increase and our worship will be far more pleasing to God.

"Oh come, let us sing to the Lord! Let us shout joyfully to the Rock of our salvation. Let us come before His presence with thanksgiving; let us shout joyfully to Him with psalms. For the Lord is the great God, and the great King above all gods. In His hand are the deep places of the earth; the heights of the hills are His also. The sea is His, for He made it; and His hands formed the dry land.

"Oh come, let us worship and bow down; let us kneel before the Lord our Maker. For He is our God, and we are the people of His pasture, and the sheep of His hand." Psalm 95:1-7

SCRIPTURES FOR
WORSHIP

People worshiping the Lord—

Gen 22:5 And Abraham said to his young man, "Stay here with the donkeys, the lad and I will go yonder and **worship**, and we will come back to you."

Gen 24:48 "And I bowed my head and **worshiped** the Lord, and blessed the Lord God of my master Abraham, who had led me in the way of truth to take the daughter of my master's brother for his son *(Isaac).*"

Ex. 4:31 So the people believed; and when they heard that the Lord had visited the children of Israel and that He had looked on their affliction, then they bowed their heads and **worshiped**.

Ex. 12:26-27 "And it shall be, when your children say to you, 'What do you mean by this service?' that you shall say, 'It is the Passover sacrifice of the Lord, who passed over the houses of the children of Israel in Egypt when He struck the Egyptians and delivered our households.'" So the people bowed their heads and **worshiped**.

Josh. 5:13-14 And it came to pass, when Joshua was by Jericho, that he lifted his eyes and looked, and behold, a Man stood opposite him with His sword drawn in His hand. And Joshua went to Him and said to Him, "Are you for us or for our adversaries?" So He said, "No, but as Commander of the army of the Lord I have now come." And Joshua fell on his face to the earth and **worshiped**, and said to Him, "What does my Lord say to His servant?"

1 Sam. 1:3a This man *(Elkana)* went up from his city yearly to **worship** and sacrifice to the Lord of hosts in Shiloh.

Matt. 2:1-2 Now after Jesus was born in Bethlehem of Judea in the days of Herod the king, behold, wise men from the East came to Jerusalem, saying, "Where is He who has been born King of the Jews? For we have seen His star in the East and have come to **worship** Him."

Matt. 8:2 And behold, a leper came and **worshiped** Him, saying, "Lord, if You are willing, You can make me clean."

Matt. 9:18 While He spoke these things to them, behold, a ruler came and **worshiped** Him, saying, "My daughter has just died, but come and lay Your hand on her and she will live."

Matt. 14:33 Then those who were in the boat came and **worshiped** Him, saying, "Truly You are the Son of God."

Matt. 28:5-9, 17 *The women had just come to the tomb—-* But the angel answered and said to the women, "Do not be afraid, for I know that you seek Jesus who was crucified. He is not here; for He is risen, as He said. Come, see the place where the Lord lay. And go quickly and tell His disciples that He is risen from the dead, and He is going before you into Galilee; there you will see Him. Behold, I have told you." So they went out quickly from the tomb with fear and great joy, and ran to bring His disciples word. And as they went to tell His disciples behold, Jesus met them, saying, "Rejoice!" So they came and held Him by the feet and **worshiped** Him. ....When they *(the disciples)* saw Him, they **worshiped** Him; but some doubted.

John 12:20-21 Now there were certain Greeks among those who came up to **worship** at the feast. Then they came to Philip, who was from Bethsaida of Galilee, and asked him, saying, "Sir, we wish to see Jesus."

Acts 8:26-28 Now an angel of the Lord spoke to Philip saying, "Arise and go toward the south along the road which goes down from Jerusalem to Gaza." This is desert. So he arose and went. And behold, a man of Ethiopia, a eunuch of great authority under

Candace the queen of the Ethiopians, who had charge of all her treasury, and had come to Jerusalem to **worship** was returning. And sitting in his chariot, he was reading Isaiah the prophet.

Acts 16:14 Now a certain woman named Lydia heard us. She was a seller of purple from the city of Thyatira, who **worshiped** God. The Lord opened her heart to heed the things spoken by Paul.

Acts 24:11, 14 ..."because you may ascertain that it is no more than twelve days since I *(Paul)* went up to Jerusalem to **worship** . ....But this I confess to you, that according to the Way which they call a sect, so I **worship** the God of my fathers, believing all things which are written in the law and in the Prophets."

Warnings regarding worship—

Ex. 34:12-14 "Take heed to yourself, lest you make a covenant with the inhabitants of the land where you are going, lest it be a snare in your midst. But you shall destroy their altars, break their sacred pillars, and cut down their wooden images (for you shall **worship** no other god, for the Lord, whose name is Jealous, is a jealous God)"

Deut. 11:16-17 "Take heed to yourselves, lest your heart be deceived, and you turn aside and serve other gods and **worship** them, lest the Lord's anger be aroused against you, and He shut up the heavens so that there be no rain, and the land yield no produce, and you perish quickly from the good land which the Lord is giving you."

2 Kings 17:34-36 To this day they continue practicing the former rituals; they do not fear God, nor do they follow their statutes or their ordinances, or the law and commandment which the Lord commanded the children of Jacob, whom He named Israel, with whom the Lord had made a covenant and charged them, saying: "You shall not fear other gods, nor bow down to them nor serve them nor sacrifice to them; but the Lord, who brought you up from the land of Egypt with great power and an outstretched arm, Him you shall fear, Him you shall **worship**, and to Him you shall offer sacrifice."

Jer. 13:8-10 Then the word of the Lord came to me saying, "Thus says the Lord: 'In this manner I will ruin the pride of Judah and the great pride of Jerusalem. This evil people, who refuse to hear My words, who follow the dictates of their hearts, and walk after other gods to serve them and **worship** them, shall be just like a sash which is profitable for nothing.'"

Mic. 5:13-15 "Your carved images I will also cut off, and your sacred pillars from your midst; you shall no more **worship** the work of your hands; I will pluck your wooden images from your midst; thus I will destroy your cities. And I will execute vengeance in anger and fury on the nations that have not heard."

Zeph. 2:11 The Lord will be awesome to them, for He will reduce to nothing all the gods of the earth; people shall **worship** Him, each one from his place, indeed all the shores of the nations.

Matt. 15:7-9 *Jesus is speaking*—- "Hypocrites! Well did Isaiah prophesy about you, saying: 'These people draw near to Me with their mouth, and honor Me with their lips, but their heart is far from Me. And in vain they **worship** Me, teaching as doctrines the commandments of men.'"

Rom. 1:24-25 Therefore God also gave them up to uncleanness, in the lusts of their hearts, to dishonor their bodies among themselves, who exchanged the truth of God for the lies and **worshiped** and served the creature rather than the Creator, who is blessed forever. Amen

Col. 2:23 NIV Such regulations indeed have an appearance of wisdom, with their self-imposed **worship**, their false humility and their harsh treatment of the body, but they lack any value in restraining sensual indulgence.

Rev. 19:10 ....And I fell at his feet to **worship** him. But he said to me, "See that you do not do that! I am your fellow servant, and of your brethren who have the testimony of Jesus. **Worship** God! For the testimony of Jesus is the spirit of prophecy."

Rev. 22:8-9 Now I, John, saw and heard these things. And when I heard and saw, I fell down to **worship** before the feet of the angel who showed me these things. Then he said to me, "See that you do not do that. For I am your fellow servant, and of your brethren the prophets, and of those who keep the words of this book. **Worship God.**"

Worship that pleases the Lord—-

Deut. 26:9-11 'He has brought us to this place and has given us this land, "a land flowing with milk and honey," and now, behold, I have brought the firstfruits of the land which you, O Lord, have given me.' Then you shall set it before the Lord your God, and **worship** before the Lord your God. "So you shall rejoice in every good thing which the Lord your God has given to you and your house, you and the Levite and the stranger who is among you."

1 Chron. 16:29 *Part of David's song of thanksgiving when the ark was placed in the tabernacle in Jerusalem—* Give to the Lord the glory due His name; bring an offering, and come before Him. Oh, **worship** the Lord in the beauty of holiness!

Neh. 9:3, 4b And they stood up in their place and read from the Book of the Law of the Lord their God for one-fourth of the day; and for another fourth they confessed and **worshiped** the Lord their God. ...stood on the stairs of the Levites and cried out with a loud voice to the Lord their God. *Verses 5-38 contain their words of worship—-tremendous!*

Ps. 29:2 Give unto the Lord the glory due to His name; **worship** the Lord in the beauty of holiness.

Ps. 99:5 Exalt the Lord our God, and **worship** at His footstool—He is holy.

Isa. 66:23 "And it shall come to pass that from one New Moon to another, and from one Sabbath to another, all flesh shall come to **worship** before Me," says the Lord.

Jer. 26:2 "Thus says the Lord: 'Stand in the court of the Lord's house, and speak to all the cities of Judah, which come to **worship** in the Lord's house, all the words I command you to speak to them. Do not diminish a word.'"

Zech. 14:16 And it shall come to pass that everyone who is left of all the nations which came against Jerusalem shall go up from year to year to **worship** the King, the Lord of hosts, and to keep the Feast of Tabernacles.

.Matt. 4:9-10 *This is the third temptation of Jesus—* And he said to Him, "All these things I will give You if You will fall down and **worship** me." Then Jesus said to him, "Away with you, Satan! For it is written, 'You shall **worship** the Lord your God, and Him only you shall serve.'" *Also in Luke 4:7, 8.*

John 4:20-24 *The woman at the well in Samaria is speaking to Jesus—* "Our fathers **worshiped** on this mountain, and you Jews say that in Jerusalem is the place where one ought to **worship**." Jesus said to her, "Woman, believe Me, the hour is coming when you will neither on this mountain, nor in Jerusalem, **worship** the Father. You **worship** what you do not know; we know what we **worship**, for salvation is of the Jews. But the hour is coming, and now is, when the true **worshipers** will **worship** the Father in spirit and truth; for the Father is seeking such to **worship** Him. God is Spirit, and those who **worship** Him must **worship** Him in spirit and truth."

1 Cor. 14:23-25 Therefore if the whole church comes together in one place, and all speak with tongues, and there come in those who are uninformed or unbelievers, will they not say that you are out of your mind? But if all prophesy, and an unbeliever or an uninformed person comes in, he is convinced by all, he is convicted by all. And thus the secrets of his heart are revealed; and so, falling down on his

face, he will **worship** God and report that God is truly among you.

Powerful worship includes physical expressions and music—-

2 Chron. 7:1-4 When Solomon had finished praying, fire came down from heaven and consumed the burnt offering and the sacrifices; and the glory of the Lord filled the temple. And the priests could not enter the house of the Lord, because the glory of the Lord had filled the Lord's house. When the children of Israel saw how the fire came down, and the glory of the Lord in the temple, they bowed their faces to the ground on the pavement, and **worshiped** and praised the Lord, saying: "For He is good, for His mercy endures forever." Then the king and all the people offered sacrifices before the Lord.

2 Chron. 20:18 And Jehoshaphat bowed his head with his face to the ground, and all Judah and the inhabitants of Jerusalem bowed before the Lord, **worshiping** the Lord.

2 Chron. 29:28-30 NIV The whole assembly bowed in **worship**, while the singers sang and the trumpeters played. All this continued until the sacrifice of the burnt offering was completed. When the offerings were finished, the king and everyone present with him, knelt down and **worshiped**. King Hezekiah and his officials ordered the Levites to praise the Lord with the words of David and of Asaph the seer. So they sang praises with gladness and bowed their heads and **worshiped**.

Neh. 8:6 And Ezra blessed the Lord, the great God. Then all the people answered, "Amen, Amen!" while lifting up their hands. And they bowed their heads and **worshiped** the Lord with their faces to the ground.

Worshiping God in heaven—

Rev. 4:9-10 Whenever the living creatures give glory and honor and thanks to Him who sits on the throne, who lives forever and ever, the twenty four elders fall down before Him who sits on the throne and **worship** Him who lives forever and ever, and cast their crowns before the throne, saying: "You are worthy, O Lord, to receive glory and honor and power; for You created all things and by Your will they exist and were created."

Rev. 5:8-14 Now when He had taken the scroll, the four living creatures and the twenty four elders fell down before the Lamb, each having a harp, and golden bowls full of incense, which are the prayers of the saints. And they sang a new song, saying: "You are worthy to take the scroll, and to open its seals; for You were slain, and have redeemed us to God by Your blood out of every tribe and tongue and people and nation; and have made us kings and priests to our God; and we shall reign on the earth."

Then I looked, and I heard the voice of many angels around the throne, the living creatures, and the elders; and the number of them was ten thousand times ten thousand and thousands of thousands, saying with a loud voice: "Worthy is the Lamb who was slain to receive power and riches and wisdom, and strength and honor and glory and blessing!"

And every creature which is in heaven and on the earth and under the earth and such as are in the sea, and all that are in them, I heard saying: "Blessing and honor and glory and power be to Him who sits on the throne, and to the Lamb, forever and ever!"
Then the four living creatures said, "Amen!" And the twenty four elders fell down and **worshiped** Him who lives forever and ever.

Rev. 7:11-12 All the angels stood around the throne and the elders and the four living creatures, and fell on their faces before the throne and **worshiped** God, saying: "Amen! Blessing and glory and wisdom, thanksgiving and honor and power and might be to our God forever and ever. Amen."

Rev. 14:6-7 Then I saw another angel flying in the midst of heaven, having the everlasting gospel to preach to those who dwell on the earth – to every nation, tribe, and people – saying with a loud voice, "Fear God and give glory to Him, for the hour of His judgment has come; and **worship** Him who made heaven and earth, the sea and springs of water."

Rev. 15:2-4 And I saw something like a sea of glass mingled with fire, and those who have the victory over the beast, over his image and over his mark and over the number of his name, standing on the sea of glass, having harps of God. They sing the song of Moses, the servant of God, and the song of the Lamb, saying: "Great and marvelous are Your works, Lord God Almighty! Just and true are Your ways, O King of the saints! Who shall not fear You, O Lord, and glorify Your name? For You Alone are holy, for all nations shall come and **worship** before You, for Your judgments have been manifested."

Rev. 19:1-7, 10 After these things I heard a loud voice of a great multitude in heaven, saying, "Alleluia! Salvation and glory and honor and power belong to the Lord our God! For true and righteous are His judgments, because He has judged the great harlot who corrupted the earth with her fornication; and He has avenged on her the blood of His servants shed by her."

Again they say, "Alleluia! Her smoke rises up forever and ever!" And the twenty four elders and the four living creatures fell down and **worshiped** God who sat on the throne, saying, "Amen! Alleluia!" Then a voice came from the throne, saying: "Praise our God, all you His servants and those who fear Him, both small and great!" And I heard, as it were, the voice of a great multitude, as the sound of many waters and as the sound of mighty thunderings, saying, "Alleluia! For the Lord God Omnipotent reigns! Let us be glad and rejoice and give Him glory, for the marriage of the Lamb has come, and His wife has made herself ready."

Call to worship—

Ps. 66:1-4 Make a joyful shout to God, all the earth! Sing out the honor of His name; make His praise glorious. Say to God, "How awesome are Your works! Through the greatness of Your power Your enemies shall submit themselves to You. All the earth shall

worship You and sing to You; they shall sing praises to Your name."

Ps. 95:6-7 Oh come, let us **worship** and bow down; let us kneel before the Lord our Maker. For He is our God, and we are the people of His pasture, and the sheep of His hand.

Ps. 96:8-9 Give the Lord the glory due His name; bring an offering, and come into His courts. Oh **worship** the Lord in the beauty of holiness! Tremble before Him, all the earth.

Proclamations regarding worshiping the Lord—

Ps. 22:27-29 All the ends of the world shall remember and turn to the Lord, and all the families of the nations shall **worship** before You. For the kingdom is the Lord's, and He rules over the nations. All the prosperous of the earth shall eat and **worship**; all those who go down to the dust shall bow before Him, even he who cannot keep himself alive *(referring to Jesus)*. (Phil. 2: 9-11 Therefore God also has highly exalted Him *(Jesus)* and given Him the name which is above every name, that at the name of Jesus every knee should bow, of those in heaven and of those on earth, and of those under the earth, and that every tongue should confess that Jesus Christ is Lord, to the glory of God the Father.) *Also see Isaiah 45:23*

Ps. 86:9-10 All nations whom you have made shall come and **worship** before You, O Lord, and shall glorify Your name. For You are great, and do wondrous things; You alone are God.

Ps. 138:1-2 I will praise You with my whole heart, before the gods I will sing praises to You. I will **worship** toward Your holy temple, and praise Your name for Your lovingkindness and Your truth; for You have magnified Your word above all your name. *Consider that this is written in the Old Testament times, previous to Jesus' coming to the earth. Jesus is the Word become flesh, and His name is above all other names–John 1:1, 14, Acts 2:38, Acts 3:6, 16, Acts 4:10, 12, Acts 10:43, Acts 19:5, Philippians 2:9-11*

Jer. 7:1-2 The word that came to Jeremiah from the Lord, saying, "Stand in the gate of the Lord's house, and proclaim there this word, and say, 'Hear the word of the Lord, all you of Judah who enter in at these gates to **worship** the Lord!'"

Dan. 3:17-18, 28 "If that is the case, our God whom we serve is able to deliver us from the burning fiery furnace, and He will deliver us from your hand, O King. But if not, let it be known to you, O king, that we do not serve your gods, nor will we **worship** the gold image which you have set up." ....Nebuchadnezzsar spoke, saying, "Blessed be the God of Shadrach, Meshach, and Abed-Nego, who sent His angel and delivered His servants who trusted in Him, and they have frustrated the king's word, and yielded their bodies, that they should not serve nor **worship** any god except their own God!"

Acts 17:22-25 Then Paul stood in the midst of the Areopagus and said, "Men of Athens, I perceive that in all things you are very religious; for as I was passing through and considering the objects of your **worship**, I even found an altar with this inscription : TO THE UNKNOWN GOD. Therefore, the One whom you **worship** without knowing, Him I proclaim to you: "God, who made the world and everything in it, since He is Lord of heaven and earth, does not dwell in temples made with hands. Nor is He **worshiped** with men's hands, as though He needed anything, since He gives to all life, breath, and all things."

Phil. 3:3 For we are the circumcision, who **worship** God in the Spirit, rejoice in Christ Jesus, and have no confidence in the flesh...

Heb. 1:6 But when He again brings the first-born into the world, He says: "Let all the angels of God **worship** Him."

ENDNOTES

1 The God Who Hung on the Cross, by Dois I. Rosser Jr. & Ellen Vaughn International Cooperating Ministries Information and Books: 1-800-999-3892

2 YWAM – Youth With A Mission books
   Their website: YWAM and YWAM Publishing

3 Down Mercy Road, by Vicki Penwell
   Mercy in Action
   mercy@vineyardboise.org

4 Understanding Who You Are in Christ, by Kenneth Copeland
   Believer's Voice of Victory
   Information, Prayer and Order number: 1-800-575-4455

5 God's Best Secrets, by Andrew Murray – Clarion Classics, Publ. by Zondervan

6 Trials of Today, Treasures for Tomorrow; by Jan Eckles
   Information: jeckles@cfl.rr.com

7 Six Steps to Spiritual Revival, by Pat Robertson
   Information and Order: CBN website, Shop, books.

8 Take the Limits Off God, by Morris Cerullo
   Morris Cerullo World Evangelism
   Information for Ministry and Materials: 1-858-277-2200

9 Oral Roberts Ministry prayer line—1-918-495-7777

10 Morris Cerullo Helpline—1-858-435-7546

   Also ask for their Ministry materials.

11 Living Beyond the Limits, by Franklin Graham—See the websites.

12 Claim Your Inheritance, by Richard Roberts—
    Call 1-918-495-7777

13 Heirs of the Promise, from the Potter's House, T.D. Jakes—
    Call 1-214-331-0954

14 The Seven Robes of Joseph, by Lydia Chorpening
    Information: richorpening@discover-net.net

15 Victory Over the Darkness, by Neil Anderson—See website.

16 Reclaiming Surrendered Ground, by Jim Logan—See website.

17 Power in Praise, by Merlin Carothers
    Information: 1-800-772-4731

18 Empowered by Praise, by Michael Youssef
    Information: leadingtheway.org

ALDERINK— REVITALIZING WORDS INDEX

MEET THE AUTHOR v

DEDICATION xi

ACKNOWLEDGMENTS xiii

FORWARD xv

PREFACE xix

INTRODUCTION 23

WORDS 25
    Scriptures for Words 31

TRUTH 43
    Scriptures for Truth 47

GRACE 57
    Scriptures for Grace 62

REDEMPTION 69
    Scriptures for Redemption 75

FORGIVENSS 81
    Scriptures for Forgiveness 87

RECONCILIATION 95
   Scriptures for Reconciliation 99

RESTORATION 103
   Scriptures for Restoration 107

RIGHTEOUSNESS 113
   Scriptures for Righteousness 118

PARTAKE 127
   Scriptures for Partake 132

REVEAL-REVELATION 139
   Scriptures for Reveal-Revelation 143

GLORY-GLORIOUS 149
   Scriptures for Glory-Glorious 155

KINGDOM 165
   Scriptures for Kingdom 172

JUDGMENT 183
   Scriptures for Judgment 187

COME 193
   Scriptures for Come 198

LISTEN 207
   Scriptures for Listen 213

SEEK THE LORD 219
   Scriptures for Seek the Lord 224

NEW 231
   Scriptures for New 238

BELIEVE 245
   Scriptures for Believe 251

FOLLOW 263
    Scriptures for Follow 270

ACKNOWLEDGE 277
    Scriptures for Acknowledge 285

UNDERSTANDING 291
    Scriptures for Understanding 296

TRUST 307
    Scriptures for Trust 312

ABIDE 319
    Scriptures for Abide 324

WALK 331
    Scriptures for Walk 337

STEADFAST 347
    Scriptures for Steadfast 353

REFUGE 359
    Scriptures for Refuge 363

DELIVERANCE 367
    Scriptures for Deliverance 372

STRENGTH 379
    Scriptures for Strength 386

REJOICE 395
    Scriptures for Rejoice 401

WORSHIP 409
    Scriptures for Worship 416

ENDNOTES 427

Printed in the United States
201871BV00003B/70-105/A